Going Critical

How To and Why To

Give and Take Proper Criticism

Thomas P. Hanna

Going Critical

ISBN-10: 1477498753

ISBN-13: 978-147749875-0

Table of Contents

"The world is a mess. They are ripping us off, playing us for fools, and poisoning us at the same time. And no one seems to know how it got that way or what to do about it."

"The world isn't really a mess, it's just misunderstood and sadly mishandled. But if you will just trust the candidate of Party X or the executives of Corporation Y and give them a free hand to do whatever they deem appropriate for your benefit, they will work it all out for you in no time. At least surely by the next election."

"The world is a mess and it is all because of a conspiracy of the rich and the powerful to have everything for themselves. Only if we follow the dictates of revolutionary group M can we correct the situation and save the planet."

"The world is a mess and it's all due to sin and human perversity. Only if we follow the moral dictates of self-anointed Righteous New Messiah Z do we have any chance of improving the situation and not going to hell where surely he won't see us forever."

The litany of laments, the explanations, and the solutions or the assurances that there are no solutions go on and on. It is practically impossible to be conscious today without being continually exhorted, warned, threatened, and badgered about these topics. The basic message is that the generally accepted conditions in the world are far from perfect or even from what many of us would consider to be basically acceptable. The analyses of causes and cures are bewilderingly diverse and rather uniformly unsatisfying. So what are we to do? Throw up our hands and conclude that it's all impossible and wildly out of control and not our responsibility anyway? The temptation to think that is certainly great. That is the one line of action (or more precisely of inaction) whose outcome is easily predictable - more of the same.

But what, if anything, can we do about it? I suggest to you that the essential first step is to take a long, hard look at how we got in this situation. I presume that will give us a better idea of whether things are really as bad as we make them out to be, and exactly where and how we let things get away from us. Actually this may be too complex a reality for most of us to grasp without long and detailed study, including the history, politics, and psychology of the persons and groups that played roles in the process.

Before we can correct any abuses and misuses and before we can reasonably argue for throwing things out and replacing them with new or different systems we need a clear view of what is involved and what the likely results of the change will be. This means we need to critically evaluate the situation. All around us there are people doing things that will directly or indirectly affect us. Some of them are trying to cheat us, use us, or patronize us. Others are working actively to be of service to us and to give us our money's worth in the broad sense. Both types need our attention: the first group so we can circumvent their purposes; the latter group so we can appreciate them and give them an appropriate supportive response. Both activities are elements of criticism.

Have you noticed how much more you bring to certain activities and how much more you get out of them once someone takes the time to explain the intricacies to you? Imagine watching a basketball or football game with no idea of the rules or objectives of the game. Or consider how much more you notice the artwork in other people's homes after you try your own hand at creating some or at least selecting some to decorate your own spaces.

We live in a world of great complexity that is daily becoming more complex. Our technological breakthroughs have permitted us, and therefore almost forced us, to live faster. On a daily basis we must make more decisions about more kinds of things than people ever had to before in the history of the world. Our situation in the world, our relationship with the environment, has changed dramatically as a result of our technologies, the synthesis and dispersion of many new chemicals, and our population explosion in the last four hundred years. Today we have to make decisions about technological matters that will have longer-lasting and more far reaching effects than any faced by man before - decisions about genetic engineering, nuclear energy, and synthetic chemicals that may cause cancer in people twenty years after they were exposed to them and by which time they are widely dispersed through the environment. Decisions that must be made in an atmosphere of urgency that has never existed before because things were never before able to reach the point of no return so quickly. Now more than ever we need to be able to sort out the facts from the fantasies and the b.s. from the bullion.

When you become critical you wonder about and often ask about things. Who is this person or group that is proposing or trying to impose this change and what are they all about? Is what is being proposed really safe? Beneficial? Necessary? Are the claims that are being made true, complete, and relevant? Do I want or need this or is it simply what someone is trying to sell me by suggesting it is a status symbol?

In cases of questionable safety is it better to be safe than sorry? After a disaster we may not be able to repair the environmental damage. Does the possibility of someone not being able to make some money right now outweigh this?

It may be consoling and reassuring to many people that change is just that, change. There is no way to prevent it from happening and not even any good reason to want to oppose change in and of itself. Change doesn't necessarily mean for the better or for the worse. A higher degree of mindlessness and anonymity are not its inevitable consequences. It is true that even when we are fully aware of the unworkability of the older ways there is something scary about the unknown and therefore a strong tendency to hold tightly to the ways we have done things before rather than to try something new.

Wanting more of the pie for yourself is natural. So is resenting those who reduce or muck up your bit of the world for their profit with no benefit to you. It is only when you become mature enough to see the bigger picture - in this case the longer view - that you can recognize that you can, should, and must take that better perspective that our other human accomplishments have made possible and restrain your actions to be a fit member of a group or society. For humans that lesson is one that we can and often do share (with more or less success) with those around us, especially those younger and less experienced.

We are consciously and unconsciously taught good manners, the techniques of lying and cheating, and how to manipulate other people to make them do what we want. Somehow though we avoid most conscious attempts to learn and to teach the techniques of good criticism, a mistake which should be remedied immediately for the good of all concerned. It may revolutionize our lives and our world but it can't hurt any except special interests, and not even them if they are not abusing the public good. In many areas of human endeavor there is no protection except self-defense. It is sad, and many of us resent it and argue that it shouldn't be so, but to a degree we are individually responsible for the conditions of the world, large and local. Every time that you vote (in the widest sense of the term) against establishing firm protections for others because it might mean putting some crimp in the way you (or the line of business you depend on for your livelihood) do things, you are voting in this situation. With the multitude of special interest groups there are around, this attitude of "I'll never agree that I shouldn't be able to expose you to risks for my profit, therefore I can't support restrictions to keep you from exposing me to risks for your benefit although I would like to" keeps us all relatively unprotected.

When you ask, "How can they get away with doing that?" several answers suggest themselves.

(1) We allow them to do it because we are unaware of what is happening, or we are too disorganized, dumb or powerless when we act collectively to do anything effective about it.

(2) Only persons (including corporations, associations, and other fictitious legal personages) with great wealth and/or clout do it and they simply buy control of the individuals that give them de facto control of the legal system to protect themselves.

(3) It is so craftily done that we seldom have an opportunity to prevent it.

There may be an element of truth in each of these responses but in my opinion the first is the major truth. I maintain that the majority of the problems are partly our own personal and/or collective fault in the sense that, and to the extent that, we let them happen. That is not necessarily as simple and as stupid as it initially seems but it is something we could prevent. I know better than to make any absolute statements and I am aware of a number of rip-offs that have been so carefully and cleverly camouflaged that it is difficult for the average citizen-consumer to learn of them - although he is almost always the one whose wealth, and often health, is paying for them.

Some people can probably never be given a criticism effectively. Others will receive them only with considerable difficulty and after long wrangling and argumentation. But many will accept criticism properly if it is given properly, i.e., in a constructive manner. Of course some people will accept anything you say to them but it has no effect. They either don't want to have to argue with anyone about anything or they don't want to be bothered getting involved in this matter specifically with you. A few people are so insecure that they will take you too seriously and completely. They have to be encouraged to evaluate, not blindly accept, the pearls of wisdom falling from your lips.

This is not a book on literary criticism, a list of complaints, or some nifty lessons on nagging. It is an attention-getter designed to try to prompt you to reflect on how critical (in the good sense of the term, as I will emphasize repeatedly) or uncritical your thinking and judgment are about the thousand-and-one events of your everyday life and how much difference that actually makes to you and to the whole of society. It is my conviction that most of us are not drilled in critical thinking so we are easy targets for a great variety of manipulators, users, and plain old con men who understand and take advantage of our weaknesses.

°This is not a book with all the answers since those must be matched to the individual circumstances.° Rather, it is intended to be a stimulus to promote discussion. I intend to confirm your right - and your ability and obligation - to consider alternatives and to decide about what you are going to try to do to improve things.

This can be considered revolutionary by some in that it promotes the notion of throwing out the ineffective even if that is traditional and the way it is usually done, but I advocate such discarding only after careful consideration and weighing of the value and effects of such changes. I strongly recommend retaining, with or without modification, whatever stands up to scrutiny as efficient and/or acceptable if for no better reason than that we don't see a better alternative for now. This book is subversive in that I propose to overthrow the status quo in whatever places or ways things are stacked against our best interests.

This book is very optimistic because it at least tries to project an expectation or belief that those who are interested in a better quality of life (which doesn't automatically equate to a higher level of consumption) can get agitated and organized enough to prevent those wealth and power grubbers who have no care for or interest in the welfare of those they exploit or the survival of life, including man, in the longer run from destroying everything for their own short-term gain.

This book doesn't have a list of formulas that will solve all our problems and conflicts. It contains my reflections on what guidelines are helpful and what predictable pitfalls should be avoided. Any real life situation involves specific people with their unique backgrounds, fears, and limitations. Of the many scenarios that might be envisioned to illustrate my points I have tended to pick ones that emphasize the critic as invited commentator rather than those situations where the critic has an obligation (as, for instance, a job supervisor) or feels he simply has the right to try to impose his views on the others in these circumstances for any of a variety of valid reasons.

I would hope that after reading this book you will be more aware of the manipulations from all around and will begin to deliberately deal with at least some of those so your life will become more *lived out* and less *drifted through*.

I hope that once made aware of the possibilities for good from effective critical thinking, more people will become better critics and will actively seek to promote the techniques among their own circle of family and associates so that the benefits will become more widespread. This book is an urging for personal change, not a call for some large scale, organized movement.

Much to be desired, but not really expected based on history, is a widespread significant increase in resistance to manipulation by limited interests, along with the development of ways to better present and evaluate ideas, policies, political candidates, etc. in order to get a more realistic adult consensus. Democratic institutions are based in theory on such a consensus but even a superficial examination shows that it is almost never actually achieved. We allow the system to continue because we have no better substitute ready. We give lip service to the idea that the practice is conforming to the theory and the ideal even though we recognize that it is only a pale phantom of what it should be.

Who is the book written for? It is intended as an idea stimulator for those who want to be less used inappropriately and to make a positive contribution to human societies and the human species. It may only confirm what you already think and know. It may suggest some new viewpoints. It may bring into focus why you feel dissatisfied with the way other people deal with you - and you deal with them. Getting you to think specifically about some of these matters is my major intention. I believe that getting enough people to think carefully about what they are doing and how they are doing it will make a major difference.

This book is not a report of a psychological or sociological study and it is not authenticated or validated by quotes or footnoted references to such works or to those with professional credentials in such areas. It is a compilation of my own thoughts on a subject I consider to be of fundamental importance.

This book is not any kind of therapy and does not attempt to deal with problems that call for professional help. I am not a psychologist and

I am not saying anything in these pages that I intend to be understood as solutions to anyone's personality or psychological troubles.

I view writing this book to be a part of my contribution to the fumbling process of the masses that overall and collectively constitutes human evolution. I am intelligent enough to think that I am as capable of making a contribution to the whole foment of human thought and behavior as many of the others who have done so, and I am egotistical enough to think my contribution might be of some real value. I am not, however, egotistical enough to believe that I have all or even most of the answers to the many, many problems that we face as individuals, nations, and a species. I also know only too well that I can be as wrong, close-minded, and blind to alternatives as anyone else.

A word about gender pronouns. In this book where a pronoun stands alone representing a hypothetical person I have used the feminine pronouns in the odd numbered chapters and the male ones in the even numbered chapters. That is much easier that simply randomizing them. That is the only significance of the gender so anyone who tries to read more into any statement herein than that is on notice that (since this is effectively Chapter 00 or even numbered) he is digging where there is no dirt to be found.

An ocean of words washes over everything and everybody. Claims, statements, "facts", positions, and "guaranteed solutions". Our only hope of making sense of the situation and gradually sorting out our options and making reasonable choices depends on filtering this tidal wave of communications to separate the facts from the foam and the options from the obfuscation. What is needed is critical thinking.

Is there any single cause of all human problems? No. Is there any single cause of many of them? A qualified yes. The qualification is that the single cause is the broadly defined *lack of critical thinking and decision-making* rather than a more narrowly definable greed or hunger for power or stupidity, although each of those is a factor in many specific problems.

Is that single cause a major factor in the majority of our human problems? This is unanswerable in an assured and objective way since it involves a large element of subjective judgment which can easily be influenced by the experience and personal inclinations of the speaker. It's also an example of the problem itself since it implies that some numerical calculation of the percentage of problems involving non-critical thinking is important, maybe even essential, to the task of considering how things might be improved by better criticism skills. We are impressed by numbers but they are not and should not be essential to getting us moving on many of the important matters.

Reality has an annoying way of not corresponding to our personal notions of the ideal world. Most of us want to believe that a majority of the population are reasonably intelligent people dedicated to making sensible decisions based on a careful analysis of the facts. However, reality, as reflected in opinion polls and history, finds that many, often it seems in fact a majority, prefer to have someone else make the decisions and then create the bandwagons that these people can climb aboard. They want someone else to establish the new *In* fashions that they can slavishly imitate (while convincing themselves that this sets them apart). Despite all the whining if they decide this is not the proper person to tell them what to do, they still want somebody else to tell them what they should or even must do and even think.

One of the questions many people have been taught to dread is, "Are you being critical?" The implication is that you certainly don't have what it takes to be allowed to do that terrible thing since criticizing is not a nice thing to do. But in fact that is the best thing you can do as long as the criticism is constructive. We tend to prejudge criticizing as bad but when done thoughtfully, which means properly, it is always a positive act.

Most of us have more than enough things that we want and need to occupy our time and thoughts with that we don't want to have to be concerned about many of the decisions being made by others that will affect us. These other decisions are distractions and interruptions but they also have repercussions on us. They may, in fact, become major matters of concern, danger, or torment for us after they are implemented. At that point it is irrelevant whether we weren't paying enough attention or we couldn't get enough detailed information on the topic. Or if we had the goods, we still couldn't get enough people, or enough of the right ones, to see what was happening and what it would mean, to join us in objecting or in trying to force a rethinking.

Criticisms are everyday events in our lives and are our lifelong occupation. They occur at several levels and with matters of different seriousness. To many people the term suggests several related but distinct activities which are often clumped together and to which we tend to give a pejorative coloring. That is sad because by so doing we miss the important point that getting and giving good criticisms can be among the most important and useful occurrences of our days. Critical thinking is good behavior that requires concentration. It doesn't happen inevitably, automatically, or without consciousness and effort.

Our word criticism comes from the Greek *kritikos*, which means "to be able to discern or judge". *Webster's II: New College Dictionary* reflects the origin of the word when it lists as its third definition of criticism "the art, skill, or profession of making discriminating judgments, esp. of literary or artistic works." *The American Heritage Dictionary*, 4th edition gives as its third definition "the practice of analyzing, interpreting, or evaluating artistic works". Both list "The act of criticizing, esp. adversely" as the first meaning, reflecting the common notion that the main idea of the term is finding fault, censuring, and giving disapproval. In this book I will make the case for the need to put more emphasis on their third definition. As Ernest Dimnet states in his book *The Art of Thinking*, "Comprehension is criticism, and criticism or judgment is thought."

Thus criticism is the act of judging and evaluating the qualities, performances, and/or the value of a person, idea, object, action, or institution. A criticism I give expresses my opinion, my judgment of the effectiveness, attractiveness, acceptability, or other qualities of the subject. It may be either approving, disapproving, or deliberately neutral. In order to remove the bad-mouthing prejudice associated with the word in common usage, we need to expand our thinking about the term to encompass this wider sense of its meaning.

On short notice, Jane, only on the job a week, had to conduct a tour of the company's main building for some visiting clients. In her nervousness she mixed up a few minor details in her descriptions. Afterwards her section supervisor, who had given her the last minute assignment, stopped by her desk and commented, "How could anybody not know the location of the video production office?" She then walked away without another word.

The coworker at the next desk said, "Now she'll know better than to stick you with jobs like that anyway."

Later her immediate supervisor asked her to come to her office. When Jane was settled in a chair, nervous almost to the point of tears, this supervisor said, "Sending you to lead that tour when you're still learning your way around yourself was really unfair of us. Especially since we didn't even provide you with a complete tour when you started here. I'm really sorry about that. But for the most part you handled yourself well. I especially liked your analogy about the manufacturing process. I suggest that you make yourself a set of notes on the different operations and keep them on index cards in your desk so you can carry them along with you the next time you have to take your turn at playing tour guide."

All three people who commented to Jane offered criticism of her performance but only one was helpful and had any real beneficial effect on her future performance. Only her immediate supervisor's was a constructive criticism, one that recognized the problem, helped her to see it as a deficiency of specific preparation rather than general personal inadequacy, and suggested how she might improve her performance next time. If only more of our critic were constructive!

Thinking critically means I don't accept too easily what others claim, think, or profess. I hold it up to the light of truth and good sense as I understand those and then form my own opinions and make my own decisions. Thus my exercise of this skill is an indication of my awareness of the people and events in the world around me and my deliberate attempt to make my life a more meaningful and pleasant experience and this world a better place by consciously striving to produce the best that is in me and in those around me.

Researchers have found that 13-year-olds allowed to calmly and effectively dispute issues like grades, chores, and friends with their parents (no whining or yelling allowed) were much less likely to accept offers of drugs or alcohol from their peers than those who quickly caved in to parental demands without being allowed to question them. By learning to disagree in a constructive way they learned how to assert their own positions and defend them in all areas of their lives, even though they didn't always get what they wanted each time. This is a good lesson for patient parents and teachers to take to heart.

Many people don't think for themselves. They suspend their own judgments until others are expressed and then repeat those. This is why open debate is seldom an effective way for opponents to present their ideas or positions to a committee or open mike small meeting. This is a sort of mental cowardice on the part of those hesitant people, but you can use it to advantage for the causes of importance to you. When you can, be the first to express a view. If you can't speak first keep this follow-the-leader pattern in mind as a potential problem Deliberately counteract it by being sure to present your own views on the main topic when it is your turn to speak and don't waste your opportunity on the sidetrack issues. Don't let the discussion bog down in nit-picking about details of whatever opinion was the first one expressed - unless that is your opinion. Prefer getting a diversity of suggestions and ideas on the table but if the others show no readiness to do more than follow along at least make sure your ideas are heard.

Criticism is a subversive activity in the sense that it helps us avoid or undermine the plans of others who intend to control or manipulate us for their own purposes. Most of the manipulations we are subjected to are both legal and moral. They are thought of as the normal stuff of life in a society. They depend on us not objecting and subsequently rebelling and most often we don't object because we don't really notice what is being done. Criticism focuses us on what is happening and prompts us to think about it, which increases the likelihood that we will decide not to go along if we don't see the benefit to us or the common good, only to the person trying to use us. Only those frustrated because they can't use us as they want will argue that critical thinking is a bad thing and try to associate it with the undesirable aspects that the word *subversive* may conjure up. That in itself is fair warning about them without anything else needing to be said.

Criticism may sometimes mean telling the other person to carry her own burdens and do her own work and not try to foist them on you. When another tries to persuade you to handle the menial or unpleasant tasks for her, you owe it to yourself to call a halt. When she wants you to do the job because she doesn't know how to do it even though she was hired specifically to do it there are bigger problems but those are still not your problems. You don't need the depression of having her burdens hanging over you too.

We are geared to be aware of and to deal with changes. That moving shadow or the new shape on the horizon is what is most likely to affect our survival in the short-term. Our brains evolved to focus on the new or different, rather than on the normal or usual. Plus we are linearly analytical. How can we learn to focus on the *usual?* We need to condition ourselves, train ourselves, to every so often slow down a bit and examine our various day-to-day activities and surroundings as if they are new. We have learned to scan the input and move on when it is business as usual but we can focus on the details of even the most usual items if we make the effort. We need not and usually should not spend a lot of time analyzing each and every move and decision every time a similar situation comes up. The benefit comes from focusing just enough on the matter to ask ourselves whether this particular situation makes sense as useful or helpful to us, or are we missing what is actually being done - that someone is trying to use us as a tool or at most an unresponsive cipher.

Criticism need not always be expressed. It is sufficient to decide whether to deal with certain people, to buy certain products, to support certain causes, etc. We don't need to announce our thoughts on these matters to anyone else, although in some instances that may increase the effectiveness of our decision either by persuading others to consider what we approve of or object to, or by making those we are unsatisfied with aware of that so they can decide whether to change how they are conducting their business operations.

Let me emphasize that criticisms are not always or even routinely the same as complaints. Those are only one subclass of good criticisms. Many good criticisms are not at all complaints and many, if not most, complaints are not good criticisms. This distinction will allow you to avoid many semantic arguments. And do note that these are usually arguments, not discussions - which in itself should be a lesson for us. Giving ourselves or others a pat on the back for a job well done is a judgment, and therefore as much a criticism as giving out kicks for not

being perfect but not as much better as we could be if we treated ourselves better. If we always kick and never pat we will be constantly
bruised and sore. There is no contradiction between being your own best
friend and being your own most perceptive critic. In fact they go together
rather inevitably.

Sometimes a complaint reflects more about the critic than it does
about the subject. I remember reading a letter to the editor of the local
newspaper by a business owner complaining about the poor skills of her
female clerical help. She blamed it on the community college which had
granted these women associate degrees. She called for the college to be
closed down since the graduates were not up to her standards. The point
of course was that this employer had hired the women, the college didn't
do so. The fact that she apparently did no screening other than looking
to see if they had a degree tells us much about her letter writer's poor
business management abilities but not much about the people she hired.

A simple example of what critical thinking is about is answering
the question: Is this a bargain? We are immediately faced with two items
that require some opinion or decision. First we must decide what a
bargain means in this particular case. Does getting good value for your
money mean an item or service is a bargain? Or must it come at a lower
than the standard cost in this area, season, and situation? Is an item a
bargain if it is marked down 15% from the list price? Is it still a bargain if
the list price this week is 25% higher than it was last week in order to
allow this markdown? These things get complicated. A savvy shopper has
to know what the usual prices are in this store and at the competitors'
stores from week to week before she can begin to decide whether the
come-on in the ad page is worth heeding.

A further consideration is whether a cheap item is truly a bargain
if it is of poor quality and is not likely to hold up well. Or is it a bargain if
the item is terrific but it doesn't fit in with the rest of your decor or
wardrobe so you will have to purchase additional items to make full use
of it? Or is it a good deal if it increases the probability of some adverse
event in your life or residence? Perhaps a lamp with defective wiring that
the store sells off cheap to you because that model has been blamed for
causing a number of house fires.

Only after we have decided what is a bargain in this situation can
we get to the second decision - whether this case fits those theoretical
expectations so we can say that this is or is not a bargain for us in the
here and now. The point of this book is exactly to note that we go

through the process of weighing those two items the moment we are confronted with the question but only when we take the time to examine the situation do we realize what all we actually did and that we could have done things differently. Once we are aware of the process though we can be more deliberate about it and perhaps do a better job of it.

We can list the traits of good criticism as follows.

(1) It should be a sincere opinion.

(2) It should be well thought out and formulated.

(3) It should point out what are judged to be the good points as well as the deficiencies, the strengths and the shortcomings of the person, deed, idea, or institution.

(4) It should usually be given in private.

(5) It should be offered as one's personal view.

(6) If possible, it should be constructive.

(7) It should point out the specific elements that are problems.

(8) When feasible, it should suggest how they might be remedied.

(9) It should be given as information which may be helpful to the other in deciding about future activities or repetitions of this one.

(10) It should not be given too often.

(11) It should, when practical, only be given when it is invited or requested.

(12) It should, when possible, be given only when the other wants our honest appraisal or when we feel the effectiveness and impact of the person, idea, or institution will be enhanced by the change.

(13) It should be encouraging and stimulating, not intended as humiliating.

(14) It should involve effective listening when that is called for.

(15) It should focus on the positive.

(16) It should emphasize cooperation, not competition and not comparisons.

(17) It should use humor when appropriate to the topic and the personalities, but should avoid sarcasm or embarrassment.

(18) It should recognize effort and improvement, not just the things done well.

(19) It should consider the feelings of the person criticized.

(20) It should base her personal worth on her being, not on her performance in a specific case, but must strive to be objective when the point is specifically to evaluate her overall performance.

Good criticism should make us so aware of unacceptably selfish and harmful behaviors and attitudes that we have to see them (if they are present) in ourselves as well as in others and prompt us to reform ourselves too.

Forewarned is forearmed. If you know in advance that the system (whether educational institutions, the I.R.S., the corporate culture, etc.) is going to try to screw you, it doesn't hurt as much because you aren't surprised by the embarrassing insult of the situation. Plus you can prepare your defenses. There is no sweeter balm for your soul than successfully sidestepping a working-over by the automatons of some system that supposedly exists to serve your needs.

An Arabian proverb translates as, "Examine what is said, not him who speaks." I would argue that if you want to protect yourself from exploitation you should be examining both what is said and who says it.

Focus your criticism on all the people or institutions involved in the problem in proportion to their roles. For instance, when legal drug rip-offs occur (for instance with drugs for abusive purposes being obtained with improper prescriptions) the drug users, pharmacists, doctors involved, and the government agencies that fail to institute proper controls, plus the legislators who fail to provide the needed legislation to establish and enforce such regulation, are all partly to blame. No one element deserves all the blame and certainly they don't all deserve the same amount or kind of blame, but if we really want to improve an important but defective system as complicated as that one, no blameworthy element should escape some censure or punishment.

We can't hope to do everything ourselves. We need to discover for ourselves a group of experts, persons wise and knowledgeable in different areas who offer consistently sound conclusions. We can then allow their opinions to guide us on many further developments. Once we have the experts reviewing their fields for us we don't need to feel obliged to attempt to analyze every detail of those matters ourselves before we reach each decision. Occasionally, when the experts or others indicate that their opinion on a point may be out of pattern for them for some reason, or when the subject is of particular importance, I will of course still want to go more critical and examine the matter in detail myself. Being guided by experts I have checked out doesn't suggest blind acceptance, only a lowered threshold of skepticism.

For humans, thought is language (even if not all language is very thoughtful). We can only formulate and express any detailed thoughts in language which means that the language we use both shapes our thoughts and is shaped by them. If we don't have words for it, we are hard put to think about any intellectual topic, let alone discuss it with others. Basic to language are words which, to be useful, must have definite areas of meaning even if those areas vary somewhat with context and over time. These areas of meaning are the word's definition(s) in general usage.

A major part of many misunderstandings - and a major tool of those who want to cheat and manipulate you - is a failure to agree on the definition of terms at the beginning of a discussion or negotiation. It is easy to assume that the other person means the same things, including the same restrictions and extensions, as you do. It's also a very dangerous assumption. If it were true, half the lawyers in the world would be out of work and legalese wouldn't be needed. In order to minimize confusion and misunderstanding it is always a useful exercise to define your terms as you go, whether you are writing or talking. Dictionary definitions are a starting point but the words we are most likely to disagree about the meaning of in a particular context are those with a ton of historic, symbolic, or political baggage attached. Any five people selected at random might, after some hassling, agree to a general working definition of a word like patriotism but getting them to agree that this particular action or omission is patriotic is much less likely.

It is valid to criticize someone for what she does and sometimes for what she fails to do. Playwrights and authors (as well as politicians and administrators) are often criticized saying they didn't work out some aspect of a topic or didn't stress certain elements in a presentation. These critiques are especially common in theater, movie, and book reviews. This hardly seems like a fair and reasonable criticism unless the author gave us a specific blueprint that she was attempting to follow when she started off. Then we can comment on how well we judge that she stuck to her announced plan. To criticize a person for not doing what you think you would have done in the same situation is not of much value. How this person's performance matches up to that of others performing the same or comparable tasks is valid grounds for a critique though.

Thus criticism means passing judgment upon the qualities and merits of anything as much as it means finding fault or censuring and it is time we corrected ourselves on this. Critical thinking is what allows us to improve ourselves, protect ourselves, and create a better world. Without criticism (in this positive sense) we can realistically hope for little more than mediocrity and lots of exploitation.

We live in a complex, fast moving world and simply surviving, let alone succeeding and getting ahead, is an everyday challenge. The world is full of fakes, frauds, and plain, old-fashioned shoddiness. That is a strong statement but the majority of people are likely to agree. In the Internet age it has probably never been truer that there are lots and lots of people looking for just half a chance to help themselves to what little you have or to use you as grist for their own operations and there are frightfully few people or institutions that are doing much that is effective to keep them from succeeding at that, propaganda and good intentions notwithstanding. (We will consider this kind of qualified statement in more detail in Chapter 20).

Most of us find ourselves thinking such thoughts with regularity. It is hard to document but to many it seems that things are getting even worse, that that regularity has increased in frequency in recent years because of the Internet and our general increased interconnectedness. Suffice it to say that, at the very least, events in recent years at the local, the national, and the international levels have all contributed to make the situation glaringly obvious.

Is there a single factor that runs as a common theme through many, even most, of the problem areas of our individual and collective lives? I believe so or I wouldn't be writing this. What has been deficient time and again has been criticism or critical thinking, the careful and hard-nosed assessment of what was being proposed, its direct and indirect consequences, and who benefits and who pays the price so that we can make better decisions.

The time has passed when any of us should be able to believe that life is simple and all we have to do is follow the rules of society and everything will be *Just fine, thank you!* It has never really been that way but there have probably been periods in history when it was easier to make it seem a possibility. The disturbing realization for many today is how often and in how many areas and ways we, individually and collectively, are being taken in by persons and corporations for their personal gain at our expense. This also isn't really new; only the extent of the consequences may be new with increases in global interconnectedness and international corporations and our awareness of the impact on us because of that intensified intercommunication and the volume of chatter.

Way back when, Socrates argued that the unexamined life is not worth living. We don't have to go that far to recognize that many of the deficiencies in our lives and societies arise from the fact that our lives and societies are unconsidered. Too often the things we do and the ways we do them are unthinking routines. We do them that way because in a sense that is how it is always done. We seldom stop to wonder why things were done that way in the first place, whether this is the best way to do them now, and what the alternatives might be. This tends to be the case even when we are well aware of the problems that are caused by what we are doing or how we are doing it. We grumble and loudly complain that somebody ought to do something about the consequences of doing this, but we don't seriously consider whether we ourselves need to do this at all or if we could do it any other way with less of what we judge to be the harmful or undesirable effects. In fact we can too easily be persuaded by those with vested interests in the matter to accept and publicly support efforts to keep anyone from changing how we do things, even if that would be for the better for most of us.

If you want a system (used here in a generic sense to signify any human-involved activity) that does the desired job as efficiently as possible and with a minimum of undesirable side effects, you need to think the matter through, generate as many possible alternatives as you can, and then weigh those and make deliberate decisions. When you allow your life or your world to develop by accident you get as fine and sturdy a structure as you would get by simply stacking a group of pre-assembled walls from different sources together and calling it your dream house. You might or might not end up with the number of rooms you wanted but their size, shape, and ability to withstand the weather will be a lot less than if you had picked parts that were designed to fit together smoothly and snugly.

The considered life is the one you can be most proud of because you know that you made a sincere effort to choose the most workable set of behaviors and activities available to you at that time to match your skills, interests, and ideals. You undoubtedly had to make compromises in the process but you did so recognizing that there are limitations that need to be addressed when your conditions will permit. You can take pride in the fact that you have taken responsibility for your life instead of letting others choose for you or having events or Fate determine things.

It is for this reason that those for whom things don't run as smoothly as the ideal have an advantage. If you have to scramble to make ends meet you may pay more attention to doing productive work and seeking the efficient tools and procedures. Those who are mediocre athletes are more likely to seriously question whether the effort needed to play on the organized team are worth it. Maybe the playground pick-up game is good enough.

To assess the possible advantages of a critically aware life you can consider the alternative, which is life as a cipher who is being gouged, manipulated, and played to the advantage of others. This is because you aren't paying attention to the treatment being dished out, are unaware and too unimaginative to consider that the situation might be otherwise, and too unorganized to do anything about what displeases you except grumble, curse, think violent thoughts, or opt out of the controlling system. Of course that last simply guarantees that, with no input into the system, you will be treated in the same unacceptable manner forever.

It' is easy to assume but often hard to demonstrate convincingly that the traditional way is the best way to do something. Too often things are done intentionally in a way intended to be expeditious and nothing more. We try to take care of the immediate problem fast. Efficiency, long-term consequences, and sociological or environmental impacts aren't major considerations at those moments.

A peculiarity of good criticism is that even when it is unfavorable, it forces honest and sincere people to reevaluate the situation and it is rather hard for reasonable individuals to completely overlook or talk around. Generalizations, angry shouts, and muddled claims can easily be met by the same; reasoned arguments which let honest people come to a better understanding of the situation, the effects of their actions (whether intended and desired or not), and the potential alternatives available must be met by intelligent and open-minded people with a reasoned response as long as the audience demands that.

Over the years we have gained insights about body language, power games, and transactional analysis. For the price of the book we have had cup after cup of chicken soup for our souls and exhortations to be our own best friends. We have also had a shelf load of books advising us on how to up the organization, and to protect the interests of old Numero Uno above all else and at any costs to others. Many bestsellers books and many of the TV talk shows hawk the latest variations on using the unwritten rules to promote ourselves and win out in the competition because, presumably, there is nothing much that any one of us can do to clean up the situation or to prevent this general screwing of anyone and everyone who will stand for it except to join the ranks of the users where the lower level users get used by the upper level users to do the grunt work of using the rest of the population. Either that or the publishers don't know how to make as much profit selling us books that suggest how to clean up the mess.

Possibly what we need is not so much to learn the rules and the games so that we can excel in the competition as to learn how to change the rules and the games to make them less destructive. Instead of simply beating others at the game wherein they are setting the rules maybe we should change the whole situation by refusing to play or to allow them to play as usual. This will shake the whole socio-economic system but we will survive it. Some things might never be the same again but as long as they get better not worse, that is a pleasant and hopeful thought. We can't lose sight of the fact that eternal vigilance will be required to make that the case though.

The contemporary atmosphere of rampant self-evaluation, self-improvement, and pop psychology has made us progressively more aware of the intricacies and often hidden or overlooked manipulative pressures of our relationships at all levels - as citizens and taxpayers, as consumers and production workers, as parents, mates and children. The list goes on and on.

We need to remove some of the b.s. from our lives, to *defake* ourselves. Initially this will be a major task but as we get into the process it will get easier. We will never get rid of all of the b.s. from the system but de-b.s.ing is good mental exercise (even if not exactly graceful phrasing). It keeps us alert and therefore contributes to our survival in all spheres.

Criticism includes analyzing the motivations and the assumptions that snap into place as soon as you begin to consider a problem, a statement, or a position. Here is where we can and should deliberately exercise our intelligence by pushing ourselves beyond our predetermined reactions and reviewing this matter again and checking whether we still agree with our original decisions.

We should be angry about the deliberate attempts by advertisers, P.R. flacks, politicians, and others to treat us as mindless and to control our thinking and/or behavior. We are constantly subjected to various attempts to propagandize and brainwash us. Not a new situation, but one that our new technologies have made easier and therefore more intensive and unrelenting. We need to question and examine all claims and be consciously wary of and thick-skinned to manipulative propaganda. If too few people give overt and critical responses, the demeaning realities and destructive changes go unnoticed and therefore unchecked.

There are many frustrations associated with being a perceptively critical person but there are at least as many frustrations associated with being a non-critical person. The differences are sometimes qualitative, sometimes quantitative, and sometimes non-existent. The frustration of seeing a wrong perpetrated but not being able to do anything effective about it is a special problem for critics. The special satisfactions for the critics in such situations include deliberately turning aside and frustrating some of the many attempts being made to impose on or to use them. Don't kid yourself that you can develop yourself into a critic without having some fairly fundamental changes occur in your personal life. But also don't be so obtuse that you think that change has to be a bad thing. In fact you will probably like yourself a lot more when you go critical and so will those people who pass the alertness and awareness screening test to remain your close friends.

There is real frustration to be dealt with as you become a more critical thinker and much of that is the lack of critical functioning in the intellectual-political lives of others. You may find yourself screaming (or at least being tempted to) when you see others taken in by propaganda about subjects that deeply concern you. I have no easy answer to relieve this frustration. I would hope that after you have gotten involved in a topic and critically evaluated the matter you will be better prepared to present your case for one side or the other. There are, however, no general rules for when, how, or if you can successfully proselytize the masses – or these particular individuals - and win them over to at least a careful consideration of the matter. Even if being called nasty names doesn't bother you, there is a danger in being perceived as an obsessed reformer since that label deadens the effectiveness of your message and may push others uncritically over to the side you oppose. (More about the power of labels and names in Chapter 26). That is their loss - but if they tilt the vote count in favors of the candidates or policies you oppose, you lose too.

Will becoming an effectively critical person solve all of your problems, resolve all of your frustrations, and make you a completely happy person? No, I fear not. It may, in fact, increase your frustration with the way individuals and institutions try to abuse and manipulate you.

Also at the way many of the manipulated allow that to happen even as they whine and complain about it. Why go critical then? Because it will help you to avoid or thwart some attempts to use or abuse you and thereby will minimize your victimization. While you may not be able to change everything you decide needs changing, it may act as a goad to get you to work at changing what is within your scope, matters which otherwise you might simply let slide by. It will also likely give you the satisfaction of knowing that you are at least aware of and wary of the inefficiencies and inflexibilities of our current social and political systems. That in turn might stimulate you to think up and suggest new and better ways of doing things that would benefit everybody. Unsung heroes still make a positive difference.

A starter project is to provide your local news media and others in decision-making positions with positive as well as negative feedback. Write, email, or call and tell them what you like as well as what you don't. Remember that, as an example, when some organized group decides to pressure programming executives to stop airing some TV show, the sound of the voices opposing it are loud and if the viewers who are not being organized by some other group don't let the executives know that they want this viewing option, the voices that are heard will generally carry the day because the deciders want to have numbers to guide them and to show to support their decisions against the inevitable complaints. You don't have to be part of an organization to let them know your thoughts on the matter. In fact not being just another name on the list attached to some communication but an individual acting alone, using your own words and phrasing and not mentioning any organization sharing some or all of your views, often seems to give your message more impact. You can make a contribution to the consideration and, more often than is generally recognized, you can make a difference to the decisions that are made.

The details of the things we speak of with the code word *values* are matters of opinion no matter how strongly anyone may argue that his interpretations of them are their true, and their only true, descriptions and designations. Their large subjective elements makes values topics almost automatic subjects for argument since few like to be designated as barbarians without sensitivity to or concern about *Right, reason, and a strong supportive social and moral order* or whatever is the current line.

For the same reason, on the local and individual level there's little likelihood that you or anyone can calmly discuss these matters and persuade the other that he is wrong. Therefore often the sensible strategy is to vigorously avoid these topics with him. When you have a zealot across the table (and they are generally the only ones who will bring up such matters which are widely recognized as private and potentially confrontational subjects) you play into a no-win game if you even engage in the discussion. This person expects to persuade you but is strongly resistant to any suggestion that he should or must be open-minded himself so do yourself a favor and say no to having such discussions before you get into them.

The other person will probably rant and rave and loudly state that your refusal to acknowledge the correctness and superiority of his position to all others definitely means this, that, and something else- all generally considered credentials for admission to hell. With people like that you can't stop that line of verbal abuse by reason, by appeal to fairness, or by shouts and threats. You can only sidestep the worst of it by refusing to play the game. You can make statements but you can't effectively engage such a person in discussion because from the start he intended this to be a one-way communication. One way to end the encounter is to simply repeat your same statements word for word until he decides that you can't be used further for his purposes. Don't kid yourself, discussing, explaining, or defending your stance slips you into the one-sided confrontation he is aiming for. Accept in advance that you won't get the satisfaction of defeating this adversary because such a person will never admit, even to himself, that he is wrong or that you are correct or even have a right to an opinion different from his. The best you can do in these assaults is to maintain your dignity and composure while holding your own ground and simply not conceding his points. Brace yourself for the fact that he is likely to claim to you and to others that you are doing precisely that by not letting him fully argue you into submission. Don't argue, just repeat as many times as needed that he is wrong.

This is a prime case where those too devoted to being *nice* get used and abused – and, frustratingly, too often leave others undermined too. The nice person sees it happening but won't stop or prevent it. They often claim they cannot do otherwise but the reality is that they choose not to. They make a choice to let it happen. "It would be hard" or "I wouldn't feel good about saying no" or any variation on those sentiments is not an excuse the rest of us should accept. If you won't risk hurting the nice person's feelings by not accepting his excuse, you are adopting his deficiency as your own. Even *being nice* has consequences so you should go critical whenever a situation develops where you think about being compliant. At the same time, don't lose sight of the important guideline: All things in moderation and in their proper place. Reducing the old man next door to tears is not the goal, only not letting his mistake make you take a mistaken stance or action is.

There will probably be some people who won't like your new critical approach to life and these persons will usually fall into one or more of several predictable categories. First are those who want to control or manipulate you because they see their power to manipulate you diminishing. Second are those who feel threatened because you are growing and they are not. Third are those who just don't want anything to change because change scares them.

These latter two categories you may feel sorry for but I hope you will realize that you shouldn't retard your own growth to console those who won't let themselves grow. Note that growth in this sense is, despite much verbiage to the contrary, essentially always a matter of *will not*, not *cannot*.

But, you wonder, suppose other people don't like me being so critically aware. What should I do then? First, I think you need to ask yourself why they object. If it is because you are no longer the sappy wimp they could manipulate and use at will, then I suggest that you are better off without them.

If it is because they now feel inadequate because they are not as alert to what is happening as you are, I suggest that you need to continue what you are doing but check yourself to be sure that you aren't, perhaps unconsciously, giving off social signals that suggest you think they are now somehow inferior to you and probably beyond saving. Of course if that is your conclusion there is little chance that you can effectively hide your thoughts so you might as well embrace your decision and accept its consequences for you and for the other person. After an initial resistance to change in you, in their relationship with you, and in the way things are being done many (trying to be an optimist I would like to think *most*) people will learn from your approach and become more perceptive and critical in the good sense themselves.

If the reason others object to your new critical attitudes is that you've been making yourself obnoxious by lecturing everyone, correcting everyone within sight, and generally acting in a "I'm better than thou" manner, the problem lies with you and you need to turn your critical skills on this personal problem. Anyone who is too pushy about minor matters is likely to find himself avoided, talked about in uncomplimentary terms, and probably ridiculed for not having enough good sense to avoid the pitfall of abusing criticism. Many of us will agree that that seems appropriate.

No one can, or should, protect those persons who are competent to do so themselves but who refuse to accept the responsibility for taking an active role in protecting themselves from the multitudes wanting to fleece them of their money, their liberties, and their dignity. Some people, like the physically disabled or the mentally incompetent, deserve more protection by governments and others because they have inherent limitations. Those persons who just don't want to have to deal with unpleasant things and who therefore sit back and expect others to protect them should expect to be victims. They are putting the targets on their own backs and asking for it.

Does being a critical person in this positive sense mean that you will do nothing all day but evaluate, weigh, and judge? Yes and no. You probably already do a lot of that if you think carefully about your daily mental activities. You probably will find yourself paying more attention to what happens to you but it should not become some kind of an obsessive behavior. There is nothing in the nature of critical thought that makes obsession more likely. You have no reason to give much daily attention to many of the routine tasks of your life once you have carefully considered them and their alternatives and consequences and concluded that your present ways of doing those things are acceptable. Periodically, especially when some new element has to be added to the task or when you detect signs that the end results are less than you hoped for, you may want to set yourself down for more thought on that particular topic but it won't serve any useful purpose to overdo the process.

You have probably noted many times the thin line between hype and outright dishonesty. What do all the hype phrases mean? Which ones actually mean anything of value? Are the rest harmless? Acceptable? How do you sort out the real distinctions between hype and small change? Lots to think about.

First, is the claim documented or documentable? Claims like *best loved*, *greatest*, and *most influential* are hard if not impossible to document. (More about superlatives in Chapter 21). They are largely a matter of opinion. Winner of X award or recipient of a degree from Y University are items of fact that can be verified and documented. Finding that the claims are accurate may or may not make much difference to your judgment about the person; finding that they are false should make a difference to your thinking about them and/or the situation the claims were made to support.

Second, who made the award or whatever? Joe Nobody can give an award with an impressive sounding title but it is still only Joe Nobody behind it giving it its only importance. What does it mean if some general circulation magazine gives out best auto salesman awards every year?

Third, what criteria were used for giving the award and is the award relevant to the present situation? Perfect attendance is one thing, academic achievement is another. An award that virtually everyone who works in an industry receives in a few years has less clout than more restricted ones. It is interesting that there seems to be a perception in some circles that TV Emmy awards fit in this *everybody gets one eventually* category. You have to decide for yourself if school events that are planned from the start to seem like competitions but reconceived so that every entrant will get an ego boost from being declared a winner are helpful in the long run.

Criticism is an everyday, positive, major, and characteristically human activity. But why criticize? In a nutshell: to protect, to perfect, and to protest.

Critical evaluation is self-preservation. It is also the best way of working within a democratic type system for the good of all. We need to question and examine all claims. We must be consciously wary of and thick-skinned to propaganda. Be skeptical of the claims, for instance, that you are being fully protected by various government regulatory agencies that are hobbled by political considerations. Don't accept the noise, dirt, and other pollution of the world around you. Assert your right to a decent world. As long as the majority of us acquiesce, things won't get better. Put at least your moral support behind changes for the better.

It often seems that the manipulators and users run the world so why not just join them and get what you can? When you think the other way - how to keep them from getting yours by inappropriate means - you are in a different (and some of us think a better) mind-world.

I criticize to set a good example as a role model of an intelligent, responsible, adult citizen. I have a duty to myself, my family, my local community, and the world community to do this. I have a duty to do the best I can and to be the best I can be and that means going critical each and every day about a variety of matters. It doesn't mean that I should be a drudge always busy calculating and weighing every decision about minor matters. I am going to have to make choices about all sorts of things all day long anyway so I make them more consciously and I am on the right side of things. What dressing to have on my salad doesn't call for great critical skill unless I have to worry about ingredients to which I am allergic or deliberately choose to avoid for some reason of symbolism or conscience . The political correctness of choosing the right salad dressing is too silly for serious consideration.

Part of the sense that comes with experience in using my critical skills is the one that semi-automatically sorts the matters I encounter during each day into categories on the basis of their relative need for close attention. Today (1) I need to write the checks to pay bills now due; (2) I would like to read the lead article in a magazine that I bought yesterday so that I can discuss it at a meeting next week; (3) I need to turn on the oven to cook tonight's dinner; and (4) I should order a new supply of items I use almost every day since I have only a two week supply left. It doesn't require a genius or a half hour of contemplation to decide that number three is of immediate concern; number one is of importance today; number two can be done any time this week; and number four any time in the next two weeks.

We are all to some extent (and sometimes quite a large extent) blind to our own shortcomings. It could hardly be otherwise. We need a good impression of ourselves for our own mental health so we overlook and rationalize and pretend. We all do it. It is the stuff our daydreams are made of and much of the time it does no harm. It is only when someone with a more objective view of us takes the time to point them out to us that we notice our attitudes and behaviors that cause friction with others and/or that honestly prevent us from accurately assessing the world. In the same way, it may be our task to make those around us aware of the way they are perceived by others and how their perception of others affects their behavior. We are each the product of a specific set of experiences at a particular time so we do not have, cannot have, substantial experiential awareness of any other people's situations with their special needs and pressures, although we can often empathize in terms of categories of experiences.

Many things in our lives are influenced (and sometimes distorted) by our preconceived notions of what they can or should be. If your idea of what happiness would mean is out of focus, you might be missing out on happiness today simply because it doesn't match the details of the ideal you have set up. An ideal which you might well have absorbed largely intact from others, including some film or novel that moved you, without ever giving it serious scrutiny.

We live in a complex world in which few of us can truly be rugged individualists. The tax collector, the government inspector, and the communications media are at everyone's doorstep. This means opportunities and benefits for us that wouldn't be possible without the civil institutions but also means unprecedented opportunities for persons, individual or corporate, to use, abuse, and confuse us. With many different agencies making rules and binding decisions that are going to directly and indirectly affect us, we need the skills that will let us maintain some kind of control over our lives. Critical thinking is possibly the most important of these skills. The fact that over the centuries many people have been subjugated by tyrants and many still are today around the world should caution the rest of us to pay close attention to what is said and done so we can keep our own leaders from abusing their power. We must force them by whatever legitimate processes are available to live up to the written rules and their own verbal promises and agreements, all tempered by the reality of human institutions.

We also need critical powers to withstand the social pressures from manipulators like religious fanatics, warmongers, and other users of all stripes. Without the confidence that comes with my critical capacities I am less than a full person.

Consider trying to drive a car across an expanse of featureless flat landscape of loose-packed sand with your only view out through a section of the driver's side of the windshield and the safely paved road has no painted center line or shoulder marker lines. That is life without the feedback provided in part by criticism.

Or consider a hypothetical case. Andrea, fifty, and looking for a hobby to give her some additional satisfaction, decides to become a portrait painter. She buys the basic supplies and a how-to book on the subject and goes to work during her spare time in a room over her garage. She sets herself the goal of having an exhibit of her original works (done using photos of celebrities as models) in the lobby of a local bank that regularly schedules such events. She works on the portraits for a year without allowing anyone else to see them. She finally approaches the bank manager about scheduling a show and is devastated when she is told that after looking at her masterpieces the manager feels they are not nearly good enough for the bank to sponsor her show.

It is tempting to say that people criticize for as many reasons as there are individuals, but that is obfuscation, not an answer. Most people, if they take the time to think it through, will recognize several major categories of motives for criticizing, some good, some bad. The "good" motives are those that involve wanting to help someone - including ourselves, the person being criticized, some third party, or a combination of these. Within the general heading of "being helpful" there are still a variety of specific intentions.

A first reason to offer criticism might be to help the criticized avoid giving offense. This person may not know, or may not be thinking about, the background of others she has to deal with and she may unintentionally cause hurt and offense by inappropriate remarks or gestures. Since she doesn't intend to be offensive, simply drawing her attention to the matter may be all that's necessary. Both she and the third party benefit from you taking the interest and the risk of precipitating a bad reaction to yourself by quietly pointing out the problem.

A second reason could be to bring out the very best in the other person. We all benefit from a loving prod now and then. It is easy to get lazy and let our performance get slipshod. As long as our performance is still adequate, most people won't say anything even though they are noting the decline in quality and/or quantity. But the person who really cares for us will say something. She will gently but persistently remind us of how much better we can do. Drawing the line between encouraging and nagging is the problem here.

When is it my business to intervene or interfere in some situation I witness? Whenever I believe that I am showing better judgment that the other and when I believe my intervention won't turn the whole thing into a chaotic shouting match that might make the situation worse.

A third reason to offer criticism might be to fulfill your duties as a supervisor. Whether you want that or like that or not, in accepting the appointment to any supervisory role you automatically take on the official role of critic. It is what the job is all about. In this case your obligation may be to be most concerned with the interests of the third parties who are at the receiving end of the work. A school administrator has to be concerned about the quality of the instruction the students are receiving and all the activities on school property. A factory supervisor has to be concerned with the quality of the materials being turned out and the safety and the satisfaction of the customers and the employees. Supervisors may take an interest in the personal aspects of the workers, but they can fulfill their contractual obligation to criticize with only a minimum of that.

A fourth motive might be to set the record straight. One may feel a duty to honesty, fair play, and objective decision-making to make an effort to get all sides of some issue and its consequences as widely understood as possible. For someone who believes strongly in the right to make informed decisions, it would be reason enough that one side is not being fully and accurately presented. She need not advocate any position or choice in order to feel obligated to inform and evaluate them.

A fifth reason to criticize might be because our carefully weighed opinion is specifically sought by those involved. Intelligent people value an objective critical opinion. They know enough to want to compensate for the inevitable subjective elements and the problems of unconscious bias in perception and interpretation when we are personally involved. If they respect our integrity and opinion enough to request it, they are paying us a high compliment as well as giving us a prime opportunity to make the best use of our critical faculties - along with the burden of getting involved.

A sixth possibility is similar. A third party may seek our opinion of persons, items, or events. Here we are being asked as experts, or at least as person of taste, intelligence, and experience. But in this case there is less likelihood of the person being criticized being affected by our observations than if she asked herself. In this case we must ask ourselves why we are being asked to do this. If we suspect that our comments are intended to be repeated to inappropriately put down the subject we should seriously consider declining the invitation to comment.

A seventh reason to go critical might be to offset the impact of the expressed views or actions of others when we believe those are slanted or wrong in some matter of significance. This is the role of lobbyist - putting words in the ears of decision-makers that are intended to influence their actions. Initially I may not be particularly inclined to advocate a position until I hear those on the other side of the question (or even on the side I favor) misrepresenting the facts or exaggerating in ways or to an extent that I feel cheats the listeners out of the honest, objective facts she needs to make an informed decision. This is also the category in which I would include any necessary defense of yourself and your beliefs, values, accomplishments, etc.

An eighth positive possibility is to go critical in order to stimulate discussion. Sometimes people don't know how to effectively evaluate a topic because they haven't concluded it is a matter of significance affecting them or something which they can really change. Making them aware of the impact and the consequences may open their eyes to its importance. Simply asserting the point may reassure the listeners of their importance in shaping policies and procedures.

Here we may also deliberately decide to play the Devil's Advocate and present arguments and positions that we don't really believe in but that fit loosely into the topic area precisely so those will get consideration and thus other people will realize the range of possibilities. Usually only those intent on distorting our message or position will miss the obvious verbal and body language signals that we almost always broadcast when questioning or commenting in this latter mode.

Sometimes we may put forth a dissenting opinion in order to stimulate suggestions when we don't feel that the proposed solutions are the only, the best, or the inevitable answers to the situations. We may want to stimulate discussion because we don't have a specific best alternative already worked out but we are convinced there must be other, and possible better, ones if enough people contribute their views.

A ninth motive might be to perform the patriotic duty to critique elements of our government - the people making decisions, the specific policies or laws in place or being considered, etc. In this case the intent is not to blindly damn the nation, rather it is to refuse to allow shoddiness to be played off as our best.

As noted above, there are also bad motivations for criticisms to which we are all occasionally tempted.

Sometimes the motive is pettiness. We hope to make ourselves seem intelligent, cultured, and informed by offering severe and non-constructive criticisms. When a local newspaper reviewer in a small city in the Midwest writes a scathing review of a performance by a ballet master like Rudolf Nureyev you have to laugh at the pretentiousness or the smallness of the event or it may raise your blood pressure and lower your opinion of the residents of whole regions.

Sometimes jealousy is the stimulus. This is the often a continuing embodiment of the mistaken notion that somehow I build myself up in proportion to how much I tear someone else down. We have all seen it done and most of us have recognized that it doesn't work out that way, but the temptation still raises its ugly head too often for us not to be aware of and cautious about it as a motive.

Hatred is a common force behind much bad criticism. Whether the focus is racial, ethnic, political, or strictly personal, the taint is much the same. Like the computer programmer's expression GIGO - when garbage goes into a criticism, garbage is also what comes out.

Some bad criticisms are sloppy and empty rather than deliberately mean or intended to harm. This is a likely outcome when the observation is made mainly to have an expressed opinion on every topic. No thought goes into it, so what comes out is froth that has little or no substance. In a similar vein we may voice views that we have given little if any thought to before this moment or even right now in order to agree with someone else. This is simply apple-polishing. The intention is to slyly insinuate ourselves into this other person's circle, not to make a serious use of our critical powers.

Just as safety requires that we look both ways before crossing a busy street, happiness requires that we consider where we stand in both directions when we critique our degree of achievement and satisfaction. If you only look at the goals above you that are still out of reach it is tempting to feel angry, frustrated, and stymied. These might include the big house, the power office with two windows, the expensive car that won't get you anywhere the cheaper one wouldn't although it might influence the opinion of some others about you. But stop and consider what you have - the roof over your head, the stuff threatening to explode out of the various storage spaces, the social status, the food on your table, and your ability to choose what that food will be. Then compare yourself with the majority of those living around the world. You may, as I do every time I reflect on this, realize you are one of the relatively fortunate ones in that you have accomplishments to be proud of and are entitled to take satisfaction in just as you are without having to give up the plans and drive to do more or to acquire more. According to CNN.com a telling statistic is that in early 2012 if your annual income is more than $34,000 you are among the world's richest one percent even if you are a ninety-nine-percenter among the U.S. population.

Critical thinkers don't try to keep the world the way it was, they plan the new futures as they adapt to the new realities. Realize that you and your government don't have to follow the trends. Recognize in particular that *trends* are artificial creations of writers and commentators seeking a way to put their opinions in capsule form that many will find too clever or convenient not to repeat and accept. They aren't necessarily reality - and especially not something inevitable or immutable.

When you are a very young child you clamor for independence and identity. This is important to your development and maturity. "I want to do it myself," and "My way is best" are the battle cries of the two-year old. Gradually we are allowed more independence, and the first steps to maturity occur when we realize from our experience that actions and choices have consequences. Independence has a price tag.

Sometimes you must choose between two good things knowing you can only have one. If you choose unwisely you are stuck. By the time we are in our early teens we are becoming annoyingly and vividly aware that the wrong choices can condemn us to lives of failure and bleakness. So what do we tend to do? Some become adept at blaming someone else, almost anyone else, for their own failures. Some let someone else tell them what to do and to think about politics and morality and other major areas of life while they fiercely defend their right to make their own choices about their favored brand of beer, their favorite sports team, and what things are going to be taught to their kids to be sure the young ones don't become threats by concluding that something other than the position being given to their parents by those they let tell them what to believe, think, and do to concur with are correct.

Often we feel compelled to reject the ideas that our parents are working hard to instill in us as old fashioned and inadequate. Which of course they are. What some substitute for these ideas and value systems are a different, or at least seemingly different, set espoused by some guru, cult (in the broadest sense of the term), or "In group" of their peers. Thus we preserve our sanity in the sense that we assert our independence as persons by rejecting one pre-packaged set of values but immediately seek the security of another set. Otherwise we have to walk the mine-fields of decision-making and responsibility ourselves. But happy and blessed indeed are those who tread that path and succeed.

We have a tendency to get stuck in outdated patterns of thinking and behaving. These may have served and even been good responses in the past, but sometimes the situations have changed in ways that make these responses part of the problem now. These aren't objectionable because they are old fashioned, but because they are non-adaptive. They make assumptions that we now recognize are not valid and therefore are not workable. For a long time it was widely accepted that dumping our sewage, garbage, and industrial wastes into the oceans was okay. It was considered a sensible thing to do because it was assumed that the oceans are so large that any harmful materials would be diluted to the point of no concern. Try telling that now to people living along many stretches of coast that see the very ocean so fouled that they dare not enter it for swimming and may be advised not to eat any fish and especially shellfish caught in many-miles-square regions of it. Read the scientific reports on large areas of ocean that are now effectively dead zones because the microbes decomposing all that dumped stuff use up all the oxygen in the water so nothing except some of those decay types can survive.

No one of us can cure all the woes of the world by her critical functioning. Only a very few people can even directly make any very widespread and significant difference by their care and precision and vigilance. But each person can make a difference in her own little corner of the world, benefiting not only herself but those in the circle of people and institutions with which she directly interacts. If many of the small, local situations were better resolved then some of the larger, more widespread problems wouldn't arise and the beneficial effects would be spread that much farther. The individual can also help make those in positions where they could change the ways we do things more aware of the problems, the proposed solutions or mitigations, and the human toll of not correcting those messes. The effectiveness of a group often depends on the number and determination of its members which gives the person impact in the collective that she doesn't have alone.

Some accept the responsibility for offering proper criticism in a timely fashion as part of their professions. For instance, there are times when a scientist must publicly offer criticism. Often she must use her own expertise to aid and support attempts to attain a true understanding of the physical world. No one can know everything about everything, or today in many topic areas everything about anything, so a pooling of information and insights is essential.

A second situation is when her critique is the necessary stimulus to prevent too easy (i.e., too critically undemanding and therefore possibly sloppy and halfway) talk among scientists in their theory-making, etc., and/or to push them to the best. When doing scientific research, a knowledge gap of even a few months can mean an immense amount of futile work and thus wasted resources that are always in short supply.

Even in America where we talk and argue about it a lot, there are limits to freedom of speech. Few will argue that anyone has the protected right to say absolutely anything anytime and in any setting - and the few who take that stance will likely start adding exceptions and qualifications before the discussion goes very far. Shouting *fire!* in a crowded theater when there is no actual danger is considered the classic example of what is not allowed. The challenge of life in a free speaking society not willing to accept chaos and total anarchy is to formulate workable principles for limiting this freedom to avoid inappropriate harm to any party while protecting the freedom from inappropriate restraint by individuals or any sub-group. *Inappropriate* is the key word and will remain a continuing source of disagreement. This will always be a problem that requires constant vigilance and adjustment as new technologies give us new ways to communicate and interact and as each new generation has to learn why the restraints that are in place were enacted since most of the younger people have until then been shielded by those very restraining laws from the harm that can result when the users and exploiters are given totally free rein.

Does it make sense that a Federal judge ruled that the cigarette makers do not have to put gruesome photos showing the harmful effects of smoking on their packages to discourage use of the harmful products as ordered by the Federal government because making them do that is a violation of the companies' right to free speech by requiring them to "say" this is what our products can do to you? Consider. Discuss.

From Day Two one person's "reasonable and sensible restraint" has been "unacceptable censorship" to someone else. Sometimes a conflict arises because of a failure to distinguish between *criticism*, which hopes to restrain by moral, social, or economic force without using the formalities of law, and *censorship*, which is aimed at restraining precisely by the power of the law.

Government regulation of industries is a special case where you owe it to yourself and everyone to consider what is involved. No industry (in a broad sense) starts off with self-created or self-imposed restrictions or regulations. Those are eventually imposed by government after the damage (or potential damage based on what we learned the hard way from dealing with the damage done by comparable industrial operations at other times and locations) has been recognized, documented, and gotten to the point where those being harmed could organize enough to be heard.

Every time you hear a politician, industry spokesperson, or tea bag head call for removing regulations you should clearly understand that they are saying in code, "We should be allowed to kill you and your kids and spoil your quality of life for our short-term profits and all the rest of our blather is to fill in the news bite time so no one who doesn't agree will be allowed to be heard." A suggestion for you, ask that person to explain to you and to the public at large in any except monetary terms why the regulations are unacceptable to her. Also ask her what her handlers or sources say are the reasons the regulations were put into place except documented damage done to people's health or to the environment. And while you're at it ask if she believes that the solutions to all problems with regulations is to toss them or gut them rather than to tweak them to deal with the kinks without removing the protection that was the reason they were enacted in the first place.

You might notice while you are considering regulations and their desirability that those who make the big profit from their removal aren't living, wouldn't be caught living, where they will be harmed by the damage they advocate. Don't kid yourself, anyone saying "Remove the restrictions" rather than "Let me help you do the tough work of figuring out how to adjust the balance between useful and harmful" is advocating the consequences - but only the money part for them, the bad stuff is for the suckers to deal with. Anyone have workable suggestions on how to change that? We need all the alternatives we can get.

Specific topics or ideas may be judged inappropriate or, in some circumstances or within some social groups, outright unacceptable. That is to be expected because social mores tend to overwhelm (although not overpower or nullify) recognized legal rights. Most of us expect a holiday celebratory ceremony or a political address to include certain types of statements and exhortations which we are then prepared to embrace or ignore based on our political predispositions. We may therefore be startled by and resent as rude and inappropriate adversarial exhortations interpolated among those we accept as the proper order of things. A person invited to say a few words during a July Fourth celebration but who launches into a diatribe against the preference in music of someone else on the reviewing stand would strike most as out of order. Often our expectations influence our openness to counter-arguments, protests, and the like. We are uncomfortable when we don't know in advance what will happen because we don't want to become publicly involved in disputes and disagreements.

Sometimes others don't want to hear criticism because they don't want to have to get involved with problems. "Don't make waves," is a dominant theme in many lives. But being appropriately critical is a job for all of us. Make these people face up to their responsibility or, at the very least, make them and everyone else aware of the harm that is resulting from their failure to do so.

You can't argue with someone who refuses to have an open mind, so there is no point in wasting your time in publicly engaging in such confrontations. You are, in fact, playing into her hands since your frustration and fumbling in an unfair situation is perceived by her and others including some of the pundits and news reporters who will originate the statement themselves or be certain to quote it from almost any source over and over and over as a victory on the field of battle of ideas and right-and-wrong which she has won.

When or why would I not criticize? Officially never. I can no more not evaluate what I am doing and what is being done to me than I can not notice whether I am standing upright or hanging upside down. Whether I decide I can do anything to change my condition and consider how I might do that is not automatic in the same way though.

Making critical judgments should be second nature to me and should become almost automatic. My reactions are flexible though. I don't have to automatically reject something even though I perceive it as being less than the best. In the social context I may allow something to go uncommented upon because that is what I judge to be the best response under these particular circumstances. If pressed I won't claim to believe the shoddy is artful or the sleazy is praiseworthy but I may elect to keep my opinion to myself if allowed to do so since I judge that being open about it here and now won't be helpful. This is part of the process of living in a society - trying to make an educated guess about when not speaking out is likely to result in more harm that sounding off and then acting accordingly.

Everything in human behavior seems to have its dark or shadow side, the less desirable or even potentially harmful price that must be paid for the objectives we value and pursue. Critical thinking is no exception to this generalization and since, as we have seen, it encompasses a variety of behaviors it can have shadow aspects of any of those. Consider some of the risks and the burden they impose upon us and you will be better prepared to avoid those.

Giving criticism to a receptive person allows us at least a less guarded if not a totally unguarded moment in that individual's defenses and it may be possible under the guise of objectivity or fair play to either deliberately hurt him or slip in our own pet ideas or causes. How subtly this can be done and the difficulty of ever being certain whether there was a deliberate attempt to betray the person's trust makes it more tempting.

You could gain the respect of others and a reputation as a helpful critic which brings with it the danger of seeing yourself in a messianic light and overestimating your wisdom and importance. You could lose your sensible humility and believe you are always right, always have the best insights, and never deceive yourself or miss the point.

You could become so involved in critiquing everyone else that you ignore or neglect yourself.

You could confuse recognizing the need for change or for better ways of doing things with actually coming up with those new ways and implementing them.

You could become an obnoxious imposer of critiques (generally in the narrow negative and pejorative sense) on everyone and everything, whether anyone invites or wants you to or not.

You could simply become obsessed with critical thinking and feel you need to know everything in such detail before you can make a decision that you are immobilized.

You could become a chronic second-guesser constantly reviewing your decisions with a view to revising them - with the result that no one else can ever consider your announced positions to be final and what you will stand behind. Or you could go over the other way and become so enamored of your views and decisions that you won't reconsider them or alter them in the face of new information, changed conditions, or an altered perspective.

Why do we so often put off solutions until a full blown disaster has developed and only then think about new ways of doing things? Especially why in cases where it has been obvious for some period of time that this disaster was likely and was directly associated with the way we were doing things? A realistic answer often is that there are limited resources and choices had to be made about which projects would get the support and more short-sighted decisions were made.

At least in part though it is because change produces stress. Therefore you need to prepare yourself for some stress as part of the process. Especially when you first start deliberately choosing to change or reject the normal or usual, you will experience stress. It gets more manageable as you get experience in choosing. Rejecting some big given of your life lets you reject many more things after due reflection later. This isn't rejection out of quirk, but rather because the reasons for accepting or believing in it are no longer persuasive to you. Good criticism is hard work and therefore a burden but one that we must agree to accept to be all we could be.

Why is criticism so hard? Because it is hard to always be fair. Hard to be certain you are right. Hard to be certain you understand and are using terms in the same way the other person is. Hard to risk losing a friend, associate, or someone else who could potentially be of value to you. And hard to risk getting stung so badly in response that you will refuse to view things critically again, even for yourself.

Part of the work is that in a sense you must do the other person's work too. You have to try to understand what he intends or intended, and what criteria he was using. Then you have to evaluate whether his objective, his criteria, and his methodology were appropriate and whether his performance was up to expectation. You have to try to go beyond the immediate events in evaluating it in the larger picture or you are probably missing the point.

We can recognize three levels of criticisms and can see that the burden imposed by each is in proportion to the importance of the matter in our lives.

The lowest level are *Superficial criticisms*. These include things like our reactions to TV shows, magazine articles, certain foods, some sports events, etc. in which we have little emotional investment.

What we might call *Intermediate criticisms* involve persons and things that affect us directly but not in an ultimate way. We pay attention to these, but we don't burn bridges or send in our main battalions in response. Minor items in the budget of the local municipality, decisions about whether we are okay with the brands they stock in the store most convenient to us or should shop elsewhere, and whether to allow outside tables at restaurants in our neighborhood that will narrow the pedestrian walkway fall into this category.

The highest level we might call *Intense criticisms*. These involve matters of long-term and far-reaching importance for us personally and/or for large numbers of people. These are events which may have some ultimate effect on our fate and well-being. We focus our attention on these and may be prepared to mobilize all our resources to deal with them.

If, as is common, our personal and corporate learning curves are sigmoid or S-shaped there is a plateau or even a decline after a period of achievement. The initial goals and insights may lead there inevitably. The way to avoid being stuck permanently on the plateau is to periodically rethink and reevaluate the whole business. That lets us reset our goals and approaches in realistic terms and according to the directions we are now interested in, no matter what we had previously intended.

Attention and critical evaluation go hand in hand. If you aren't paying attention to what it happening around you that affects you, there is no opportunity for you to react to the events critically. But there is also little motivation for you to be attentive if you are only going to passively acknowledge whatever happens. This doesn't, however, mean that you must, should, or even can become directly and significantly involved in everything that affects you. For the majority of us, our worlds have gotten more complex but our days still have only twenty-four hours.

There are limits to the number of areas that anyone can keep tabs on. You destroy your own potential effectiveness when you spread yourself too thin because it quickly becomes obvious to all that you simply don't know what you are talking about and therefore aren't someone to be taken seriously.

This is a major problem that needs careful consideration. In the modern world we are affected by a spectrum of technical problems, many of them deliberately complicated by those with a vested interest in keeping us from understanding the details. How can we organize ourselves to pool our resources so we can keep abreast of the advancements and potentials in the important specialized areas, since it is impossible for any one of us to do it all? Can this even be done? How do we select the individuals to become our experts in each area? The people whose opinions we will take as our principal input in making our decisions? How do we certify for our own purposes that they are basically objective, aware, informed, and aren't seeking this position precisely in order to influence us for their own political or economic agenda? It is important to recognize that those intent on slanting the expert condensations of information are potentially more destructive than those who are simply ignorant of the complexities of the topic they purport to know about.

Is it even theoretically possible for any person or group to obtain sufficient detailed and objective information about any technical field - whether electronics, economics, politics, soil fertility, or what have you - to make genuinely informed decisions? Is there such a thing as *objective* information or is that a meaningless concept? Are reports from the individuals who produce them ever complete and impartial? Could they be? Do the information output centers - the technical journals, the government sponsored studies, the privately owned news media, the privately funded think tanks - allow even the possibility of intelligent citizens who are working at the task being able to get enough of the pro's and con's and verified hard data to make free and informed decisions?

Critical awareness has a down side in addition to the dark side noted above in that it is will likely increase your sense of anger and frustration because you will recognize incompetence, manipulation, and disinformation at every turn but won't be able to do a lot about much of it. It is to be hoped that this annoyance will transform itself into a compelling drive to become more active in the political arena (in the broad sense) but it also must lead you to some accommodation with the situation itself lest you go bonkers because of the strain.

You can't change everything or even everything in any one area. That means that within the limits set by your time, skills and capacity, and by the circumstances beyond your control, you must develop techniques for keeping yourself calm and under control while you carefully evaluate what you can change. There is a satisfaction in seeing through the fog and recognizing situations for what they are, and another and somewhat different satisfaction in doing what you can to make things better.

The world will be a better place when more of us look critically at the myriad claims being made by those proposing to sell to, govern, or represent us. When we begin to express ourselves as incensed and repulsed by the ad makers' attempts at manipulating us and *developing a need* for their product no matter how exotic or useless, the market place will be less of a viper pit. Don't hold your breath though.

The game of politics will have to be played by modified rules when we become exasperated enough to refuse to tolerate the stupidity of listening to all of the political managers and players explain openly to the political analysts and news media people how they are going to adopt some position, make some statement, or support some idea in order to win our support because we will fall for this maneuvering and see it as reflecting the real candidate and his ideas. We have done half the job when we make a regular practice of holding up to the light and actively criticizing the claims of these persons. When we pressure them into honesty and sincerity by refusing to buy their products, support their election or reelection, or tolerate their continuance in office, we will have done that much more of the rest of the job.

But let's not fool ourselves, this is very hard work and not a task that will be accomplished overnight - and not once and forever. It won't be easy because people, especially those with something to lose, are skilled at artful deception if not outright lying. Also because we all have many other matters of consequence to concern ourselves with. We may be surprised and saddened to learn how little consensus we can put together on most any topic. We each have our prejudices, our ignorances, and whole areas of human concerns in which we have no direct interest. What may be a burning issue to you may well seem unimportant to me until and unless you convince me that it actually affects me enough to merit much attention.

We can't always be certain we are correct (whatever *correct* means in the context) but we can reassure ourselves that we have tried to make rational decisions based on as much information as we have available to us. The reliability of that information is always a matter we need to keep in mind and regularly assess. Those who insist on certainty in their lives create their own problems. They seem to pick out some system and then insist that it must be accurate in all of its details because otherwise they would either have to make some decisions or they would be obvious fools, even to themselves.

Are our standard ways of action compatible with and supportive of critical thinking? Not necessarily. Sometimes the format gets in the way of the desired result. For example, panel discussions seldom cover much ground or do so very effectively. Organized debates are for winning points, not making a sound presentation. For starters, Deborah Tannen's books on how we don't speak the same "talk" even when we use the same language should be on your required reading list if you are intent on doing better. I list some of her titles at the end of this book. The "objective" presentation doesn't exist. None of us is completely objective, our good intentions to the contrary notwithstanding. We simply have too many conscious vested interests and semi-conscious prejudices.

We are also burdened by the fact that almost nothing in the world of human behaviors is absolute. The existence of underlying absolute moral principles is a fiercely debated topic which is not within the scope of this book and I prefer not to be interpreted as suggesting or supporting any side in that discussion.

Consequently I must argue that even ambiguity has its place in human affairs. Our word ambiguity comes from the Latin *ambi-* and *agere*, "to go around" and refers to something that can be interpreted in more than one way, something that is vague and doubtful or uncertain. But ambiguity per se is not the problem; abuse of it is the problem. When we use it as an inappropriate shield or smoke screen to prevent access to information that the person asking has a right to or when we rely on it too much of the time so that the very basis of communication is thwarted, we have problems. The difficulty is to define the situations when it is appropriate and to try to devise strategies for preventing its abuse. Ambiguity can be deliberate or incidental and it can revolve around definitions, intentions, consequences, or data.

When the ambiguity results from inconclusive data, too little data, or biased data the situation is frustrating but we have little choice but to live with it until better input can be obtained. When it is thrown up as a smoke screen to hide incompetence, illegality, or personal scheming it is intolerable but at least in the short-term we may have little remedy for the damage it is doing.

The middle ground is when more precise information might be available but it better serves some proper purpose not to be specific about evaluations, intentions, and the like - the position of Wikileaks to the contrary notwithstanding. Diplomacy, at both the interpersonal and international levels, is the most frequent justification for deliberate ambiguity. When your opinion about something non-essential will cause hurt, strain relations, or generate a distracting argument and none of this will serve any useful purpose it makes sense to hedge. Diplomatic reports are where the true evaluations and thoughts of those involved are communicated to those far away who must decide how to proceed based on this input. What kind of fools think there is no valid place for keeping such messages within the group?

Your neighbor's first grandchild may seem totally unremarkable to you but what purpose will it serve to deflate his genetic pride by saying so when you meet him on the street? If called upon to testify to a world body that this is the genius child that has come to lead us all to new heights you would be compelled to say honestly that the kid seems as ordinary as they come, but for the small audience of a doting grandparent you may restrain yourself to something noncommittal. "He certainly is something" or "Yes, he certainly has big eyes" are honest without committing you to anything. (More about artful dodging in Chapter 14).

In a comparable situation, a national leader who while attending a lavish celebration like the Bicentennial of the French Revolution of 1789 tells an interviewer that the French Revolution has no real value or meaning for the modern world inevitably generates real antagonisms among the celebrants and hosts of the event by saying so unless really pressed by that interviewer to make a contrary statement that might have significant consequences. Otherwise the statement may reflect the leader's honest opinion but it fails the test of diplomacy because there doesn't seem to be anything constructive in the utterance. Here the complication is the questioner. Since a response for public consumption was being requested it is possible to imagine ways of asking a question of a major political figure so that you put words into that person's mouth. Especially in a public situation where neither refusal to respond nor long and detailed qualifications would be accepted, it becomes possible for reporters to lay verbal traps for newsmakers. We can't escape the fact that this is an age of sound bite electronic news reporting.

An honest but negative response in such a situation could reflect any of several reactions from the political figure. First, he might detect unemphasized implications in the question that he knows full well may or will subsequently become the center of focus leading to claims that "although not in so many words" he made undesired or unintended statements. Or he might be using the question as an opportunity to state his opinion that any fuss about this matter is a waste of time, a statement that might be viewed as out of place if he were to initiate the topic. Or he might have decided that the statement would have a beneficial domestic political impact for him and would cause only a minor diplomatic flap so he comes out ahead by making it. Or he simply might not care about any diplomatic or political repercussions of his statement.

He might also be new at the game of being a public figure and answer off the cuff without thinking about the fact that the whole world might read of the comment in the next few days. For a public figure, whose every word can become news, there are potential pitfalls in any utterance within direct or indirect hearing range of his competitors, opponents, or reporters - or these days, bloggers, open microphones anywhere nearby, and almost anyone with a picture cell phone. As a result, blatantly innocent and/or ambiguous statements are the safest.

It also seems acceptable for those public figures to hide behind fog expressions when asked leading questions or when asked for yes-no responses to complicated questions that properly require qualifications. The reality is that the questioner argues time and page space limitations as the excuse for such unqualified responses yet those same people and lots of others will be in the front lines of those arguing and accusing about all the details and implications that the public figure couldn't be given a chance to deal with initially.

There are also those times when the responsible decision-maker is evaluating the information he has received on a matter and considering the ramifications of the possible responses. During those periods it would be inappropriate for him to make final and binding responses about his intentions precisely because the best decisions require some study and thought. The flip side, of course, is that often the unpopular policies have already been decided on but admission of that fact is delayed to limit the time those opposed to the plans have to prepare their responses. A danger with this strategy that is routinely shrugged off is that at least some of the public will detect the lies and as a result the person and his cause will lose credibility about all topics.

Which brings us to the problem of how do we devise guidelines or regulations that assure proper consideration time but minimize the abuses? I have no ready solution, only a caution that there are many levels and ranges of situation where the need to set limits may arise and there will not be, cannot be, any single guideline that will apply to all of them.

History warns that there will be a strong push to apply whatever guidelines, good or bad, are developed for one area to a variety of other but significantly different situations. We must resist this trend. *Follow the leader* or *one size fits all* are the easy ways out of some of our problems but they are seldom satisfactory ways. Harder but ultimately necessary is the task of formulating separate workable guidelines that fit with each type of situation.

A commonly considered case where ambiguity often seems to be desirable is in the specification of responses or punishments to violations of rules. In international affairs it probably is better not to spell out too precisely what retaliation will be administered for acts of terrorism, failure to act in a civilized manner or in our best interest, or other generalized occurrences. If you promise massive retaliation and the subsequent precipitating action is minimal, you look to the world like a bully or a group of power mad lunatics. On the other hand if a massive provocation brings only a wimpy response you are a laughing stock around the globe. A danger of huffing and puffing but not being able to actually do anything effective is a real threat to personal and national dignity and prestige. Better to design your response after you have measured the assault. Better to keep as many options open as possible as long as the offense is still to come. On the other hand, for specified acts it makes the administration of justice more even-handed if there are a range of preset penalties for each type of act, always with allowance for mitigating circumstances. For instance, zero tolerance policies are the work of fools and a burden on every reasonable person.

Federal penal guidelines may considerably limit the discretion of judges in passing sentence on convicted felons. They are intended to minimize the disparity in punishment for the same crime under the same circumstances depending on whether you are tried before a hanging judge or a bleeding heart judge, or in Texas rather than Connecticut. They also seem intended to simplify the onerous tasks of judges and prosecutors. They are far from perfect but are an attempt to deal with a real problem. Such ideas are always works in progress, requiring more refinement in the search for the balance between fair and effective. These rules are a stark example of that need.

It is possible to group or classify criticisms based on the subject being evaluated as we will do in this chapter. It is also possible to classify them by type as constructive or destructive, or by specific sub-heading such as superficial, job-related, personal, sexual, or self. From a different perspective they could also be classified as anticipatory, participatory, or post-action or reactive.

An *anticipatory criticism* is one that is presented before some action, but based on previous ones by this person or others, in the hope of improving this performance. This is the coach reminding the athlete of the plays they have been practicing (perhaps with a more or less explicit mention of how she messed up in previous games so she will avoid those mistakes today).

I am calling criticism given on the fly in the sense of during the action (but not in the sense of off the cuff and without adequate thought) *participatory criticism*. This is the commentary from the woman in the back of the canoe as the two of you enter white water. She reminds you of the standard procedures for getting through this, shouts out when you need to pay heed to the protruding tree branches coming up fast on the left while you are so focused on the rocks to the right that you may not notice them, and gives you a word of praise when a well-timed maneuver with your paddle steers the canoe safely around a hazard.

A *reactive criticism* is the most common form. It is the recap after the game to emphasize which moves worked and which ones need to be scrapped or need practice since they didn't yield the desired results this time. The time frame for such analysis is very flexible. If there is some reasonable expectation that rehashing it might benefit some of the participants, the option remains open. It can be done fifteen minutes after the game, or fifteen days, or fifteen years later.

When classified by subject, criticisms fall into four major types, with inevitably some overlap where we need to make working rules of thumb to draw the line.

A) *Criticisms of a product* - which might be of an art object, a literary creation, an athletic performance, a meal, an article of furniture or clothing, or anything else crafted or modified by one or more persons. These are a matter of deciding how we think the product matches up with some theoretical ideal or some actual model we are comparing it to. The judgments are mainly yes or no on whether it is as good as or better than other products of the same type. There is some implied evaluation of the producer, but the focus is on the product.

Some products are more obviously associated with and reflective of a particular person's talents and labors than others. For instance, an actor's performance cannot be viewed as an impersonal event although to a degree the meal prepared by a particular busy chef might be. The workers in a factory who assemble the pre-cut pieces and tack on the padding make a chair but we think of their work as less creative and therefore subject to a different sort of criticism than the artisan who shapes each piece from the raw wood and may spend several days making a single chair. The two chairs serve the same purpose but the handmade version is more valued (and therefore more expensive) than the factory mass-produced version because it is seen as the result of a personal investment of talent. The factory worker is evaluated but on different (although not totally unrelated) criteria.

An athletic or artistic performance is seen as an event that may be talked about for years but which is also understood as transitory by its very nature. You can stand a chair or a statue by the wall and look at it for the next sixty years; a stage performance lives on only in memory (unless filmed in some fashion but even that is not quite the same as the live event). There will be another game next week or the curtain will rise again tomorrow evening. Our critique of the person should factor in this latest performance and those of the individual's whole career - and in a less personal scope, those from all the people who participate in the activity around the world and over the years.

Joan scored two points tonight but her average for the season is four per game and the team average for the last thirty years is three per game. Harriet gave an adequate performance tonight but she was more on the money last Thursday night. Compared to other Ophelias over the years though she isn't in the top twenty.

Some product performances are quantitatively or mechanically rated. She scored seven hits in twelve times at bat. She completed the course in five minutes, 26.7 seconds. More tickets were sold for her performance tonight than for any other event in the history of this theatre. Others critiques are more subjective and therefore more open to disagreement. The pro baseball player with the most home runs in a season is a fact; the "best player to ever swing a bat" is only an opinion.

Generally speaking, artistic performances and unquantified sports and other performances can be, and possibly will be, argued forever. That is part of the reason some want to quantify things as much as possible, even though that focuses the attention on parts of the performance rather than on the whole, which may include such intangibles as grace, verve, and good sportsmanship. A desire to avoid subjective disputes may also partly explain the seemingly obsessive fascination of some with the statistics in sports.

There is a blurry line between criticism of the creative products of a person and of the person herself. When the main emphasis is on the product with only incidental attention given to the longer scale (career or multiple repeated events) I am considering it under this heading. This meal, this book, this performance. The longer scale criticism like, "Is she a great actress or only one who gave one great performance?" I shift over into the next heading. Products that can stand alone are likely to be subjected to a simple assessment. "Is it superior to others I am aware of, yes or no?" Those that require a weighing and judgment by the critic that can't be strictly objective will always require more detailed, and probably qualified, statements.

B) *Criticisms of a person or an institution* are the second important category by subject. The judgment of a person might focus on her habits and mannerisms, her projection of herself, her presentation of material when lecturing or teaching, her performance in some artistic activity, and the like. For an institution, the focus is on how well the individuals who make up and represent the institution are doing the job that this artificial person the institution is set up to do.

Criticism of a person is the area that we should approach most cautiously yet it is often the topic that we launch into most readily with little or no preparation. We all have the right, duty, and need to form some critical opinion of the people with whom we interact and associate. This is necessary to decide how your relationship will develop and whether it will continue. It is necessary to decide whether or not you want to deal with these people and how to do so if you have to do so because of your social, economic, or political situation. These include the business interactions of any kind that may involve friendly interactions but are not primarily social ones.

For instance, Mrs. B. had an unpleasant experience dealing with a bank teller who was too busy having a conversation with a co-worker to do things correctly and who then belittled the customer for causing the confusion. She has a valid basis for having a negative opinion both of that employee and of the bank that hired her but does not provide adequate supervision to prevent that kind of lousy business practice.

You are judged by the company you keep so if you have a choice about being seen in public with her, you want to consider at the start if this is someone with whom you want your name associated by others.

These interactions include all of our personal and possibly even amorous relationships. The person you meet for the first time or only occasionally by chance at large group social events is not seen as part of your inner social circle, but the person you make specific arrangements to meet somewhere is. You have no control over chance encounters but you made a deliberate connection in the other cases. First impressions may be lasting, but they also may be wrong. The person you initially instinctively shied away from will probably never become a close friend but some of those you were favorably impressed with at first may also prove to be disasters whom you need to avoid once you are better acquainted with their behavior.

If a politician advocates some policies of which you disapprove but also champions some that you are eager to support, you must decide how to work with her without being perceived as approving of all her positions. It is necessary to decide on possible endorsement of the person, her personality, her quirks, and her works - which will then reflect on you since others will judge you by how well their judgments about this person correspond with yours. There are no firm guidelines about such matters.

It may also be necessary to critique this person because your job calls for it. If you are in a hiring/firing or other supervisory capacity regarding this person you have no choice about it, you must judge her performance on the job, in the classroom, or in whatever situation you are overseeing.

This all pretty much boils down to three questions we may have to ask ourselves. First, do I want to associate with this person - and therefore be known by the friends I keep? This is either me-you or me-she depending on how well I know the other.

Second, do I have to evaluate or rate her from a business or an occupational point of view? This is mostly me-she. I react to the person or to a third party at a level other than that of our personal relationship, but it may include my supervisory duty to give her and others feedback on how I think she is doing and how she would be more effective.

The third kind of situation is when this is my friend and I must ask myself if I can I point out her strong and weak points to her and to others and make it work to her good? This is mostly me-you. It can also be me-she when I am attempting to defend or explain her to others. It is most important to remember that this can never be a fully objective evaluation. My personality, likes and dislikes, background and experience always influence my evaluation of anyone else. I should state that often so I won't take myself too literally.

C) *Criticisms of an idea* are the next subject category. This includes our evaluation of the interpretation of facts, of any original correlations, conclusions and extrapolations, and therefore the criticism of opinions.

This is another somewhat nebulous area, but one where rational arguments carry more weight. While there will always be room for disagreement, there is a more solid basis for criticism when we can point out that either there are flaws in the logic of the opinion or that it is based on false assumptions, data, or interpretations. In many cases we do better to oppose our opinion or our interpretation to that being offered with specifics about what we think doesn't work and suggestions for what might do so, rather than trying to show that the other person is wrong. It is always more acceptable to offer an alternative rather than sheer negativity. Once you have loudly asserted that she is wrong, there tends to be a vacuum where there should be room for discussion. If my opinion is better thought out, substantiated, and presented then the points I make will have more weight with those open-minded and sincerely interested in the matter. Why bother discussing the point with anyone else when you won't get anywhere or do any good?

Sometimes we will feel it desirable to express our own opinions while granting the other person hers precisely because we want to go on record as being unconvinced by her arguments. This is good. We still have to use our own judgment about how strongly to make the point though. How much are we willing to lose in rapport in order to make this point? That is a basic question that we are constantly being called on to answer.

You are usually in the position to decide whether to discuss or debate any topic with someone else. Unless your job or the law requires you to otherwise it is wide to do whatever you can to avoid being forced into public debate on controversial topics with those who evidence less that open minds. You can't win over such people with logic or with eloquence. They are determined not to be open to other ideas. They don't engage in discussions to enlighten or persuade, only to subjugate others to their own thinking. Those willing to sit in on these contests, for so they inevitably are, aren't usually about to be confused by logic or facts either, so don't feel too much obligation to them. They are likely there to watch their side win another battle or to have a diversion from the competitions on some TV show.

In general, our criticism of opinions will be closely allied with the problem of evaluating ideas. This would involve: (1) the interpretation of facts and statements, and (2) original correlations, conclusions, and extrapolations. In these areas a good critical reaction can be immensely helpful and is much to be sought from knowledgeable persons who are also good critics.

Finding a good critic for our original ideas can be more difficult. We need someone who can appreciate the logic, see how well it fits into the larger picture, and who is secure enough not to feel threatened or jealous because of our ideas. A good critic will take her time about reacting to our ideas. Maybe she will only nod that she understood what we said. An hour from now or tomorrow or next week she may have worked her way through it enough to see its strengths or its weaknesses. On the spur of the moment she may not be able to give much useful help.

Her task is probably one of three - or some combination of them. One, she may have to point out errors or deficiencies of your logic, your data, or other elements. Second, she may reaffirm you in your views and their soundness by allowing you to refute and reject her objections to your own satisfaction. And three, she may give you new insights and point out that others may see it differently - and clearly suggest to you how they might see it. She may succeed thereby in making you consider more of the possible areas that might be affected by your action or decision.

One of the great thrills of reading widely in many areas is when you come upon an author who has reached a conclusion either similar to your own or one very different from your own but it gives you new insight into the matter. A good critic can often help precisely by directing you to these sources so you can profit from them immediately rather that when and if you happen to stumble on them yourself. This is the type of help that a good academic adviser or teacher among others may be able to provide. She gives you the benefit of her years of reading as a short cut to relevant sources.

D) *Criticisms of facts* are the fourth subject category. The focus here is on their accuracy, completeness, lack of bias, relevancy, etc.

A good critic considering your interpretation of facts or would-be facts will help by checking your logic, your sources of information, the actual data, and other details. Often we are so wrapped up in our brain-child that we overlook fairly elementary errors or deficiencies of logic or fact. A good critic can point these out to us in such a way that we can't avoid them (because we may try, consciously or unconsciously, to do exactly that). Often she can lead us through our arguments, questioning each point in turn, so that we must verbalize, and therefore somewhat formalize, our ideas. This often will make us aware of the shortcomings. Perhaps she will force us to state the several points of our argument that contradict one another and lead us to see the contradiction.

A well chosen critic will have enough background knowledge in the area of thought to: (1) question our sources, (2) question our data, (3) question our interpretation of the data, and (4) suggest other sources or interpretations. Unless we have worked in a particular field of endeavor for some time, and especially unless we have actually done the kind of work that goes into the writing that we depend on for information and ideas, the professional literature of the subject area, we may give that information more weight that it deserves. With most research reports you have to scrutinize the data closely and not depend too completely on the conclusions of the author or the blurb prepared by the abstracting service. Sadly some researchers develop reputations for generating questionable data but still get published by reputable outlets. Their studies are then quoted in textbooks and used as the basis for elaborate theories and future research, often because they are the only ones or the most cited ones in a formerly obscure topic area. Here is where we need good critics and where the consideration of someone with experience in the field is most helpful.

A good critic will want to check out your data. Did you get it right when you copied it from your cited source? Are you sure that you are making the same claims for the data that the person who collected it made, including the same or comparable assumptions? If it is your own original data, can you defend it? How much fudge factor is there in it?

E) *Criticisms of taste* are the other subject category. The Romans maintained that in tastes, whether for food, clothing, life style, etc. it was every person for herself. They said that *De gustibus non est disputandem* or "There is no point in arguing about matters of taste.") Therefore, beware.

Criticisms offered in such matters are only avenues to controversy. There are no universal norms to refer to. In fact, there are seldom even very widely accepted local norms or conventional mores. Especially today, unless you are a demigod or a politician you are probably kidding yourself if you believe that "everyone agrees that..." *anything*. So go easy in this area. Step out boldly or tentatively as you choose, but be aware that you may generate a lot of unresolvable controversies which will serve no useful purpose, accomplish no good, and may cause you much trouble. The on-going problem of trying to establish community norms about what is pornography illustrates the problem.

Questions relating to taste will often involve you being asked your reaction to some product - an art object, a meal, or a TV program. This is the type of criticism which you are asked or invited to give, explicitly or tacitly, every day. While most people would argue that when they ask your opinion they don't want to influence you, that they really want your honest reaction, even those who might not turn on you in a rage if you say something negative often are made uncomfortable or hurt by such a response. Accept that often you are actually being asked to give your approval to it and nothing more. For one thing, this may be because it makes them uncertain about their own reactions. They liked it but they felt that you were supposed to have better taste in such things so they sought confirmation from you. Now they may feel that they made a serious error of taste and that this must be obvious to all because of your comments. Or perhaps they feel that you made your point unnecessarily strongly or suggested by some comment that you didn't really understand the thing at all or that you are just throwing your ego around. This will tend to make them consider your evaluation as having less value and therefore their overall opinion of you will also suffer which may reduce your ability to influence them for the better in future matters of real significance.

In many cases the best reaction to such invitations is to demure and artfully dodge by making some non-committal statement and trying to move on. "Very interesting." "It certainly is different." Sometimes something like this works fairly often. After a while many people will see the pattern and accept your refusal to get in the middle of such situations but they will usually tacitly agree to your decision.

There are always those who will insist. They are to be avoided whenever possible. They will react badly whether you refuse to comment or you comment negatively. Nothing but enthusiastic agreement will do for them. (Why do they always seem to pick the weirdest and ugliest things to champion?)

What matters or topics are there that cannot be (re)examined? *Cannot* could imply that it is beyond human comprehension or even detection and therefore, at least at this period in our history, it is literally beyond the reach of investigation by human intelligence. By their nature these items cannot be known now and that is the simple fact. Three hundred years ago many of the technological fields of today would have fit into this category. Radio. Recorded sounds. Lasers. Antibiotics. Gene splicing. Orbiting satellites. Without the basic science to comprehend and explain the phenomena there were no mental images or models to use to think about them. There probably are such things today but since they are unknowable today they are not a major concern here.

What I wish to comment on are those bits of human belief or knowledge which one authority or another attempts to place beyond the reach of intelligent scrutiny by edict. Is it appropriate that religious doctrine, government policies, or scientific facts and "laws" should be sacrosanct? It must be frankly admitted that questioning may be the first steps to rejecting. If dogmas or policies have a foundation in sound theology, rational political theories, or reproducible scientific experimental evidence there should be no problem. Nothing confirms a person's belief in and support of a position as much as seeing for herself that it makes sense. "Taboo! You cannot examine it!" smacks loudly of cover-up and fraud. A religion or a government founded on carefully concealed fraud is going to crumble sooner or later but it can still abuse a lot of people for far too long. The effort of those with vested interests in keeping those institutions operating to quash honest and open discussion and evaluation of the claims and policies should be an immediate and loud warning that such examination is definitely called for.

Are religious disciplinary policies immune from scrutiny and thus from criticism? Should they be? This is an important topic that needs to be considered at greater length than is possible here.

In theory everything and anything is fair game for criticism; in practice though there are levels or modes of criticism and some subjects are generally considered okay in some modes but not in others. Highly personal topics that are not the subject of public scrutiny (for instance, what consenting adults in their own homes with the shades drawn) are generally not appropriate topics for comment or inquiries by strangers. The important exceptions are those outside parties who are operating in some official capacity, like police officers or social workers investigating a report of illegal activities.

Government programs and policies are properly subject to full criticism in the broad sense as well as the negative sense that we all know is a national pastime in most countries with enough organization to have government programs.

Personal criticism, even if constructive and well thought out and well founded and intentioned, is always a bit hard to take. That's natural. That's human. Even when we know full well that we aren't perfect we hate to have the fact noted by others. Yet we have all learned that a bit of pain is often the price for improvement. "No pain, no gain," applies to some criticisms although it is not as universal a principle as in the context of exercise programs (where it should be questioned too).

When we are numbed and lulled by the status quo, we are little inclined and poorly equipped to consider alternative ways of doing things. But when we focus our critical skills on any matters, we open the possibility of finding the present ways unacceptable or at least imperfect. That may then lead us to think in terms of improving on the system to remedy the defects we have detected. That in turn might lead us to recognize and consider alternatives, at least some of which might be workable improvements.

In matters of global or national importance it is easy to conclude that you as an individual can have no significant input on them - and you may be right. But since the people who can have an impact are basically the same as us in many aspects in spite of having been raised into high places, we can know that we could make a dent if we worked our way into similar positions. Whether we would want to do that is another matter. The impact we might have in our local circles is usually more obvious. But even here it may be useful to differentiate between the actions that have value for you and those that alter the external realities.

How much involvement is enough is a complex and very human question. The all too human but nonetheless accurate answer is *it depends.*

It depends in large part on how important the present issue is to you, how it stacks up in your consideration of priorities. It depends on your realistic appraisal of what effect you can hope to have on the matter. You might for instance run for political office, locally or on a larger scale, in order to influence the decision. You might file a lawsuit to block an issue on which you have no other effective leverage. If you don't live in a municipality considering a new trash disposal scheme, you may get involved in the educational phase of supporting or opposing it even though you can't vote on it.

Lukewarm enthusiasm tends to produce mediocre activities. It also depends on what and how much you have to gain and to lose. The higher the stakes, the greater your determination is likely to be and the greater the commitment you will likely be ready to make. People are different. Among other large categories, some are theorists, others are activists. They perform separate functions and most of us are to a large degree primarily one or the other. You are likely to find that you are comfortable with some tasks but not with others among the list of things to be done to achieve any large-scale goal. You may try to force yourself to do what you aren't comfortable with - and you may do a credible job of it - but you aren't likely to be happy doing it or with the results and you aren't likely to be willing to do the same thing again.

How much involvement is enough also depends in part on your other obligations - as parent, mate, and member of the community.

Part of honing your critical skills is developing an appreciation of the fact that everyone does not think in the same patterns and have the same interests, priorities, or experiences. So not everyone is going to agree with your evaluation of any particular situation or your proposals for improvements. The realization that others with the same general concerns as you do not view the specifics in the same way can come as a surprise or even a shock. The acceptance of this fact is a major step in your maturity and adaptation to reality.

This realization that honest and intelligent people can come to a spectrum of views on the same matter is broadening and enlightening because it forces you to look for explanations and that leads you to appreciate the importance of information inputs and of the impact of the individual's experiences in forming his expectations and interpretations. A man who has observed several instances of harsh authoritarian put-downs of dissent will expect a similar response to even a peaceful demonstration against a government policy; the man who has lived in a society where such protest activities are a normal part of social life will argue that such fears are unfounded and paranoid. Therefore their expectations will probably prompt the two to favor quite different approaches to problems arising from government policy.

In spite of the fact that it deprives us of the feeling of security and the comfort of feeling that we need only to agree with the group-think to be correct, the benefit of this awareness is that it pressures you to face up to the necessity of each person being an independent thinker and critic. It also emphasizes that even among seemingly like-minded people you need to be prepared to explain and perhaps defend your views and decisions.

Who gets to decide who can offer criticism? Ultimately it is the audience, since the impact or effect of the views are what will make the difference - depending on the specifics and how organized the situation is. There may of course be various arbiters before that.

Can just anybody be a good critic or does it require some special talent? Who may criticize? Essayist and literary critic Joseph Addison (1672-1719), claimed, "It is ridiculous for any man to criticize the works of another if he has not distinguished himself by his own performance." I respond that as a universal statement that one is baloney! I suspect that were he around to clarify his broad statement he and I might find middle ground wording we could agree on though.

If there is a moral duty to be critical in certain circumstances, are there no reasonable limits on who can criticize and who or what they may critique? In practical terms, no. In reasonable terms, yes of course. We all too often encounter people with no knowledge, license, or good sense criticizing anything and everything. In America we generally concede that there is nothing to be done about this legally as long as they are not disrupting traffic, endangering others, or violating specific laws while doing so.

There is a distinction to be made between those who can offer criticism and those to whom the rest of us will pay attention when they do so. This is where we impose the restrictions for which there is no mechanism in law or official procedures. Virtually anyone can offer criticism but those on the receiving end don't have to be receptive or attentive when what we know about the critic and his background and agenda forewarns us that the criticism is unlikely to be constructive and helpful. A stranger we are more likely to hear out and then weigh his observations, I hope with an open mind, since we don't know his agenda to start with.

Those from whom we accept criticism separate into those who offer it unasked, those who offer to give it if we wish to hear it, and those from whom we solicit it. Those who offer comment without asking if we are open to it are the potential problems because they disrupt and distract when there is little if any chance they will have a useful or effective impact.

There are those from whom we must receive criticism on certain topics and then there are those from whom we choose to accept criticism on certain topics. The obligatory cases are those involving persons with some legitimate authority over us - like parents, on-the-job supervisors, and teachers. The topics on which we must hear them out (even though we may let it all go in one ear and out the other) are determined by their role in relation to us. Parents have wide leeway; supervisors, teachers and the like are restricted to subjects fairly directly connected with the job or the classroom.

It is appropriate to ask who can and who must criticize. In some cases criticizing is an option but at other times it is an obligation. Parents, for instance, have an obligation to educate their children in the socially acceptable behaviors for their stratum of humanity. Once they know what is expected, the children may decide not to go along with it but that is then their decision based on knowledge and they are properly held responsible for their subsequent behavior. The parents often have little culpability for subsequent behaviors of their children despite much shouting about this when someone is determined that *someone* must be punished for what the kids did or he won't sleep soundly since the law shields the under-age perps themselves. On the other hand if the children are doing unacceptable things out of ignorance of the social expectations the parents are very much responsible.

A worker who sees things on the job which constitute a present or potential danger to the health or welfare of the workers or the general public has an obligation as a responsible citizen to take whatever steps are possible to correct the situation, whether directly or by bringing the matter to the attention of the proper authorities. Persons who have accepted positions that include the responsibility for monitoring the performance of others (supervisors, principals, etc.) have a serious obligation to give individual critiques and, when necessary, to root out those who can't or won't perform to reasonable minimum standards.

When his supervisor, who had carefully kept his distance until then, took Jack into his office to offer some personal comments about Jack's personal appearance "to help in your dealings with the ladies", Jack politely declined his help. When the supervisor persisted Jack told him his actions were inappropriate and insisted that this line of talk cease. A co-worker who heard about this argued that Jack should have let the boss have his say, thanked him and then ignored him. Jack maintained that to do so would signal to the supervisor that the man was free to comment on any aspect of Jack's life and since Jack didn't intend to send that signal he needed to speak up.

There is probably no reliable objective data on such a matter but I am comfortable saying that I believe anyone can develop a degree of critical sophistication, although some people will always be better at it than others. Part of what will hold some back is that they consciously or unconsciously restrict themselves. They won't allow themselves to question authority, to accept responsibility for themselves, or to consider any idea that doesn't come with a stamp of approval from the proper people in society (whomever they perceive such persons to be). Effective criticism requires an open mind and a willingness to take some risks. The ideal of the fully mature person is the one who forms his own opinions rather than letting another totally dictate or shape them for him or just going along with whatever other opinions are expressed.

As in any complex topic, there is a simplified answer and a more complicated one to the question of who may criticize. The simple answer is anyone. The better answer is - all those with the appropriate background and who are prepared to accept the responsibility of the task. The best answer is that only a discriminating few in each case are qualified, since the task calls for someone acquainted with a lot of specifics if it is to be done to full advantage.

A good critic must be someone who: a) knows the topic; b) knows the specific details of this case; c) knows the persons and the situations (even more specifics); d) is aware of the basic do's and don'ts as suggested by this text and other sources; and e) is willing to do the task correctly, but is not being forced to do so against his wishes.

He must also be someone without: a) prejudices, although pre-formed positions that respect the rights of others are okay; b) an agenda that takes precedent over truth, objectivity, or fairness; c) a personal history with this case that might diminish it by raising questions about the fairness and honesty of his critique; d) a personal situation that might be complicated or compromised by the wrong response in order for him to act fairly and be perceived as having done so by those with open minds.

Sometimes the critic cannot be a disinterested party but then a person dedicated to fairness and honesty should suffice.

Not everyone who may properly offer criticism will choose to do so. Someone who shouldn't be considered qualified may still wish to do so and it will be necessary to deal with that. Someone too eager to criticize probably should not be invited to do so unless somehow it can be determined in advance that he has valuable insight, not just a desire to sound off or to praise or to put someone down.

Most often we can't keep someone from criticizing; we can only decline to pay attention or to allow that criticism to be the official or most influential word.

When we restrict our consideration to *good* criticism I think we can argue more strongly for some basic qualifications for a person offering criticism that we will agree to pay attention to (which is not the same as agreeing in advance to accept his views as valid and compelling, or to act on).

First, he should have a reasonable knowledge or experience of the subject area. Those who have never done any interior house painting aren't people whose opinions about that should get much consideration. For matters of procedure and technique it would make no sense to pay attention to any critic except a person who is well versed and probably experienced about the details. When Aunt Suzie, who has never even driven a car much less had training as an auto mechanic, tells you why your car's motor is not running smoothly you aren't likely to take her opinion seriously, even though she might be your source of preference for information on topics she is familiar with. We know that no one is knowledgeable about everything and not everyone is knowledgeable about any particular topic. We match expertise or experience to the needs of the topic to sort out reasonable prospective advisers and critics.

Second, the critic should have a reasonable degree of knowledge of the local situation that he is critiquing. For matters that are partly or completely within the public arena, a total stranger knowledgeable and appropriately motivated may be suitable critic, but for local and personal matters a total stranger is less likely to be acceptable or useful. The more intimate and personal the matters needing a critique, the more we should expect the critic to be aware of the details of the relationships and histories. The exceptions are the "distant intimates", those authors, lecturers, etc. known for dealing with these types of problems. They will be readily listened to and their generalized evaluations accepted because of the aura of authority and specialized knowledge the listener has invested them with. But think about your own experience. When a stranger who happens to overhear your conversation chimes in with advice during a discussion between yourself and family or friends it is virtually guaranteed that you won't give serious consideration to his suggestions because you are overwhelmed with resentment that this person dared to intrude uninvited into a private matter even if with the best of intentions.

General purpose *one size fits all* criticisms are seldom more than superficially useful and almost never of major importance until all the qualifications are added to fit them to the specific case. An informed critic does that automatically from the start. Is there reason to believe that this person knows what he is talking about? Don't assume that everyone with some kind of an advanced college degree or other training or experience talks sense and is knowledgeable.

Third, he should be clear about his agenda in doing this. To be useful, criticism must be accepted. To be accepted, it must usually be perceived by the person receiving it as helpful and probably constructive. Few of us are dumb enough to give credence to the opinions of those we know want to harm us or our causes or even to those indifferent to us or the matter being discussed. We don't let our enemies call the shots without protesting that and neither should we let the indifferent party who routinely rattles off some commentary on any topic presented to him without care or concern try to influence the decisions that affect us.

The verbal laceration intended to deflate your ego and destroy your good name that is delivered after protestations that this is being said only to make things work better for the group is cheating. Someone intent on destroying you but who claims to be interested in building you up can never be trusted again and that word needs to be spread. Is this person a representative of a group that stands to profit from persuading you - for instance an industry spokesperson? If so, be doubly critical. And doubly resolved about spreading the word by all available avenues once it is clear how his agenda shaped his comments.

There is no reason why you cannot impose reasonable limits or restrictions on the critic when agreeing to hear him. If he violates that agreement, his testimony is ignored so he had no effect.

The generally negative reputation of criticism raises the question: Can friends be critics and critics be friends? The answer is a definite yes. Many of your best critics will already be or will become your friends because these are the people who care about helping you become the best you can be. With a deliberate attitude of openness on your part, your true friends can be encouraged to offer constructive criticisms when they think that is appropriate. But those who are friends in name only won't fit into the scheme.

Not everyone who has the right to criticize and/or the right stuff to do so is always obligated to do so. There are other considerations that might argue more strongly for the person to keep quiet. For instance: he may be barred by law from discussing this topic or he may feel too close to the situation to be as objective as a good critic needs to be.

He may avoid the topic lest some information that must remain secret be revealed by things he might say even tangential to the matter.

He may have inside information that could cause the recipient to suspect that the critic's agenda is not what it is presented as being and therefore waste the opportunity to have a good effect.

He may opt to stay on the sidelines and reserve his impact for another topic if he judges that the matter is not of sufficient importance or that there are others competent and ready to deliver the needed critical message.

Or he may be deeply involved in this situation and have strong feelings about what is planned or was done but, at least at this time, he doesn't see how to make his comments constructive.

Or he may know his grasp of the subject is basically competent but the specific topic in question demands a superior knowledge of the details and he isn't certain he has that much information which leaves open the danger that he could as a result mess things up rather than help.

Or he may simply not care enough about the person and this case. We can't all be police-person to the entire community and still have a life of our own.

Or when the importance of the matter isn't that great, this critic may decide not to get involved because it would expose him to too much backlash, would require that he distract himself from things he values more, or would put him in a no-win confrontation with closed minds.

Motives that those wishing to reject your criticism may attribute to you are the same ones you are tempted to toss out when you find yourself on the receiving end of an unsolicited and unwelcome critique. By considering them up front you can make sure they aren't true and avoid unnecessary conflicts. At least they let you brace yourself in advance for the possibility that your attempt at being helpful won't bear fruit.

There are a litany of claims or suspicions by the recipients against accepting your criticism in this instance.

1) You lack the necessary skills or knowledge so you overstated the negatives because you don't really have any expertise. This is an attack on your critical skills.

2) You overstated the negatives to inflate your own ego. This is an attack on your honesty.

3) You didn't understand the true situation and critiqued one that is only in your imagination. This is an attack on your grasp of reality.

4) You have a hidden agenda to promote others and/or put down this person. This is an attack on your true intention.

5) You are talking about the wrong subject matter. This attacks your intelligence.

6) You have the wrong attitude about this. This is an attack on your objectivity.

Those determined to justify not being open to your criticism come up with lots of defenses. A particular case is a useful example of the complications built into offering and accepting criticism and why I say that *it depends* is the appropriate answer.

Should the *good sport* criticize his teammates? 1) To improve their game - even if they don't ask for his input? Yes. 2) To let them work out their frustrations as aggression toward him? Yes, if he feels that is what they need to do and he can withstand it. 3) To give vent to his own drive to win? Only if his observations are correct and constructively presented. 4) To make it clear that he knows more and is a better player than any of them? Even if this is true, it is unlikely to have beneficial results.

A caution to keep in mind is to consider what your criticisms say about you and your prejudices and intelligence or lack thereof. Especially about your grasp of or acceptance of basic realities. For instance, do you insist that officials should "simply do..." things you favor even though their positions don't give them any authority or power to do those things? Do you really want anyone in that position to simply do whatever he or his cronies want about anything and everything? Have you seriously considered that you might be crazy?

Typical of how critics tell everyone else about themselves are those who criticize the president, any U.S. president, for not making everything change – even though from moment one anyone who understands how politics works knows he can't do most of that by fiat, much less force the opposition to do what he says when they are fighting him at every turn because they don't want him in any position of power or influence.

The major goal of criticism in the good and positive sense that I am recommending is to supply useful feedback to the other person. We do so with the hope of influencing her decisions and therefore behaviors, which in many cases will necessitate that we motivate her to improve her performance. "You stink at that!" is a kamikaze attack with no further contact needed or wanted. "You might get better results if you tried..." requires some additional time and effort from the critic to spell out the why of the assessment, to suggest alterations in the behavior that might change the perception or the impact, and to encourage her. It requires more effort on the part of the critic but usually yields better results.

Effective criticism is desirable because it helps you the one who is offering it, the person criticized, and the community at large. You by alleviating an irritation; the recipient by helping her do things to better effect; and the community because dissensions or problems have been resolved without violence or unnecessary agitation. Poet Alexander Pope advised, "Get your enemies to read your works to mend them; for your friend is so much your second self that he will judge too much like you."

A fringe benefit of making the effort to effectively criticize another is that the insights you both gain from the experience are likely to make you so aware of what you judge to be unacceptable or harmful behaviors in others that you will find it harder to slip into them yourself. Thus you will reform yourself in the bargain.

Conveniently, most of what we are usually interested in criticizing are our own and other people's behaviors since these are the only things that can really be constructively criticized. Our behaviors, what we actually do, are responsible for much of how we are perceived and affect others. They are also to a high degree changeable (even if not necessarily easily changed). We learn behaviors and therefore can learn to do things in a different way. They aren't genetically pre-programmed into us, although some predispositions like an ease of doing certain patterns of thinking (math or music for instance) or a tendency to do things a certain way (like right or left handedness) do seem to be inherited.

Performance of any sort - whether athletic, artistic, or on the job - is an exercise of behaviors so it fits this generalization. Who you are, in the sense of personality and your degree of success in interacting with others, is a compilation of your many behaviors. Institutions are in effect interacting groups of people and the composite entity is characterized and largely limited to its corporate behaviors which are implemented as behaviors by the individuals so they fit in here too.

Ideas or proposals are capable of being altered because they are behaviors in the larval stage. To get beyond this stage they will be and must be translated into behaviors whether that will mean guiding the production of some non-living structure or affecting the behaviors of those making decisions and carrying out actions. Thus ideas fit into the generalization that behaviors are what we criticize.

Since it shifts our focus from fault-finding over to problem-solving, constructive criticism is the best kind if we want to change behaviors, not just gripe about them. We don't stop noticing what isn't up to par, but we concentrate on persuading or inducing the responsible people to change that without threats or ineffectual blather that only makes us look silly. But by shifting the focus we also take on a new burden of responsibility. In deciding to be constructive critics we take on the duty of doing that well. Our doing so, however, doesn't make the other person less responsible for her actions nor alter her need to change them if she agrees with our assessment of things.

The preliminary consideration is whether I as the critic believe change, some improved behavior in this other person, is possible and likely. If I don't see how the desired change is possible in this person in her circumstances the critical process can only cause hurt not benefit and I shouldn't do it. If it seems possible but unlikely that she can change, I must make a judgment call about whether I would do more harm than good - and proceed or not based on my conclusion.

Those who haven't gotten beyond the idea of criticism as fault-finding may have trouble envisioning how it can be constructive. The word itself suggests building something and that is what constructive criticism is intended to do. It builds a better person or institution. In much the same way that remodeling a building often involves removing, rearranging, or consolidating structural elements, the improvement of yourself or of someone else is a remodeling of a behavioral edifice. Like successful remodeling of a house or repair of a malfunctioning or less than fully efficient machine, constructive criticism aims to remove damaging non-essentials while replacing any faulty important elements with better working replacements. It requires careful surgical work using precision tools, not a hacking apart with a cleaver on a butcher's block.

Sticking with that house remodeling analogy, constructive criticism requires that what is to be removed be thought out in advance. No contractor will be in business for long if she enters a house and knock down two walls before she considers whether those are weight-bearing. And when you are removing substantial support structures, you must have some sort of substitutes ready to put into place so the roof doesn't collapse while you are placing an order with the supplier.

Destructive criticisms are like wrecking balls. They smash and shatter and hope to bring the structure crashing down. They are often big, brash, and impersonal. Constructive criticisms may ultimately remove almost as much of the structure but they do so bit by bit so that the rest doesn't fall apart in the meantime and they replace the defective or inferior structures with new and better ones rather than just leave behind a heap of rubble.

Sometimes in cases that involve replacing what was excised (even if it is smaller and of a noticeably different configuration) the end results of destructive and constructive remodeling may end up the same. The difference is that a destructive approach leaves it to the owner to find and put together the replacement on her own or with the help of advisers recruited after the demolition dust has settled. A constructive critic has the plans for the replacement ready to lay out for inspection at the start of the process and she is ready to help in the work from that early point in the process.

A main difference between destructive and constructive criticisms is in the critic rather than in the person or thing criticized. The difference is in how she goes about it - which depends on her intentions. Even if the recipient is not receptive (which means the criticism isn't likely to have any real beneficial impact), the constructive critic will offer to provide the feedback without intentionally raising hackles or trying to publicly humiliate the recipient, which should minimize the danger of damage being done. Most of us standing in the recipient's shoes will recognize the good intent of the critic even if we choose not to be open to her comments. Thence we will know this is someone we might approach about this or other matters later when and if we are in the market for some safe and helpful feedback. Someone intent on giving real help will almost always provide a constructive criticism, observations that may note deficiencies but which will at least offer some kind of encouragement, not just jeers and calls to go hide in a hole as a failure.

Constructive criticism may not be as satisfying to some people as complaining because it requires some thought from the critic, rules out demeaning and abusive name calling as counterproductive, and of necessity requires that the critic get personally involved with the person she is criticizing. When one is irritated but doesn't expect or especially care about soothing the itch, it is common policy to "bitch up a storm" because of some imagined superiority this gives to the whiner.

From the very beginning we learn how to do things and how to become the person that we will be by a process of trial-and-error. We do things and then evaluate whether each attempt works in the sense of producing the desired results with a minimum of negative side effects. Perhaps even without being fully conscious of it, we then try it a bit differently the next time and consider whether that gives better results, more negatives, or no apparent difference. We start learning this process as we swing our hands about trying to grasp that brightly colored toy suspended over us in our cribs without hitting ourselves in the eye as hard or as often.

The adults in our environment begin to apply criticisms early on. *No* becomes a dreaded word and therefore one we begin to wield with great fervor ourselves at about age two. Some older people (since siblings who are not a lot older than we are may be an important component of this category) are better than others at making us understand and accept limitations. In our early years a flat prohibition is often the message that works best. The assumption (probably correct) is that toddlers aren't interested in or able to follow the rationale for the decisions. But even at this stage the best nurturers are encouraging us as often as restricting us. They also redirect us to acceptable or safer activities rather than just put up roadblocks. Chances are that even as a toddler you had some sense that certain people were more constructive critics than others, although you would have scratched your head in puzzlement if asked about it in those words.

We can critique an action as either a stand-alone, one-time event or as one of a series of outputs of a person or group. Unalterable things most often can't be constructively criticized because they can't be modified in response to the feedback. Non-human, and especially non-living, items are criticized by rating them. They are accepted, rejected, or given some grade on a prearranged scale. Such critiques are valuable but in different ways than those involving behaviors. Even a book or film is set so we can only grade it, not alter it by our expressed opinions, although those might affect future works by those producing the items. Things that are alterable can benefit from the feedback in that the persons behind them and capable of changing them may decide to do so even though the object itself can't respond on its own.

It helps to cite specific actions as examples of your generalized observations, but from the start you need to phrase things to emphasize that it is the pattern of actions you are concerned about and not just this particular event (if that is in fact the case) which the recipient might want to reconsider. It often seems petty and unhelpful to harp on some past event, however it is something to listen to and consider when a good criticism makes us see that it is an example of a continuing behavior pattern that is producing undesired (and perhaps unrecognized until now) effects on others when we intend to impress or influence them for our benefit.

A common strategy is to attempt to sidestep into a constructive criticism by asking questions in the hope that those will open up the topic for consideration. This may represent a valid desire of the critic to understand the other's thinking or motivation in order to decide whether or not some revealing comment on the subject is appropriate. Or it may simply be a verbal strategy for saying something without having to actually state it. You let the other person draw as a conclusion what you wanted to say but couldn't bring yourself to or have decided is best not stated too explicitly by you.

The complication here is that you, the critic, know where you want your question to lead but the other person doesn't and she may be confused, alarmed, or angered by what may seem like an unwarranted intrusion into her private affairs or an off-the-wall probing for deep, dark agendas or hidden meanings. There is a time for questions but that usually comes after the basic exposition of the critic's intentions and interests. Don't ask questions if you aren't prepared to have them rejected outright, shunted aside, or laughed at. Your intention doesn't control the other person's responses.

All criticism aims to communicate. Whether your point is to help or to hurt, why bother making it if you don't get your point across? Well-intentioned criticism also aims to influence and motivate the recipient.

Feedback requires communication whether that is verbal or body language (both categories in the widest sense). I am including spoken, sung, or written words under verbal communication. Plus of course we often depend on our tone and phrasing to say more or give a different message than our words by themselves do in order to send one signal (usually a warning or a denial of what the words say) under cover of a routine social noise.

Body language would include everything from a raised eyebrow through hand movements intended to be out of view of some other observer, the kind of semaphore we sometimes practice behind the back of the person we are trying to deceive while keeping you the person facing both of us in the know. Body language can also send a different, and often contradictory, message than the words we are uttering at the time. Often when we are unwillingly making a statement under duress, we deliberately use our movements to get across our true thoughts or what we want to have taken as such. More often we are unaware that our unconscious is revealing our true thoughts in this way while we are consciously trying to lie our way through a situation.

When we want to offer good criticism we want to influence the recipient, hoping to prompt her to change some part of her behavior. Otherwise why do it? In this context *influence* means that we hope to alter some behavior of the recipient when and if it is repeated. That requires altering her thinking. That could mean either getting her to think it is better to not do certain things, or to do them in a different way, or to just get her to think about them rather than act in a mindless daze. Note though that influencing her to decide to change doesn't in itself dictate what alternative path she will or should choose to follow.

In some instances we want to influence an audience beyond the prime recipient because the lesson to be learned would profit them all. This is a valid aim but usually only workable or a good idea in limited circumstances. Most often the direct criticism will have the greatest beneficial effect if it is given in private and nothing is said that might embarrass the person or intrude on her privacy beyond that. However, when an offense committed in public view prompts a criticism, common sense and circumstances may dictate that your response be delivered in the same space. When the person deliberately acts to be seen as giving offense in public, she has no right to expect only a private response.

Motivation is the other aspect of helping the recipient improve her performance. Motivation is about choosing a path to follow from among the possibilities available to you. It is about getting you from the point of recognizing that what you have been doing causes problems for you and others, to the point to deciding to do some things differently. Motivation is about role models, cheerleaders, and leadership.

First you use your influence to get her attention and lead her to decide to make a change, then you offer suggestions on what changes would be more effective in getting her where she wants to be. This is where the critic must be most conscientious about suggesting what seems to be best for this person rather than simply what the critic might like to see even if it leaves the recipient in midstream. I might want to motivate this person to find some activities to help her make social contacts but the fact that the choral group that I direct needs members isn't enough reason to try to steer in this direction despite the fact that she indicates no real interest in singing.

There are three distinct phases to the process of giving a useful criticism, each with its own potential problems. First, the observations must be made; then those observations must be crafted into constructive criticisms; finally the criticisms must be received and then accepted.

Observing the behavior or performance of others seems simple enough. We do it every day. But observations that are to be the basis of valid criticisms must be accurate, detailed, and reasonably unbiased. Many times we at least begin to make the observations that will lead to a criticism because we are detecting something dissonant in a person or situation. Things aren't going as expected, or we are being irritated when the situation shouldn't have that effect on us.

Once the observations are in order we can decide how and if they can be cast into constructive criticisms. In Chapter 08 we will consider the qualifications required to merit that designation

Ideally, before you speak you will rehearse what you intend to say. Good criticism isn't better delivered off the top of your head. In fact it is seldom half as good when done that way. It needs editing to try to make your points clearly and in a logical sequence so that cause and effect are obvious. You also need to consider the terms you intend to use to avoid expressions that carry unintended baggage or that might suggest you are hinting at further actions when that is not the case. "You need to pay more attention to your feet when dancing" gets across the same basic point as "You have two left feet" without the baggage of "You're a klutz with no chance of getting this right." And "After the way she treated you, it would certainly be okay for you to go to the party with someone else" might seem like a subtle (or not so subtle) hint that you are open to being asked to be that someone else.

Even the best constructive criticism will have little effect unless the recipient is open to considering it. This is why the opening phrases of the conversation, in which the critic proposes to give feedback if the other wishes or is at least willing to hear it, are the point at which it needs to be emphasized that this is a voluntary activity (if it is). The critic must make clear her respect for the other person and her reasons for offering to do this task, which are to help, not hurt. There should be an overt acknowledgement that the recipient is in no way obligated to agree with what you say or to change in any way if she doesn't find merit in the observations. In many cases you as would-be critic already know the potential recipient well enough to gauge how much preliminary softening up is called for and there is no profit to overdoing it. When you feel the need to offer your observations to people you know little about (for instance, the officers of some organization that you are acquainted with and care about even though you have had no direct contact with these individuals) you may need to lay out your intentions with more detail before you get the go-ahead to present your critical observations and conclusions.

Your basic task is completed once you have presented your views. You overstep your position if you attempt to coerce the other to even respond to you beyond asking for a playback of what she thinks you said to her and what that meant, much less to say she agrees with you.

It is important that your points be understand the way that you intended them therefore it is always a good idea to at least request a playback of what the other person thinks you said. It is often awkward to do this during the uncomfortably tense recital of your observations, but many hurt feelings will be avoided if any misunderstandings can be clarified then and there. Remember that each of us hears what is said through the filter of our own experiences and often the words that imply one thing to you imply other things, even contradictory things, to your audience. You can usually only find out what the person receiving the critique *heard* you say by asking.

Understand that agreeing to listen to someone's critique because they might have some valuable feedback to offer does not commit you to do anything more than listen. You may disagree with the critic's views but if they were presented privately and only as personal observations intended to be helpful, you may feel that it would serve no purpose to argue the points. Or you may simply want some time to think through what has been said and its ramifications before you react to it.

Even the best criticism carries no guarantee that it will make the beneficial difference that was intended. In spite of your efforts to avoid that happening, it might be misinterpreted. Or for any number of reasons the recipient might not be capable of making the required change even though there are no outward signals of that fact which might have alerted you. Or the recipient may say she is open to your words but not be. Or maybe you just weren't persuasive even though you did your best.

One of the worst things you could allow to happen is to let yourself develop into a nag. Good and effective critiques are only given to those at least partially disposed to listen with an open mind. You can't shove your opinion down someone's throat and expect positive results. Just think for a moment about how you would react (how you *have* reacted) to someone doing the same to you. If no case springs to mind, consider the hypothetical one of someone trying to browbeat you into admitting that your religious beliefs are erroneous or crazy, or that your ethnic heritage automatically makes you untrustworthy.

For your criticism to be effective don't exaggerate, emphasize. It is all too easy to mentally multiply the size of the impact, the costs, and the perceived or anticipated horror caused by whatever it is you are opposed to before you spit them out and then give a quiet "my mistake" (which will get two lines on the bottom of page 26 of the newspapers to offset your original statement which merited banner headlines). Only emphasize the aspects that make your point, which are normally the exact points the other side is trying not to have anyone notice at all.

Sometimes it is desirable or even necessary to address the matter of responsibility directly and it certainly can be done in a constructive way. There is hope for a good resolution when the emphasis is on making all parties see and agree that there is a problem stemming from this person's actions, rather than on just branding the person as a failure or worse.

Our world and each of us in it is imperfect but we each want to be the best we can be and to have as perfectly humane and as stable a world as possible. Changes are needed if we are to go from imperfect to more perfect and often we aren't aware enough (or honest enough to admit we are aware) of our own behavior and performance. The most effective way - and sometimes the only practical way to get a clear focus on what we are doing, how we are doing it, its effects on others, and what other ways of doing it might be possible - is to have an independent observer describe it for us. Unfortunately, as often as not, we will then begin to quibble with or reject most of the observations because we are too proud to admit we could be doing *that*.

Our most important criticisms are those we communicate to the others involved with the intention of improving their effectiveness, performance, or behavior. These are constructive criticisms. If well done, they are always positive interactions. But because they often include an element of fault-finding, they carry with them a risk. They can do more harm than good if handled poorly and over the years they have been the cause of the break-up of many friendships. So why risk it? Why not just leave well enough alone. The only adequate answer can be that you care enough about this person or organization or about their impact on your life and on others to run that risk. And the risk can be minimized by having a clear idea of what you want to do, how to do it, and (very important) when it can be done most effectively.

Beth is convinced it is just bad luck that she has gone through four receptionist positions in a year but her friend Mary knows that Beth's overly informal manner in answering the company phones and her failure to take accurate messages is the problem. Mary is in a quandary. If she says something and Beth insists on the bad luck explanation she will feel like a fool and a meddler but if she doesn't say anything Beth may not figure out how to improve her performance so she can keep a job.

Ethel M. took continuing education courses in art appreciation and considers herself to have a well-developed taste in art. Her sister-in-law has just purchased several inexpensive oil paintings to decorate her home and Ethel thinks they are "dreadfully common". Ethel is trying to decide if she should straighten out her sister-in-law and get her to discard the paintings before anyone else sees them - and maybe suspects that Ethel had something to do with their selection.

Mr. C sees his daughter, a recent high school graduate, preparing to go to a job interview for a bank teller's position wearing the jeans and hiking boots she has adopted as her uniform for the last two years. Should he suggest that more formal attire would be more appropriate?

In each of these cases an individual is deciding whether to offer a criticism. In two of three cases the people have an opportunity to perform one of the most valuable and helpful services any person can provide for another - giving useful and constructive criticism. Ethel should just mind her own business.

Distressingly, most criticisms, in the broad sense of the term, are neither helpful nor sound because they are simply derogatory grumblings stimulated by our prejudices and peeves. For instance, the comments that racial or political factions shout at one another almost always fail the tests for being constructive criticisms.

What basic traits make a criticism constructive?

A) *It is the result of careful observation and is carefully thought out.*

Very few people are wise enough and experienced enough to give good constructive criticisms on the spur of the moment since it requires thought and effort. Instant commentary is almost always seriously wanting; off-the-cuff critiques too often miss the mark and then cause misunderstandings and resentment. The supervisor who sits the new salesman down to give him "the standard pointers since you all make the same mistakes" isn't helping much. The "Oh, yeah, let me see now..." commentary made on the run isn't usually even worth listening to. The would-be critic who doesn't have the time, or won't take the time, to prepare is worth about as much as any professional who doesn't bother to prepare for the job. He can't give a best performance. You might go to the hospital for abdominal pain but if some intern ordered you to surgery to have your appendix removed without the appropriate specific lab tests and examinations and you might question his decision even though you would agree it is an appropriate course of treatment once the diagnosis has been confirmed.

Observations that aren't accurate aren't observations at all, they are daydreams. They are reports of what the observer expected to see or wanted to see and they often have surprisingly little relationship to actual events. If you propose to suggest that someone stop doing something or do it differently, first be certain that they actually do it.

It is not possible to give the best criticism without preparation, but when you have thought your way through a particular matter at least once you may be able to operate at an acceptable level in critiquing other examples of the same class of situations. This is what allows professional counselors and various supervisors to deal with numbers of clients or employees without an elaborate ritual of preparation for each meeting. When the person and situation being critiqued fits within generalized parameters, criticisms can be reasonably nicely molded to the individual cases. When the matter is highly personal in that it arises out of the experiences, expectations, or intentions of this person though, a more hand-fitted response is required and that does call for some specific preparation.

But even here a person trained and experienced in dealing with cases of this nature won't require as lengthy a preparation, which may complicate the situation because to those not knowledgeable about such things the professional may seem not to have given it any thought at all. A physician reviewing a patient's chart before he says much more than hello has his mental computer processing the data in there, checking his mental files for standard therapies for the diagnosed conditions or the next tests in the process of eliminating possibilities in order to arrive at a diagnosis. An experienced M.D. may do this dozens of times a day, focusing a bit longer on the data for patients new to him but only needing to trigger his memory files of what he has learned, said, and done over months or even years to this long-time patient.

B) *Constructive criticism is presented as this one person's observations and evaluations being offered to someone he respects.*

When someone invites or allows you to present a criticism they don't automatically agree to accept that you are correct, or empower you to attack or abuse them. Especially when we are dealing with people younger than ourselves there is a tendency to pontificate and to claim a greater share of wisdom and common sense simply because of our age and experience - although we may find those factors less compelling when we are being criticized by someone older than ourselves. As soon as a critique takes on any element of "Now I'll straighten you out because obviously you need it", it is on the wrong track. A constructive criticism is always a "You might not be aware of how this looks to others and you might want to do it differently if you did" type presentation. To be fully effective, criticism must be well received and that usually means it must be willingly, even if hesitantly, invited rather than imposed.

It must be offered cautiously to avoid misunderstanding and to be sure it is taken as intended. If the recipient interprets it as just another attack it will be of no worth.

Hard as it may be for you to accept, you are not the universal person. Your opinions and observations were shaped by your education, experience, and prejudices and do not reflect those of all people or even of all right-thinking people. Therefore it is inappropriate to present your views as being universal, absolute, or unquestionable. You may validly reflect the general values and thinking of a particular religious, social, or ethnic group (although even this is difficult outside of a few narrow topics) but be far off the mark for many other groups. Leave it to the person receiving the criticism to decide how widely to generalize your observations. Whenever you overextend your scope, you reduce your credibility and your usefulness as a critic.

This is where the advice to walk a mile in the other's shoes before you judge him resonates. You don't have to agree with his thoughts or have the same respect for things in his background as he does, but until you understand his point of view you can't grasp why and how much his decisions are influenced by factors like his religion, ethnic upbringing, and other expectations and experiences. When you recognize those barriers and gulfs between the two of you, you have a better chance of finding ways to bridge or minimize them to be helpful to him.

Because of its interpersonal nature there are practical limits on who can offer constructive criticism to whom. People who can't tolerate being around one another are unlikely to make it happen. If you don't approve of a particular person, of some ethnic, racial, or religious group, or of those who engage in specific activities, you are unlikely to be able to offer valid criticisms of them that can lead to improvement. For example, someone who tells his friends, "(insert the name of the group of your choice) are just dumb, they can't help it," isn't likely to suggest or to support better on-the-job training for new workers of that group. Even persons who might be good at the task of offering criticism under some circumstances won't be in the heat of strong disagreement. Effective criticism requires mutual respect even though affection isn't necessary.

C) *Constructive criticism is presented in a friendly tone and atmosphere, if possible in private and in person.*

Keep in mind that this may be embarrassing and uncomfortable for the person being criticized so help him out as you will want to be supported when you are on the receiving end. There are professional situations, like medical staff conferences in a hospital, where criticisms are normally given before a group so that all can benefit from the observations involved. But that case is the exception, a situation where, more or less willingly, the members of the group have agreed to submit to this public appraisal of their work.

Most often criticism is more appropriate and is better received in private and in peace. Recognize that you too probably reject out of hand most critical comments made to you in the heat of anger, therefore expect others to shrug your words off in the same way under those circumstances. Until we adopt a deliberate policy of at least listening to criticisms, it takes a brave friend and a sideways approach added to the always necessary diplomacy (and perhaps a touch of guile) to even bring up a touchy subject. Any criticism should be accepted or rejected on its merits, but first it must be listened to and heard.

A quiet, neutral time and place are the setting most conducive to open, thoughtful consideration of one's performance. No one can seriously be expected to give careful thought to your comments while dinner is burning in the kitchen, the washer is overflowing in the basement, or the boss is giving strong body language messages of "Where is that report?" from across the hall.

D) *Constructive criticism deals with something that is capable of being altered or corrected.*

It isn't helpful, and is often downright cruel, to criticize someone for things they can't change like their looks (as opposed to their attire, hair style, and the like) or their ethnic background. It also shows a lack of good sense on the part of the critic to find fault with people on the job about third party matters that this person can't control. Pity the assistant who has to listen to tirades about company policies or about the bad manners of his boss. Behaviors of most types can be changed (although not easily) but his physical features or third party items are beyond this person's control.

Harry had a chance to arrange for a job interview and he flubbed it but doesn't know what he did wrong. When he hears of this, co-worker John decides that he should straighten Harry out for his stupidity. Should he say something? Not if this was a once-in-a-lifetime opportunity. If Harry won't have a second opportunity there is no way for him to do better, John will only rub salt in Harry's wound. But if Harry might have another chance at it and will benefit from knowing what to do or not do the next time, John can be helpful by offering a constructive criticism.

E) *Constructive criticism is given in a time frame that will permit the person to alter his behavior and possibly avoid some undesirable consequences.*

Past events that are not likely to be repeated are worth criticizing only to the extent that they are examples of continuing patterns of behavior that should be reconsidered by the person. Past failures are the standard fare of *destructive* criticism. How many people do you know who even years later keep bringing up some mistake from your past not as a humorous reminder of those dumb things we have all done that we thought we would never be able to laugh about, but as demeaning, hurtful put-downs? When was the last time you did the same thing?

F) *A constructive criticism must be specific enough to be dealt with.*

We can't deal effectively with generalized criticisms. Altering our behavior requires that we reduce our intentions and expectations to specifics. A major problem in any self-improvement program is to get yourself from the "I'm going to be a better person" stage (which is valuable for general motivation) to the "This is how I'm going to do that" stage. This, especially, is where a good critic must spend some time in preparation. Be clear that by accepting the role of critic you accept also the responsibility to be as specific as possible. It is here that valuable insights can be gained by both parties. As community activist Saul Alinsky phrased it, "The price of a constructive criticism is a creative alternative."

A criticism couched in too general a manner is not only worthless but potentially harmful because it does not give a reasonable indication of what specific changes might improve the situation. An office clerk who is simply told, "Your work is unsatisfactory," is in a sad position. He has no idea what behaviors or job performances are considered deficient. He is reduced to two options. He can either try to change everything he does - which is actually impossible and will probably make some of the things he has been doing well now unsatisfactory - or he can do nothing. But he is still subjected to the psychological burdens of disapproval, rejection, and fear for his job.

Similarly an entertainer told his performance "lacks sparkle" has little to help him improve since there is the immediate problem of what is this thing called *sparkle* and is his definition of it the same as his critic's? Otherwise he is in the same changing-the-good-things-to-bad bind as the office clerk. The psychologists G.R. Bach and H. Goldberg in their book *Creative Aggression: The Art of Assertive Living* call such situations "crazy making."

A dancer told that his gestures aren't broad and emphatic enough, along with a demonstration of what is desired, knows how to practice to improve though. The office clerk who is told that his finished work often has smudges and sloppy corrections knows what he has to watch out for. The child told that leaving dirty socks in the living room is a no-no, rather than simply "not to be such a slob", can alter his behavior and make his parents and himself happy since he wants their approval

G) *Constructive criticism should only be offered by someone with the necessary competence to evaluate this subject.*

In theory any mentally competent person could offer helpful and constructive criticism; in reality it is a task that requires more skill than many are prepared to offer or even willing to invest the effort to prepare for. When you have the option, you want to choose your critics very carefully. If they can give you helpful insight into your behavior in ways that don't threaten you, they may make a bigger difference in your life and performance than almost anyone else.

Someone with a decidedly inferior grasp of grammar is hardly the one to be correcting another's speech patterns. The person wearing three different plaid patterns isn't to be taken seriously as a critic of your attire. Knowledgeable and intelligent people should be sought as one's critics. An expert in a credentialed, licensed sense isn't always needed even for specialized topics but people who are ignorant of the subject must be avoided. Few people are in a position to critique you on everything in your range of decisions and behaviors. The wise person who will make a good critic will tell you quickly enough which areas are beyond his competence. There is no reason why you can't include both general practitioners and specialists on your roster of critics.

When you have decided that surgery is probably necessary for a medical condition, you don't want advice on the surgical procedures from anyone except a certified physician. Still, a layman knowledgeable in this matter may have prudent suggestions based on his own experience regarding which doctor can give you a good second opinion about whether the surgery is really needed.

A critic you have imposed on you or who comes at you in the wrong way is likely to make you feel you must instantly and automatically reject his observations. That means that even if he had something valuable to say you will refuse to recognize it because of your universal rejection of this person or this attempt at criticizing you.

Realistically most of the people who are authorized by society to routinely offer criticisms (e.g., parents, teachers, bosses and managers) are poorly prepared and inadequately motivated for the task. This doesn't mean they are incapable of the task, only that they need to give it the time and thought appropriate to an important undertaking. Otherwise, as is often the case, they will be ignored or repudiated, or have effects quite different and often contradictory to those they intended.

H) *Constructive criticism must be intended to improve and therefore to enrich the recipient.* It isn't constructive if it is intended to or is likely to only hurt the person or puff the critic. The hurting types of criticisms are what give the practice of criticism its negative connotations and bad reputation.

The positive side of criticism is giving credit where it is deserved. This means praising, complimenting, and encouraging to an appropriate degree. It runs the full flip side and is as important as the other. How often have you been told in a frank and pleasantly offhand way that you are attractive or intelligent or hard working or have great potential? Do you remember how you felt and what you resolved to do about it? I am willing to bet you resolved to make the most of whatever talent or faculty it was that was complimented. Not in a selfish or narcissistic way, but in a positive way. Resolving to use your talents rather than hide them under a basket. There is a lot of talk of narcissism and of a "Me generation" and some people use that chatter as an excuse to avoid giving and receiving proper and meaningful compliments.

Even when criticism is of the complimentary type (as it ought to be more often) the right time and atmosphere are needed. We tend to be wary of flatterers because we have learned that, as often as not, they are just buttering us up to impose on us. We enter any social situation with psychological expectations of what is going to happen, what types of topics will be discussed, etc. When events don't match our expectations we get uneasy and cautious, wondering whether we misread the social signals or if something unusual, and even potentially problematic, is happening. Even compliments on past events can have this disquieting effect because the recipient starts to wonder where this conversation is going and why you brought up this topic in the middle of this social situation. The person may be so busy trying to figure out what your true intentions are that he misses the sincere compliment intended.

Compliments of one person delivered publicly during either a celebration or a commemoration for another person are highly likely to seem inappropriate and divisive.

A full consideration of the effects of going critical requires that we recognize that, despite the best intentions of the critic, any criticism may cause pain. Like most tools, criticism can be used to do harm as well as good. A knife is useful because it cuts and it is up to the user to decide whether to use it on a nicely cooked leg of lamb or on the raw leg of a rival. A hammer can smash fingers or glassware as well as drive nails.

Distinctions often help us organize our ideas and sort out the complexities of behaviors so I suggest there are three categories of criticisms that have hurtful or harmful results: misfires, painful criticisms, and destructive criticisms.

A *misfire* is the term I am applying to a criticism intended to be helpful and painless but that for any of a range of reasons ends up having mostly harmful effects. No pain-inducing elements are deliberately included but they may slip in without being intended or possibly even recognized as such until too late.

Misfires are a common and not completely avoidable risk in the process of helping to improve one another and the world around us by good criticism. The person to receive a constructive observation may not be receptive. The facts on which we are basing our observations may turn out to be flawed or false. Or what we say may be misunderstood or misinterpreted. For these or a variety of other reasons a particular criticism may have unintended negative effects despite a reasonable attempt on the part of the critic to avoid that and to only do good. There are no general application ways to avoid these beyond the obvious. Make an honest attempt to assess the other person's openness before you get into it. Check your facts before you get to this point – or start off by asking about those rather than asserting their truth or accuracy. Make your best effort to phrase things so you say what you mean to say with the least opening for misunderstanding.

A *painful criticism* is one intended to be constructive and helpful that includes some elements that are expected to cause hurt but which are unavoidable since the desired change requires facing some unpleasant facts in the process. Hurt is an unavoidable part of the improvement process in these cases but the final and intended result is benefit and good.

All complaining is criticism (in at least a broad sense) but not all criticism is complaining - although in some cases they would be the same. Depending on the intention of the complainer, complaining may qualify as either painful or destructive criticism.

I am not downplaying that it is possible to give hurtful or even harmful criticism inadvertently. If I don't know the person involved and the specifics of the situation, I might make comments that prompt the other to abandon something good or jump into trouble. Comments can have consequences and if the critic hasn't thought those through she may say hurtful, confusing, or insulting things while trying to do good. Such inadvertent harmful effects are hard to prevent since the only decision the critic can make to avoid them is to resolve to consider each statement and its possible meanings to the other person before she makes it. That sounds simple enough but since in the majority of cases the hurt arises from real or perceived slights or insults that are tangential to the main discussion points, this means you need to consider the background and politics of the audience at each juncture and that is a lot of work.

Most of us fall down on this job periodically because we have other things on our mind that limit our concentration on this incident. These other things include the consideration of our own background and politics and whether we can take a particular stance without contradicting things we have said earlier or without seeming to embrace a philosophy or policy we have reservations about. Deciding not to say deliberately destructive things is fairly simple (although reaching the point of making that decision may not be) but trying not to do so inadvertently is not so simple. In the deliberate case you are focused on exactly the things you must absolutely do or say or must avoid; in the inadvertent case you have to try to focus on everything you say and do - and there are always lots of opportunities to make a mistake on that.

Can a negative report be a constructive criticism? Absolutely. These are included in the group I am calling painful criticisms. If not, there could hardly be any criticism worthy of the title *constructive*. Making the point that you feel needs to be made so it will get enough serious consideration and without unnecessarily hurting feelings takes skill and good will on both sides, but if the focus is on improving the performance rather than simply dumping on it and trying to terminate it, the results may cause pain but are not destructive in the sense that I am using the term in this chapter.

How do you do a good job of giving a negative report when that is what you want to do and do that while trying to remain ethical yet doing it without leaving your position so obviously flawed as to prompt rejection by most intelligent hearers? A major mistake is to deny that your conclusions are negative. You want to emphasize that you have tried to be objective and you want to present what evidence you have that influenced your analysis but intelligent people know you are blowing smoke up their skirts when you try to maintain that any negative in the report is only in the mind of the listener.

If you were asked to evaluate the case in point, you were given permission, even expected if the evidence points that way, to decide against it. There are after all only three basic stances (under all the qualifications): you favor it, you reject it, or you claim neutrality on the topic. The latter is useless to those looking for guidance in making their own decisions and if that is all you can offer (especially if from the beginning you felt it was as much as you could bring yourself to offer or were allowed or intended to offer) you have nothing useful to contribute. Why agree to offer criticism if you don't intend to be honest about it? Doing a good job in this case means presenting the reasons for accepting some points and rejecting others and then tallying up the columns to arrive at a decision that can lead to action.

A *destructive criticism* is one intended by the critic to have exactly such damaging effects. These are the only category that are likely to be motivated by hostility or animosity and to be genuinely hate-filled.

The intention is the fundamental difference between these three categories. Only a destructive criticism is intended to do harm and no good. This isn't a question of a critique that is poorly presented or received being fully responsible for the harm. The critic knows what motivates the criticism, whether or not she is willing to admit it publicly or even fully to her own consciousness. The bad aspect is entirely hers. She may be able to persuade some others that she wanted to do good by her deed but she knows better and so do those who are really tuned in.

The distinction is fairly easily made by the critic when the focus is on her intention since she, and she alone, knows for certain what her intention is (even when she is working hard at not fully facing that due to psychological stress). The distinction is fuzzier at the results end because in some senses the critic has lost control and the various receivers, each in her individual place, are interpreting and reacting to it.

Destructive criticism tends to focus on punishing people for past actions rather than on changing their future ones. It tends to be a one-way diatribe, critic to criticized, rather than a dialogue. And it tends to be selective and to imply general failure from specific instances, ignoring all the cases that inconveniently don't support that attitude. It works against the system. It is a perversion of the system, a wolf disguised as a ham sandwich. It is what gives criticism in general a bad name.

A working definition of a destructive criticism contains several terms that warrant some scrutiny. It is (1) *intended* to influence the hearer's opinion about the subject (2) in a *negative or damaging way* (3) with *no intention or expectation that this will be beneficial* (4) to the *hearer or the subject*.

Destructive criticism more clearly than constructive (although it is true of both) can have an intended effect on the subject or on some other audience or on both. Our intention is important here since we may wish one or the other of these audiences to hear our views but not both and if those we didn't intend them for do hear them and feel hurt we may be upset by that effect but unable to deny that those are our views. We can only emphasize that we didn't intend them for these ears since we didn't think there was a greater likelihood of benefit rather than pain from them.

Deliberately poisoning the opinion of others against someone is certainly destructive behavior. For example using war titles in political rhetoric is destructive. So too is lowering the political discussion into the gutter as, for instance, when in the 1990s Newt Gingrich produced a list of words for Republicans to use when talking about Democrats to push the buttons of certain types among the public. The idea was that if you call your opponents *dirty*, *sleazy*, or *cheaters* - without having to prove anything or cite specifics - you smear them without getting your hands dirty among those you know how to and intend to incite to righteous disdain for those who don't agree with you. The distribution of talking points and loaded terms likely didn't start with that list and certainly continues since then. It is unabashedly destructive but happily embraced by those for whom winning at the polls is everything, making the country and the world a better place for honest discussion and negotiation apparently hardly even a consideration.

That said, deliberately poisoning the opinion of others against someone is destructive behavior in the usual sense of the term but it may be justified and a good thing for the listener or others if the subject being warned against or her policies or actions are harmful to the general good or specifically to these others or people they care about. When it is intended to steer others away from what the critic believes are bad people or policies it can indeed be justified and positive things said about it, even though not everyone will agree with the position being taken. On the other hand, when the destruction is incited by pettiness, a self-serving agenda, or some motive that will lead to benefit for the speaker or her people at the expense of others involved but not the common good, it is hard to justify it or find positive things to say about it.

Destructive criticisms are where we are often our most creative. We exaggerate, twist facts, lie, and omit vital information in the interest of shaping our hearer's response. All of which emphasizes our choice to be dishonest and our true intention to do harm.

What is intended as a destructive criticism must operate through negative reactions. It aims to persuade you to reject something whether or not it also hopes to get you to embrace some specific alternative. The end effect might be the same if the primary focus is on persuading you to join the one side, which inevitably will mean rejecting the other, but the approach will be different. You sell what you want the other to embrace, you don't come at it from a negative stance. It is generally intuitively understood that if all your program offers is that it is an alternative to what you proclaim to be a bad program, you have little going for you. You have to offer more than that. Negatives are used to persuade people to reject; positives must be used to persuade them to accept and embrace a person or idea.

I emphasize throughout this book that the intention of any good criticism is to help the recipient and perhaps others who are negatively affected by the actions that have provoked the criticism. This assumes that the perpetrator is not knowingly and intentionally causing the harm. I would argue that feedback that doesn't intend to be useful or helpful in resolving some real or perceived problem doesn't deserve to be called criticism. It is carping or complaining or insulting but it isn't valid criticism.

I may give a criticism even if it won't be well received when my offering these comments is as much as I can do under the circumstances precisely because I suspect my words have little chance of having the desired effect. I have the right intention and I am doing a good thing by making my observations part of the process and the record even if they don't carry the day. There will likely be other days. It is always useful to know there are people who are opposed to what is being talked about or that there are alternative views and proposed procedures. My time and effort are even more helpful, however, when I have some reasonable expectation that things will improve if I can make this person aware of the harm resulting from the way she is acting, and point out that there are ways for her to achieve her goals without those bad side effects. Most often a destructive criticism is deliberately that and the words are chosen precisely with the intention and expectation of doing harm and causing unhappiness exclusively, or at least to a degree that will outweigh any good that happens in the process.

The receiver of the destructive criticism may be the person who is criticized or a third person. If hearer and criticized are the same person (and assuming that she alone is exposed to it) the harm is focused on and intended to reduce the self-esteem of that person. If a third person is the receiver, the intention is to diminish the standing of the one criticized in the opinion of the receiver and those she may pass her reactions along to.

It is possible to spot a few strategies used to construct criticism of a destructive type that are intended to have an after-life because there are some valid facts at their core. One procedure is to comb the subject's comments for tidbits that can give a warped impression of her meaning and intent when quoted out of context. Especially if you can claim to be quoting some published text or recording of the person speaking you have considerable credibility and few of your listeners may bother to verify what was actually written or said. I cite a specific and striking example of this in Chapter 22. Also many of the minority who do check will often scan the text to locate the words in question but won't read the whole thing and recognize the actual meaning. The more explicit the statement made in the critique, the more vulnerable it is to widespread discrediting. Like fog, mere hints and "It seems to say", are almost impossible to strike back at effectively. Think of the various claims made about any politician of stature for examples of how and how often it is done and ask if those say more about the targeted person or the ones pushing these (mis)quotes at you.

A somewhat similar and highly successful and often used strategy is to *interpret* what the person being criticized said rather than to quote her. This approach is often used to conceal a twisting of the person's statements or positions in truly preposterous ways without losing much credibility with some part of the audience. It is also a highly protected maneuver since you don't risk being shown to be incorrect about what was said or done when you present your comments as your interpretation of what you heard or read. We all highly value our right to interpret as we please so to a large degree we grant that same right to others. We also know from experience that it is possible to honestly misinterpret someone and conclude that she meant the exact opposite of what she wanted to get across or some other outlandish ideas wide of the mark so we are partly protected by society's forgiveness and aren't automatically exposed as liars and deliberate detractors even when we should be. Only the critic knows for certain what her true interpretation is (unless she tells that to someone else. Ah, the powerful ego allure of the blog!)

Few of us can resist a good quotation, especially one that plays off the basic cattiness that most of us contain within ourselves even if we try to control and camouflage it most of the time. If there is humor in it too – a biting play on words or on the usual expectations - we have to laugh and will probably repeat it even if it attacks people, policies, or institutions we are otherwise defensive about supporting. The only defense against this fact, which is the basis of the success of editorial cartoons, is to condition the audience to respond negatively to all cheap shots. But that isn't an enterprise that promises much success because it doesn't seem possible to do it deliberately on any wide scale. It can be distressing to see a cartoonist lampooning some item from the news when you know enough about the topic to know that the point suggested by the cartoon is widely off-base, for instance by suggesting that there is a health hazard where there is none, or vice versa. The distress comes from recognizing that often the average newspaper reader knows little if anything about the topic and therefore will now have a negative attitude about it because she will base her opinion on the matter entirely on this cartoon. Such a reader won't try to learn more about it because she now has formed an opinion and therefore in her mind the topic is closed. There are too many new things in the news every day to spend much of our time on most of them beyond fitting each into a personal opinion profile – yes; no; not worth considering; *yuck!* Editorial cartoons are hard to nail down. Did this person intend to influence opinions or was she only desperate to get some laughs no matter how dumb or cheap to convince the editors to print (and therefore pay) her? Only a study of the output of such a person over time will let you draw a more definite conclusion about that although you are as free as the cartoonist to draw your own conclusions whenever you want. In this case about her and her intentions and about the newspapers that publish her work.

Destructive criticism often involves outright falsehoods. In the political arena (in both the narrow and the broad sense) especially, we all recognize that, on average, the public has a short attention span and a short memory. The false claim that gets prominent display leaves a deep impression but counter-arguments, proofs that the claims were lies, or even retractions seldom have much impact on the public opinion in the short run. The reality is that politics is always restricted mostly to the short run. Things may live on for months or years in the courts or reappear later as fodder for historians but in the day-to-day reality where the decisions are made that shape our world for today and for the next week they hit and fade, helped out of memory and attention by the next pseudo-crisis, the next juicy scandal, or the next spate of hard facts.

Doing destructive criticism is simplicity itself. Doing it well takes more effort but the techniques are widely known. Stopping it is possible for the critic involved but very difficult for anyone else. Fortunately (until recently) only a relatively small percentage of the population had the status to get widespread attention so larger scale and more political harm was a matter of raising awareness of those few when they stepped over the line of honest and impartial commentary - unless they admitted they were partisan which by itself reduces their audience and their credibility. Today, with even the most obscure tidbit that someone captured with her camera cell phone able to go viral on the Internet and be seen by millions in a single day the terrain is changing and we need to develop new kinds of defenses.

The one good thing about deliberately destructive criticism is that it can be avoided from the moment that the critic has a change of heart or that a third person focuses enough attention on the unacceptable behavior to compel the person to stop it, at least in this instance. Not so good is that once launched into the social ether the observations may take on a life of their own and spread far and wide as they are repeated by others who may be taking them at face value and not recognizing the full motivation behind them. Or they may be gleefully repeated exactly because they seem effectively destructive.

A different approach is called for to deal with any small scale or personal destructive criticisms. These are sometimes correctable to a degree that the large-scale political ones aren't. A one-on-one destructive criticism depends on the receiver to take the opinion of the critic to heart so it is simple to say, *Don't fall for it.* The catch is that only those too vulnerable to easily protect themselves from this critic to start with are likely to be harmed but they are exactly the ones who can't bring themselves to reject what is said.

Parent-to-child cases are particularly distressing. Why would a parent or anyone acting *in loco parentis* want to harm the young person? It turns out that, although they are pathological and likely to reveal the adult as pathetic, the reasons fill books. And the harm is real and difficult to correct. For an unfortunate group of those susceptible to this harm, the problem is that they won't bring themselves to defend themselves and consequently there is little that anyone can do for them short of taking over and running their lives for them. The degree to which they are psychologically able or unable to say no and protect themselves is an active debate. Let me emphasize that I am not sympathetic to those who don't defend themselves. "I just can't say no" doesn't carry weight with me. The fact that it's hard to do doesn't remove your obligation to do it. If you don't defend yourself probably no one else can do it for you effectively and you have partial responsibility for your own abuse or even destruction. That doesn't justify the abuser or reduce his burden of responsibility, but it recognizes that someone must help keep such abusers under control and the one directly involved (and too often the only one who knows what is happening) has the burden of doing that even though it isn't easy and it isn't fair.

Is it more useful to accept a minimum number of rather fuzzy categories for bad criticisms rather than to define a longer list of more precise cubbyholes? Experience with other aspects of complicated activities like human behavior suggests that there are always going to be too many distinctions that could be made. The choice of those to be made in order to group subsets are too arbitrary to allow exact fits with no lap-overs in any except very limited groupings. Since it seems that broadly applicable categories are the ones of most practical value we need to accept some fuzziness and the degree of uncertainty that goes with it.

It could be said that the best friend of a young evergreen longing to achieve perfect symmetrical shape is a skillful gardener with sharp pruning shears. In the same sense, if you are serious about developing yourself into the best and the happiest that you can be, critics are your friends. And the pick of the crop of those critics should be yourself. You should be and can be your own best friend and, in some aspects, also your best critic because no one else knows your conscious motives, desires, and quirks quite as well, or in the same manner, as you know those yourself.

Let us immediately agree that it is certainly true that we can, and often do, fool ourselves about our deeply buried motivations. Various unconscious or unacknowledged elements of our personalities may work at odds with our conscious selves and it may require a person with special insights or professional training to help us see that. Consequently that kind of special skilled help should be sought out when needed. However, such problems are beyond the scope of this book and I assume that the reader doesn't have such burdens or at least isn't looking for those answers here.

Only you can give yourself permission to live to the fullest that is possible for you. You are accountable primarily to yourself (among humans, I am not disputing any beliefs in higher moral obligations) for what you make of your life. You are responsible for your own happiness. Ordinary existence may be bleak and gray so we need to make deliberate efforts to bring color and light into our own lives and those around us. Not much will happen if we wait for it to occur by itself. We have to be open to it but we should also be prepared to actively initiate activities to bring color to our days. Don't sit waiting for someone else to make you happy or it likely won't happen.

Don't kid yourself that being your own critic is easy though. In spite of our claims, we usually don't want to face up to the fact that we are less than perfect. One consolation in doing the critique yourself is that you can give yourself a less than perfect score and no one else ever has to know about it. Certainly, since criticism in the full and healthy sense means praising our successes as much as noting our failures, any of us should be giving ourselves more pats on the back than swift kicks below that level anyway.

Assessing your assignments is an exercise essential to being a good self-critic. We have all made plans and mentally written scripts for ourselves to live out. These limits and directives are assignments we have given to ourselves. *Do this. Become this. Work at that. Don't kid yourself that you can do that other thing.* Since often these assignments are unrealistic or become out-of-date, periodically we need to take time with ourselves to work through who we are now and where we are aiming to go from this new reference point. This is a major part of what growing up is all about so it needs to be done on an on-going basis throughout your life.

There are two major elements to consider in self-criticism: your motives and your behaviors. Our motives are the driving forces behind the actual actions that are our behaviors. Our motives are the goals we set out to achieve; our behaviors are the actions we use as the means to achieve them. They are closely related but still separate. Only you can get at these. Other people supply the essential feedback on how you come across to them, but only you can say what you are trying or hoping to do.

Are your motivations reasonable and suitable? A problem for all of us is a tendency to hold onto ways of acting long after they stop fitting with our current motivations. Why? In part because it is a familiar way of acting. There is always an element of risk in doing something new or in doing the same old things in new ways. But you can let your maturity take you beyond the fears, peer and family pressures, and other factors that formerly shaped your actions.

Sometimes your motivation is appropriate but your choice of specific behaviors is counterproductive. You want to get to know someone you are meeting for the first time but to impress him you come on so aggressively or clownishly that you scare him away.

At other times you may be performing behaviors for motives that are different from those you claim are your intention. You join in the volunteers clean-up project "to help make the neighborhood a better place" when what you really want is an excuse not to be elsewhere with relatives you don't like to be around. When this motivation is truly unconscious you may well need professional therapeutic help to change, but often it is just less than fully accepted into consciousness. You may nudge it into that mental closet with the glass door where you are aware of it but refuse to let yourself think much about it or acknowledge it. These situations can often be dealt with by self-criticism.

A useful technique to force yourself to focus on what you really think about a subject is to make yourself write out your position. It is fascinating how long and how tenaciously we can hold an unjelled opinion in our minds. We have a general sense of whether we approve or disapprove and some loose ends of reasons why, but until we must put it concretely into spoken or written words it can be a hodgepodge of images and impressions without being distinct positions and ideas. It is only when we must define and defend our positions, at least to ourselves, that we have to really marshal our thoughts and make recognizable patterns that will constitute a position on a topic. "I just don't think so" boils down to the fact that you don't know why you are taking a position and that should warn you that you are acting dumb by flying blind. Putting it down on paper means you have to put it into words. You can't dodge it anymore. You need to list the pros and cons as you see them and explain why you consider those to be points for or against. Be firm with yourself - make sure you put down your position, not simply a more or less random collection of thoughts on the subject. Think of it as preparing a position paper to be presented to the world even though you will probably never show this to anyone and maybe won't even discuss the topic with anyone.

Self-criticism should generally lead to changes in your motivation or behavior. Of course if you are truly perfect you won't want to change but, despite a lot of claims, few of us are saints even in our own eyes. For many aspects of your life however, you hope and expect to eventually identify the behavior patterns that will best help you achieve the goals you have set for yourself. Then you periodically review your objectives and decisions and each time reaffirm your commitment to these goals and methods.

Keep in mind that criticism means evaluating and choosing, not change for its own sake. Most certainly not non-conformity for its own sake. You may feel that your illusions and fantasies and your sense of being right about yourself and the world are threatened by change, but actually only your self-defeating, self-destructive elements are likely to be attacked.

Many assume that taking charge of yourself always has to mean rejecting the commonly held views and attitudes of your social circle but that is not true. Good criticism means evaluating and holding onto what conforms to your criteria of acceptability as well as rejecting what does not. It always leaves open the possibility of seeking alternative ways of dealing with the matter without automatically committing to them. Liberate yourself by calmly and deliberately deciding on your own positions on life and its events. You'll feel better about yourself and you'll inspire others to follow your example and think more deliberately about their lives too.

As you get older you may find that you become less idealistic and more practical. For better or worse you accept that time, circumstances, aching joints, and human nature will only let you do so much. It took you a lifetime of trial and error to select the repertoire of behaviors and attitudes that you now use, so don't expect to change everything over-night. Don't even expect to do a complete consideration of more than one aspect of your life-pattern in a single critique session. You have to go about it bit by bit. Self-criticism is an on-going, lifelong activity. You will need to spend more time and energy on it when you begin to do it deliberately, but that is true of almost any activity.

First, establish the mindset that the present and the future are what matter. The past is important, but only because it gives you insight into how you came to be who you are right now. Recognize and accept that you can now consciously decide to become somebody different and better. You can also decide to stick with what the years have carved out in you because it doesn't seem half bad. I like to think this condition is true for most of us.

From a consideration of the past you can recognize how others manipulated you and how you tried to manipulate them. It is a valuable lesson, but only that. Don't keep going back to your past failures. They are now history. Profit from them and move on. The special magic of this kind of criticism is that you can turn your worst faults and failures into something positive by learning to become a better human being from them. It is like using manure to grow cabbages. Things are recycled and re-formed.

It takes great courage to accept responsibility for yourself. You have no one else to blame for your failures but you also get the full credit for your successes. Be clear with yourself that when you are responsible for yourself, only your own opinion about what constitutes success and failure is important. You say to the world, "This is my position on things so take it or leave it." That is scary because it may bring disapproval from others and we were raised to need the approval of others. As infants we were totally dependent for our survival on making ourselves acceptable to those who could feed, clean, and protect us. As adolescents we experience strong social pressures to conform in order to be accepted by our peers. By the time we are mature enough to take care of our own survival the lessons of conformity and group decision-making about values are deeply implanted in us. Maturing means that you accept the responsibility for being yourself, so the most mature persons are those who most fully accept the responsibility for all aspects of their lives.

This isn't to argue that you can just throw off your burdensome responsibilities as mate, parent, or employee but it is a suggestion that you can alter many of the specific details of your life. A man with a family to support can't honorably walk away from a reasonable job simply because he has always dreamed of being a rock star and is going to go live hand-to-mouth to see if he can achieve that dream and too bad about his family. But taking the initiative of joining a music group in his free time and developing his musical skills and working with the group to develop a band persona and identifiable sound which might lead to a professional career may well be within his reach. The housewife who abandons all attempts to keep the house in reasonable order because she wants to spend all her time reading romance novels is going too far if that housekeeping is her acknowledged contribution to the family process. But that is no reason why she might not set herself a period every day for her reading. Or for learning auto mechanics or computer repairs if she is inclined. She is certainly free to throw off the shackles of dumb restrains like "jobs appropriate for men only".

Try new things and let go of the old ways of thinking and acting, but only after you have scrutinized them and decided that you know of ways that you judge seem more likely to produce better results for you. In many areas of our lives changing just for the sake of changing isn't reasonable or responsible. Changing for better and attainable alternatives is. But let the old ways go in bits and pieces so you have continuity. Aim for improvement and development, not just rejection. Replace the old living room furniture and decorations a few items at a time, don't toss everything at once and then live with the bare walls and floors for months as you get new items when your budget allows.

Our ways of acting reflect our attitudes and values and we may be reluctant to admit that these have changed. The fan who was ready to swoon over a favorite performer as a teenager may feel compelled to wax enthusiastic about the idol whenever his name is mentioned long after the fan has concluded that such teeny-bopper behavior is absurd and the idol's performances weren't really all that good by objective standards. It is perfectly valid to decide to maintain this fiction as a monument to who you were - as long as it doesn't weigh down who you are now or want to be from here on.

Self-criticism is a progressive operation. The more you do it, and the better you do it, the more willing and able you are to do it often and better. It takes some experience at doing it to let down your defenses even with yourself. To be convincing to others you must feel thoroughly convinced of your defensive excuses so you practice believing in them and convincing yourself of them. Think of how many times you have rehearsed in your mind your explanation of why you do what you do. After a time you act like you believe your own explanations. Deeper inside as you continually try to assess your success in convincing the others of them and by preparing alternative defenses if these prove to be ineffective, you give away the fact that you know these are mainly defensive reactions. In the calm and privacy of your own mind you can admit what was happening and decide to do things in other ways.

You don't have to make decisions this instant. It may be more helpful to put off most of those criticisms and decisions that don't require immediate action until a regular self-criticism session so you can think things through more calmly and completely. Establish priorities, sequences of actions, and timetables. Then be prepared to ignore them. They are helpers, not jailers.

Don't be obsessive about intense, *stop everything else while I do this* self-criticism. It is a tool, not a major occupation. Do it periodically, not constantly in a 24-7 way. Surely there are other important things that require your attention and unless you are a total mess you are operating in at least a minimally workable way.

A nice balance is needed in assessing your goals. You always want to set your sights high enough to stretch you and develop you to your limits. Unrealistically optimistic or ambitious plans are double trouble though because you can't achieve them and thereby you also set yourself up for the negative feedback of failure. Don't lose your dreams, but don't get completely lost in them either. Any of us should be capable of more than enough solid accomplishments to give us satisfaction. Figuring out just where the dividing line between achievable and impossible for us lies is the work of a lifetime and not a task we can let others do for us.

Constantly test and urge yourself on but generally make progress in small, sure steps to minimize the impact of failure when it comes. Once you know where your current limits are, you can work at expanding them. Limits aren't carved in stone, they change as you do. The range of your possibilities gets wider as you get better. But a big disappointment, especially one involving efforts made very publicly, is likely to discourage rather than encourage you to further growth in that activity.

Meet your own expectations. Set realistic goals and give achieving them priority so you get the positive reinforcement of success. Be positive and constructive. Encourage yourself to do better rather than put yourself down for failing to be perfect. Be self-centered enough to care for yourself and to take care of yourself. That way you will make more progress in your self-improvement program and you will like doing it more.

Be your own savior! I am not being sacrilegious, I am talking about savior with a lower case s. I am talking about being your own best resource and supporter. So many people seem lost in a "somebody has to help me" mentality which not only diminishes their self-respect but also makes them obvious and willing victims for every manipulator who comes along. My point is to emphasize that many of us have found that some seeming disaster proved to be a blessing in the long run (although it was agony in the short run) because it forced us to try something we hadn't thought of before or which we were afraid to let go of our security blanket in order to try. Security blankets are important, but at some point they have to be left behind.

Can you laugh at yourself? This doesn't mean that you put yourself down, only that you can admit that sometimes you don't manage to achieve what you set out to do and sometimes you simply act in ways that look and maybe are silly. Check when you become defensive and analyze why. As a bonus, recognize that beating others to it takes the sting out of the words they considered using to hurt you, which is a sort of sweet revenge.

Jim was distressed that he was passed over for promotion when that had seemed assured until the last month. When he calmly thought about what had happened in the office in that month he recognized that his former boss had retired and from the start he dealt with the new boss in the joking way he and the old boss had been comfortable with. He now realized that there had been clear body language clues that the new man didn't understand or appreciate this way of being dealt with by a subordinate as he was trying to put his mark on the job. Jim realized that since he had been busy working on a project he had sidestepped the other man's signals as unimportant but now he knew they weren't. He conceded that if their positions were reversed he would have been confused by the subordinate's attitude and behavior and wouldn't have recommended him for promotion either. It was too late to change the promotion decision but now he understood why he had messed up so he could start to rebuild his relationship with the new boss.

As a teen Richard borrowed a phrase from his grandfather which he twisted out of context for his own purposes. Years later he realized he still dragged it out almost reflexly although his attitude on the subject had shifted almost 180 degrees. He had told himself it was deeply ingrained now so he couldn't stop himself from spouting it out so everyone else would just have to read it as the reverse of its obvious meaning so that they wouldn't be confused by him - but they didn't do so and concluded he was a fool. Finally he admitted what he had known all along but didn't want to admit – that he could stop using the phrase in contexts where it would be confusing if he made enough effort and only doing that would solve his problem.

To others Nancy came across as brash and pushy but when she forced herself to look at why she acted that way (swearing herself to secrecy for life on this matter) she admitted it was because she feared being ignored as she had been during her early years. Finally she accepted that she had reached a place in her life where she could now get noticed without trying so hard and things got better in her dealings with others.

Ruth would have bitten off her tongue before she would admit to anyone else that she often lied about the credit due her for organizing parties when others actually did most of the work, but once she could face up to the fact with herself she could piece together the reasons she had started to do so and could then bring herself to make the move to stop doing it and substitute a more helpful response to those situations. She even found that sharing the plaudits and taking credit only for what she actually did resulted in more social benefits overall since most of the time she hadn't been fooling many others anyway.

Self-criticism is only one part of a full on-going improvement program. There are aspects of your impact on others (and this impact may be essential to some of your goals) that you simply can't discover by introspection. You can get insights into these aspects of yourself only by having others relate their perceptions of and reactions to you. It may surprise you, but I hope not shake you too much, to learn that others don't always see you as you see yourself or as you want them to see you. A friend who is willing to give you constructive criticism is a most valuable asset. After you have reviewed your position on various aspects of your life-pattern, you may want to ask someone else whose good sense you trust to give you some feedback on how they see those areas of your behavior. You should be confident enough of your own decisions, however, to trust yourself as your final authority. Don't ask someone else to second-guess you, to tell you how to live your life, or to approve your conclusions. They are only supplying one view into the way others see and evaluate you. Remember, your opinion about you is the one that counts the most.

Start your self-evaluation by asking yourself to list what you have accomplished today. This is fresh in your mind and also nicely illustrates the pitfalls to be avoided. Sit back, get comfortable, and really consider that question. What have I accomplished today?

Right from the start it is most important to stick to the question that you asked. Don't waste time on others. You didn't ask what you *didn't* do, what you *might* have done, or what you *should* have done. Concentrate on what you actually accomplished. The ordinary everyday things. Save the earth-shaking things you have fantasized about doing for your daydreaming sessions, this is a serious self-criticism exercise right now. Tally up everything you did, big stuff and small. No one else will see this record (especially if it is only in your mind) so nothing is too trivial to include. A task doesn't have to have been completed or done perfectly or even correctly to be listed. The incomplete task will take less time to finish now and you did put effort on the botched job so it was an accomplishment even if you need to focus on doing that task better next time. Give yourself appropriate credit for all the tasks you made at least some progress on. The letter you intended to write doesn't count, but the one you jotted some notes about or set out paper and envelope to remind yourself about does.

Include everything on your list that you consider was constructive and appropriate, plus those things you are embarrassed to admit to because they weren't constructive or appropriate. Making the beds, washing the dishes, cleaning your tools, or handling the routine office paperwork are all accomplishments

If we consider that very few of us can do special things for ourselves and humanity at large until we have taken care of the routine necessities of our place in this world as parents, employees or employers, and just reasonably neat and organized adults, we see that taking care of the dull, routine things is a large and important part of each day's tasks. You can't effectively devote time to political or charitable work, artistic endeavors, or athletic pursuits if the day-to-day world falls down around your ears in the process. To paint a masterpiece you must first assemble your supplies, prepare a canvas, and find a place to work. It is the same with any activity. Getting the ordinary and necessary under control is essential and a major accomplishment in itself. How many harried parents or businesspersons would and should consider that a good day's work in itself!

List your strong and weak points. The chances are good that you know what they are although you may not have forced yourself to (or even allowed yourself to) examine them this closely until now. Strong points you probably have thought about; weak points you may have struggled to keep yourself from recognizing or admitting to. You may need to take some time to formulate the impressions you have of your thoughts and actions into categories that you can put labels on, but it is a useful exercise. Those general *I'm not sure what to do or say so I try to delay making a choice* ideas may simply boil down to your discomfort about having to accept responsibility for and live with your decisions. And the fact that people empty the dish you brought to the potluck dinner early on supports the conclusion that you're a good and imaginative cook.

You might find it helpful to put your list on paper. It's fascinating how much more of an impression many things make on us when we see them written down. It is as if they are now official and need to be taken into account whereas thoughts only in your mind are insubstantial and therefore seem not so important. Such a list is only a tool to help you focus so it need not be saved, although some will want to do so to reconsider it later when they need reinforcement or a pick-me-up.

You may recognize that an aspect of one of your strong points is actually or also one of your weak points. You are not all black and white, not all that simple to understand after all. Thus, being self-assured is an asset in many situations but it can become unseemly arrogance if you don't pay close attention. A willingness to laugh at yourself must be used carefully since it can also be raised as a shield to deflect honest but embarrassing self-criticism as well as that given by others that you don't want to face up to.

It is eye opening to compare your perception of your strong and weak points with the perceptions of others. If you have someone you trust who has agreed to give you constructive feedback, check that person's perceptions against your own. But remember that your critic is probably as likely to be wrong as you are. She is also likely to be reluctant to be completely honest if she has doubts about whether you really won't take offense or react badly to hearing what you would prefer not to.

The Golden Rule holds in self-criticism. Be as tough on yourself as you are on others. Consider how you try to manipulate others. You resent it when others try to twist you to their advantage, so why do you let yourself act this same way? Tit for tat is childish; being properly critical is a specifically mature activity.

Sometimes it is enough to see certain behaviors for what they are to prompt us to modify or drop them. Sometimes they result from ignorance, inattention, unanticipated circumstances, mistaken identity, weariness, or other weaknesses. We fall into them for these reasons ourselves so don't make too big a thing about it when someone else makes the same mistake. By being aware of what is happening we can prevent the other person from harming or using us - and then shrug them off. We don't always have to correct them, but there is no excuse for condoning unacceptable acts as repeated behavior. No good reason to suffer because of them either.

Be considerate of yourself. Don't try to impose your critiques on yourself when you are in a highly emotional state, whether of zeal or disappointment. Good criticism needs calm introspection and evaluation. That could in fact be used as a guide to identify any good criticism. Harsh, hurting, and sloppy criticisms are the ones that people shout at one another in the heat of an argument. The word of encouragement and the suggestion that "You might find it works better if you try it this other way" are almost always given quietly and privately. There is no reason for it to be different when you deal with yourself. The quiet voice of reason has more impact than the shouts or frenzied exhortations of those little voices in your head (unless you do have serious problems).

Love yourself. Accept yourself as less than perfect but willing, even eager, to improve. Accentuate your good points. Dwell on them. Don't keep punishing yourself for your failures. Forgive yourself for them and then concentrate on the things that make you feel good about yourself. Give yourself comfort and reassurance. Be positive and be constructive. Encourage yourself to do better rather than berate yourself for failing to do so. Keep in mind the important principle that in many circumstances a pat on the back is more effective than a slap in the face.

It takes more than sheer will power to change yourself. Enlist all your capacities but be realistic in your goals. You can choose to be only what you can be. You have to know your strengths and weaknesses, what interests and involves you and what doesn't. Trying to be things you don't really want very much to be in order to please or impress others won't work well and won't make you happy.

Self-criticism aims first to get you to know yourself as you are and then to help perfect you. This is not a cut-and-dried process. Each of us is unique and therefore has unique considerations to make. Some of what you may objectively conclude are flaws in yourself you may not know how to alter and improve on in the context of your present life structure.

For some people the requirements of certain tasks may make those unrealistic goals. For instance, if you are someone who finds it hard to sit still and concentrate on anything for more than a few minutes at a time you are a poor candidate for a job where your task will be to continuously monitor a bank of security cameras feeds for full hour with no breaks shifts or to be a quality control person assigned to spot and remove the slightly defective items from the continuous stream of items passing by your station on a conveyor belt. If you dislike having to deal with young children, don't volunteer or even agree to babysit except in close to emergency situations.

Or you might recognize that your shyness is a hindrance to your career goals but find that no matter how you try, the pounding heart and feeling of intense unease when you must meet a stranger for the first time still makes it so hard that you will sacrifice real benefits to avoid those situations. That is where self-criticism helps by guiding you to look for alternatives rather than to make yourself unhappy trying to do what you won't do satisfactorily. Maybe you can handle the matter with a letter or an e-mail. Or maybe there is someone who knows you and the new person who will be willing to introduce you and help make the first contact less uncomfortable for you.

Once you have let down your defenses with yourself and gotten a better understanding of you, you are better able to let down some of your defenses with other people. You find you can be more honest and open because you know who you are. You know that yours is the opinion of you that counts to you even when the opinions of others have significant impact on the job or in social situations.

When you are accepting and supportive of your attempts at self improvement there are fewer psychological barriers to your success. The physical barriers - and I include here the actions and decisions of others that are beyond your reasonable control - may still block the way but now you know what you want to accomplish and you will have a better idea of how to get there. The narrow definitions fall away and the range of possibilities, all leading to satisfaction, become more evident.

For most people the very fact of succeeding on their own will give them immensely more satisfaction than acting as an agent of others and carrying out that person's instructions and achieving that person's goals - even when doing those things is thought by some to be success that is measured by yardsticks like annual income, honors, or awards.

Warning! Honest critical evaluation will probably force you to see that some of your cherished positions don't hold up. Are you prepared to grow enough to shed those things and go on to better things? It is common practice for youngsters to adopt some of the ideas of their elders without fully understanding them and without considering their negative side or the arguments against them (which may be two different things).

Prejudices are commonly passed along in this fashion. But when they mature each generation should eventually review whether the traditional views make sense in their current age and world. If they then opt to continue to advocate and support the ideas, they take on full responsible for the consequences to themselves and their own children because they have moved the prejudices, pipe dreams, or mindlessness into deliberate acceptance. It's uncomfortable to reach a stage of maturity where you see the wrongness or the intellectual feebleness of your predecessors since that must reduce your opinion of them - but not to reject those points is to reject your own intelligence. What is the gain in that? Is family or ethnic loyalty to the point of bigotry worth embracing when you must live with the fact that you see it as such?

You are also likely to decide that there are some aspects of you that you don't like very much. When you look at yourself objectively (to the extent that you can do that), you may well recognize prejudices and weaknesses you aren't proud of. You may have to admit that there are periods of your personal history during which your actions were very unacceptable by your present standards. That is all behind you now. It doesn't have to be aired publicly. There is no need for you to discuss it with others in some sort of a self-debasing ritual. Not even with the person who has agreed to give you constructive criticism. It is behind you so forgive yourself and resolve to do better. But don't forget it. As long as you remember how even you could sink to that behavior, you will be more sympathetic to the weaknesses of others. You won't accept their poor behavior as okay, but you will be able to accept them as persons with faults in spite of those actions. It also allows you to be a better critic for others because you know from personal experience how people may hide their real motivations from themselves.

Beware the urge to make excuses rather to than face up to your intentions or failings. Excuses are thought inhibitors. We use them to cut off further consideration and therefore to cut off the process necessary to improvement. As soon as you find yourself thinking *I only do that because...*, you are on notice that this is a topic for careful reevaluation.

The decision to not stay fixated on your past deeds doesn't cancel your responsibility for your previous acts or remove the obligation to pay for them in whatever form that may take. Through self-criticism you may alter your views and positions but that doesn't automatically alter the perception that others have of what you said or did in the past. We have seen far too many sham conversions by politicians and celebrities only intent on winning acceptance for the moment and among the less attentive members of their audience by taking some new position. The vehement segregationist who now runs for public office as a civil rights advocate will find it difficult to recruit the support of those he fought hard to suppress in years past. He may be sincere but we all carry our handmade baggage with us and the rest of the population is well advised not to believe too quickly in a major change of heart. Maybe your words and actions over time will convince others, maybe not, but you know who you are and that is what is most important. Being aware of your own baggage may help you figure out how to distance yourself from it.

Part of maturity is accepting that there are some things you can't control so there is no advantage to beating your head against a wall about them. Some claim that dogged determination and unblinking resolve are signs of great *heart* and are to be praised and idealized. I would moderate that position with the conditions that the deeds must be ones able to be done and that this obsession doesn't distract the person from doing the other things that are effectively within her reach. The difficult task that periodic reconsideration can assist with is to differentiate between the achievable and the impossible, and how to keep hope alive without being destroyed by false expectations. We admire the patriot who perseveres through persecution by a tyrant and finally helps bring that regime down, but we also know of those for whom some impossible dream becomes a trap that drains their energies for no useful purpose. The woman living on the edge of starvation so she can devote all of her time and resources to building a perpetual motion machine is to be pitied, not admired. Not even when her obsession makes a nice TV news show filler on a slow news day.

Other flaws you may feel are not considerable enough to be worth the effort of changing. You may be content to be less organized or neat than you think would be ideal. You aren't totally disorganized and you aren't dirty, you just have sort of a *lived in* look and air about you. Recognizing the patterns in yourself may be enough. You are now aware of the fact that they might be influencing how others react to you so you can decide whether that is important to you. The chances are good that if you are content to be slightly disorganized you are not going to be overly distressed by the fact that some other person doesn't approve. But if that other person is someone who really counts with you - and that person's objection is more than just personal fussiness - you may decide to make some changes in your behavior. You can do so at that point because you are aware of what you have been doing and how you have been doing it as a result of your self-criticism.

Some of your supposed flaws may be very deliberate and positive decisions that are deficiencies only to those with specific expectations. Your inclination not to dress in the latest fashion may be a refusal to follow the dictates of the fashion designers when you don't find this year's offerings attractive or worth changing to, rather than your inability to determine what is *In* this season. Your associates probably won't appreciate or profit from a lecture from you on lack of imagination among those who let the designers do their thinking for them, but they may come to respect your independence when you calmly go about doing things your own way. Do you really care about staying in good with them if they are determined to deal with you based on their shallowness? Or in having any more than the absolutely essential association with them for the job or whatever reason forces you to do so?

Talk things over with yourself. Argue and debate as needed. Tune in to yourself. Reassure yourself and explain things to yourself. Make yourself think things through and formulate specific positions. How often and about what do you dream but refuse to take the actions that might let you achieve those goals? Why? You may get important insights into who you have allowed yourself to become if you can bring yourself to explore this topic. When you recognize how you came to be as you are, the choices you made and the factors that prompted or influenced them, you will be better able to redirect yourself down the paths that you now more consciously want to follow.

Throw off all the resentments you have carried since childhood. You can't change the past but weighing yourself down with it means you may not succeed in the future either. All those people who abused you - let it go. You don't even have to forgive them if you don't feel that is the best way to go - and you shouldn't forget what they did if there are ever legal questions about that, but throw off the burden of resentment because it is hurting you more than it is them. You owe yourself better. It isn't fair, but life seldom is. You have let them make you unhappy all this time because you set yourself up to fail by keeping revenge as an unrealistic goal. Let yourself succeed by restricting yourself to present and future goals that concentrate on making you happy. That doesn't have to mean only selfish goals. It means striving for things you can succeed at whether that is winning a talent contest, reading lots of mystery novels and recommending the good ones to others based on how much you enjoyed them, being the friendliest and the most encouraging person in your neighborhood, or the best salesperson in the store.

Ted was seen by his supervisor berating a minority co-worker in strong language away from the factory after hours. The next day it was obvious that the supervisor's opinion of Ted had taken a nosedive and that this was going to affect their interactions on the job. When Ted learned from someone else the reason for the change in attitude he could point out to the supervisor that she had seen Ted repeating a scene from a recent film as part of a discussion of the topic with that co-worker, not presenting his own views. When the co-worker confirmed this, the atmosphere between Ted and the boss improved rapidly.

This example points out the dangers of drawing conclusions and altering your evaluation of another person without knowing all the relevant details. It is easy to imagine how often comparable things might happen but in many cases there is no correction or clarification which means that the misguided misperception persists and harms someone.

Mac was surprised to learn that he had a reputation for making threats of violence against women who wouldn't agree to do non-sexual things his way. He now realized that the pattern he had observed in a drunkard of a neighbor when he was young, a man whom he thought of back then as the epitome of the tough guy macho man, had seeped into his own reactions when he got annoyed and feared his own masculinity was being questioned. Aware of the pattern, it is now up to Mac to slow down his mouth each time he starts to get annoyed and to make certain that he only says what he is prepared to stand behind as his true thoughts and intentions.

Here are some additional questions it might be useful to consider during periods of introspection, the answers for yourself alone.

How has your family background, education, and experience shaped your thinking and your values? Are these the values you would deliberately and objectively support and adopt if you were considering them for the first time or are they just the ways you have gotten used to thinking and reacting without reexamining them? We start off as infants helpless and ignorant of the worlds of Nature and human society. Our survival depends on learning some rules in a hurry and imitation of those caring for us is the fast track to that knowledge. A social species like ours passes along important information that can't be coded into genes by our various forms of learning, much of it by imitating the actions and words of our elders. But the species also needs to be able to change to adapt to new situations since nothing in Nature or human society stays the same for long.

Thus adaptability requires that we be able and willing to rethink the rules we have learned once we are independent enough to survive on our own. That means we continue to learn, modifying the rules to make things work better for us. We then transmit these modified ways of thinking and acting to the next generation and perhaps laterally to our neighbors who decide the new ways they see us acting are better. We don't discard all the rules and start over from scratch each generation, we review and revise them, in the process moving away from our past and toward our future.

Do you like yourself? Would you be friends with you if you were someone else? If you have reservations about part of how you act, what parts are those? Why do you act those ways? Is it possible for you to act otherwise? Are any of your personal habits actually intended to put off or repel others? To manipulate others? How did these develop? How do you feel when you encounter comparable behaviors in others directed at you? What can you do about these behaviors? What in your behavior puts limits on you? What of that can you and do you want to change in yourself?

How do others perceive you? Must you live with this or can you change either their perception or yourself? How important is that to you? When you have become aware of how others perceive you, there are several considerations. First, are you comfortable with what they think you are about or do you wish to change that? Second, if you want to change it can you do so either by changing their perception (for instance by making it clearer what your actual intentions are or why you do certain things the way you do) or by changing your behavior?

You can dream castles in the sky but if you aren't willing to do the things necessary to achieve those dreams you are only making yourself unhappy. Having fantasies is universal, although their specifics tend to be highly individual. As long as they encourage, reassure, or comfort us even though we know they aren't possible because we don't have and won't develop superpowers, they serve a useful purpose and usually aren't harmful. Getting lost in our own version of them can certainly be a fun way to spend some downtime anyway.

It's helpful to be able to set aside a day or more each year to relax in a quiet atmosphere away from your regular hustle and bustle to do this reflecting as some people do in a retreat, whether of a spiritual nature or simply as R and R. Unfortunately many people either can't get free for those days or think they can't. Often after the first experience of such a self-renewal day they decide they can't afford not to do so regularly.

We have considered what a good criticism should be and why we should be good critics, now let's put the shoe on the other foot. What about the criticisms directed at us? One of life's less pleasant experiences is receiving negative criticisms, personal or professional, so why should we put up with them? It would be difficult enough if they were all good criticisms in the sense that we have defined since even when we would never in any way describe or even think of ourselves as flawless, it hurts to be told that we or what we do are less than perfect.

Constructive criticism properly presented has the minimum threat to it. But, having the delicate egos that we do, there is still some apprehension. Even when we sincerely request the feedback we secretly hope that it will all be enthusiastic praise without a single element of "It might be better if..." You have probably experienced that little skipped heartbeat when you know for sure that the other person does have something in some way negative to say about you. Unfortunately the majority of criticisms leveled at us aren't constructive and aren't properly presented so too much of the time we are right to be apprehensive about the whole business.

For my purposes here I define *accepting* criticism to mean hearing the observations through without serious interruption except to ask for clarification. This doesn't mean that you pledge to agree with or to implement any of the observations and suggestions that might be made.

Why should you accept criticisms? Let us consider some reasons.

1) They may be true and correct and therefore you might learn something valuable from them that you are unlikely to find out in any other way. That new awareness will then give you a chance to shape yourself up.

Especially, the criticism may give you an insight into the way that you are projecting to others but aren't aware of. This is valuable feedback because we all assume that others are seeing us as we want to be seen (which is often not as we see ourselves) but they aren't. They often don't understand our motives, aren't taken in by our attempts at deception, and aren't being turned to putty in our hands by our attempts at being charming. We all stand and watch others going through their acts and read right between the lines and fume or maybe smile at their attempts to manipulate us, yet we seldom reflect on the fact that we do the same thing to them. It is a peculiar type of blindness.

Maybe I don't realize that I smack my lips when I eat and make enough slurping sounds for a herd of hogs. I am so used to the sounds that I don't focus on them. But everyone else does. And not with relish.

Or perhaps I don't think about such things very often and I don't realize that I walk like a human question mark with shoulders slumped and hips thrust forward. I would probably look better and feel better if I paid more attention to my posture. I definitely would project a better image of myself which might influence how others meeting me for the first time will judge whether they can trust me to be useful ally in the projects they are looking for help with if I am this bit more self-aware. Most can easily recognize when I am physically impaired versus when I am simply careless or subconsciously projecting that I consider myself to be a loser with nothing much to offer.

Or maybe I was trying to impress somebody and I allowed myself to talk beyond my expertise and made some foolish statements that the other person, better versed in the topic, knows are wrong or misleading. The only way I will avoid that trap again is to learn that I was incorrect - and criticism, properly done, is a useful and often powerful learning experience.

It can be startling, even frightening, the first few times that we find out how differently people perceive and receive us than what we thought we were projecting. For instance, many quiet, shy people come across to others as arrogant or haughty because of their reserve. Or that what a person feels is his dignified reserve may be interpreted by others as coldness. Or the one concerned about making his position on a topic very clear because he has been misinterpreted in the past is now judged to be pushy or obsessive by this different audience. A very concerned and helpful person may come across to others as a busybody and a snoop, even though he never intends to be so. It is an eye opener to learn that the enthusiasm for sports that you cultivated at great personal expense in time and effort because you believed it would make you a good conversationalist and one of the boys comes across as a constant endeavor to outdo everybody else by knowing more of the scores and knowing them sooner than anyone else. Maybe the image of you as a compulsive competitor is obvious to everyone except you.

2) You might accept criticisms because they are well-intentioned constructive observations by someone who cares about you and who is

willing to run the risk of being hated, attacked, or rejected by you in order to try to help you be better.

3) Maybe you accept them because you can't do anything to avoid them. Sometimes it would cause far more misunderstanding, hard feelings, and fuss to defend yourself from listening to them than to let these things be said and then passed over. It takes a very strong and mature person to let someone else make critical statements about him in public and not fly into a rage or a rush of denials and excuses, but only quietly deny any untruths that were cited, correct any misrepresentations or misinterpretations, and let everyone judge it for himself.

4) You might listen to the critiques because in your judgment this critic simply isn't worth paying attention to even to the extent of actively rejecting him.

5) Or to pay your dues so you can return the compliment. If you have a mutual support arrangement then you must take criticism as well as give it.

6) You might accept a criticism because it tells you a lot about the thoughts and expectations of this critic and may be worth accepting as the price for this window into this person's values, attitudes, and thought processes.

Neither the fact that criticism was invited nor the fact that it was given in good faith imposes any obligation to accept it or act on it. Inviting it, more or less willingly, obliges you to listen to it and consider it but that is all. Until and unless you decide which suggestions will be helpful, listening doesn't commit you to anything. Not even to respond.

Critiques imposed upon you without your agreement (by anyone except a person with a legal or societal obligation like a parent or job supervisor) don't even carry an obligation to listen. Even when you agree to listen, that is all you must do since, except under a dictator of one sort or another, no one else has the right to force you to think by to his personal rules or whims. Of course that doesn't keep many from trying.

Remember that reactions of the other person are subjective and what one person is sure and adamant about, others may not think is true at all. Sometimes a person is simply wrong in his criticism. Perhaps he assumes you accept positions or ideas that you don't accept or agree with. Or perhaps his observations are in error - you weren't the one he thought he saw do that stuff he is upset about or thinks paints a picture of you that others should know about.

Sometimes the criticism is inappropriate because the critic isn't in a position to offer one. For instance, a co-worker who assumes to himself supervisory prerogatives is overstepping his bounds.

If you want another's criticism of you to be constructive and helpful, then you must deal with him in kind. That is, you can't meet a name-calling attack with a name-calling attack. Some will argue, "He should be more aggressive and give those people just what they're giving him. An eye for an eye." How often we hear that said about some politicians from the same people who two breaths before condemned all politicians without exception for fighting all the time so they get nothing constructive done. If you feel that the behavior of the others is boorish and unacceptable, why would you let him set the pace and bring you to his level?

You may decline to respond to a criticism at the time it is given but still give it serious consideration. Your refusal to respond may or may not be stonewalling and only you will know for sure until there is clear evidence of a change in your actions that would be the obvious result of a revision of your ideas about things.

Some critics will push for a reaction to their comments (beyond a restatement of what you understood them to say and mean to be certain that you got the point they were trying to make). This is where the individuals and the situation draw the lines. Person A may insist that you made an agreement to respond when you agreed to hear him out. Unless that was very explicit in what you said, you didn't accept any such burden and can stand your ground on the point. After a single unpleasant incident of this kind you will likely learn to avoid this argument in the future by stating in advance the limits of your duties if you even agree to hear any criticism from this person again. You also need to consider how you think you should react to criticism of you for not meeting the critic's pre-conceived ideas of what you should have done?

Why would the critic want to hear your response?

(A) To be certain that you correctly interpreted what he said. This is commendable and even desirable. It makes it worthwhile to discuss the matter further. But you have no obligation to do so if you don't feel that more discussion will be useful.

(B) To give him a continued open line of communication so he can continue to try to persuade or cajole you to his point of view. This is probably exactly what you are trying to avoid. His wish is not your command or obligation.

(C) To get the satisfaction of making you admit your mistake and acknowledge his intellectual and/or moral superiority for catching you in your error. Needless to say you have no duty to give him this satisfaction. Not even if he is right.

If you have the self-control to do so, just hearing the other out, then walking away without comment deprives him of the satisfaction of getting you upset - if that was the critic's intent - while still indicating your willingness to listen to reasonable feedback. It isn't easy to do, but it has its benefits.

Depending on circumstances, it may or may not be helpful to tell the critic when you are rejecting his offered views. With someone in a position of authority or control over you there will often not be much benefit to doing so and possibly a lot of unnecessary aggravation if you do. Why make things more unpleasant when you can just nod your head in a noncommittal way and then go do what you intended? But with someone on a peer level there can be advantage to clearly and explicitly rejecting their criticism when you judge it to be improperly motivated, inadequately considered, or inappropriately presented. You are then reversing the situation and acting as a critic of that person's skills as a critic. Remember though that you then have the same obligation to be constructive in order to be effective.

When you are rejecting a criticism because you feel it is mistaken or misdirected, you may want to state your position rather than keep quiet. It is important to emphasize (and be sure) in your own mind and in your words that it is the content of the criticism or its presentation that you are objecting to, not simply the idea of being criticized or of this person doing it. It would be inappropriate to maintain that you are above criticism as long as the criticism attempts to be constructive and is given in good faith by someone who believes he is trying to help. If these basic conditions don't exist, however, you might well react negatively to the very fact of being criticized by this person. You can also refuse to accept a criticism by threatening to beat the stuffing out of the critic if he continues, but this is not the recommended way to respond.

Remember that in many topic areas there can be a big difference between your taste and *universal good taste*. Don't too readily equate the two. Also don't confuse (or let your critic confuse) tastes with substance.

If you reject the criticism offered of your behavior or work, then you and the situation determine how you should act. It is often simplest to thank the critic for the observation and promise to give it some thought and then walk away, literally or figuratively. You can then forget about it if you choose. As long as the critic is willing to let it go at that, the case is closed.

It helps the situation to thank the other for his concern even if you reject his comments. Accept that a good criticism required good observation and some thought in preparation which means the person cares about helping you. Encourage those who are thoughtful and helpful enough to be willing to give you feedback, but limit it to matters of consequence. Don't expect or even tolerate intrusive feedback on every little point.

There is also a time to tell a critic where to get off, but that is a very different situation. Unjust or seriously erroneous criticism should be corrected as quietly and bluntly as possible, but don't feel you have to absolutely convince the other - since that may be impossible. When the criticism isn't constructive or isn't intended to help, there is little point in arguing your point. The other's mind is obviously closed.

You have the right, maybe even the duty, to correct the bad manners of the critic - for instance, in publicly discussing private matters when it could and should have been done in private. A flawed criticism bestowed on you in a public forum may, and often should, be answered in that same public way. If the critic naively mistook this as a time and place to offer personal criticism, he will learn from the experience. If, as is more likely the case, the critic made the observations under these circumstances precisely in order to embarrass you or damage your social standing, you have the right and the obligation to defend yourself against the attack and can do so with confidence that what was offered was not intended as constructive criticism.

Sometimes a crude or negative criticism is given in order to draw you into an argument. This is usually done to embarrass you by having you seen as someone out of control. Marty McFly, the Michael J. Fox lead character in the *Back to the Future* movies, demonstrates the way that some people can always be manipulated by calling them names like "chicken". A caricature for the sake of the movie action, but many of us have met people who are as knee-jerk in some reactions.

Some criticisms are angry responses to the failure of others to let themselves be manipulated by this speaker. I remember a man at a seminar who, while asking questions at the end, tried repeatedly but unsuccessfully to put words into the mouths of the speaker. Later outside I heard him loudly denouncing the speaker as arrogant because he wouldn't agree with this man's attempts to recast the speaker's ideas to make this questioner's point instead of the speaker's point.

You have a fundamental right to ignore or reject any inadequate or inappropriate criticism. It may also be difficult. Difficult because you must determine that it is inadequate or inappropriate without letting your own ego and prejudices blur your vision. Difficult because often the criticism is imposed by someone who had societal authority to do so and who has the power to impose penalties on you if you don't comply with the changes in behavior called for. In more extreme cases he may even be able to penalize you if you won't publicly state your agreement with and acceptance of his positions and ideas. Difficult because if you're sincerely looking for help you may not see any others you can turn to so you might feel depressed or inadequate to the tasks expected of you.

When your sincere criticism is rejected it is important to keep in mind that this person has the same right to say "No, thanks" that you do. Rejection of the criticism you offer isn't necessarily rejection of you and your caring and concern. Often there are reasons that you don't know about and which the person doesn't feel at liberty or obligated to let you in on that influence his reaction. You have done what you could, the rest is up to him.

There are those who consider it heroic and truly loving to badger or batter someone until they do what the other has decided is best for them in the long run. I feel strongly that you have the right to fail in every way if you don't make the appropriate decisions for yourself and I for one will stand by and watch you self-destruct if that is what you choose to do. I won't force my thinking on you although I will certainly impose the very letter of the law on you in terms of your obligations of child support, civic responsibilities, and the like. Don't bother me with your arguments that you couldn't help yourself. You made decisions, just not good ones, and then hoped someone else would take control of your life and make it all good for you. You elected to act like a loser, so I am willing to concede your right to end up like one.

I offer the following general guidelines for reacting to criticism.

1) Don't refute a statement until you can restate it and thereby prove to yourself and the other that you know what he meant by his words.

2) Don't beat around the bush and end up saying nothing unless there is good reason to do that. Either make your point or keep quiet. (See Chapter 14)

3) Don't make generalized statements or contentions unless you offer some corroborating evidence or specific examples.

4) Be prepared to accept even sharp rebukes and evaluate them before you decide whether a reply is necessary or would be helpful in solving the problems.

(5) Avoid the temptation to explain it all away. But do, in the same helpful manner adopted by the critic, point that out when he is missing some significant point or is misjudging some relevant factors.

(6) Listen for the little clues that indicate the things the person can't bring himself to say but really thinks you should be aware of.

(7) Criticism of personal matters like hygiene and manners are better received from older to younger, rather than from peers but that doesn't mean they are ever going to be welcomed or heeded.

We react to non-praise criticism with a range of responses.

A) We reject the criticism and the person. We attack the critic, questioning his intelligence, knowledge of the subject, intentions or reasons for criticizing, his credentials for criticizing, or his right to criticize.

B) We reject the criticism but not the person. We claim that the criticism is worthless and not worth considering, but we appreciate the concern of this person.

C) We stalk off and/or sulk. The childish reaction.

D) We conclude that he must have misunderstood what we did, said, or intended. We assume that we are all thinking on the same lines and using terms in the same way so the other guy is all mixed up, stupid, or a troublemaker.

E) We consider the possibility that he is correct so we stay open to thinking his points through in a cooler moment and then we may reevaluate the situation. We need not (and should not be too quick to) capitulate immediately. It is enough to simply agree that the matter calls for some rethinking.

Critiques can be good or bad, well done or poorly done. For us to evaluate the critiques given of us and our work, our ideas, or whatever is the subject we need to consider some basic guidelines of good criticism.

a) Is it a criticism of the person per se or of his mannerisms, deeds, or performance? Either might be appropriate under specific circumstances but all too often we allow them to become confused and this eliminates much of our would-be objectivity.

b) Is it a generalized statement? These often prove indefensible. It is usually safe to presume that if the claims could be made specific they would be or can be when you raise this point.

c) Does your critic have facts or only rumors, deductions, and suspicions to go on? Each may be valid but they have different weights.

d) How emotional is the comment? The more agitated he is, the more suspect his critique is. High emotion leads to easy exaggeration.

e) How important would this criticism be if it were valid? Is it a major or a minor point? Is its effect transitory or long-term?

As both the person offering a criticism and the one receiving one, ask yourself three questions.

1) What did the words used mean? What were their connotations and the denotations for me? What code words or references intended to color the meaning were included? What did his facial expression, body language, or tone of voice add to the message (whether he intended that to be detected or not)?

2) How did I feel? What physiological responses were happening in me that might give me some useful feedback? Fear? Recognition that he is right but I thought no one understood certain things.

3) What did I do? What was my immediate response? Positive, neutral, negative? Verbal and/or physical?

Insist that criticism of you be constructive, that you won't accept anything less.

Insist on specifics and as much clarification as you feel you need to accurately understand what you are being told or accused of.

Insist on a specific statement of whether this person is saying you do or don't do the things being discussed. General "people sometimes do such things" comments don't help because you may waste your energy considering critiques that don't actually apply to you or weren't intended for you.

Ask for suggestions on alternative courses of action and insist on a detailed answer or make it clear to everyone who can or will hear about this event how inadequate the critic is without picking a not helpful fight.

How good are you at facing and admitting your own mistakes? You know you aren't perfect so why fight it? Laugh at yourself in a supportive, never a derisive, way.

Remember that you are the whole you, not just the point being criticized.

Making value judgments is one of our most important activities. Every day in every encounter with other persons or the results of their work you make many value judgments. You like some things, you feel uncomfortable about others, and you decide that certain actions are unacceptable for whatever reasons and resolve not to support or give approval to them. That is criticism or critical thinking. It means as much shouting "Bravo!" for a great performance as it does saying, "There's no way I'm going to pay for that sloppy job."

It is certainly a personality defect when a person always finds fault with everything. Having unrealistic expectations and standards assumes both that the person won't be satisfied and that she won't be taken seriously by others for very long. The result is that the individual has no significant long-term impact on how things are done. But for many areas of our lives and societies we can argue that there are real shortcomings and we ought not to accept the status quo too easily. Hitting the balance requires care and effort. But everything of real value as a human endeavor requires care and effort.

I need to recognize and accept the fact that some things I can change myself, some I can influence change in, and some are beyond any direct influence from me. I can't do everything but I can do some things if I am willing to make the effort. That means I need to develop some skill at differentiating the situations. Anything that is a human institution was made by humans and therefore can be changed or even unmade by them. However, changes in the physical world resulting from men's actions may not be able to be changed by us. Once a species is extinct it is gone forever. Once a tropical forest is cut down and burned it is unlikely that anything more than a poor approximation of it will regrow for many decades, if ever. Once a hill is deforested and erosion begins there is little likelihood the soil loss can be stopped without a large scale investment of resources that will seldom be judged doable.

A major problem in the evaluation of government decisions is that we don't have all of, or perhaps even enough of, the facts to make a sound judgment. This is further complicated when some of what we are told are lies and distortions. Critical evaluation will tend to make us aware of this, even if it won't give us the reliable facts. At least it protects us from swallowing the falsehoods and will prompt us to keep up the pressure for the truth. Also, practice in critical thinking in areas in which we have some expertise will make us better able to cut through some of the smoke screen generated to confuse us in other areas.

Informational presentations should be truthful, fair, and as much as possible objective. *Truthful* seems self-evident - and I consider it at some length in Chapter 24.

Fair is complicated because it is rooted in a judgment call for which we don't have universal and enforceable criteria. I may consider what was done fair but others, equally honest and sincere, may disagree. Fair is generally understood to mean providing a level playing field for all participants, giving all sides equal opportunity and an appropriate share of the resources needed to succeed. Presenting only one side of the story or structuring the information to emphasize one side or make it seems clearly more believable or desirable rather than allowing the audience to decide that unassisted is unfair. Providing presentation time to only one side or significantly more to one side in what is represented to the public as a nonpartisan event is unfair. Permitting repeated interruptions of one speaker but not the opponent is unfair. I urge you to add your own observations about unfair tactics to the list.

Objective is a special quagmire because claims and wishes of the philosophers and others notwithstanding there are not universally agreed upon guidelines for what this means in practice. That's why there are so many tomes on the library shelves presenting this person's or that one's interpretations, corrections of everyone else's misreadings, and new insights and understandings of the alleged authentic realities.

Objectivity is complicated both because it's hard to agree on an effective definition of it and by the difficulty of rising above our own interests, experiences, and drives in the way we shape any comments that we make. You may believe you are objective but because you don't know the alternative ideas you may be giving a slanted view as the only one.

This question must be seriously considered. Can you give truly objective information to help others form their opinions or is it inevitable that you will try to influence and shape their opinions? I believe it is possible (although not easy) to achieve a reasonable degree of conscious objectivity when we firmly set our minds to doing so. I have serious doubts about whether we can achieve what the majority of honest and reasonable people would publicly agree is total objectivity. I'm quite confident that universal agreement on this point is not possible.

Should you admit to a desire to influence your audience if you are questioned about that? That would be the most honest response and, since you probably can't deceive anyone who has gone so far as to raise this question, it is the response most likely to preserve your credibility. Forewarned, the person can apply her own critical skills to sort and weigh what you say and decide how to act. An alert and intelligent person would be doing that anyway so the main thing you do by owning up to it is to admit that you favor one side in the matter and therefore want others to profit from it, support it, or appreciate the advantages of it. Even if they don't favor your side in this matter, few will object to you admitting your intention if you state it up front since it is the way most of us operate most of the time when we are dealing with matters that only some embrace.

Should you volunteer the fact that you hope to influence your audience? That is a separate judgment call. You probably aren't deceiving the critically alert people but you might be slipping under the radar of some others. You must consider how important it is to you to influence as many as you can in the short run and weigh that against the likelihood that those persons will become aware of your strategy for dealing with them and resent it and therefore the possibility that this will reduce your credibility with them over the longer term.

If questioned, is it ethical to deny that you are trying to influence them if you are aware that you are but that isn't your prime intent? You might claim that you are doing all you can to be objective and mean it. If however you deny that the idea of influencing or directing their response is part of your motivation, then you are lying and that's not acceptable. Accepting that it can happen, without having it as your prime goal, is standard middle ground. The danger is that if you deny any thought or willingness to influence their thinking in this matter few will believe you then or in other matters later.

We communicate for a variety of reasons. Sometimes because we want to impart information for its own sake (*informing*) and sometimes because we want the information or its implications to affect decisions and reactions of our hearers (*persuading*). These are both valid uses of our communication skills but when we are the ones on the receiving side of the message it will be useful to know which result is intended.

The differences between informing and persuading include the selection of the specifics and the illustrations or comparisons used to reinforce the points being made.

Depending on the complexity of the subject and the background of the hearer, we might simplify the presentation or we might work through all its complexities. For those with no particular experience or training in the subject and therefore probably with little interest in a detailed description of the processes or events, we will give a bare bones outline that gives only the general picture. This is the task of the headline writer who boils the entire story down to a few words that give the core bit of information. But a superficial blurb won't be satisfactory for the person who is knowledgeable in the field. This person wants all the available data and theories so she can draw her own conclusions. She wants to see the facts, figures, charts, and photos.

When the intent is persuasion, however, the information will be doled out carefully since much or too little will diminish the effect. With too little to go on, many intelligent people will delay or even decline to make a decision on the topic. Too much, however, will give away that there is more to it than you wanted them to recognize and that may lead them to different conclusions than you wanted. Told that "not much" of the money given to a charity goes to the professional fund raising group that set up the campaign, some may still decline to contribute suspecting that they will be helping the money collectors more than the charity. Being above board and saying publicly that more than half the money collected will go into the collection group's pockets will possibly turn off many more potential contributors. It is hard to assess how many people suspect that "not much" means about half and won't contribute without a more precise and verifiable figure.

Persuasion is the heart of propaganda, a term heavily burdened with overtones and baggage from misuse. Persuasion is a valid and appropriate use of verbal and non-verbal communication but not every-one who wants to persuade us has our best interests or even a legal and moral objective in mind. Trying to talk a friend into seeing a film with you is persuasion of an innocuous sort. Trying to talk the population at large into voting for a particular political candidate or program is a different level of persuasion but a phenomenon we are all familiar with. Trying to whip a crowd into a frenzy in hopes of inciting them to some act of defiance or even violence - or trying to dissuade them from those acts and quiet them - is another example of the spectrum of uses of this communication form.

A tricky problem is how to deal with hard to define and evaluate matters like intelligence or sanity for which we have standard operating procedures that are convenient but that we know full well are inadequate for the job yet because of the complications of the task we think we need or want to perform, we know of no alternative techniques. This leaves us with the unhappy choice of performing a task in what we know is an inadequate but routine way (even if we know it is sometimes harmful or meaningless) or not being able to perform the task in an objective way.

We regularly and routinely try to evaluate people's intelligence, honesty, and reliability in order to predict their educational potential and their future on-the-job performance. It would be so convenient if we could sit everyone down and have them take some standardized test and from the result accurately and realistically predict who will perform well in particular job areas, who will come up with the new ideas that will make life better for everyone, and who will steal you blind if you put her on your payroll. But humans are complicated and changeable. Their performance at any task may be affected by a wide range of motivational and social environment factors. It is impossible to reduce the individual to a single number on a scale or a single category box out of a matrix of possibilities but we do it in many situations anyway. Every day and in a dozen ways.

We use I.Q. scores to determine which class an eight year old will be assigned to. We use S.A.T. scores to decide who gets a chance to enroll in the supposedly better colleges. High school and college grades often determine who gets the good jobs and the best pay. Supervisor evaluations make or break careers and determine the speed of career advancement. Treating people as ciphers that are picked to fill specific roles sidesteps the messiness of dealing with real people who have bad days, may be late bloomers, or who may not be motivated to perform up to the potential they displayed when younger - or the reverse. Of course we don't want to think of ourselves as ciphers and we know very well that having the flu on the day of the big test does make a difference in your score but it is easier to try to deceive ourselves that no one will be dealing with us as a number on a paper while we ourselves are dealing with these other people in exactly that way.

Some of the contests we hear about regularly are built around such silliness that one can only wonder about the supposed intelligence of the businesses that operates on the basis of these distortions. A conspicuous one is the TV ratings system. Absurdly, it equates the statistical estimate of the number of viewers of a show as approving it. According to this estimating system you can't watch a new show without automatically approving of it, even loving it. That's even if you decide never to watch it again and to speak of it with scorn tomorrow to any who will listen. For the ratings records you approved of it when you (or your statistical stand-in) simply turned it on.

This unavoidably is also taken to mean that for the semi-official record the two-thirds or more who turned on their TVs but didn't watch this program disapproved or rejected it without making any reasoned judgment on it because they never saw it. Under this system, choosing any alternative - like watching another show, knitting a scarf, or reading a newspaper in that time period are all *No* votes cast against this show. The only thing viewers have to go on is the advertising (or more accurately, hyping) of the show, word of mouth, and, if it is a weekly series, their estimation of previous episodes.

Things are further distorted when the show's airers add together the guessed numbers who turned in for at least part of several different episodes and tell you that that total number watched the show. This implies, without actually saying it - since that would nullify the intended effect - that those were separate people who all watched every one of the episodes included in this count. It's up to you to decide which distorted claim to believe. That little asterisk at the end and the tiny print some-where else on the page are important if you want at least some hint at the real situation. The idea seems to be, "Hey, be a good dupe and only pay attention to what's in the full size font and accept the distorted view".

Particularly the first week of the TV season it is stretching things to say that the public has selected a favorite among the channel programs when no one can have seen more than one of the programs in any time period (even if she taped something else for later viewing). To make matters sillier, the channel with the overnight (and weekly and annual) highest viewership percentage is declared the winner with fewer than a third of the guesstimated viewers. The other channels are "losers" although there often are only one or two percentage points between them - which since those are statistical points means they are often not validly any different. That means more than two-thirds of the viewers are officially designated as losers because they didn't choose to watch the winning program or channel.

The most remarkable part, however, is that business people will pay a premium rate to advertise on the channel declared the winner in this fashion. For instance, if you were (or are, since many brand name battles are quite comparable) ready to make a major purchase for your home like your very first thingamajig you might be impressed if the salesperson tells you that brand A sells more thingamajigs than anyone else. If you pushed for specifics and were told that brand A sells an estimated 30%, brand B 29%, brand C 28.5% and a group of smaller brand the other 12.5% your amazement might diminish a bit. But what would you say when told that because brand A sells more it costs more? If you said *Fine, that's how it should be* you are ready to be a business executive or a consumer dupe. The task is to try to learn if the top seller is better in various objectively measurable ways, not just more intensively advertised.

In chapter four of their excellent book *Nobody's Perfect (How To Give Criticism and Get Results)* Dr. Hendrie Weisinger and Norman M. Lobsenz offer some helpful guidelines to use in appraising the validity of criticism made of us.

1) *Importance.* How important is this criticism? To start with, is the subject a significant one? There are cranks among us ready to work themselves into a lather about the most superficial or plain dumb matters but we are not obliged to join in those fusses. Think hard about it since you get to make this call, is the specific topic one that we should make a big deal about? Our experience with the long list of political questions should cause us to think long and hard before muddying the waters mainly for the sake of doing so if honest communication is our true interest and intent - or tolerating others doing so.

2) *Source.* Does this person have the knowledge and position or authority to make this judgment? Not everyone willing to criticize you deserves a serious hearing. What are her motives in criticizing you? We may only be able to guess at these but if there is reason to believe that your benefit isn't uppermost in the listing, you have good reason to ignore or reject what she says.

3) *Gauge the emotional context.* Is this the critic's way of venting her aggression about something else? There is no profit in paying serious attention to complaints about something that isn't really the subject inciting this person's strong desire to have some say. If she is angry that her proposal was rejected by others, her attack on your proposal may have little to do with its merits. You owe it to yourself to judge the critic and her agenda before you take her claims or observations seriously.

4) *Consistency.* Is the same criticism offered repeatedly? If so it is more likely to be valid. Once in a lifetime mistakes may evoke criticisms but those are of little value. The repetition of a mistake that we could

have avoided by paying more attention to the feedback is an extra mark against us. The same observations by several critics or from the same person on separate occasions (without any indication that this has become a fixation for this critic and is therefore not connected with a real desire to help) deserve serious consideration.

5) *Cost.* How much energy would you have to expend to change this behavior? Is it worth that effort? A cost-benefit analysis is as valid and valuable in your personal life as anywhere. It may not be a good investment of your psychological energy to go to a lot of trouble to change some item that you consider to be of only minor importance even if it seems to annoy someone else - especially when that is someone only at the fringes of your social circle

6) *Benefit.* What effect will changing have? This is the other side of the coin from cost. Sometimes you can see (and the critic could not) that altering your behavior in this situation will have further ramifications for your life, either positive or negative.

Eating more slowly so that you don't go rushing off before those joining you for lunch are finished may make it hard for you to get done all that you are obligated to do even though slowing up might make you a more desirable lunch buddy. It might also affect your appreciation of food and cause you to either gain weight because you continue to shovel it in but for a longer period or to lose weight because you savor each item more but don't feel compelled to jam in those extras that you thought might be needed to give you the energy to get through the afternoon. Thus consider the benefits to others as well as yourself, but don't automatically think that giving precedence to the benefits to others is the best way to act if that means shortchanging yourself in any sense.

You can generate some basic criteria for evaluating the success of your own critical decisions.

A) Did you focus on the matter with enough intensity and duration to make a reasonable evaluation of the pros and cons, the consequences and the alternatives? This is the *preparation factor*, what you did to get ready to give a useful and constructive criticism.

B) Did you find or create the opportunity to present your views and reasoning to those who had to be involved in the decision-making and/or implementation in a non-threatening way so they would hear you out? This is the *presentation factor*. The most insightful criticism in the world is useless if it falls on deaf ears.

C) Did you give an open-minded hearing to any objections and alternative proposals made in response to your criticism? This would be the *reciprocal receptivity factor* that is essential to making the process a dialogue rather than some would-be authority handing down edicts.

D) Did you accomplish what you wanted to? Did it get done whether you did it yourself or persuaded others to do it? Was it done in what you felt was the best way rather than in a less effective compromise way? If not, did you manage to introduce your idea into the agenda so it will be considered in the future? This is the *success factor*.

It often takes time and maybe repeated tries to get your criticism seriously considered and acted on, but if it is important it is worth that effort. If you give up too easily, you aren't a good critic. You need not, in fact usually should not, make yourself obnoxious about the matter, but you should use the routine procedures to keep it before that relevant audience and make it clear that sooner or later they will have to deal with it and sooner is better.

The answer to whether you accomplished what you wanted to is in the actions. A change in the behavior that precipitated a criticism is the main sign of its success. In some cases we can readily see the changes (like the way important papers are shared in an office), in other cases they may be more subtle (like the attitude of a person to members of some minority group). It is possible that we had an impact and now have the other person thinking about the matter but so far she hasn't chosen to implement a change of behavior or perhaps she hasn't had the occasion to act in that area but she intends to do so in a changed way when the situation calls for that behavior. Unless we are in an official supervisory capacity for this person, our duty is done once we have made the critical comments. Implementing them or not doing so then is her decision and her responsibility. It is appropriate that our evaluation and opinion of her should be affected by whether and to what degree she changes now that we have made her aware that her behavior is less than the best though.

The answer is in our own actions when we assess the success of the decisions we have made about changing our own behavior and attitudes. We should find ourselves giving more consideration to what we are about to do before we make the decision about whether and how to do it. We may decide to fool ourselves about this, but we know what we are doing even if we manage to keep ourselves from fully acknowledging that.

Don't settle for imperfect best except as a step along the way. Ideals are wonderful and yet terrible things. Wonderful because they give us a view of inspiring, encouraging possibilities, but terrible when they become so rigidly fixed in our minds that we lose sight of the fact that reality almost always falls short of our views of the ideal and can't reasonably be forced into that mold. Terrible also when we must face the reality that many of the conditions we consider ideal and highly desirable aren't attainable in anything like our existing world and society.

Accepting and acclaiming the best of what is currently available as the best that exists is honest and makes good psychological sense; acclaiming it as the best there can be is shortsighted and pathetic. That is the approach taken by persons so desperate to claim superlatives for themselves that they are unwilling to recognize and admit their warts and too insecure to believe they can allow, much less participate in, any process that questions or alters the status quo they have accepted.

Part of the frustration we set ourselves up for is expecting perfect answers to our questions when only adequate ones are likely. In an ideal world it might be realistic to believe that every question can and should receive a full, detailed, and perfect response but our personal experiences should make us aware that this seldom happens. Sometimes nothing more than an adequate response is possible. Sometimes it isn't necessary or appropriate to demand more before we make decisions.

To say that an answer is an adequate one isn't to imply that there is anything incorrect about it, only that it doesn't deal with all those innuendoes, extensions, and implications that the original question stirred in the mind of the person who asked it or the ones who listened in on the exchange. What is an adequate answer will always vary with the audience, the intent of the question, and the moment in time. For instance, giving an elaborate answer to a tangential question while more immediately relevant matters go unanswered because of time constraints would be undesirable. It is also a common tactic in persuasion.

A technical question asked by someone without the information background to understand the technical terminology and its implications can only be answered with a simplified response. That might seem blatantly inadequate to a trained person but it will tell the untrained one as much as she wants to know or will be able to deal with comfortably.

A mixed audience of well and poorly informed listeners always presents a speaker with the problem of selecting the level to which she will pitch her presentations and answers to questions. There are no universal rules that can be used, only a few generalizations. Unless she is facing a meeting of technicians, a speaker will probably find it hard to underestimate the comprehension and background of the typical group on any specialized topic. But if you aim your presentation at the bottom row you run a great risk of being perceived by many as treating the audience as a crowd of idiots. The most workable suggestion is to aim for the middle level of the group as you understand them. Especially if you are aiming to influence as well as inform (and most speakers are hoping to do both) you have a better chance of success with the largest number of the audience with this approach.

The most effective and therefore successful responders find the words, examples, body language, and tone to make it clear to an audience that they are giving a simplified answer but have the fuller and more detailed one available for those prepared to understand it after this presentation.

Everything has it limits, including proper criticism intended to be helpful. The reality is that you can't help some people. Despite their protestations if too publicly challenged on the point, many people do want to be told what to do and to believe. Accept the fact that this means you can't help those people to "get free". You can calmly present facts and authoritative source paths for them in case they ever decide outside the spotlight to question, but don't expect any public statements that can be used to document your success in persuading them to change. Be aware of their need and allow them room to keep their thoughts and decisions private to evade some social pressure, especially of the types intended to keep them under the control of others.

Unless they are publicly proselytizing or at the very least actively supporting such activity, it is seldom fruitful to put people on the spot about what they do or will agree to. If they are advocates or activists, they are fair game for wounded feelings so you must decide how much you are willing to give them those. Putting them on the spot is of course a standard tactic of exactly the people you would be trying to get these people beyond so how are you different from those except that you want to squeeze the victim to say no instead of yes?

Change always requires an open enough mind to recognize and accept that there are other possibilities. That is the step that must come before any evolution of what are better, more correct, or whatever criteria are important to those involved in the particular case.

The human population is too diverse in every aspect for us to have realistic expectations of more than working majorities on any matter. That is a hard fact to accept but we need to face up to it lest we become discouraged, even defeated, by disappointment. You have an agenda whether you have ever thought of it in that way or not. You would like society to operate in certain ways and to not operate in certain other ones. The specifics are particular to you although you may share general ideas with whole groups of others. The specific combination of the minutia is where you are likely to be in only a small group or even unique.

For many it is startling and disappointing to realize that you (as an individual and as part of most, if not all, collectives) can't make everyone else see the errors of their ways or get them to recognize that many of our problems are the result of the ways we do things and that we can do those things in other ways that would minimize or even end the harmful effects. We can note succinctly here that there are a range of reasons for this and each non-responsive person likely has her own combination of reasons underlying her decisions to stay with the outlook, attitudes, and methods that she has adapted as her own.

The temptation, largely based on doubts that these persons who don't understand the realities and viable options as well as we obviously do, is to keep on preaching to the whole world no matter how much negative feedback comes from various quarters and no matter how much evidence there is that doing that is a waste of our energy and resources - or even fully counter-productive.

All of which should prompt us to reevaluate (which does not mean reject, unless that is the end conclusion of that process) our own thoughts, beliefs, and expectations on these matters. This is useful to sharpen our vision. Doing that, we may spot the places where we have not thought through all the factors and potential consequences. We may realize or at least face up to the fact that we are operating on the basis of the positions and beliefs we ourselves inherited from our parents and others we accept as authority figures or gurus but which ideas may be riddled with holes and contradictions that we either had not noticed until now or that we deliberately overlooked because we earlier refused to question or contradict our authorities. That is likely exactly the accusation we suspect is the deficiency of many of the non-responders to our enlightenment.

As we acquire new information and more clearly see the effects and consequences of some of what we previously decided seemed true and trustworthy, we confirm or adjust our views. Since our "minds" (which I am defining here for the sake of easier commentary as the totality of our biological machinery and all of our experiences in all aspects of our lives) are vast and getting more so with each day's new experiences and exposures it is unrealistic to expect to review the totality of ourselves in one session. We need to sit quietly (if possible) and work our way through our thoughts and decisions about particular topics. First we are likely to realize, maybe for the first time or the first time in some period of time, that no topic is likely to be an isolated point. If it is isolated though, then we can quickly and easily reevaluate our thinking about it. For those matters that we recognize as more complicated now that we are focused on them, we must try to force ourselves to identify and lay on the table the many associations that have touched on that topic area in our experience - the good ones, the bad ones, and those seemingly irrelevant ones. We should never forget that we are works in progress. We acknowledge that that means we are always able to improve if we see the need for and the route to that. The key to fullest success in that is to do such reevaluation regularly, not just when we face an emergency.

Being responsible for our decisions and actions is scary. Almost paralyzingly so for some people. There is a social price to pay for always being able to point to someone else as the source of the wrong or ineffective decisions or positions you can be associated with (without, of course, explicitly admitting that you made the decision to accept that person or group's stance). For some, that price is the lesser of the burdens - "I am responsible" versus "She is the one really responsible and calling the shots that I then slavishly embrace".

To a degree (that constant and important qualifier) most of the time (another common qualifier when we are talking in general terms) we all adopt positions suggested or advocated by others. Once we go critical though we do so (A) with the various adjustments or qualifications needed to fit the generalizations into our particular worldview, stating that explicitly if our doing so is appropriate or called for, and (B) we accept personal responsibility for the ideas, claims, etc. as if they are our own unique creations since we embraced them.

When we want to or agree to give criticism it is important to say what we mean in the critique clearly, constructively, and in a context that the other person can appreciate and profit from. When we don't want to and aren't prepared to agree to give a critique it is useful to have some skill in sidestepping, saying nothing, and putting the other person off. Since the whole basis of the process is to provide honest and where possible useful feedback it is not acceptable to give empty, or worse, lying critiques in order to wiggle out of the situation. But it is acceptable to many people to use various schemes to keep ourselves from being cornered or pressured into offering the analysis when for any reason we don't want to do so. Especially in minor matters it is often easier and better all around to avoid the issue so that no feelings need be bruised or backs arched more than is often unavoidable in such matters.

The artful dodge is acceptable behavior because it functions as a social escape valve. It lets you avoid getting drawn into contentious or potentially hurtful discussions that you have no obligation to engage in and does so without having to resort to lies. A lie is a statement that has substance and can therefore be used offensively or defensively by the other person beyond anything you envisioned or intended. It can also hang around for a long time or pop up to haunt you at inopportune moments. A dodge is a mirage, a fog bank that the other can't use very effectively and that evaporates quickly without leaving much residue.

You aren't required to offer an opinion every time that someone asks for one. Even when you feel that a well-honed critical observation might make the solution to a problem clearer to the others, you may estimate that they are not really receptive and therefore it will be wasted on this audience *at this time*. Once presented, your views will instantly become old hat to these people. That increases the chance that repeating those views later to another audience who might have influence in this matter but have heard them and seen them fall flat - or to this same audience when circumstances have shifted and made them receptive - will have less effect than the observations deserve. The obvious way to preserve the impact of good critical comments is to keep them in reserve until the appropriate audience is receptive. Therefore we need to have ways to sidestep the topic at other times.

When you are tired, distracted, or otherwise having a hard time caring about this person, topic, or situation you should insist on being allowed to excuse yourself from this task. If you feel that you have an obligation to yourself as well as to them to only give your best as a critic there is little choice except to dodge if the other is determined to get a response from you right now.

The simplest approach is a flat refusal but often that is not the most workable one. Saying nothing comes easier to some people than to others. For some it is the most natural thing in the world. I am tempted to suggest that this makes them naturals as politicians but I am going to restrain myself from making that seem like a slur. In fact much of the time when among the public an effective politician has to listen to righteous dawdle and self-serving prattle and still give the impression to most observers that he is taking it all in, still being civil and interested, but without making any commitments. This is a skill that many of us don't possess in abundance.

You can say nothing by literally keeping silent. This might be an effective way keeping yourself out of some conversations you choose not to participate in, but unless you are or want to be known as someone who sits around wearing a vague smile that suggests you have a vacuum between your ears it may require some artful techniques. Your silence can be supplemented by moving away from the speaker, by sprinkling your comments with non sequiturs, by saying only innocuous and unfocused stuff that is minimally arguable by even the most determined person, by firmly redirecting the conversation to topics you are willing to engage in, or by speaking total nonsense (although this has severe limitations if you aren't willing to be branded a fool).

Why would you want to say nothing? Because for any number of reasons you don't want to get into a critical discussion of this person, performance, or item or don't care to discuss anything or some things with this particular person or group.

You may not know enough about the topic in general or this case in particular to make a useful contribution and would prefer not to pretend otherwise. You may not be convinced that this audience will take your criticism well if it is less than a rave approval. You may believe that the asker only wants to learn what you know or think about the person or performance in question in order to use that against you or against the person being critiqued - or both. Or you may not agree that a supposed association between items or events that this discussion is suggesting is valid but realize that to speak on the matter is to give tacit approval to the notion that such a connection does exist.

Sometimes it is possible to discuss the pros and cons of a subject without offering a criticism. Here you speak out loud the analysis you would go through to draw your own conclusions but you stop short of that final step and let the other person draw his own without overtly expressing yours. I qualify that because if it is a topic of importance or any that you have a strong position about, it will be unlikely that you will present the analytical points without your audience being aware of your leaning. The artful dodging here is to resist the temptation or pressure to articulate an opinion rather than just list the points of consideration.

Saying something worthwhile is an art; so is deliberately saying nothing. The skills required are much the same since both call for careful consideration of our words and their impact. We usually sound serious and thoughtfully involved when we say something profound but to deliberately say nothing effectively we must come across as casual and ideally disinterested or even disconnected. Coming across as too serious about a matter of no real consequence is not a good way to go if you want to be taken seriously at other times.

Diplomacy is desirable whenever it is feasible. Diplomats speak in bland, measured opacities. They are "encouraged" or "concerned". They say that on-going negotiations are "candid" or "useful" or "productive". They don't let themselves get nailed down on what they mean by those terms. In this context we can define diplomacy as the strategy of verbal gymnastics in which one avoids saying explicitly what one thinks, relying instead on polite statements that can mean nothing or have strong meaning but whose intended meaning in each instance of use is unclear and vigorously kept unclarified so it can be disputed and explained away as a misinterpretation at some later time if that seems useful. The heart of the art of diplomacy is to dance around sensitive subjects without giving offense and in a way that keeps the door open for future contacts and discussions.

It definitely means that you don't publicly call your opponent nasty names, you don't impugn his intelligence, his parentage, or his intentions in your negotiations even if you think such comments would be justified by his attitudes and actions.

In many diplomatic situations saying nothing is not an option since that in itself might say a great deal about the conditions between the parties so saying something that means next to nothing is the artful reaction. A saving grace of diplomacy is that even when most people recognize that it is in play they will decide it is acceptable and go along rather than create a fuss demanding total honesty or take offense at your decision not to be explicit with your comments since you obviously think those would cause a problem or you wouldn't be hesitating to voice them.

In some instances you may judge that the best approach is to state clearly (although you will possibly be exaggerating for effect) some reasons why you aren't equipped or able to give criticism of this event. You may not always be able to avoid it, but if you phrase things carefully you will try hard not to introduce an at this time qualifier which might lead to you having to fend off the matter again later. You can hope the topic won't come up again, but if it does you start over again from square one and do the sidestep waltz.

Ignorance of the technicalities is a good and valid reason not to offer criticism of many subjects. Lawyers are expected to know the law in general but most of the rest of us have only a smattering of tidbits about it that we have picked up over the years. Most lawyers, however, know little about microbiology so someone seeking a second guess about which antibiotic a doctor should have prescribed for them can quite rightly be told by a lawyer that he simply has no opinion on that matter (but he can consult with someone who should know - at your expense). In the same way most microbiologists can't offer much useful comment on the risks of various surgical procedures. "I don't know enough about the details of that area to have an opinion," is a prime way to avoid giving a reaction without giving offense. Most of the time that *is* precisely why the person doesn't want to comment on the matter, especially to someone that he knows from reputation or experience will soon be blabbing whatever comments the critic makes around as having been made with great show of authority by the reluctant consultant.

In most technical areas there are more than enough complexities to allow any except the known world authority in the particular special topic (and often even him) to claim that there are too many possibilities and ramifications for him to comment without an extensive briefing by experts on the particular case. Few will push the matter after it is made clear that the authority isn't willing to say anything. Those few are likely to need the simplest approach which means being told explicitly and emphatically that no answer will be provided.

Sometimes we don't wish to offer a critique because we don't feel we are adequate to the task. Perhaps we don't know even the generally accepted criteria used by those interested in the subject. Do you have any notion of what the judges are looking for at a cat or a dog show? Or a juried art show? Do you know the moves and their relative weight in the scoring that the judges in a gymnastic or diving competition watch for?

Sometimes we don't wish to comment because we know that the person asking is looking mainly to find negative reactions to repeat in order to try to diminish the subject being critiqued. Much of the time these aren't total strangers asking for our opinion but persons whose agendas we have some idea about so we can often make reasonable predictions about what use is going to be made of whatever we say.

Sometimes the subject of the requested critique is the work or some personal aspect of the one requesting it. If we could only honestly give a mediocre or worse rating we can predict that will not be helpful and might well be damaging to either the person's self-image or his relationship with us, we may urgently want to avoid responding and having those effects but once we have been asked we realize we must tiptoe away from the idea, but subtly. If we believe he can't do better than he has in this case we can say so but if we believe he can do so we want to encourage him and not throw cold water on his early effort and let that be the end of it. These are among the more difficult cases and the ones where artful sidestepping is most called for.

Sometimes we may be reluctant because, having considered the matter, we can't come up with a constructive response and we see no point in offering any comment that doesn't meet that criterion.

Sometimes we simply don't want to be lured into a pattern of routinely coming up with a critical reaction on demand because we fear it will set us up for troubles in any or all of the criteria listed above in the future.

In some cases you can use some real or potential controversy about the matter as your reason to reserve your opinion. This is a refusal to respond but it is softened by a reason that many will accept as valid. There will be objections that you were willing to make strong comments about other controversial topics in the past but the simple response to that is that you, and only you, decide which topics you are willing to risk getting caught up in a public fuss about.

There is of course a vast difference between saying nothing and *deliberately* saying nothing. The latter is a crafted message intended to lead the hearer to the conclusion that the speaker has no thoughts worth pursuing about this topic. It is a way to avoid more serious engagement without risking a confrontation by overtly refusing to respond or by presenting arguments for you not getting into a detailed critique. Note that both of these are valid stances but more open to argument from the other person because they are obvious and open to reaction. *Deliberate Nothings* (DNs) reduce the likelihood of an argument because, like a mist, they obscure your intent but provide no solid target for attack.

Effective DNs have to make at least minimal sense in context. They might seem a bit or a whole lot contrived to those who are alert, but if they are obvious nonsense to even the least tuned in members of your audience they won't stand up to scrutiny without signaling that you are a babbling fool - and establishing that isn't usually the point of the exercise.

It is helpful to develop a list of noncommittal statements that you can trot out when you want to avoid saying anything you can be nailed down about. Over time your associates may become aware of how you use these and may groan or mildly protest when you use one as a dodge but generally even then they serve the purpose.

One of my favorites is to describe as *interesting* things that I don't wish or intend to describe my reaction to more precisely. There is nothing inherent belittling or negative about the word yet it says nothing very specific. What does it mean? Attractive? Looks like it was made by a drunken monkey? Clever? Bordering on the monstrous? Perhaps any of these but no dictionary will catch you out so it means whatever the other person chooses to take it to mean (without him being able to quote you as saying it was other than interesting) or nothing much at all. If you use it as I do, you are content to accept that ambiguity.

Say Nothing statements need to be vaguely approving but not committed. "Nice", "terrific", and "Oh my, yes" can all be quoted against you as approval. "Not likely", "*ugh*" (especially when accompanied by a facial expression reflecting the discovery of a rotting corpse and fingers-down-the-throat gesture), and "Are you kidding?" all reflect disapproval. But "interesting", "thought provoking", and "I'll have to think about that" all convey the desired sense of openness without passing judgment.

We all recognize at a fairly early age that some of the responses we get to our questions or actions are hollow. The words are those used to convey praise, support, or conviction but we sense that there is no such feeling behind them. They are nods to social convention, not sincere statements. As you recover from your disillusionment, you realize that life in human society is more complex than you had realized. You also realize that there are socially acceptable ways for you to sidestep when you don't want to comment on some topic. The essential element of a hollow comment is that it is noncommittal, neither clearly nor emphatically for or against, since either might bring with it an obligation or an undesirable association in the public mind with someone or some group or idea that you don't want to be misunderstood as connected with. The irony is that what you inadvertently convey may well be exactly what you were trying to avoid with your hollow response.

In some cases you can start with the request made to you and talk around the subject enough in generalizations and hot air that the other person forgets that you didn't offer the requested critique. Martha asks John what he thinks of a new CD that she has recently plunked down her hard cash to buy. John notes that the group who made the recording were recently involved in some legal case that made the news and they played at a multi-group concert in another city the year before, then he shifts them off to another topic. Unless she is really concerned about or enthusiastic about the new CD there is a good chance that Martha won't press for John's more judgmental reaction to them and if asked later will claim that she has a vague sense that John did answer the question but she can't remember exactly what he said.

Non sequiturs are tricky but they can work if they are not too humorous and are not too blatantly a defiant refusal to give a more meaningful answer. They need to be chosen with care since too weird a departure from the context of the discussion will focus attention on itself and the speaker. Then the evasion has the opposite effect from that intended, which was to be like a stealth aircraft and fly undetected through the radar of conversational conventions. Too peculiar a response attracts attention and, worst of all for what was intended, it may evoke guffaws and laughter. Those are a disaster at this juncture because nothing focuses attention quite like laughter at a nonsense statement that now itself becomes the momentary topic of conversation. Whether it was said with forethought, what exactly it was meant to mean, and what message it was sending between the lines are now being scrutinized by those present and the speaker is pinned to the exhibit board in the spotlight when he intended to blend inconspicuously into the background. For better or for worse, laughter is a powerful tool for turning not-too-discerning people away from something.

The usefulness of a well-chosen non sequitur is that it closes off a conversational pathway with a dead-end sign. No dispute. No quibbling about terms. Simply no place to go from there. To be effective it must be maintained as such. It is not open to probing questions or requests for clarification. The statement stands on its own and you move on. If you allow the other person to drag you into a defense or an explanation, you have relinquished the safe ground and wasted your effort.

The change of topic strategy probably dates back to the first caveman who shouted "Sabertooth!" when pressed on a point he didn't want to answer about and it continues to be used because it works. The strategy includes crude moves like creating a panic to distract and shift your audience to the subtle (and therefore more effective) sidesteps. Such shifts depend on you using words or topics from the matter you are pressed to give a reaction to as the path to redirect the thoughts of all concerned onto something else. If well done (and if the other person isn't too hotly determined to get the sought after reaction from you) the audience hardly even realizes until later that you changed the subject. Then they can't decide if it was done deliberately since such shifts are normal in conversations.

You start to make a point to Albert and you evoke an image that has meaning of a different sort for him, which he therefore comments on. You are pausing in your presentation to get back to your point but chances are you are also trying to keep up with the social flow by reacting to Albert's story (since not to do so shows you really didn't listen to him and are only waiting for him to stop talking so you can continue). If you now react to some element of Albert's new story with an extension of your own, things sideslip away from the original topic. An hour later when you are alone you realize you never did make your initial point but you doubt that you were deliberately sidetracked; rather it must surely have been the common give and take of conversation.

When all else fails, try excess. Talk the matter to death. Examine the pros and the cons, the history of the subject, the personalities that are involved, the hypothetical consequences if a similar situation were to arise with various public figures as players, your own vaguely related experiences - all without ever taking a stance even though you mention all of those that could be taken. With any luck your audience will recoil in horror from this torrent of nonsense and change the subject (if not flee the scene) before you yourself can't stand it a moment longer and are struggling not to strangle yourself with your own tongue to shut you up.

Depending on the situation, your cleverness, and perhaps your brazenness, you may avoid sticky situations by having to rush off to an appointment you had forgotten about until just this moment or to go find a pay phone to relay some important information to the C.I.A. without the call being traced back to you by the enemy. Or perhaps you can have a sudden attack of half-hour laryngitis. There always seems to be some of that going around. How obvious you are willing to be about this type of dodge depends on you and your assessment of the situation. Sometimes you can take the edge off the blatant rejection of the request for feedback by trying to turn the whole thing into a joke. You sent your brain out to be dry cleaned after seeing the latest scandal mongering on the TV news and it hasn't come back yet. Or you would answer that question but the response is classified so then you would have to kill the questioner to maintain the answer as top secret.

Telling a story by way of a response lets you avoid the personal element of the situation while either making a point you think is relevant or one that is innocuous but meaningless to this discussion but which will discourage the questioner from pursuing the topic with you. Those who cultivate a reputation for meeting all requests for personal feedback with hot air stories won't be asked often but then they also won't be given the openings to make pertinent and useful observations that might profit the other and/or themselves. Everything has its price.

Even when no individual actions are elicited (whether those are solicited or not) it doesn't take an especially adept public relations person to convey the impression to less than critically alert news media (and thus to their even less critical audience) that at least the majority of those physically present were also supportive of the positions presented by the organizers. It is here that the manipulation occurs. It is simple and straightforward. Bodies present at the event are said to equal persons who support the proposals since those attendees didn't clearly indicate otherwise and they don't have a P.R. person buttonholing the media reps and whispering spin control into their ears and microphones.

To some people negativity of any sort is considered suspect, if not on the face of it bad. But, at risk of being thought of as negative, I am compelled to tell you that that simply isn't true. There are times when a negative stance or response is the most sensible and appropriate one. At the right times a negative position is good, useful, and even necessary. So are skepticism and suspicion. I prefer to say that being negative means not feeling guilty without good cause.

Because *being negative* is widely misrepresented and is too often misunderstood as a bad way of acting, it is a useful bugaboo. The threat of being publicly accused of being negative can be effective in shutting up some people and putting others on the defensive but there is a triple Catch-37 here. Depending on the sophistication of the audience, a person might be intimidated into silence by the threat of being branded negative. Or she might waste her time wrestling with the label of *negative* rather than with subjects of more relevance and importance so that she effectively hands control of the topics in the event over to her opponent.

Or she might lose some impact because a naive audience decides she is being arrogant for not taking the charge of being negative seriously and answering it in detail and they decide to favor the "Gal that ain't bein' negative." They are likely to pay a price for that in rip-offs and lack of responsible people in leadership positions later, but they are not astute or perceptive enough to likely ever recognize that fact. If the person being accused of negativism is intelligent and self-assured she will shrug the charge off as meaningless and recognize that with an audience like that she didn't lose much by not stooping to their expectations.

It shouldn't come as a surprise that much of the persuasion that goes on is slanted, twisted, and clearly deceptive. It is a kind of selling and if the details were clear cut, universally known, and without doubt or dispute no persuasion would be needed. Therefore you have to do what you can to protect yourself directly by your own actions and to protect yourself from the effects of the actions and acquiescence of the uncritical members of the masses.

The main strategy to avoid these pitfalls when the audience is of questionable sophistication about such tactics, and the outcome is important and depends on audience reaction, is to keep the discussion moving briskly and not allow it to become fixated on the question of negative actions or attitudes. You may not be able to keep an opponent from throwing the words into the ring of contention, but if you sidestep them by immediately throwing out a more relevant topic that needs hassling out, most people with open minds will concede that you did the sensible thing in focusing on the relevant matters and not taking what is always limited time in any public discussion for what is only a tangential item. The partisans will yelp and the give-us-controversy-at-any-cost portion of the news media will waste everyone's time on these bits, but until enough of us ignore those attempts at deliberate distraction and those who repeat them, our responses are limited to not responding to them.

There is the risk that if you specifically mention the distracting and disruptive matter and assert you won't take time for it, you will thereby focus everyone's attention on it and give it the status of a real topic. In order to avoid sinking into this quagmire, the ideal is to stick to the other topics and emphasize their relevance to the subject under discussion or the reason for having organized this public event. The call on whether you must give any attention to the charge of negativity depends of course on the specific factors and must be made in each situation. In the *sound bite, one news cycle of focus and then discarded from much further consideration* state of contemporary presentation and persuasion, with every topic quickly reduced to declaring winners and losers with little or no coverage or concern about the meat of the topic, this isn't easy and may not be viable for some situations. It is certainly unsatisfactory to those interested in honest communication but you should never lose sight of the fact that the commercial news sources are businesses. Hence the guesstimated audience numbers are a prime consideration. To bring them back tomorrow, how well those people are being informed or educated seems to have lost ground today to how much someone judges that they are being *entertained* by the news.

Criticism is not a nasty, nagging activity. If it becomes something like that it is only an empty caricature of what it can and should really be. We often make negative reports but seldom reflect on the fact that they can be either of three types that I am going to designate as punishment, documentation, or constructive criticism. If we confuse the categories we are less likely to make something useful out of a bad situation.

Punishment reports are sometimes the most satisfying in the short run because they let us blow off steam at the person whose actions have made us angry. When you are being yelled at, accused of all sorts of stupidity and perversity, what is there to say in response? You might claim innocence or extenuating circumstances but generally by the time the yelling has begun, the critic is beyond paying any heed to these interruptions. The intended and primary message is that you are a lousy person and are not worth much. A pretty weighty condemnation for what if objectively considered was most likely a relatively minor offense.

Punishment reports are dead-ends because they address the past and not the future so they don't have any positive effect in the longer run. They are concerned mainly with making this person suffer for what she has already done rather than with preventing future defective acts.

I am labeling as *documentation* the cases in which one person calls attention to the deficient actions of another with the primary intent of motivating the other to not repeat those deeds. Unfortunately, too often this is what the critic intends when she starts to give a documentation report but she loses control of her words due to anger and what comes out is a punishment report instead.

A documentation report is more useful that punishment because it focuses on the future which can be altered rather than on already fixed historical facts. It also may focus on the deed rather than the doer, which is usually more workable and less psychologically damaging. But as long as it goes no further than an exhibit of the evidence of wrongdoing and an exhortation to not let it happen again, it misses the chance to be more helpful.

Only when the emphasis is on how to avoid future misdeeds and specific alternative procedures or pathways to that end does the pointing out of deficient deeds becomes *constructive criticism*. The focus is then on fixing what was not right rather than simply dwelling on it. Depending on the individuals and the situation, it may or may not be useful to focus on culpability in the discussion. Often the mistake is understood by both parties and if the person in the wrong indicates that she recognizes and regrets the error it will serve little useful purpose to emphasize that and to do so risks generating destructive feelings for no good reason. When the person is involved with politics the situation shifts of course since too often any misstep that can be exaggerated to make the opposition look bad is considered usable by her opponents, even if it isn't fair, relevant, or meaningful.

Freud recognized that there is no negation in the Unconscious mind so when we operate on mental automatic pilot we get automatic affirmation. Negation is impossible to our Unconscious mind as well as uncomfortable to our Conscious so we must proceed more deliberately when we intend to take a negative stance. We have to focus on what we are doing and work through the discomfort. This prompts us to try to find a fault in our thinking and decision-making so that we can persuade ourselves to abandon the negative position. But since focusing our attention is exactly what allows us to sidestep the Unconscious, this is what we want to do. We turn the inhibiting barrier into a stimulating goad. Focusing on the fact that we are likely to feel this discomfort can be a helpful reminder of what we are doing and can help our resolve to act deliberately rather than automatically.

This built-in tendency to resist negatives can help us in positive ways as long as we have a reasonably good opinion of ourselves and a strong drive to be precise and accurate - which will have us point out the exceptions to our generalizations. When we frame our personal failures and weaknesses as simply stated negatives (for instance, "I always get phone messages wrong") we focus the automatic rejection apparatus of our minds on finding the error in that statement and in the process we may get some insight into how to truly correct our deficiency. Or we may run some negative generality about ourselves through the process and be forced to recognize that it is true and therefore we are not going to change it without great effort or maybe no matter how hard we try. That is also useful because it saves us the wasted effort of trying to correct what we aren't willing or able to change. We accept that element as important to our goals or to who we are comfortable being. We can use the time and energy to seek compensations instead. Changing how we do things usually has a cost and when we clearly see the price tag attached we aren't always willing to pay it. But even then we've made a deliberated choice so we are better off.

Genteel society has long pushed the idea that approval is shown by applause but disapproval is shown only by silence. It's not nice to boo a sloppy performance or to give public display of the fact that you don't like whatever is being done to you. I say *Do Boo!* Let your disapproval be known. One of the few ways we have in our culture for doing this is to boo, literally or figuratively. So when that is the message you want to give, this is the appropriate method to use.

At a public meeting a businessman introduced a speaker who was out on bail while appealing a conviction for bribery and racketeering and several members of the audience booed. This horrified some others present who agreed that the woman was a convicted criminal but they disapproved of this public display of disapproval even though they were uncomfortable that by being here she was being given the appearance of their approval. Who is being responsible here?

It is all well and good when you are rich or powerful to sit silently through some offensive situation and then go out and use your wealth or influence to destroy the career or business of the offender. There is no need to give voice to your disapproval in an "undignified" public display (which might also focus undesirable attention on you and cause those who can harm you to notice what you did to this person who offended you). But when you are one of the little guys and you don't raise a ruckus you can be pretty sure that nothing will be done to remedy the situation, especially if it's some wealthy or powerful person or organization behind the action.

You can also be sure that those in charge are going to great lengths to convince themselves and everyone else that your silence constitutes approval. For instance, note how many times on the TV news, lack of verbal disagreement is reported as being tacit agreement. They may also add insult to injury by using you statistically to their advantage even though you don't approve of them or actively disapprove of them - but you do so silently and without letting that show. You are part of the constituency that hasn't taken a public stance against them, therefore you can be counted in the *approving* column for their P.R. and planning purposes.

You always have the right to decide what is appropriate. You might show disapproval of an overblown and overpriced professional's sloppy performance but politely allow a comparable performance by an amateur to pass without undue comment. If you use the same scale to rate pros and amateurs, top seeds and weekend warriors, the rest of us can be comfortable about ignoring all of your evaluations.

Being a good critic requires work and often even some expense. Refusing to buy a product or support a position is only part of the task. To be fully effective you need to take the time and trouble to let those you are rejecting - whether manufacturer, advertiser, media outlet, or politician - know that you are doing so and why you are doing so.

We often complain among ourselves about the poor quality of service in restaurants and stores but those responsible for maintaining that service can't hear us. We bear a significant responsibility for the situation if we don't make them aware of the deficiencies as we perceive them. At times their stance of ignorance of the customers' discontent is real - the management level may truly be unaware of what is going on at the service level. But often it is a defensive lie. In either case if we the consumers make enough noise and make it long enough, we will be heard. Note that I'm not advocating making loud and disruptive shouting scenes but I am recommending that within your personal comfort level you repeat your complaint firmly and insistently until you get a response from the manager on duty or whoever is appropriate that indicates you are being taken seriously, not just shrugged off as another complainer of no importance. Especially when you combine your complaints with action - withholding your business or your support and letting others, especially those at higher levels of the company, know that this is being done and why - you will eventually be taken seriously. Shout a warning about rip-offs from the rooftops (not literally of course, that only works in certain movies) as fair warning to everyone else. You would want to get the hot tip about what to avoid, so give it when you are in the position to do so.

With lots of invitations to give feedback and ratings on a slew of Internet sites these days this has gotten easier. As you are likely to find if you look through a few of those, a few who list complaints about the products or service may not sway your opinion or decision but they are educational in that they represent a more complete range of the reactions to the company, topic, or whatever. For instance, I noted that a seed company I'm delighted to have around because they offer so many less commonly available species had 46 ratings, 45 of them positive. That reassures me that they are doing a good job. I also have found a problem with ratings and comments on the Internet that since they are more or less eternal a posted claim tends to hang around long after it was either disproven or corrected so it becomes my responsibility to spend what turns out to be unnecessary time checking details like that. With anything you see online, remind yourself that the system is designed to facilitate and then preserve postings, not to verify or delete them simply because they are wrong or unfounded or outdated.

The adage, "If you can't say something nice about a person, don't say anything at all" is not always prudent advice. Sometimes the negative things you know (if accurate and relevant) may save someone else from harm. It is tempting to immediately qualify this and say you shouldn't say anything negative about a person, only about a situation, performance, or idea - but many times the person is the root of the problem, deliberately and even maliciously so. In such cases the criticism of that person is not only appropriate but necessary. The adage is good advice though when it is understood to mean you ought to avoid mean gossip and irrelevant character assassination. Like everything, it must be considered in context.

If you know that a doctor is incompetent, you should report that to the medical association before she harms her patients. If you know that a bus driver is drunk when she arrives for her shift, you should report that fact so she won't kill herself or someone else on the road. If you know that a woman was part of a con scheme that cheated people and you now see her involved in some new investment scheme, you would do well to inform the investors of the woman's past so they can double-check the validity of the present deal. You would certainly be appreciative of the same information if you were in their position. Part of the reason that so many con schemes and rip-offs occur is that the people who have learned about them, often by suffering losses, keep quiet about them whether out of embarrassment or to not get involved. This then leaves the perpetrators free to repeat their scams, victimizing others. The scammers and thieves depend on this to keep doing what they do as long as possible before they have to move on to a new state and must adopt a new alias.

Not every critique you give or receive will allow for a positive orientation. Sometimes the point is precisely that an unacceptable or dangerous deed was done and something needs to be said about it. Even in this case, however, the criticism can be constructive if it focuses on the deed and doesn't impute unresolvable evil intents to the performer - unless that seems to be the situation, in which case your warning is potentially a heroic public deed.

Beware of the tendency to let your negative reactions mushroom to become more inclusive than is warranted. The other side of the mentality of seeing everything as either black-or-white is the tendency to let one's negative responses to some aspects of a system poison your emotional reactions to the whole system. It is easy to resort to gross generalizations and grumble about the whole system in negative terms when you are angry. This is an emotional rather than a rational reaction and we need to be guard against it since it is not a best performance from us. Even as we do it, we often recognize our error but we may either feel compelled to go through with what we have started or may simply refuse to think about the subject more rationally in the heat of our emotions.

People attempt to make demands on us all the time and too often they succeed. The problem here is a distorted idea of *niceness*. We fear we may shock the person if we say she is rude or pushy for asking such personal questions or trying to get us to do her work for her. The person attempting to impose the burden is in fact depending on our reluctance as victim to call her to task or to tell her to go fly a kite.

Betty was asked by a co-worker to do some extra work to help her associate finish up because the other woman had been late getting back from an extended lunch hour shopping trip. When Betty refused to use her own break for this purpose she was bad-mouthed as being negative and selfish. Way to go, Betty! After her follow-up comments there seems little doubt that the co--worker fully intended to use Betty like a sucker from the start.

Insecurity often leads us to say yes when we ought to say no. We are concerned that others will think less of us because we wouldn't do whatever was asked of us. We may be right about that. Many people will indeed think less of us because while they wouldn't put it in so many words they may want to use us themselves at some later time. Or they don't have the self-confidence to say no either and it would accentuate their lack of resolve and self-possession if we stand up for our rights in situations where others see them meekly capitulate time after time.

Not everyone will think less of us though. Some will respect us for protecting our own interests and some will even draw inspiration and determination to do likewise from our example. Think of the many times you have heard someone praised with words to the effect that, "She knows where to draw the line so she has the time, energy, and resources to accomplish her primary duties."

You have no obligation to allow most of the infringements on your privacy but if you do allow them you have no one to blame but yourself. You don't have to answer your doorbell when you can see it is a salesman or a nosy neighbor. You don't have to answer any questions, or all of the questions, that a pollster asks on the telephone or on the street corner. You don't have to answer any questions that a TV reporter wants to ask in order to have filler for the six o clock news. These are all cases where you decide whether you are going to allow these people to intrude on you. Take this simple fact and mark it in large letters across the back of your mind: *I don't have to answer any questions except those from proper authorities functioning in their official capacities.*

Typical is the person who asks some personal question about matters she has no proper right and need to know about and when you decline to answer she acts insulted and hurt. Then she starts in with, "What's the matter with you? What are you afraid of? Do you think you're somebody special? What kind of a weirdo are you? Everybody asks and answers questions like that." You may be tempted to snap back that she should reveal the same kind of personal information about herself if this is such a standard topic of conversation but in doing so you will have lowered yourself to her level and significantly diminished any right you had to be upset or insulted by her rudeness. Tit for tat always runs that risk. Laugh her off or walk away.

There is a school of thought that maintains that your outlook must always be positive, which is interpreted as meaning that you should always proceed as if everything were fine and not waste energy on complaining about what is rotten.

One place where this position tends to be strongly held today is in environmental policy. If you claim that there are serious problems and we ought to be reevaluating our technologies and ways of doing things, and therefore questioning the status quo, you are a doomsayer. The argument goes that if you are a *positive* thinker, you keep repeating that this is the greatest nation in the world and technology and the free enterprise system (in the form that we have it, not the real thing) has made it that way so unrestricted use of both is the best thing for all concerned. These positions are, of course, slightly overdrawn here to make my point. Not too many people are quite this neatly *pro* or *con* but in my experience there are more than enough to make it a viable point of discussion.

To some people being skeptical and suspicious about claims and promises is negative. They maintain that we should always aim to be trusting and accepting - and therefore positive. My reaction is that blind trust is the stuff of sheep being led to slaughter. Like most things this topic is a matter of degree and situation. In a one-to-one personal relationship a large amount of trust and acceptance may be appropriate; in a politician-to-electorate or business-to-consumer relationship it is often an open invitation to abuse.

Pollyanna types never want to accept the fact but there are some unscrupulous, sadistic, and truly evil people among us. These see-no-evil people always feel compelled to argue that the person's childhood traumas, family background, or socio-economic condition make it difficult for her to act properly so they will expose themselves, and the rest of us, to the same damage from those unrepentant crooks again and again and expect us to go along with that yet again.

Taking the negative view doesn't mean you are rejecting all the good things or the idealism of the Nation, it means you aren't content with it in its present imperfect state. You want to make it better. Until you recognize and pinpoint the defects in a system you can't correct them and may not even realize that the system can be improved and is correctly viewed by those less smitten as defective in various ways. If you never inspected your house you wouldn't know there are cracks in the walls and termites in the timbers until the place literally comes falling down around you. Does that make you a better person than someone who wants to improve things?

Some will maintain that criticism of any part is condemnation of the whole effort. Mature, independent thinkers don't fall for this kind of argument even when the news anchor repeats it. The smart people know from personal experience that it is possible - and desirable - to pull any complex situation apart and evaluate it item-by-item. The fact that you find the soup too salty but the rest of the meal just fine isn't a rejection of the cook's whole effort. Similarly you may reject or give a poor evaluation to some elements of any system while still feeling that the system overall is workable or the best that is currently available. Those who can't divide their criticisms can only accept or reject; those that can give reactions to individual elements can improve the system without destroying it.

Some are trained to think that skepticism and suspicion of claims made without verification are negative and bad because it means you don't trust others. I don't know who proclaimed naiveté to be the cultural goal, but I recognize that this attitude of constant trust is an open invitation to disaster.

Checking claims and being less than overwhelmed by promises that can hardly be verified (and then only too late to make any real difference) is a sign of maturity. It is an indication that we have gotten beyond child-like acceptance of whatever authority figures tell us, usually because we have recognized enough times when the assurances and claims were deliberately used to lull us so we could be taken advantage of in some way. Note that child-like behavior becomes childish behavior once we have to start to accept responsibility for ourselves.

Certainly skepticism and suspicion, like anything else including trust and non-critical acceptance, can be carried to extremes and become impediments to social and professional communication and interactions, but the extremes are not the norm. In a world full of people with vested interests ever ready to use and abuse others for their own short-term gains it smacks of walking into a pride of hungry lions freshly anointed with steak sauce not to carefully consider everything that is happening around you that might affect you and yours.

We want to aim for and actively seek a happy medium between believing nothing at all and believing everything and anything that anyone says. The tools of the process are the critical skills - verification of facts; realistic assessment of potentials; imposition of accountability and obligation on claimants; assumption of unspoken qualifications, etc. It takes mature intelligence to get beyond the starkly black-and-white stage of thinking into the real world of many shades of gray. Because you don't give unconditional approval to some policy doesn't mean you are totally opposed to everything involved in the whole system, but being skeptical is always sensible as long as you don't take it to the extreme.

Skepticism about promises falls into two categories. First, does this person actually intend to do what she is saying? Second, is this person capable of actually doing what she promises?

Do not take any claims of authority on verbal face value. When the person at your door says she represents the county and is checking all houses to see if they meet specifications (and if not she'll give you a good price on fixing it up for you) insist that she leave immediately if she doesn't have credentials from the county in her possession. And check on them. Have her wait outside while you go and call the county offices. Look up the phone number yourself, don't just call the number she may give you - which may only connect you to her accomplice. If she comes when the county offices are closed, order her off until a day when she can be verified. It's also a good idea to call the police immediately to report that this supposed county employee is making threats if she does so and perhaps to have them check her claims about who she works for even if she doesn't make threats. But don't expect the police to do anything about this now unless there is a continuing threat to you. The call is to make sure there is an official record of your complaint and possibly to alert the authorities to an on-going scam in the community.

Critical thinking is related to a healthy sense of skepticism. How many problems we would spare ourselves if we would believe what we actually see (although we need to be more skeptical about that than ever before in this day of digital image manipulation) and not what we want to see (which is all in our minds).

You're wrong! Most of us take some secret satisfaction from saying it but we all hate to hear it so let's consider some related topics. When may you say, "You're wrong"? When should you say it? When should you accept it?

Despite the experiences almost all of us have had of different people, both those in superior positions (parents, teachers, and bosses) and our peers, telling us we were wrong about various matters it is one of the things we most hate to hear and even more to admit. Part of it is the initial confusion of possibilities. Do they mean you are incorrect in your claims or your calculations or your citations? Or that you did or said something generally considered unacceptable and bad. Or that you are simply on the side of this issue that the other person disapproves of. Each situation has its burdens but some might be harder for this person to take than the other accusations.

We may get some hint about the weight the other person places on the matter from the way the words are delivered. "You're wrong" can be said with glee, suggesting the other has caught you in a mistake and expects to embarrass you. If said in anger the person probably thinks he or those he cares about - or maybe justice and fairness - have been damaged by what he is accusing you of. It can be said in a correcting way, which hints that the aim is to help you, not to humiliate you. Or it might be given in a cautionary way as a helpful warning, which suggests that you still have an opportunity to prevent the worst damage.

Why do we enjoy saying it? Because it puts us on the side of those knowing what is good, better, and best at the same time that it lets us bring the other person down a notch and shows that he's not perfect. Why do we hate to hear it? For the reverse reasons. Because we don't like to be less than perfect and therefore incorrect, especially not in the view of others. Also it lets others gloat at our mistake and therefore we lose face. Plus the other person might be wrong and we must now attempt to prove that which can be a special challenge on the spur of the moment.

Censure isn't the same as censorship although they are related. You may, perhaps you even must, point out what you believe are any unacceptable acts or proposals by others. You may also attempt to focus public pressure on those involved if the matter calls for that. You are not attempting to censor them as long as you or those you attempt to recruit to your position don't try to use the force of law to block the acts. Of course if the acts are those that the law regulates, then censorship is sort of unavoidable but that is probably as it should be.

Using the pressure of the marketplace isn't censorship, it is the appropriate tool of the community to express its collective response. It is a self-regulating method as long as those who want to support one side of the issue can direct their support or money elsewhere, while those who want to support the other side are free to continue to do business with these people.

Must telling someone that he is wrong always be a constructive criticism? No, because that requires the recipient to be open to it. If the matter is important - especially for the welfare of yourself or others - I think it needs to be said in whatever context is appropriate whether private or public. For the best effect on someone who may at least be willing to improve, there is little reason to doubt that private correction is usually best though.

In very public cases of abuse you need to give a public criticism to make the others present aware of what is being done even if this will make it harder for the miscreant to change (which is a substantial doubt anyway). Too many times keeping bad stuff covered up in the hope that the perpetrator will reform leads to more and therefore preventable bad stuff happening. A judgment is called for in deciding how to proceed, but erring in favor of the majority who will be harmed if they aren't warned seems to me like an appropriate rule of thumb.

Telling someone he is wrong in his specific statement or action does not require that you add any other comments giving your opinion regarding the person's intelligence, social status, or ethnic background. Adding such stuff is a sure indication that your correction was not intended to be constructive.

Be realistic when you ask questions, especially hostile ones, in a public forum. Don't expect to get good answers. Be content to publicly and explicitly note aloud that you didn't get an adequate answer. The makers of products aren't going to tell you about the risks from their wares except as required by law and then only expect that information with a lot of fuzz and equivocations. They have probably studied those risks closely and discussed them in detail with their clever lawyers before deciding whether they would open themselves to too much liability by even selling the products but they never intend to share those discussions with the world at large. It's not good business to scare people away from your products as long as you can convince yourself that what you make or sell does more good than harm and that the risks are only to a few and not all that great. Focus on the fact that that is part of the reason we have those regulations that some keep insisting are ruining their chance to get rich so that this idea will keep popping into your consciousness waving a red flag. Politicians aren't going to spell out the details of how they will fulfill their campaign promises because those will depend on future circumstances and are also, to some degree at least, hype to get your vote, not firm commitments to do what no one can guarantee can actually be done, although many of them will routinely and regularly claim to. You may notice that that won't stop them from deriding their opponents for not making the same kind of empty and windy generalized promises though.

If you are convinced that you never make mistakes, you must live in a very small world. You can always test your breadth and depth of specific information from thermodynamics to trivia in various textbooks and self-quiz books if you chose to prove your claims to yourself. If you are convinced that your positions on all matters of opinion are the only correct ones and are not open to challenge you have likely noticed that few people are willing to talk to you and then only about the most innocuous subjects.

If it is correct that you are wrong in a criticism you have given or other statements you have made, and if you want to be the best you can be, being told you are wrong may be helpful and useful information even though you probably won't eagerly seek it out. The unavoidable fact is that you can't correct your performance until you know that you are wrong (whichever sense of the term applies). Since being wrong means you are not getting the approval and acceptance that one needs to succeed in some areas, and maybe even just to survive in society, this is a dead-end situation. That leads to the logical but uncomfortable conclusion that if you truly are unwilling to be told that you are wrong, you accept the fact that you have little chance of success as more than a cipher in society.

You should also recognize that by taking the stance of rejecting any claims that you are wrong you remove yourself from the rolls of the correctible people and close off major avenues of learning and thus improving yourself. It is a common although not universal phenomenon that as an individual matures and then ages his support for various political and social policies changes. On average, people are more liberal when they are young and become hard-bitten and often narrow-minded conservatives by retirement age. Part of this is that our priorities change along with our life situation; part is that as we witness more of the consequences of particular policies and learn about more options and alternatives and that new information affects our decisions. We also tend to be less willing to hope that this time a large segment of the population will act in more sensible and selfless ways than they have repeated in the past. If you're not willing to see the possibility of shifting your own thinking, you block yourself from possibly improving your position or coming to support policies that seem to better reflect your current thoughts. Failure to make adjustments leaves you vulnerable. Maturity is about recognizing the appropriateness of and the need for change and then shifting your stance based on an intelligent analysis of what will best serve what are now your goals and priorities.

If it is true that you are wrong and you know that is true, you can't gain anything substantial by denying it. At least not if someone is intent on making the point against you publicly. In these cases what are your response options? First, and most defensive, you can get angry and vicious and attack whoever dared to note your error.

Or you can downplay the significance of the matter. This is a standard defensive maneuver. "You're gonna make a federal case out of that? Don't waste my time on the little stuff." And all too often the additional wish that, "Therefore you should forget about those many times in the past when I did or called for exactly what I'm telling you not to do now."

Or you can argue for reduced or shared responsibility due to the circumstances. "Yeah, I did it but as the part of the team taking orders, not the part giving them." "Everybody was doing it" is a classic defense, but seldom effective.

Gracefully accepting correction when it is warranted speaks well of you. It also reflects the attitude that you are correctable, that you can recognize when you made a misstep and bring yourself back onto the right path. Those who will never admit they were wrong are forced to keep walking in the rough because to step back over onto the path is to acknowledge that they stepped off it. They operate as if they don't think anyone else will realize how dumb they are being, but that is seldom the case.

The non-defensive and most useful response is to acknowledge the error as soon as possible when there is enough evidence to convince you that you did err and in the process indicate that you hope to learn from it. Remind yourself that mistakes of this type can happen and set a good example by correcting yourself. Also apologize, if possible as publicly as you made the criticism, because that is part of the openness that supports good critical functioning.

In matters of facts, you have to discover that you have them wrong before you can correct yourself, so it is helpful to have that pointed out even if it is done in an unnecessarily embarrassing way (which may be both deliberately and spitefully chosen as the mode of presentation of this information). Still, be sure to promptly thank the person for helping you out in this manner. Perhaps even express the hope that you haven't misled anyone else by your erroneous statements.

Best of all, laugh at your mistake and at the embarrassment it is causing you. Most of the audience will like you for taking the correction well and will be forced to recognize the smallness of the accuser if he has overdone the role of protector of the truth. It takes self-control, but it turns a potential debacle into a minor event. A solid sense of your own worth makes allowance both for having incorrect information and ideas based on such, and for publicly airing that stuff so that you can be seen as wrong. To err is human, so welcome to the species.

When you find yourself in the wrong you should analyze the case to try to understand why you made the error. If there is bad information out there, say so to alert the person you misjudged and any audience. If someone influenced your conclusion by words or actions, point that out to those wronged to alert them. Ask yourself if you believe that someone deliberately spread incorrect or false info and if so identify them. At least avoid their inputs in the future yourself. Depending on the specific circumstances, maybe even spread the word that they are unreliable or worse. But don't do any of these things just to excuse yourself.

Also review whether you spread the wrong information and ask yourself the following or similar questions to decide what else, if anything, you should do to correct or offset the harm you may have done in addition to spreading the correction with as much diligence and to the same sources as your original but incorrect message.

A) Is this about something that is now history or is it something that might occur again? What is done is done and probably can't be undone, although some of the consequences of it might be subject to alteration. Don't waste much time on what you can't change.

B) Is this wrong in a factual or in a moral sense? Errors of fact can be corrected by study, but errors of morality may require rethinking of your motives and values. Facts may be considered largely fixed and verifiable, but morality is a personal thing with many sincere people disagreeing about the particulars so what is morally offensive to some may not be to others and any person might change his view of these matters after full reconsideration.

C) Did someone else get hurt because of the error? What you do that harms only you may still be unacceptable, but at least the damage is contained. Your responsibility increases when others, especially innocent people, are adversely affected by your decisions and actions. The follow-up questions are whether the damage can be corrected or compensated for, and if so how?

D) Did the error become enmeshed in on-going activities so that it will continue to cause trouble until corrected? In the most obvious case, an error in a computer program will cause the same glitch in the data every time it runs. But a written company policy that bans the use of certain brands of supplies because they have been shown to be defective, but misidentifies the brand names, will also keep repeating the mistake until corrected.

A second stage of self-examination would then attempt to understand what exactly you did that was wrong. Was it the action itself or the intention that was at fault? If you misunderstood or misinterpreted something, what was it and why did you go wrong? Is there a pattern that might reoccur and is the warp in the information you used to reach your decision, or in you and the way you weighed the information and other factors to make your decision?

If you made an honest mistake there is no reason to hesitate about taking action in the same arenas again. At times we all get our information confused, or attempt to operate on too little information, or just follow the wrong impulses and premonitions. If the error indicates a significant lack of information or understanding you are put on notice of the need to seek instruction or clarification. Sometimes you miss the mark because you read too much into the question or situation. Give yourself credit for knowing enough to know too much about the subject, while you look for the verbal or other signals that indicate the limits being set by a question or a questioner.

When you hear the dreaded words "You're wrong" you should run through a mental checklist. First, is the comment really directed at you? If so, are you being targeted personally or as a representative or simply a member of some group?

Second, do you understand the specifics of what is being referred to? You can't profit from any correction unless you know what it refers to so that you can decide whether you agree. Only when you accept that you need to change something can you decide how to change it and whether to do so now that the price of doing so is clearer and can be better weighed against the cost of not changing.

Third, is this an honest correction or mainly an attack? The most normal response is to accept the former (whether or not you ultimately decide you should change) and to reject the latter and I see no argument against that.

Fourth, could this person be correct? Could it be that either your information is faulty or that you misstated it? Finding out that you are operating from defective information is embarrassing but essential so you can get back on course.

And fifth, what are the consequences of you being found wrong by this person and in this social situation?

The vulnerability of our self-image, a personal variable, will often determine our reactions. Three considerations feed into that.

First is the identity of the critic and the manner in which he tells us we are wrong. How much we respect this person's opinions or how much he can affect our image in the public eye is important. We instantly ask ourselves whether he delivered the message to help or hurt us.

Second, who and how many other people were also told about our error? Our attitude and vulnerability to these people and their opinion of us can be a major factor. This may tie into our underlying belief in the necessity of being approved of by specific individuals or groups.

The third consideration is our immediate perception (that could be modified when we have an opportunity to think it through) of the correctness of the points charged against us, the appropriateness of the way we were informed, and the consequences of the fact that we are wrong (i.e., of the erroneous act itself) and of that fact becoming known. We may modify this initial perception when we have an opportunity to think it through with the pressure off.

The sting from being told you are wrong is ultimately self-generated and therefore you can moderate it when you resolve to do so. Why is it that one person can be publicly pointed out as being incorrect and he hardly lets it ruffle him, while another man in exactly the same situation and using the same words feels humiliated and devastated? It is obviously not the matter on which they were in error, who pointed it out, or the words used in doing so (although those are all factors of substance that could make a difference), it is the person receiving the criticism that decides its emotional impact on himself and reacts accordingly.

The social impact may be beyond his control - and recognizing that is part of the process he is undergoing - but he and only he decides how he will respond. There are likely to be physiological reactions to the social and psychological impact of what may seem like an attack and he will experience those, but they don't produce an automatic decision or response beyond the possible blush and rapid heartbeat. The person still decides whether to feel devastated or to accept his imperfection and get on with other things.

What are the most useful reactions to being informed that we are wrong? We agree to consider whether the claim is accurate and agree to do what we can to correct any correctable consequences. We thank the critic for pointing it out, recognizing that it may have involved risk on his part to do so. If it is immediately obvious that the critic is misguided or misinformed (i.e., he has confused you with someone else and you didn't do what you are accused of) you can point that out. This is worth doing but we all know that there is a tendency to promptly deny even what you are fully guilty of doing, so don't expect everyone to believe you simply because you say it's not so.

We are often able to fall back on the possibility that our accuser (for so they always seem to us to be in this context) is in fact the one who is incorrect and we are off the hook. Sometimes that is the case. If we are said to be wrong about some agreed upon fact - say the dates of some eighteenth century battle in Europe - a trip to the reference books should settle the question. Things are stickier when the matter is one that involves a judgment or opinion since what you are ready to agree is correct may depend on which of two or more different opinions or theories you choose to accept. For example, which side in that battle was more to blame for it happening? Even in situations where there isn't complete agreement, there is often a consensus of knowledgeable or educated opinions. You can soothe your ego and bolster your reputation, if you think that necessary, by making it known to whatever audience is involved that there is lack of agreement among the experts and perhaps point out whether your position is more widely accepted than your opponent's. This is most often required when an audience unfamiliar with the details of the topic has been told that you are wrong on a matter of importance. If the conversation is only between you and your critic, or if the audience are people in the know, it is recognized without anyone emphasizing it that this is a difference of opinion, not a verifiable error.

It is also possible that the accuser is using a slanted definition or selected data to make the claim which will not stand up to close scrutiny but which gives the momentary appearance of substance that is needed for him to wound your credibility or reputation in the eyes of this audience. Those people probably won't remember any of the details an hour from now so presenting a refutation later has only a minimal effect since by then they have formed an opinion about you that will guide them in describing you or deciding whether to vote for or otherwise deal with you. To keep the audience in a state of doubt and confusion about the matter and the claimants so they won't easily come to a conclusion too soon it is important to challenge his claims and data on the spot.

Many witnesses will be left with no unspoken negative attitudes toward you if the accusations are promptly disputed, but will give the benefit of the doubt to the accuser if you say nothing or simply protest that he is smearing you without going right to the specifics. If you can instantly point out the actual slant or the unrepresentative data, that's wonderful. But at least put your own accusations into play. All the better if you can do so in a scoffing manner that paints his claims as silly or stupid (and hints but doesn't outright say that that extends to any who believe him or his claims).

What are you generally better off not doing the moment you are accused of being wrong? Denouncing the critic is especially bad when you are inclined to heap on comments about his parentage, intelligence, ethnic or other connections, and vile comparisons with lower life forms. These are tempting but they don't answer the question of whether the claim is true. They do though say more about you than his questioning of you did and that will only help form an impression and opinion about you and the topic among the less perceptive and less honest portion of the population.

Also don't raise undisciplined questions about the facts of the claim and those on which it is based. Lawyers get paid to do the nit picking and equivocating. Consider the popular opinion of them before you put yourself in their company.

It probably won't help if you storm away - except to avoid a physical confrontation that won't help and may seriously complicate things.

What can you do to most effectively make the point to someone else that he is wrong? First, when it's not a matter of great importance, do it privately if the claim was delivered in private or if his position is an error of fact and any other audience can see that or can check on the facts and discover that. Even then, preface your point by a remark that reflects your recognition that you might be or be seen as being incorrect. However, be sure to mention whatever evidence made you aware of the error or supports your claim. Be as explicit and detailed as possible about the items in question. If the matter must be brought up publicly, then emphasize that your focus is on those specifics and not a general attack on this person's intelligence or credibility. Unless he's running for the same political office as you, of course. In that case being polite or sensible will be used against you as a sign that you're soft. How low we sink in the political arena.

When feasible, make the point and move on rather than try to force a confrontation or an admission of guilt. If the situation can be corrected but the solution may not be obvious, point out what might work as a constructive contribution to the process. Don't however make a case for the obvious unless the situation requires you to, since that is rubbing the other person's nose in the stupidity of the thing and, despite how satisfying that might be in the short-term, what doing so tells everyone else about your shallowness is likely to hurt you more than him in the longer-term.

Words of apology can be powerful utterances. They may forestall a fight, heal a break-up, destroy a career - or make one. Statements with that much impact must be used carefully. The power, of course, comes from the overtones and attitudes we associate with them. It is what they imply happened, not their explicit meaning, that gives them impact.

Depending on your attitudes, offering an apology is either one of the hardest or one of the easiest things to do. Some people seem to be constantly apologizing for any and every little thing; for others an apology is an admission of error or wrongdoing that they will offer only under great duress or when they are fully convinced that they made a significant misstep, not just made someone who is overly sensitive feel better. These different reactions are rooted in personality factors, social conditioning factors, and in the different meanings the individuals associate with the social signal called an apology.

To the ancient Greeks an *apologia* meant a formally stated defense or justification of some policy or position but the primary meaning of our word apology today is *expressing regret for an offense or wrongdoing.*

An apology is more than a comment on the weather or a casual nod to a neighbor or a confirmation of a meeting appointment, it is an interpersonal signal, an important social interaction. As such its meaning depends on the context and on the intentions of those involved. No two apologies are the same because each is a different social interaction with consequences for the future dealings (or non-dealings) between these individuals - and possibly the large groups whom they might represent.

Part of our social education is learning that signals like apologies don't have automatic effects or universal meaning. Apologies are peculiar things. Sometimes they will ease our anger; at other times they will increase it. Sometimes we expect an apology and will be hurt or angry if we don't get receive it; at other times we wouldn't accept one if it were offered most sincerely. For some individuals though, offering an apology will be the final admission of defeat on some point.

There are a few fairly formalized expressions that, depending on context, will be understood as a valid apology although this is not the only way to convey the social signal. Generally the expression is only considered to be a valid apology if it is expressed verbally, even if only muttered or the word inaudibly mouthed. A wave of your hand in acknowledgement of your culpability is not usually sufficient, although a public bow of humiliation might be. Depending on circumstances, the words of apology can be whispered as a minimum and very unpublic concession, blubbered abjectly, spoken in firm, sincere and personal terms, or shouted in frustration so that all within earshot will know it is said but only meant most begrudgingly and therefore not very sincerely.

Interpersonal friction may occur at any of several levels and the importance and the method of offering an apology shifts accordingly. We can recognize several levels of apologies that have increasing greater impact and consequences for all involved.

Social lubrication apologies are the ones that require the least thought and are most freely offered because they have the least consequences. The simplest and least complicated situation is an inadvertent literal run-in with someone, whether stranger or acquaintance. The bus lurches to an emergency stop and you are thrown against this person; in wending your way through a crowd you misgauge her intention and zig when she zags and the two of you collide, you brush her with your packages, or step on her foot. There was no real physical damage done and anyone rational understands there was no malice or premeditation involved. A quick and sincere "Excuse me" or "So sorry" is as much as normal people expect or want by way of apology in such a case. This is the only level at which an apologetic gesture alone is sometimes sufficient since you don't know the other person and introductions are not expected. Only if you are obviously negligent about watching what you are doing is this, or should it be considered, a problematic occurrence. Even so the failure to mumble an obligatory apology or to make a properly apologetic gesture without breaking stride if, as is often the case, you were bustling along and this event doesn't call for bringing everything to a standstill might be perceived as rude or at least a lack of good upbringing. In somewhat public-touch-resistant cultures like ours it's expected behavior. Not to say the words (or at least mouth them) is an attack not against the individual but on the social conventions and that failure may be viewed negatively by many of those who see it not happen.

There are always people with their own problems who will want to make a public shouting match out of such accidents which they will proclaim as deliberate and premeditated upon themselves. I recommend that you walk away from them without comment. You cannot explain or defend yourself in any satisfactory way to such a person because you are only an excuse for her to go on this way hoping to get public attention which equates to her as satisfaction. You make your simple statement of apology and move along. Don't play her game. There is no benefit in it for you or for the general public.

Another area where a social lubrication apology may be helpful is when the words function as a peace offering intended to reopen the channels of communication when another's reactions suggest that she feels you did something wrong but you don't know what. Such words may be a sincere attempt to soothe anger or hurt feelings and make amends when what you said or did gave offense, whether that was your intention or not. But they can also be a smug sop to the hurt ego of someone you judge to be enough of a fool to take the words at face value despite all of the sarcasm in your delivery.

Private personal apologies are the next level and a somewhat more consequential one since these may be of great importance to your relationship with this person, and even a whole social circle. They don't usually have a wider impact than the circle of those who know you personally and fairly well though. They require a more elaborate apology. A social lubrication "excuse me" may be muttered without conviction and in a distracted manner and still touch the social base, but the same tone used in a one-on-one "you done me wrong" situation will likely stimulate rather than stop negative reactions. In the personal apology the other person's ego, reputation, and social standing are all on the line and failure to make what is perceived as a proper apology may release angry, hurt, or vengeful reactions that can easily expand the scope of this negative interaction to all levels of your relationship with her and beyond. In these cases a degree of informality may be accepted but words that reflect that you and the other are more than strangers passing on the street are called for. Calling the other person by name is common, and the name used may be a friendly and informal first name basis one. This is the level of interaction where comments about your own klutziness or some brief explanation for your misunderstanding or distraction if those contributed to the situation might be appropriate as long as you are not trying to blame others or simply brush off and explain away or duck your responsibility for what happened. The apology may need to be more abject, even a bit groveling, depending on the particulars of what you did or didn't do and the consequences to you of your relationship with this person.

An example of this level would be when you interpreted what this person said to mean there was no need for you to do anything about a matter, so you didn't. She, though, feels that she clearly asked you to do particular things and is upset that you didn't do those. Or you told a waiting group that she called and said she wouldn't make the rendezvous so they left on an excursion without her - but you were confused and it was someone else who sent that message through you.

Or she feels that a story you told to a group to much appreciative laughter didn't name her as the butt of the joke but anyone who knows some of her embarrassing past moments, (although there aren't supposed to be any others who do) might recognize similarities between your story and what she stumbled through and therefore she concludes that you were actually trying to bring that all to public attention. Depending on how far she has to stretch the story elements to find a comparison to events from her life, you might or might not succeed in convincing her that you didn't intend what she is suggesting. The best path may be to apologize and, to be on the safe side, post a mental note inside your head to never again tell that or any similar story to any group that know her.

Public apologies are of at least potential greater impact although the consequences of making or not making the move may be of limited reach. These are the cases where there is some official element or you erred in the carrying out of some duty or responsibility beyond those of a circle of acquaintances. In these cases a public acknowledgement of the mistake is important along with prompt efforts to repair the damage, if that is possible. These situations are *stop and stand still to show they are important matters*, not things acceptable dealt with on the run. They need to be dealt with audibly, publicly, and in their specifics to detoxify them.

For instance, an agency of a local municipality messes up and must correct the mess it made. The local tax assessor hit the wrong keys on her computer and sent bills for three times as much as they should have been to the residents. A notice of the correct amounts is essential. An added note of apology is expected. But there are no aspects of the matter than will make it of more than local effect within that municipality as long as it seems clear to all that it was a simple clerical error and steps to correct it were started as soon as it was noticed.

Another example of the same level of apology would be if a state's governor got confused and rattled off the name of the wrong group as the ones being investigated or charged while answering a question in a news conference. As soon as this mistake is brought to her attention (since she probably doesn't realize at the time that she said that name rather than the correct group name) she apologizes and corrects the record so only those determined to make a fuss about her original statement and ignoring the follow-up have anything to get excited about. This may be a much ado about nothing in that state but is unlikely to be a topic on the news beyond that state's borders or beyond that day's news cycle.

Formal apologies are the most consequential level. These are seldom personal ones, they are usually gestures made officially in the name of a government or some other large body of people. One government formally apologizing to another is a major event. The head of a family apologizing for the deeds of herself or some other member(s) of her family to other families is also generally a matter of consequence. These are the cases where careful consideration needs to be given to whether an apology will be offered and exactly how and when. The wording is most carefully chosen to avoid legal and long-term problems and often these presentations have a ceremonial aspect to it. Diplomacy is in part the refined art of apologizing, usually without quite saying you were wrong.

A formal apology may be a requirement of a treaty to end a war or for a nation to be admitted to membership in some international organization. An apology for the past policies against specific other groups by a major church made by a local pastor speaking on his own authority, not as a designated spokesperson or representative for the leadership or the majority of the congregants, is not inappropriate but it is inconsequential as long as there are a hierarchy of church officials keeping mum. That same apology offered by the recognized head of that church has the significance called for to express to the whole world the recognition that things done in the past are at this point acknowledged and admitted to be unacceptable now and in the future. At this level an apology is a group or corporate gesture. The decision to offer it and the exact wording is approved by the group's top leaders and announced as an action of the entire group as a group.

Like any other corporate decision there may be many members of the group who oppose making the move at all or object to the precise wording, but the group's internal authority structure gives those top people the say. This recognizes that in any group of more than a handful of individuals allowed to think for themselves and express their opinions, there will seldom if ever be complete agreement on any specifics and therefore an authority or power structure is agreed to so that things can get done.

Why might you offer an apology? When you recognize the potential social power of making the gesture you might decide to use one in a variety of cases in which you judge that the potential benefits outweigh the social and personal psychological costs. If you decide to offer or accept an apology it makes the most sense to so in the way that you are okay with that has the likelihood of producing the most beneficial effects for all those concerned.

You might, for instance, offer a sincere apology to defuse a fight that won't profit you in the long or short term even if you win the battle. Maybe in your opinion this other person is making a big fuss about some point of minor consequence or is misinterpreting what you said or did, but the friendly atmosphere of this dinner party or other social situation will be unnecessarily disrupted for you and the other guests if you engage in an argument with her. Your role as controller of your social world may take precedence over making some minor points with this person who probably is not of major consequence to you and your social circle anyway, so you may shut her up by offering a blanket apology for whatever she thinks you intended as offensive. The witnesses to such an encounter will have little doubt about what you are doing and will usually appreciate your efforts to keep the whole event from turning into some kind of a shouting match about something of no importance to anyone except this individual with a chip on her shoulder.

Often a vague apology is offered to clear the air of any feelings that I hurt you even though I know that I did nothing deliberately to do so and see no basis for such a feeling on your part. We quickly identify those in our social circle with whom virtually any discussion of personal interactions is likely to turn into a litany of imagined rejections and hypersensitive examination of every word and action for subtle negative messages. Interestingly, these same people may be fine social companions as long as you can avoid these topics. Eventually you recognize that with such a person it is counterproductive to try to explain that the obvious meaning of your statements was what you intended, not some obscure reading between the lines, and that you actually did have an dental emergency and were under the drill and not just trying to use that as an excuse not to meet her for lunch. The only workable thing to do (other than to drop her from your social circle, an alternative to be seriously considered) is to throw a blanket apology over the topic and immediately move onto something else.

Often an apology is offered when in that specific social situation not to do so might seem rude when that is not my intention. If, for instance, I discover only as it unfolds that the "surprise" of the party I was invited to join is a crude practical joke on the guest of honor by the organizer of the event, I will certainly join in the litany of apologies if serious offense is taken even though I was not in any way responsible for what happened either actively or passively. On the other hand if I had made a deliberate effort to prevent the jokester from ruining the occasion but she had slipped something by me anyway, I would probably not feel that an apology from me was appropriate - except perhaps to say that I tried but failed to squelch the action. To do otherwise is to assume responsibility for the actions of others that are beyond my control and doing that makes no sense.

Sometimes an apology is applied as social balm in case you have taken offense at something or have concluded that I am culpable for what offended you (whether I am or not) when it would be awkward or even impossible to explain in detail what actually happened. In this case I know that you are not being overly sensitive but rather that a complex situation has left you in doubt about my involvement and about who is responsible for which events. Especially if legitimate personal or business privileged information is involved, I may not be at liberty to explain everything at this time but I don't want you left feeling that you are being attacked for unknown reasons so I quietly say a few soothing words.

Why might you demand an apology? An apology does not right the wrong done to me but it may help me to deal with the situation. I might, in fact, demand an apology to force you to admit out loud that you have caused me harm. But since a public apology is usually intended as a social signal to others as well as to me, I will weigh the social consequences in deciding whether to demand an apology and how and where it is to be offered.

I might demand at least a private apology from you to counterbalance your demands that I publicly acknowledge some social obligation to you. Or to try to determine your motivations in the act in question. Or to test your sincerity and willingness to be honest about your actions. Or to help me vent my feelings about the harm you did to me.

I might demand a public apology in order to let third parties see that I was wronged and that you are forced to acknowledge your part in that. Or if you normally make a point of requiring one from me or others (and therefore seem to want to use one as a brand of defeat for the apologist).

I might demand a fully public apology if I feel that your act was deliberate or culpably negligent although you would like everyone to believe otherwise.

Why would you or should you accept an apology? You are certainly under no absolute obligation to accept an apology just because it is offered - although social conventions might pressure you to do so. This is sometimes a difficult point in disputes in the public forum because third parties may feel they can gain some political advantage by pressuring the sides to make public statements saying that they have reached agreement even if this ignores important points of disagreement. It takes courage and determination to stand up for what you believe in and are intent on signaling to the world and to not allow the desire of others for a social veneer of agreement to pressure you into consenting to give a false appearance of consent.

I might accept an apology in order to allow the other person to make social amends. We speak about the "social fabric" to suggest a continuous entity formed by the interweaving of many individuals and organizations that makes each a part of a larger whole while preserving each one's distinctive features. Such a unity in diversity requires some constraints on each participant. Each must adhere to certain social conventions and rules intended to keep interactions polite and non-aggressive. Failure to follow these rules rends or shreds the social fabric. A tear needs to be repaired but if there is no mechanism for undoing the damage there is no long-term prospect for a social fabric. An apology is recognized as an effective needle and thread for making such repairs. It is the socially approved and even mandated way to acknowledge a failure to adhere to the rules or conventions and a proper way of closing the wounds produced. It may leave scars, but it stops the hemorrhaging of distrust and the refusal to cooperate. I accept the apology for the good of society.

Binding up social wounds requires cooperation from both sides. If I am the injured party and I refuse the apology, the tear in the social fabric cannot be properly closed. On the other hand, even though I recognize that an apology won't rectify all the damage done, I may well decide that it is better to get life back on a more normal and productive path by accepting the apology and letting the other make the proper social gestures so that the formal requirements are met. I take this action for the sake of the apologist and any others being affected by the rift.

Or I might accept an apology so that I can let go of my anger and resentment without feeling I am inappropriately abandoning my rights and letting you undermine the social expectations that require you to accept responsibility for what you do. Anger is a powerful emotion and some people are good at nursing grudges and keeping their anger alive for long periods, waiting for the opportunity to get revenge. They find satisfaction in being able to thwart the other person weeks or months later and take pride in a reputation for never forgetting a wrong done to them. There is a price to be paid for harboring that anger though. A price in physical well being and psychological distortion. The irony of the anger is that you do more harm to yourself because of the constant physiological stress such a strong emotion generates than you are likely to do to the person you are angry with. Constant mental replaying of the unpleasant happenings also makes it hard to move onto other, more pleasant thoughts and possibly useful plans. By holding too tightly to your anger you may peg yourself to the ground and frustrate your own longer term aspirations and possibilities. That's a big price to be pay for a small satisfaction that may never even be yours.

It's not fair that someone should be able to harm you and then only offer a few words of apology as reparation but the simple fact is that life often isn't fair. If you try to hold out for more fairness you will likely be unhappy all your days. It is not easy for some of us to accept the fact of the lack of fairness but we still have to do so. You can't rationalize your way through it, because unfairness isn't rational. For your own sake you have to simply take a deep breath and move on. It doesn't mean you have forgotten what happened or that you may not gladly grab at a chance to balance the books, but it does allow you to put it out of mind and get on with your life. That is made just a trifle easier if you get at least the minimal satisfaction of an apology to list on your side of the ledger of social happenings.

In this case the apology is for you. It is to vindicate you. You were correct in feeling wronged and that has been acknowledged. Now you have to take yourself in hand and make yourself move on for your own sake. What offering the apology is causing or not causing the other person is irrelevant to this purpose. It is the ritual of letting go because the minimal social signal has been given that is important for you to feel you can move on. You must try as much as possible to ignore the tone if it sounds insincere, and close your eyes to the facial expression that may belie the words the other is speaking. You owe it to yourself to move on and need only think of that. Do it for you.

You might accept the apology to give public testimony that you and the other person are working together again. Sometimes it is third parties who need to be able to get on with things and I can release them from a restraint by giving public notice that a dispute I had with someone is formally ended with a public acceptance of an apology. If these people have been avoiding social or commercial contact with that person out of a sense of loyalty to me or to the principles and positions I represent, I now clearly signal that such distancing is no longer necessary or expected.

Since alliances shift and antagonisms develop in both political and business situations where factions strike deals with one another, it may be important that all who have an interest know the current terrain. Formal social signals help to keep the channels of interaction clear.

You might accept the apology to defuse the feelings of others. Sometimes those associated with us by blood or politics care more about the way others deal with us that we do ourselves. Family or members of an ethnic group may be sensitive to insults we personally pay no attention to. They feel harmed because they consider themselves to be part of me and they see me as having been wronged. In this case the most effective way to quell the hot tempers of these third parties may be for me to clearly signal my acceptance of the offered apology even though I personally don't consider it necessary or don't care enough about this person to have taken any insult from her actions. In this type of situation the group calm is probably a higher good than a precisely stated personal position and would prompt more ready acceptance of a properly offered apology.

Are there situations where I might appropriately decline to offer an apology? Of course. For example, if I take myself seriously then I must accept responsibility for my actions and that includes my words. If I want others to take me seriously I must take pains to make my words and actions reflect my thoughts and strongly held ideas. I can't expect anyone to conclude that I am a person of substance if I won't take a firm stance about what I find acceptable and unacceptable in the face of opposition.

Therefore I may decline to offer an apology if I don't believe I did anything that can properly be considered insulting, harmful, or wrong. That means that if I believe that words of apology have sincere meaning I must use them only when I am sincere in expressing that meaning (recognizing that context will often make it obvious when I am speaking in a teasing, ironic, or joking way and do not intend that my words be given serious weight). I recognize that some people are ready to claim injury at any juncture because they feel that forcing an apology from someone else somehow makes them more powerful and respected. I also recognize that there are some who are supersensitive in their perception of slights or insults. I see no reason to accommodate such people in their self deception and I point out that going along with them only encourages them to become even pushier and more obnoxious, it doesn't solve the problem of them doing that.

In the same vein if I don't see an apology from me offering any remedy for a problem, I may decide not to offer one. Empty words indicate that I don't think that words have meaning and that therefore nothing I say is to be given credence or taken seriously.

In the same way, if I am not sorry that I said or did something, and especially if given the same circumstances I would say or do it again, it would be hypocritical for me to offer an apology for the sake of avoiding the consequences of my actions. Disharmony or controversy make social and business gatherings uncomfortable, but if I have strongly held beliefs that differ from or even contradict those of others - and these views are a significant factor or focus in the gathering - then I owe it to myself and everyone else to stand my ground and maintain my independence of mind.

There will often be considerable pressure to make a conciliatory gesture by offering an apology and getting out of the way so the steamroller of the other people's ideas can flatten everything into uniformity and conformity, but I owe it to all to refuse. If this idea, this group, or this particular gathering is so flimsy that a bit of opposition is going to unsettle it, then it has no substance to start with. If those who organized the event only wanted backside-kissers they should have kept it small and private enough that I wouldn't find myself there and only then be learning what it is really about. If this more open event was arranged precisely to give an impression of widespread public agreement or support, this will be an important learning experience for the organizers and all the observers they drew there. Not to stand my ground means that I am agreeing to being used by them to help disperse a lie, and no matter how I try to cover it over with empty words, that is how it will be widely perceived. That simplifies the situation for me since if I don't distance myself from the setup the consequences of not letting myself be used are then as obvious as the ones of allowing myself to be used. Taking the stand for my integrity is then easier to stick with even if not pleasant.

Even when I might have readily offered a sincere apology under more honest circumstances I might vigorously and vocally decline to do so in a trumped up situation or where the other has exaggerated the actual events to make a big fuss. If I capitulate and apologize there is no way I can effectively establish my point that the account of the event is being distorted. By keeping the topic open and attempting to get more people involved in the recitation of events, I increase the likelihood that the distortions will become obvious to more of the audience (since such cases are virtually never going to develop unless there are third parties, many of whom were not eyewitnesses to the alleged objectionable action, around to be influenced by the claims).

The other side of the coin is that I might decline to accept an apology for any of several general reasons. The most obvious would be if I don't believe the person offering the apology is sincere in doing so. I don't have to concern myself about identifying her agenda or who or what is pressuring her to do this, if my perception is that she is insincere I may decide not to go through the social motions. Also if I believe she will do the same offensive thing again when it is of some advantage to her I won't go along with the charade.

Similarly I may decline an apology if I feel that it doesn't settle the matter or release you from other social obligations to undo the harm you have caused when I may be able to force you to complete those steps by standing firm.

There are social consequences to publicly accepting an apology so I may say that I am not accepting the offered one if I don't think you are a basically honest and sincere person and therefore I don't want to be identified to anyone as a person giving you even limited approval.

Since words have meaning and impact, I can't truly forgive you for something that either didn't happen or that did me no harm or caused me no distress. I could accept your apology to make you feel better but when I do that I run the risk of having you conclude that my doing so means that I really was distressed or harmed, otherwise why would I accept your apology? In such a case I can add a comment to that effect while letting you complete the social ritual. I don't always have to outright refuse to accept a sincere gesture.

One of the best things you can do for someone is to pay him a sincere compliment. It doesn't cost much to give, yet it is immensely helpful and valuable to receive since it makes him feel good about himself and that is one of the healthiest states of mind for any of us.

Can you remember the way it made you feel the last time someone complimented or praised you beyond the routine and entirely appropriate and to be encouraged minor key instances? Think back over your life and you can probably remember at least a small number of instances when someone took you aside and said a few words to you that had a great positive impact on you, maybe even influenced how you view yourself right up to this moment. If the number of such instances has been large in your case, you should be even more thankful. The rest of us are jealous of your good fortune.

Now think about the last time you praised someone else. Wasn't it nice to see the pleasure it gave him? In view of the pleasures that both giving and receiving it allows, it is hard to explain why so many of us praise one another so infrequently.

A sincere compliment (Would that this were the only kind!) is an appreciation, a positive feedback or evaluation of this person and/or his performance that is intended to reinforce the individual's vital and proper positive self-image. It is our celebration with him of his success at being an effective person.

Of course there are Compliments and there are compliments. "That's a nice shirt," is typical of the social lubrication and flattery compliments that we sling around rather loosely, the lower case c type. We may or may not mean it, and even if we do we aren't making a big thing of it or committing ourselves to anything by it. We aren't even admitting that we gave this person's appearance more than a superficial glance. Usually we all recognize the latter for what they are even as we graciously respond to them as if they were significant without being fooled for an instant into thinking they were heavier weight than that.

In this discussion I am referring to Compliments with a capital C, the more personal, in-depth kinds of positive reinforcement that we may give and receive. The multiple messages in a compliment like, "That outfit accentuates the dignified look that I always find so attractive in you," is more what I have in mind here. It says first that I'm taking notice of your attire which you obviously spent time and thought selecting. Second, it indicates that I am more impressed by you than by the pieces of cloth. Third, it acknowledges that I have paid attention to your appearance and the impression it creates before. And fourth, it says you have specific qualities that I admire and can specify, like dignity, so you know what your strong points are in my view. The Big C compliments we remember, cherish, and try to live up to. They are the ones that change our lives.

Big C compliments have recognizable characteristics.

(1) They are *sincere*. Many of the complimentary statements that people exchange are transmitted within a context of social convention. We are expected to pay tribute to the graduate or the birthday girl or the wearer of the new clothes. A real compliment is given because we feel genuine admiration for the person being complimented and for the feature mentioned. We want him to grasp the fact of our approval and admiration.

(2) Big C compliments are *significant*. They make an impression because they note and celebrate the speaker's perception of the other's impact on the world. They are about who you are, how that affects what you do, and how you do the things you do. Your momentary appearance alone, your attainment of the conventional milestones like birthdays, and superficial critiques of your performance are the usual stuff of small c polite compliments. "I love your dress." "My, don't you look nice in blue." "That was a wonderful recital." Flattering fluff. Always welcome and to be encouraged as the start of more significant comments, but generally having the impact of a cream pie tossed by a toddler.

(3) Big C compliments are *personal*. Paying compliments is paying attention. It can only be done credibly when you know who the players are, what the actions and the intentions are, and who has done what. Big C praise is focused on the person rather than on the deeds done (even though it doesn't ignore or reject those) so it's always essentially personal. We regularly discuss topics like his physical attractiveness, his manners and the way he deals with other people and the way he comes across to others about others as third person subjects but, largely because of their personal nature, we seldom discuss them with the person himself.

(4) Big C compliments are *gratuitous*. Neither the situation nor my involvement with this person requires that I say this. There is no social expectation that needs to be met. It's not said to trigger some reward, to

win some concession, or to persuade the other to compliment me in return. All of those might motivate others at times so the wording alone isn't the whole point, the intent is the heart of the matter. The direct beneficiary of big C compliments is the person praised. I offer the compliment simply because I want to. Spontaneous praise is thrilling and moving precisely because if truly spontaneous and gratuitous it has to be genuine and heartfelt.

Because of their personal nature, Big C compliments are usually delivered in different contexts than flattery or social lubrication noises.

A) They are generally offered in private. They are very personal observations and the context contributes to the recipient's perception of their sincerity. This also spares the startled or the shy recipient any embarrassment he might feel if placed in the public spotlight to be praised. They can usually be repeated in a public way if the recipient wants that or agrees to it.

Giving sincere compliments, especially to shy persons, requires tact. When any recipient is caught by surprise since he was not expecting anything like this he may be momentarily flustered and that in itself might be more embarrassing for him than it needs to be if it is a very public discombobulation. It is fine to have others know of and possibly agree with and reinforce your view but it may make the recipient of the compliment uncomfortable. For the really important compliments and observations, the important thing is that the direct recipient receives the message. It is less important that others do so. The positive impact will be mainly on this person, although it can't be denied and shouldn't be underestimated that hearing compliments given to others can have a salutary effect on the hearers by prompting them to act in similar ways, both as those giving compliments and as those acting so they deserve and will receive them.

B) They are offered quietly. Some messages are shouted with horns tooting in the background but strongly felt personal messages like these are best delivered in an intimate you-me context.

C) They are offered without expecting a response. Don't feel hurt if you don't get one, especially if you don't get a compliment in return. This doesn't mean the other didn't hear and accept your words, nor does it mean he rejects them or don't care about them. He may simply be overwhelmed and at a loss for appropriate words at the moment.

D) They are offered mainly to give the person receiving the words of praise a better appreciation of his strengths and potentials. They are intended as useful feedback, someone else's perception of him and his accomplishment and promise.

F) They are reinforced regularly but unobtrusively. Once the words have been spoken in an appropriate situation a wink, a touch in passing, or a smile may be sufficient to indicate a reaffirmation of the sentiments for years to come.

F) They are as specific as the situation will allow. Generalizations have their place but in a compliment they suggest that the praiser hasn't taken much time to think about what he is saying and therefore they reduce the value or impact of his words. A real compliment is hand-fitted to the individual rather than a statement that could possibly be applied to half the people within a radius of a country mile.

Superficial compliments are typical of what are offered to new acquaintances and desirable in that setting. Often when boy-meets-girl or peer-meets-peer there is a tendency to try to get off on a good foot with some innocent compliment. Significant compliments, though, are usually only exchanged between people who have gotten to know one another in some depth. Significant and sincere compliments help to develop and deepen these special relationships that are usually the most important ones in our lives. When you feel you can express your admiration for the other without fear of being taken advantage of or put down for it and without your observations being misinterpreted as simple flattery, you have established a good rapport with that person.

You don't have to be very old or worldly wise to recognize when the commendations you receive are routine and carry little weight. The grandfather that you almost never see because he has no interest in children may make the proper social noises when you are brought into his presence at some family gathering but you know he would say the same thing with as much feeling and conviction to literally anyone the family paraded before him. Such social lubrication praise isn't insincere, it is just not very personal or serious. You would be laughed at for taking such statements personally and getting a swelled head about them but it is considered appropriate to get a bit of an ego boost from them within the family circle.

Social obligation praise is similar to but a bit more formal and impersonal than that used for social lubrication. This is the gush of polite well-wishing that relatives and neighbors lavish on the graduate, birthday boy, or whoever is the focus at this time in order to stay in good standing within the family circle. Politicians of all stripes use it on those same occasions to ingratiate themselves with these persons and their families and friends. It's not undesirable or inappropriate but these comments will seldom be confused for more enthusiastically personal feeling by any except those intent on fooling themselves.

Giving small c praise to stroke someone's ego is on a par with giving him a dish of ice cream to please him. It will soon be gone but it's a nice little treat while it lasts and not to be bad-mouthed or rejected. The big C considered praises we receive (always too few and too long in between) are more like giving him a prepaid card for a kazillion visits to the ice cream store in that the good effects can go on and on because the memory stays with him and the resolve he made to live up to the praise continues to motivate him.

Being able to pay sincere, in-depth compliments also puts you in a better position to offer constructive criticism that may contain some negative elements. Actually the two functions are closely related. If you care about this person and want to help him be the best he can be, you want to do two things: make him aware of his strong positive points and encourage him to continue those things and, if possible, point out his weaknesses or failures in a constructive way so he can correct them and be a better and more effective person. You aren't being fully helpful unless you do both - if the situation allows (a very important and basic modifier).

Negative feedback has a tendency to leak out and filter through to us either verbally or non-verbally. In the heat of an argument or when someone wants to hurt us for whatever reason, observations or opinions designed to make us aware of our faults and negative aspects may be spoken with vehemence. But positive feedback often doesn't come through as well because it is less often articulated and therefore must be inferred. Unfortunately, without specific reinforcement we may have only our own judgment to go by, and self-delusion is a well-recognized problem. Consequently those who are not so egotistical that they could never doubt their own successes are left in a state of doubt. They want to believe they are succeeding as social beings, but they can't be sure.

Of course what seems like praise may not really be praise. Words that are superficially compliments may be self-serving, backhanded, or even poorly disguised negative reactions. False or negative praise is a backhanded statement phrased to appear superficially as a compliment, but intended to be understood by at least some of the hearers as actually an insult or put-down. Sarcastic praise may be genuine, but it's seldom enthusiastic. It recognizes the other's accomplishment but does so only begrudgingly. Praise given for deeds the speaker knows were not done but finds some reason to mention, possibly to force into the open the fact that they are fictitious in order to embarrass you, is not true praise. These types at least point out that there is a social *face* and a standard format for true and sincere praise.

False praise is the weapon of the person who wishes to harm but chooses not to be open about that. The tone used is that more or less appropriate to praise but the words are carefully chosen to have an overtone of quite the opposite meaning. "Your new sweater looks great" said with the right tone and a roll of the eyes to the by-standers shields the speaker from any claim that he attacked the other guy's attire or style but it lets everyone know that that is exactly what he is doing (and will be very sensitive about having done to him).

False praise differs from flattery because it is not an exaggeration of true praise but specifically a statement trumped up to look like it is approval that is on close examination actually disapproving. The falsity in this case resides mostly in the choice of words rather than in tone and mannerism of delivery. It is a complex maneuver since to be effective the statements made must simultaneously be worded to be taken as true and as false with no signals of which is preferred or actually intended. We learn at an early age that communications signals can have more than one level of meaning whether they are spoken, written, or expressed as body language. Our success in fitting into society depends in part on learning to distinguish between the levels and in accepting that contradictory signals must sometimes be allowed to coexist in order to convey the contradictory feelings of the communicator who may feel social pressures to give one message while being pushed by personal considerations to maintain a different position. The ambiguity in the signals allows the viewers to accept that social correctness is being maintained if that is what is critical to them, while also recognizing that it would put them in a position of disadvantage if they acted as if they believed the signal were the true controlling influence in this person's future responses and secret actions.

Praise or approval seems vitally important to our proper psychological development if we are to be happy, but is insincere praise as good as the real thing? Unequivocally no. It not only isn't as good, it may be absolutely harmful. It isn't even better than nothing unless we have a sad situation where the individual literally doesn't receive any positive reinforcement feedback from anyone. We generally know when we are being patronized and when the compliments or approval we receive are sincere. When we receive what we perceive to be insincere praise, the message we receive is that this person has to go through the motions for some reason but we aren't really considered commendable. Or that our accomplishments aren't really of any importance. Or that we are being played for a fool by letting ourselves feel proud and happy when these people are only teasing us and therefore we can't expect any good things to follow from this.

Flattery is praise twisted out of shape. It is praise exaggerated in form, elicited by inadequate or inappropriate actions of the other, or both. It also has degrees and may be viewed in specific instances as anything from joking social lubrication to vicious irony to sycophantic bootlicking.

There is a double edge to flattery which makes it a tool of choice for those intent on scoring points off those they dislike because it offers what the intended victim, and any witnesses, will probably recognize as exaggerations of the facts and certainly of the reaction to them by the flatterer. Those at whom it will often by directed but on whom it will have the least effect will take the exaggerations as entirely correct and appropriate. A person who takes the flattery seriously or at face value has by that fact alone revealed himself to be foolish, but to reject flattery as such requires a strong enough and realistic enough personality that it is beyond the capacity of some.

It is awkward to reject flattery but generally possible to sidestep it. To reject an expression of praise tends to come across as an argument that acknowledgement and credit for something are not deserved, when what you are trying to deflect is only the misstatements or exaggerations that you fear will come back to haunt you later if not challenged now. No matter how precisely you and the flatterer understand the distinctions you are making, rejecting flattery outright will tend to sound (or can too easily be made to sound) foolish, ungrateful, or hopelessly befuddled to those watching from the sidelines.

There is a place for both public and private praise and in the ideal situation both will be given. They are not the same, however. Private praise is more intimate and emotionally intense. This is where we are likely to give free rein to our affection, admiration, and appreciation. This is also a one-on-one atmosphere in which we can feel and measure the intensity and sincerity of the praiser.

When public praise takes place in the context of a formal awards ceremony or testimonial it achieves a high degree of collective approval which adds a dimension that individual responses can't achieve. The award may or may not actually reflect the majority opinion, but at least it is more than a single individual giving approval.

Not all praise is really directed at the person on whom the words are focused. Private interest awards are often mostly an excuse to get public attention for the group giving the award and this person is only the current filler of that space. This is often the case within minority ethnic groups, social or sport clubs, and the like. The praise is not insincere but it is not of the same quality as more specifically personal acknowledgement because there is always the unspoken admission that some other member of the group would get exactly this same celebration for almost anything of note he had done and someone else would have been chosen to receive this award and this praise if this person were unavailable on the night of the awards ceremony. These are often annual events so someone will be chosen to get the award each year, truly outstanding accomplishments are not required.

Therefore this also reveals a different side of praise - that it can be, and often is, used to build and maintain group loyalty. It is a social binder that simultaneously recognizes personal achievement but then binds that into and associates it with the group and its ideals or goals. As a social glue it may have considerable power and is certainly a positive way of playing up the group's message. How better to assure that the important historical deeds aren't forgotten than by including them in traditional rituals of praise and celebration to which each new generation or new group of inductees will be exposed?

Ceremonial praise often involves some element of selection of those to be praised from a group by a specified competitive activity. This adds a new element and somewhat changes the focus. Praise showered on the winners of competitions is not invalid or any less important or sincere than that bestowed on individuals in other contexts, but it does have a different quality about it. Ceremonial praise for contest winners is also limited by the time factor. There will be another contest and a new group of praisees next week or next year and this event will be history. This type of ceremonial praise acknowledges and is a large part of the reward for the achievement of the moment, *this* game or performance (which may well be the end point of a long and exhausting period of training and elimination contests) which this person may not be able to repeat during the next competition. Athletic competitions are prime examples. This year's champs can be and often are next year's has-beens.

Idealistic praise publicly applauds those persons and the elements of their positions and actions that we perceive as implementing or supporting our strongly held philosophical or religious views. The flaw here is that often in order to have a chance to crow about our pet ideas, especially if these aren't mainstream views, we are tempted to close our eyes to behaviors in the person being extolled that we aren't proud of or have even openly condemned at times. This is certainly not effectively discriminating praise.

Tunnel vision praise is real and possibly even enthusiastic but very narrowly focused. This is directed at a specific accomplishment and makes little room for the person involved. Essentially, the action is praised, not the person. Usually this is a reflection of a praise-giver who has a generally negative view of life and people, but is forcing himself to be honest and to acknowledge that for a change someone did something right.

Some claim they fear paying compliments lest they somehow be suckered into granting concessions they would prefer not to in regard to this person. I find such claims unconvincing unless the speaker is some-one who knows from experience that he is not able to hold his own and is often taken advantage of, then I must concede the risk. For those more adept at dealing with social stress I suspect this is just an excuse not to go to the trouble of being nice to others.

Praise is amazing stuff because few other things most of us can generate can do so much good when given in the right places and yet actually do harm when slopped around indiscriminately.

Praise makes us feel good about ourselves by confirming (or maybe making us aware for the first time) that we are carrying our portion of the burden of making the world a better place. It assures us that our actions are not useless and in vain since others are aware of them and seem to be benefitting from them while it reassures us that we are having something like the effect we aimed for. It prompts us to resolve to keep up the good work and it encourages us to aim for a similar level of achievement in our future actions in this and in other arenas.

There is Praise and then there is praise. I certainly hope we have all been recipients of at least the routine and automatic praises that are doled out along the path of life since these are the minimum of approval and encouragement that we need in order to be happy as well as to be psychologically and socially healthy. I am not arguing against such comments at all but I am suggesting that the words and gestures we long remember and that have the greatest positive effect on us are the ones of considered praises we receive. Note that praise is most often given in the form of words rather than actions, although applause, hugs, handshakes, and trophies certainly count. Such compliments are thought out and deliberately formulated rather than off-the-cuff and generalized. The person who acknowledges that she knows what efforts and sacrifices you made to achieve your goals or who recognizes that this particular feat is not a one-time-only thing, but the fruit of a talent in you that gives promise of continuing and even expanding accomplishments, is giving you the highest praise and the best encouragement.

What people of all ages and degrees of success want, need, and relish are words of encouragement. A cheer and a "go for it!" from someone who matters. This is confirmation that what you are doing is seen, recognized, and approved of. Few inputs can have as much of a beneficial effect. It removes the feeling of acting in isolation and, without depriving you of the glory of your talents and efforts, makes you part of a society. You are not alone and you are not really a stranger. You belong.

Encouraging another means literally, from the derivation of the word from the Latin, "to pour heart into" her. This is closely related to the activity of paying sincere and significant compliments. The purposes are virtually identical. You want the person to feel good about herself and to use her gifts and talents for the benefit of herself and others. The main difference between encouraging and complimenting when they are not synonymous (which they often are) is that we give compliments for what the person is or has accomplished, while we often give encouragement in spite of what the person has not become or accomplished in the hope of helping her to reach the desired goals in the future.

Very often encouragement is needed precisely because the person doesn't have enough self-confidence and this may be because she hasn't been given enough positive feedback in the form of more or less explicit compliments in the past.

Like a compliment, encouragement has to be deeply sincere to make a real difference. A "stick to it" from a casual acquaintance has about as much impact as a "great game!" from that same person. It's not a bad thing or something to be rejected, but it's not of much substance. It's the friend that you know is really behind you and really cares that has the big impact on you. This is the person whose words and non-verbal messages give you the determination to keep on and make the best effort you can. It is this person that you know will still think well of you even if you don't achieve what you wanted to. Too many people are only interested in you if you are the winner, this person will appreciate that you made the effort. There are always lots more also-rans than winners, but they all tried.

So whenever the opportunity arises, try to give others the benefit of your observations about their strong points. Simple flattery puffs the ego but has little lasting value as it rolls off us, but thought-through words of encouragement can have considerable effect because we try to live up to them.

Some people indulge in superficial flattery because paying out compliments tends to also make you the recipient of them. Those folks shouldn't cloud our recognition that a mutual admiration society, when sincere and substantial, is a wonderful thing. How nice this world would be if we had more cases of people who sincerely admire and love one another regularly encouraging one another to be the best they can be. Indiscriminant praise isn't real praise at all, but encouragement for all is great.

Each of us lives in her own private isolation chamber or bubble. We interact with others all the time but we seldom get the full message about our impact on those people. In part this is because we have too many other things to do. We can't efficiently generate our output and simultaneously focus on the feedback. In part this distancing is because few of us fully project our sincere reactions to others. We have learned not to do so as part of our social training. In the social arena, honesty and openness are not considered to be the best policy. This leads to the peculiarity that we may talk in detail to third parties about our reactions to some person when we wouldn't say the same things to that person directly.

There are some things about ourselves that we simply can't learn by analyzing ourselves. One of these is the way we come across to other people, the impact we have on them. We ourselves are largely unaware of some of the things about ourselves that make the most impression on others. We try deliberately to project certain traits that we want to be identified with - the strong, silent type; the ready wit; the smoldering sex symbol. Consciously or unconsciously, once we have accepted these self-images we physically carry ourselves, talk, and generally play out a role that we think fits the image. How our projections are received and interpreted by others may be very different though.

There seem to be two major classes of second person perceptions that we can only learn about if others tell us about them. First are the things we have done deliberately that are interpreted as meaning something very different than we intended. Some shy people, for instance, when they are in an uncomfortable social situation having to deal with strangers, may put on a mask, a sort of frozen facial expression, to hide their distress. This mask may, however, be interpreted by others as arrogance, idiocy, or physical ill health. Or the body builder who flexes a bit to make herself more impressive to others may intimidate them instead or be laughed at (behind her broad back, of course) for being so obvious. Or the person who tries to imitate the class clown because she sees that person elicit sincere laughs and be accepted for that reason, but she doesn't have what the role calls for and flops or even offends those she wanted to win over.

The second class are the perceptions that we aren't conscious of, often because they result from what we don't do rather than from our actions. This is, for instance, that wonderfully attractive person who simply puts you immediately at ease because she's not trying to compete with you or to use you. These unthreatening individuals can be very effective in situations that require personal interaction because you sense that she isn't laughing at you, challenging you, or trying to rip you off. Such a person can be even more effective if she knows that she comes across this way because it then becomes a tool she can use in making situations work by putting others at ease.

There are also those who have good looks, a good speaking voice, or other attractive physical or personality traits, but who are not quite sure they are perceived as having agreeable features. Their all important healthy self-esteem may be less than it ought to be for their fullest happiness simply because they literally don't know that others find them attractive and nice to be around. We all want to be loved and admired. A great part of our behavior is directed at exactly that end. Knowing that others enjoy your company and think well of you doesn't automatically make you an egotistical and aloof bore; rather it often makes you a healthy, productive person. Similarly, not knowing that you are well thought of may make you unproductive because you may not be egotistical enough to assume that you are loved and admired when people don't make the point of telling you so outright.

In moderation, it is useful to praise someone a bit more for what we believe they can do and would like to see them do than for what they have already accomplished. This on-going praise assures them they are on a path we consider to be desirable and it encourages them to keep repeating the good deeds and working on even more of them. One common result of praise (and therefore a valid reason to give it) is to prompt the individual to resolve to press on in spite of hardships and less than complete success.

There is commonly a distinction that could be made between the person praised and the deed praised. Each could be praised but only sometimes do both deserve it. A lousy performance that was a sincere effort by an inexperienced person should get praise for her effort in order to encourage her, but if praise is given to the performance itself why would she make any attempt to improve? Why would anyone else pay attention to the value judgments of a person who can't distinguish between a hesitant amateur performance hitting most of the notes and a master performance by an accomplished professional? The praise you give says as much about you and your intelligence, honesty, and critical faculties as it does about the person or thing being critiqued.

You can't live someone else's life for her. You are responsible for you and the other person is responsible for herself. What you can do is offer assistance and support from the sidelines. This gives you some input but still leaves the other in charge of her own affairs. Young people in particular resent being told what to do at every turn because the clear implication is that you are so almighty smart and they are so assuredly stupid that they'll fall on their faces without you making all the decisions. Unless you are a pathologically inadequate adult (in which case, thank goodness, you are probably not trying to run anyone else's life) you certainly resent others trying to manipulate you and to make important decisions for you or without consulting you, so it shouldn't surprise you that others feel the same way.

Encouragement can be equally effective in either verbal or non-verbal form. The wink or touch in passing may speak volumes. Even when it is verbal, it tends to be short and simple. When her fifteen year old son finally gets to move from the bench to the game the proud parent doesn't spend five minutes spelling out the details of what needs to be done. Mom says, "Get out there and give it all you've got. I know you can do it." Fortunately the non-wordy nature of encouragement often allows it to be freely given even by people who find it difficult to articulate emotional or personal things.

Whether given to an individual or a group, encouragement always has a personal element to it. You can cheer for an idea or philosophy but you can't encourage the idea itself, you can only encourage people to accept it or fight for or against it. You can cheer on a team but that won't make much difference if the players don't take the message of your cheers personally.

Public praise not only serves to acknowledge this individual's (or group's) accomplishments and encourage her to further successes, it also offers a challenge and hope of some praise and achievement to others. It gives exposure to the actions and behaviors that we want to encourage and this serves an educational function in the midst of everything else.

Encouragement can be offered but never forced on someone. For it to affect you, you must be open to the feeling. No one can make it happen if you aren't willing, although there are time honored ways of persuading you to open yourself to it. Playing rousing or patriotic music or reading lists of names and events from history that are associated with this activity are standard ways to do that.

The task of encouraging others has no bounds of age or social position. A girl can encourage her grandmother as truly as the older woman can encourage the girl. Supervisors can encourage the workers and vice versa. This is because encouragement doesn't imply greater wisdom, experience, or social power, only a desire to see the other perform well and possibly succeed.

Who offers the encouragement is important to how much it means to me and is likely to truly affect me because it is a personal effect. Someone whom I admire from afar but who doesn't know me personally can still give me great heart and someone whom I know very well may not move me at all with the same words. A fan doesn't know the team members in detail, and the general doesn't know the soldiers under her command socially, but your family and close social circle know you, warts and all. Therefore when they take a stand to support you it is because you are you, this unique human being. There is no better or more important feeling than being recognized and accepted for who you are. The boost may have even more value and impact when it comes from someone whom you recognize as having more wisdom or experience.

At any level, the effectiveness of encouragement depends on the importance to those listening of the one who gives it. John Doe, local minister, could do little to boost the determination of the British during WWII but Winston Churchill could get them to grit their teeth and fight on despite the hardships. The school principal's words to the basketball team are nice, but it is usually the coach that gets them fired up and ready for the game.

It is hardly possible to effectively encourage someone that you don't like and don't want to be associated with in your own or in the public view. The words will stick in your throat or will be recognized as counterfeit and ignored by the recipient. One can attempt to fake a wish of encouragement because of some social pressure but it is unlikely to have much good effect because the b.s. detectors will be going off in the recipient and probably in the audience. Only the very best liars will be able to get their body language in synch with their words during such an attempt so that they don't give themselves away.

Encouragement emphasizes the possibilities. It is given before or during the competition, not afterward. You don't encourage the winner, you congratulate her. Healthy encouragement isn't tied to the outcome of the activity but rather to its performance. For those for whom winning is the only thing, life is guarantee to be filled with failures. But for those who recognize that giving their best performance is as much as anyone can do - no matter how it compares to the best performance of someone else - many successes and satisfactions are in store. It is a pathetic coach, parent, or friend who rejects the player who doesn't win each and every contest.

Encouragement is warm. It feels good. It is one of the better human interactions because it is a willing connection between these people. They open themselves and link their humanity and a bit of their species destiny as social animals, which reflects the essential oneness of the universe.

Encouragement is open-ended. It's not restricted to specific competitive events. It can be offered for particular activities or more generally for whatever life is throwing at you now and has in store for you in the future. I can encourage you in your tennis game about to start, in your academic semester in the fall, or in your new job or marriage. Or just in living your life. Be happy. Be good. Be attentive and properly critical.

When that is necessary, encouragement can be effective even when given second hand. If the person who means much to me can't be present at this time or get through a personal communication to me right now, I can draw strength from the knowledge that she is thinking of me when someone else or even a card in the mail gives me that message and assurance.

The dark side of encouragement is when it is used to recruit less discriminating people to a particular position more than to induce individual thought and action. There is always a strong social urge to join in when some group that you are part of, whether formally or simply because you are physically part of an audience, is collectively applauding a person, performance, or event. It is awkward to not join in since that signals that you disagree with what those all around you are doing. You may feel anti-social. It seems inappropriate not to go along with the crowd. You have the sense that everyone is focused on you and they are wondering what is the matter with you. It takes a strong person to stand her ground and not be induced to even nominally agree with what she has major reservations about or has fully formulated objections to.

The desire to be one of the gang is a strong psychological pull for some individuals, especially those who have few clearly defined or strongly held beliefs or positions and for those who have only a weak sense of their own uniqueness and worth. Such persons are unable to give themselves approval because they don't accept that they're intelligent enough or important enough for their opinions to carry weight. They require a seal of approval from others to feel secure and good about themselves. An encouraging word or nod fills the need.

There is both the comfort of anonymity in a group and the real possibility of being manipulated precisely because of that anonymity. Group or peer pressure seems irresistible for many. When surrounded by others who might notice, some simply won't bring themselves to stand out from the crowd by taking any stance except compliance. (Note that I don't say they *can't*.) This makes them first class dupes because they can only too easily be induced to sign petitions, contribute cash, or otherwise put themselves on the line in a more individual way by encircling them with a few true believers and a larger number of bandwagon recruits like themselves. By creating an event and gathering a crowd, a dedicated person can make a real contribution to her own or her group's cause, whatever that might be, because of the flock mentality of many. A joiner or follower might achieve a limited degree of critical maturity by selecting the right groups to join, but her unwillingness to consider the facts and make independent decisions about an appropriate response still leaves her at a disadvantage to herself and to the causes she might wish to support or advance.

A factor that often makes crowd mentality effective in controlling the overt actions of many is precisely that each person who is unwilling to admit to being unconvinced by the position being pushed acts as an agent of repression for each other unpersuaded individual by at least giving tacit approval to the purported group viewpoint. Thereby she adds herself to the number who must be opposed (and in theory at least argued with and against) by anyone staking out a different opinion.

The individuals who do ask questions or who do raise objections encourage the silent ones to do likewise - which is why those who insist on thinking for themselves and letting that be known are so unpopular with those intent on manipulating the masses for their own ends.

In crowds without a narrow political orientation - like those at some parade, holiday concert, or other festivity - following the lead of the crowd is easy and generally acceptable. Your degree of enthusiasm in responding is your control mechanism so that no battle lines need be drawn up if you disagree about the worthiness of the persons, ideas, or performances presented for approval. As long as everyone agrees to an "each to her own thing" atmosphere, those who have some need to express more enthusiastic support can do so to the bemusement of those less blown away and no one's enjoyment needs to be diminished.

But when some person or subgroup decides that everyone must react as they, the self-appointed leaders, choose to react there is no hope for the situation and the others must quickly decide whether they or the enthusiasts are going to be the ones to move along. There is little value in any other decision because compromise requires participation by both sides. One-sided "compromise" is called capitulation.

We live in a world overfilled with detail. Our minds can't handle all of the raw data so we have evolved to be intellectual sorters, people who classify the input and combine like items into categories. We can then deal with the members of each category as if they are more or less alike, although we never completely forget they have many differences, some major and some minor depending on how far down the sorting tree those are. It is a less than perfect system but it makes an otherwise unworkable mass of information more comprehensible.

Our languages reflect the same solution to the inevitable problem in that we speak in generalizations and find it hard to communicate without them. We can't speak about anything of more than very local and personal importance without using them. One person doing one thing and that only in one particular instance greatly limits our thinking and our social interactions.

Plus we usually try to quantify our opinions and statements for effect and a generalization lets us multiply the supporting evidence without having to actually produce any.

There is a continuum of generalizations and we all use the whole range regularly. They stretch from "I love chocolate ice cream...(but not with pickles and sauerkraut)", through "Airbags save lives", to "All politicians are crooks." We are likely to agree that different levels of generalization are acceptable in different situations. Usually the more immediate and personal their impact, the less general we want the statements to be. For example, depending on the context and/or the intent of the speaker or writer, *all* can mean a true majority, a perceived majority, some or a majority of those in the public eye or in some group with no qualification attached, some or a majority of those in the public eye with specified qualifications, or some group who have written or commented publicly on the matter.

We tend to be more conscious of how often generalizations are used by others than of how often we use them ourselves. Their use is as common as breathing but it is often still a type of social deception. That is not a major problem in itself but it does set us all up for the more serious and deliberately harmful deceptions pulled off using language as a con artist's sneaky but effective tool.

Generalizations are the necessary common currency of discussion yet they carry within themselves an inherent inaccuracy that can easily destroy the very communication that requires their use. Stop and replay the last conversation you had, the last item you read before this book, or the last news program you heard on radio, TV, or the Internet. How many generalizations were involved? Now try to imagine communicating the same messages with all those generalizations removed. Some of the statements become completely impossible and many more become useless as effective communication.

To illustrate, consider this statement that you might find in a newspaper article. The *politicians* want to claim credit for *greatly improving* the national economy but *budget analysts* are likely to point out that a *resurgence* of the economy which has boosted *federal tax revenues* while it raised the incomes of so many *families* and *firms* is *more responsible* than any policy changes." Eight generalizations in a single sentence but it would be all but impossible to convey this message on that wide a scale, even if questionable on the details, without them.

Generalizations are almost always inaccurate because they create categories but not all the members of the category fit this specific description. Neither the natural world nor the cultural world is so regular and predictable that unaltering patterns are to be found. Only the most general statements, and therefore the least informative and useful ones, have much breadth of application - and even they have exceptions right and left as soon as we stop to examine things closely.

Often we tend to think in universals because we are discussing problems and seeking solutions for which it would be simpler if we could find answers that are *one size fits all*. But only at the most general levels are there such answers. "Everyone should live a moral and considered life" is an example of such a generalization. It sounds good and, if widely implemented, would solve a laundry list of problems. But to do anything about such a pious exhortation we must reduce the notion to specifics and there we find no single universally acceptable or workable set of do's and don'ts. Thus the generalizations make it easy to talk about the need to and the ways to resolve our many problems, but often they don't help and may even complicate actually resolving them.

Why do we generalize? Let me suggest a non-exhaustive list of some of the good and the bad reasons.

(1) Sometimes we rely on generalizations because we intuitively believe them or we "have the sense" that they are true. The speaker

sincerely assumes that his ideas, feelings, or experiences are shared by many others. Often, in fact, he asserts them as the majority opinion, but when challenged he can offer little objective evidence of that. When we are not certain how wide an application an observation or principle has, we tend to assume it is broad spectrum if it supports our ideas or our positions, but is narrowly restricted if it doesn't.

(2) We also use generalizations when we intend our comments to be taken as applying to the wider group or situation. This is the most valid use since we are then using a generalization in order to generalize.

Losing the personal *in this case* point of why the event can and should be commended or condemned may sometimes be a problem though. Generalizations can also add praise or blame that may not properly apply to this case.

But beware of articles and books that purport to discuss a serious personal topic like a problematic aspect of behavior mainly by using anecdotes about specific cases, actual or fictitious. An example is not a principle. Your problem is not the same as that of the person in the anecdote so hearing about his case is largely irrelevant unless it is clearly labeled as just one example of some general principles that have been described. The potential stumbling block is the difference between what the speaker means the example to illustrate and what the listener takes him to mean by it.

(3) Similarly we use generalizations to explore whether some principle that we ourselves have deduced has wider application. We do this tentatively, with on-going active evaluation to see if we agree that things hold together if that idea is in fact valid. In this mode we restrict ourselves to considering the subject, rather than advocating a position we have already arrived at. These cases should not lead to misunderstandings as long as the restriction that our ideas on the topic are works in progress is made clear. The shift of focus from the specific to the generalization does dilute your thinking about the particular case or situation though.

(4) We resort to generalizations when we are trying to make a point with some impact. Overly limited or specific statements often carry little weight in an argument or to a particular audience not focused on that narrow point.

Part of the attractiveness of generalizations is the temptation to escape into the anonymity and fog of pious but loose verbiage when you don't know what you are talking about and you suspect your listeners don't know much more than you do. Often it is uncertainty about the extent of the audience's knowledge that prompts these generalizations. Even though the more specific argumentation might be more precisely applicable, in many cases we feel safer throwing out a loose statement that we can't be nailed down on and thus have our lack of knowledge documented, rather than offering a bunch of loosely gathered specifics and "facts" that may be fabricated to meet the occasion but which can be challenged and checked. We do this recognizing that even though there is always the risk of a partial loss, we can never lose completely with a generalization because we weren't a hundred percent committed to an incorrect statement.

(5) We use generalizations to hide our true intentions when we want to deceive (or at least to avoid scrutiny) or to confuse an issue and distract from the counter-arguments. For instance, we often depend on generalizations when we want to shape the facts to meet our purposes by quantifying an opinion but without giving any verifiable data. Often this is because the necessary data doesn't exist. Sometimes it is because the speaker knows the data won't support his claims if someone checks.

These are often attempts to shape the facts and the "truth" to fit a particular agenda rather than let the audience arrive at their own impartial opinions. Depending on the audience, this may be a desirable effort on the part of the speaker - like making use of an extreme example to shock people into recognizing an impending but preventable disaster – but it is still less than the ideal objective presentation. Most often they are used wrongly to build a case when we can't do a better job of it. It is an unwritten adage of advocacy, *When you don't have solid facts or data, generalize.*

Sometimes by design, sometimes by accident, generalizations may be influential but not instructive. For instance, those statements that suggest a quantified fact but supply no actual quantities to examine. "The voters voted overwhelmingly to keep the nuclear power plant." Whose *overwhelming* is this? What were the percentages of the votes? We are led to a conclusion - big win for nuclear power - but left wondering about its accuracy.

Another potential hazard is that generalizations are a common element of communication, but communication is often used for one-sided purposes like lies, propaganda, and advocacy. Particularly in contexts where we would hope for or expect a neutral presentation of facts on which to draw our own conclusions, the misrepresentations that can occur are a problem. The more important the communication is, the more necessary it is to scrutinize any generalizations that are made in the testimony and perhaps insist on more specific statements or explanations before accepting the claims or making decisions.

Generalizations used in obvious attempts to gloss over serious wrongs or deficiencies or to avoid a proper question are unacceptable. The food manufacturer who refuses to disclose his ingredients except to say, "It is filled with only good things," should be quickly put out of business by widespread consumer rejection of his products. Likewise the politician who assures us that he has fixed a problem that is within his area of control but won't give the public details on how he fixed it and who was involved doesn't deserve to taken as credible. "Trust me" is too often a fool's game and too seldom a best choice.

(6) Generalizations may be called into play in order to try to lump together and try to connect the present case or situation to famous or infamous ones in order to incriminate a whole class or to incorporate them collectively into the consideration on the basis of a small number of cases. I will consider these situations in more detail in the Chapter 21. Similarly they may be used to suggest that a minor infraction by an individual is part of a pattern of defective actions by him. In this case the generalizations multiply the infractions in the minds of the hearers without changing the facts or telling an outright lie.

(7) Often our generalizations simply represent incomplete or sloppy thinking. The critic hasn't given the matter much thought and consequently hasn't even recognized that there might be any other possibilities. Or he is trying to avoid having to make tough decisions.

(8) Generalizations are often used as a politely inconspicuous way to avoid getting entangled and possibly bogged down in details that are not relevant to the main topic of discussion without admitting that up-front. Specialists of all sorts utilize this type of generalization regularly when trying to communicate with persons outside their own discipline. As a teacher of introductory college biology I found it necessary to alert my students at the start of the semester that I was going to be skimming over many minor qualifications and exceptions in order to present the big picture in the time we had available. I told them that meant I would be lying to them much of the time because the general statements don't apply always, in every case, and without qualification. They seemed to get my point and to remember it because of my warning.

Often we slip into this mode in order to be cooperative in the sense that we agree without too much quibbling to the generalizations made by others with whom we want to stay friendly or to influence in a positive way. We maintain the implicit understanding that we may disagree at some other time but are going to hold our tongues in this instance with no more than a body language signal of reservation about the point being made.

Some people deliberately abuse those common sense flexibility limits that we regularly implicitly agree to for their personal gain. Most of us recognize that the allowance we make for generalizations ought not to be universally applied. The consequences of the point being made determine when we can let it pass and when we have to question and even reject it out loud and pointedly. When this or that claim will have only a minor impact or is an item in only a private conversation that won't be reported to the world as reflecting an official or fully committed position, we may choose to let it slip by. It is often annoying to let falsehoods or misstatements stand even in a casual conversation, but the alternative is constant bickering and nit-picking so we have to make a critical judgment in each case about how much to tolerate

(9) We also use generalizations to avoid specific cases when we are not free to discuss or are not comfortable discussing particular details that are likely to come up. A vague statement lets us move on without disrupting the social context while keeping secrets that might embarrass someone else but that those we are talking to at the moment have no right or need to know about.

(10) Some generalizations are conscious or unconscious ways for the speaker to express his biases and prejudices - whether those are racial, ethnic, cultural, or intellectual in nature. Such biases are brain-stoppers that interfere with the speaker's judgment by prompting him to either reject the perceived accomplishments of this hated individual or group, or to argue for unrealistic performance criteria that are required only or mainly of them. This is where the labeling of persons, ideas, and groups comes in. "Faggots are sick." "Environmentalists want us all to have to live in cold caves in the dark." "Blacks are all welfare cheats." "Liberals are crazy." If you have ever tried to reason with such a biased person you know it is futile. In his mind the case is closed the moment the subject is identified as part of the group he chooses to hate or object to.

Generalizations are valid, valuable, and acceptable when there is not a need for greater precision and when existing exceptions won't be a problem. Or when used to make a point or to win some points when it is essential to get an audience's attention to deliver an important and non-self-serving message. The generalizations are exaggerations, deliberate obfuscation, or attempts at mind control when the speaker knows that they exceed the facts and opts to use them for that exact reason. You might notice that generalizations are seldom misused by accident in discussions of important matters.

Generalizations about improper conduct require greater precision than those about many other topics in order to avoid making claims that have not been upheld or which you are not prepared to prove in a court of law. "The Defense Department spends millions of dollars a year..." is okay, but unless that allegation has been or can be proven with hard evidence, "He is responsible for paying himself thousands of dollars in unearned overtime" is not.

Emotion-charged generalizations are very often invitations to participate in garbage thinking. If you choose to go along with the lead, you can't avoid the taint. "This assassination says something about us as a nation..." "These teenage criminals are the product of our society and they are the real victims..." Pundits who can't distinguish between the actions of individuals and the traits of the collective don't deserve respect. In fact we should be wary of them since by their public statements they admit that they think in violent ways (otherwise they couldn't imagine that everyone else must do so) and are warning us that if they get pissed off they might do terrible things while telling themselves they are just being like John Doe, citizen-whacko.

Beware of the generalizations that defy logic and/or good sense. "Some students will abuse any privileges, so no student can be allowed to do anything." And an old favorite from too many elementary school teachers at one time, "I must punish all of you to get the few bad ones whom I haven't been clever enough to catch."

A particularly interesting but confusing claim is that, "We can't allow pornography because soon we'll all have to look at it and the majority don't want to do so." Who can even envision how people can be compelled to watch pornography against their wishes? Have they been forgetting to take their meds? The same people often insist, "We parents cannot permit any adult material on TV because our kids will see it." But of course this will only happen if they cannot/ will not/ do not control what their own children watch but making it unavailable to anyone relieves them of the burden of keeping their children, or at least the TV sets in their residence, under their control. There is the added satisfaction that they are able to dictate what you and your family can watch that they don't want to see so they don't want you to see either. The fact that much of the adult material is readily available via the Internet further undermines these anti-pornography crusades, The fact that these campaigns often seem more focused on collecting money and public attention for their organizers is another matter that is hard to miss.

Watch out for attempts to hoodwink you when anyone uses a mix of specifics and generalizations. Beware of the ads and articles that give you detailed information on some percentages, but fall back on generalizations for others. For instance, (please note that I made up these numbers) "Print advertising has dropped by 16.5% since 1967. The amount of radio advertising has increased by 23.7% in that time but the cost has increased only moderately." How much is *moderately*? If the writer could find specifics for the other data, why not for the last point? Does it make you suspect that the numbers would make his use of "moderately" look silly? Or that he knows there are no numbers to support his claims but doesn't want to admit that? It should at least make you wonder about it.

The big question is: What can we do, individually and collectively, about the abuses of generalizations? Sorry about that but I can only make a few general observations here.

We are often told that we should have known that a qualification like "In my opinion" or "According to... (name the source)" was to be "understood" when someone made a public statement. I won't disagree that those few little words would make the speaker's intent clear but I will argue that a stronger case can be made that the confusion and discord that resulted from that not being stated explicitly as a clarification and reminder to all audiences is often the cause of needless harm and misunderstanding. The simple solution is to explicitly add the qualifier right when the comment is made. The way to pressure more public speakers to do that is for the individual audience members to decide - and whenever possible let the speaker and everyone they talk to about him and his positions know this directly and explicitly - that if the qualifier is not explicitly included they are going to interpret that to mean he intends his statement to be taken in the more universal way. If he can't bother to include "In my opinion" or "According to..." at the start of any comments that about debatable or controversial subjects he is going to being taken as meaning more than he wants to communicate. Many speakers will learn in a hurry to automatically add the qualifier once the immediate effect of those words not being stated is to raise questions right there on the spot about their reliability as communicators rather than later, when it may be too late to avoid the problems caused by the miscue.

To assume it was meant even though it wasn't said is a radical suggestion because it recommends the reverse of what we usually take to be the norm. In this stance we assume it wasn't meant if it wasn't said explicitly. Will many who make comments they intend to be heard and noticed by a wider audience than those around them at that moment adopt this strategy? Probably not. Initially only those who are aware and focused on what they and others, like the person addressing them right now, are saying and intending may extend the effort to think this way. But this is one tool for that group to use to hone their critical skills. Will enough adopt the strategy to make a significant difference? Stepping over the matter of how we would measure a significant difference in this matter, there is no way to tell except in retrospect. Is it worth doing? Yes, if you want to hone your awareness and critical muscles.

Is there a downside or price to pay for routinely including such a disclaimer? As far as I can see only if the speaker actually intended to be understood as making a more universal claim but knew he needed to have a ready escape clause if he was called on that. "I assumed you understood that was included" might be lame but it is easy to drag out when questioned. Those editing the sound bites for news reports will hate it because it lengthens the bites unless they cut that part out. Doing that though puts their heads squarely on the chopping block when the first objections are made by those who didn't have access to the unedited statements that the qualifier wasn't there so they are taking it as not said and therefore not intended by the now appropriately irate speaker.

At the most personal level you can make an effort to be more aware of the generalizations being lobbed at you from all sides. Once you have them in focus you can evaluate them. Are they appropriate and necessary? Do they reflect a situation with validly too many possibilities to be boiled down to a single yes-or-no answer? Are they actually smoke screens intended to cover-up, if not outright deceive you? The best defense is awareness. Since the goal of the abuser is to mislead or fool you, your focused attention makes it more unlikely that he will succeed. Like the flu types you have developed immunity to, each re-exposure, each misuse you detect, stimulates your defense system and makes you more alert and resistant to any you encounter later.

The more you are alert to the misuse or many outright abuses of generalizations by others, the less likely it is that you will misuse them yourself. Shame on you if you do so deliberately after thinking about this topic. May you fail in your attempt and suffer the consequences.

Generalizations are like some mineral nutrients in our diet and bodies. In the proper dosage they are essential to keep things working, but an overdose can be harmful or even lethal. We need trace amounts of copper and selenium, but too much of either will poison and maybe kill us. Since we are not totally passive receivers of messages, we can make it harder for speakers to hide important stuff behind generalizations by publicly asking questions or voicing objections immediately (when possible) or while the topic is still a matter of discussion (if no questions are permitted by either the speaker or the circumstances). Push forward to be the "man on the street" that the TV crew will be looking for to get reactions to fill out their report and then use your comments to focus attention on what wasn't said or the facts that can be readily verified that were misstated or slanted. Write a letter to the editor. Add your voice to the cacophony on the radio talk shows. If you can anticipate the points likely to be glossed over in a public address, having prepared signs like *How? How Soon?* and *Paid For By Whom?* ready to hold up for the speaker and the TV cameras to see should help.

If your local TV or radio stations incorporate listener feedback messages into their reports on controversial topics, that is another place to make your points and get them heard.

At first these tactics will have limited success, but once enough of the public catch on and start to pay attention to the use of hot air generalizations, the media will focus on these questioners in the audience. The media can then be expected to usurp the strategy of calling speakers on such points, since they always want to take credit. Don't fight them on that. They can have the access and the clout to do a better job of it than most of us can as individuals. Just keep them on their toes by providing them public feedback about their own failing when they settle for froth instead of solid answers, and when they don't at least publicly emphasize that that was all they got.

Train yourself to pay attention and notice and then to evaluate and question all generalizations, but especially those about important matters. Evaluate their validity and their use whether they are made in defense of or in opposition to the topic. Get yourself out of any pattern of automatic or too-casual-for-your-own-good blanket acceptance or rejection of the ideas presented.

You don't learn any significant skill without at least a bit of focus and some practice. Good critical thinking is a skill, so practice it regularly until it becomes routine. Don't tie yourself in knots, but train yourself to be aware.

Put up mental caution signs. Generalizations are not necessarily universal and are easily slanted to mislead and persuade unfairly and only you the listener/ reader can decide. You as the presenter get to decide if their use is fair play so that you are ready to support other people using them on you or on this audience. Try to focus on the presenter and his awareness of the fact that he is using broad claims and what you can determine of his intent in doing it that way.

When using generalizations yourself, recognize their limits. Also recognize that others are likely to misunderstand or deliberately distort them and the alert people will question them and therefore you and your credibility. Don't refuse to admit that such wide open statements may be the same as sloppy thinking and poor preparation on your part. Spur of the moment comments or arguments are more likely to include broader generalizations than are likely to stand up to scrutiny than prepared statements so be ready to cut a speaker some slack. That doesn't mean you should believe or accept those overly broad generalizations, only understand why he might not have made a more tightly reasoned and supported presentation. Don't automatically reject him or his position because of such a lapse but let it make you cautious about him and prompt you to hold off making a decision about him until you hear more from and about him. This also means you should ask yourself if you are proud of your own statements as your contribution to the discussion and are prepared to stand behind them when they are challenged.

The limits and the potential for distortion are good reasons for you to hesitate and to question whatever you are told. Carefully note the exact wording of the claims and don't accept b.s. dismissals of your questions or objections.

If the matter is one of consequence, raising doubts within a larger group by publicly questioning the claims and asking for clarification and citations is a good thing in itself, even though it slows up the process. Applying that pressure immediately in the public forum will sometimes squeeze out the details and confirmations that were being evaded or often simply overlooked in the interest of keeping it short. You do everyone a favor by applying the pressure to get the verifiable facts and details – or the recognition that those aren't available or are being hidden

- right then and there before some to many in the audience have made up their minds and are ready to move on without thinking more about the effects this decision will produce. That means especially how they will be able to bitch about it but not change it later, but can change it right now.

That also means you should ask for references to support claims made and, if the matter is an important one, take the time and make the effort to check them out. It should often be acceptable for the person to refer you to a website for the citations and details. If however the information is not where he said it would be that is another warning that he is not to be trusted.

As practice, get in the habit of rejecting twisted claims in ads (where they are often used to get your attention without really intending to mislead you about some of the details). The ad that says that the Newtonian law of physics that a body at rest tends to remain at rest means that without their pills if you live a sedate life you won't become active is distorting the physics in a cutesy way – but it is also misteaching everyone what the physics is really about. Is it any wonder that so many have such mistaken and distorted understanding of basic science? Seldom take ads as accurate presenters of facts – but always be aware of, wary of, and annoyed by those that teach false lessons as their way to get attention for some other purpose.

We can't do without generalizations but once we start to sensitize ourselves to recognize and pay more attention to them we are less likely to be led astray by them. There are always going to be people who insist that the widest application be accepted for the generalizations they use for their purposes but part of the benefit of reciting the heading of this chapter as a mantra is that we know to decide what dimensions we will allow them. Don't bother arguing about such details with the speaker as long as you are the only audience or you trust any other listeners to recognize their potential distorting effect and to be correcting for that too. That is always the correct strategy. Sorry, I couldn't resist - but see how useful they are but not automatically a problem if we're alert.

This chapter title is intended to make the point of the topic here while being pretty certain to grab your attention. In my original notes this was to be *Generalizations II* since it builds on that start, but that title doesn't describe the focus as pointedly. I considered *Hollywood This and Washington That* because the focus here is exactly on how potentially misleading and therefore undesirable but probably unavoidable it is that we depend so heavily on identifying positions as those of whole groups even when both speaker and audience know that many, often even most, members of those groups don't in fact support or advocate the positions we are attributing to them collectively.

The use of straw men to make points in an argument is a strategy as old as debate. The use of dummy groups, collectives with some interest in common and able to be represented as if they were unified and acting in concert, is probably as ancient. For various purposes we hear or read regularly that "Hollywood thinks...", "The current administration said...", and "The trucking industry proposes..." The more intelligent and aware people know these are glosses or generalizations that are not absolute, all inclusive, or even halfway accurate characterizations. Making the statement using a broad generalization gives it an air of authenticity and authority among the less wary though. Since *science* and *scientists* are particularly important and dangerous instances of this I will discuss those and the pitfall consequences of misunderstanding them in Chapter 23.

The common starting point for polemics is to postulate a unity among those you want to attack so they are all equally deserving of any blame that any one among them has earned. Do you remember when you kids were indiscriminately blamed by a teacher, neighbor, or parent for the misdeed of one of your number? How did that make you feel? You may have thought you had grown beyond the stage where that could happen by now, but think again. Remember that now at least you're in a better position to defend yourself.

Particularly when politicians are making public comments it is important to keep in mind that many (most?) of their generalizations about groups they oppose (and therefore who are likely ones who oppose them or their positions) are mainly intended as code words to rile up and give their own constituents targets for their aggression and thoughts of rejection and to get the speaker's name and statements into the day's news reports. From there they can expect to influence those who draw conclusions by simply having computer search engines tally the number of times those words were subsequently posted online in any version and claiming that by doing that they took our collective pulse and can tell us what we are thinking collectively. The initial comments are not all that frequently presented as information or even persuasion, they are capes waved at the angry bulls to incite blind, thoughtless reactions.

The flip side of the identification of claims made about some group with every aspect and application of the group is the common tactic of asserting that finding a flaw in any statement or claim that can be attributed to any member of the group automatically disproves or throws out all claims and statements by any and all members of the group. And it makes little difference whether the flawed item was a collective official statement of the group leadership or an off the cuff remark by someone in a private conversation overheard by an opponent. That is nonsense heaped on top of the nonsense of the initial total identification claims. The same tactical rules seem to apply to both sides of this deliberate misidentification strategy - although those rules likely aren't written down and made available in any format to those uninitiated and unvetted for loyalty and therefore who have not promised and been judged able to keep silent about the very existence of such guidelines at any personal cost.

Dummy group generalizations are virtually always erroneous. If we are being honest and open-minded, as soon as anyone says that, "Americans think/feel/do..." or "Women/ African-Americans/ Blue collar workers/ liberals/ people of faith/ college students (the list can be very extensive) feel that..." we know we are about to be told a mistruth since there is no universal agreement in any group of significance and of significant size on any topic whatsoever. The group may have "official" positions if they are organized and those are legitimately cited, but those are not universally supported or endorsed so they are still not accurate at the individual level. There may also be poll results but they are also often seriously off base and almost always at least flawed, as we will consider in Chapter 25.

When you get to the specifics, where the useful stuff is found, there are no "Black leaders", "environmental freaks", "conservatives", or "right wing fundamentalists", as categories of people thinking and advocating precisely the same things. Beware. The speaker referring to them is saying they are that collectively uniform and is urging you to accept or reject those who have any feature or interest in common as an interchangeable group without deeper consideration, but the people are not in that much agreement on details and specifics so the claim is flawed although it may have some limited reality to it. Identifying the heroes or the culprits with that kind of generalization gives the statement more weight in some minds though. "Jane and Sally claim that..." seems less attention-worthy than "Women claim that...", "Female politicians support...", or at least, "The women in our office agree that..."

Why do we so often use this dummy group approach and why do we allow others to do so? There is an inherent (and somewhat elliptical) understanding built into the use of such statements that says, "We are talking about a fraction that we would like to believe is a majority of those included in the group we are citing, not necessarily a completely unanimous opinion - although we will be happy if you decide to take it as unanimous." Who can argue with the validity of that? It is necessary not only in order to facilitate, but even to permit discussions of group opinions. Whether you choose to believe there is an addendum like "We don't intend to be bothered making our intended limitations on the terms clearer to make our thinking also clearer" is your call.

Unquantifiable (or at least unmeasured) quantitative statements are basic elements of discussion and we need to allow a reasonable degree of flexibility in order to grease the wheels of communication. Try to imagine the news reports if we couldn't make comments about categories like politicians, Republicans, rock bands, taxpayers, or dupes. It is when someone tries to associate this person with every item or at least every carefully selected item from the generalized group description without specific evidence to support that claim that miscommunication occurs, whether that effect is intended or not. Or when she claims that every member of the group she named does think, act, or agree with what else she mentioned. This is a common strategy but one more likely to stir up rejoinders and denials and to fail in the longer term. When all you care about is the irreversible effects in the short-term, like the voting results in the primary election tomorrow, it can be effective though. That seems to be why all sides in a political battle are likely to try using it in that time frame.

Why are references to corporate entities or dummy groups such a common strategy? Because even though there is a price paid in accuracy, they simplify communication. The use of such a target involves a loss of exactness in the statement, but any simplification inevitably has that effect. In fact without some generalizations like dummy groups, many statements would become very cumbersome. The conspicuous fact that corporate entities like these have been the fodder for discussion since forever indicates that the strategy is not a lethal one. That they are often the basis of negative criticisms and outright attacks that are inappropriate and inaccurate when applied to many of the individual units within the group indicates that they are far from a trouble-free method.

One large dummy group or another is often "recruited" to support particular policies or positions in order to give the impression that their members in their countless thousands have a clear preference for a particular action or program over some opposing one but with no formal statement from them available to say that because they have no group structure to make statements about any topic at all. They are straw men even when they are useful to your own purposes.

The biggest risk in the use of dummy groups is that people who should know better will start to think in such oversimplified patterns when they make important decisions and they and others will suffer because they made plans rooted in a world that doesn't exist. To speak about dummy groups is to risk thinking of them as real. To speak of them in that form in conversation increases the risk that you will slip into talking about them as factual entities in important discussions. The more people who are thinking about them without qualifications or without quotations marks around the labels stapled to them, the greater the likelihood that other people will be led to do so.

Accusations that are untrue are unfair. Guilt by association is the stuff of small minds and those with a low opinion of the intelligence of their audience. If you can't or won't specify the particular individuals or groups (companies, committees, etc.) thereby you are advertising your failure as a critic and the unworthiness of your comments for serious consideration.

Straw men are not going to disappear any time soon but at least if we insisted on accuracy they would become rarer, especially in public discourses - by which I mean political debate in the wide sense. We find generalizations so easy to use that we can forget that many could be avoided if we made the effort, but then some of our praise and much of our complaining would become too much trouble to be bothered about.

As with many communication problems, dummy groups are best dealt with by paying attention so that you are not led to believe they have more inclusive reality than they do. It is not realistic to think that they can be banned from public discussion or even that much pressure can be focused to effectively discourage their use by those looking for the short cut to their point or those who are deliberately intent on giving the overblown impression even though they recognize the loss of accuracy. In most of the cases, several companies, agencies, or other entities are engaged in the same type of activity but they are completely separate and often in competition with one another. Law and reality dictate that such units will not sit down and work out agreements on which will produce or propose what.

When people criticize or attack a dummy group you can either laugh or cry. You laugh at this fool who doesn't know that the entity on whom she is heaping scorn or accusations doesn't exist. You cry because many of the individuals, companies, or other units enclosed within the dummy group are not guilty of what is being alleged but they are being smeared by someone unwilling or unable to make the distinctions required for intelligent discourse,

Hollywood is a geographical place and a state of mind. It is not a coordinated group of people deciding on policies, approaches, and content. There is no organized group making industry wide decisions so to talk about that happening is simply wrong and therefore stupid. Thus every time you hear someone say "Hollywood wants this...", "Hollywood doesn't have a sense of responsibility or...", "Hollywood advocates..." you know you are listening to someone who seemingly doesn't know what she is talking about and you need to ask yourself what it says about your intelligence that you are paying attention to this person. If you suspect or you're convinced that she knows what she is doing and is deliberately setting up straw men to attack, you have even more reason to question why you are giving her any attention except to counter her at every turn.

Movie producers and the Studios are looking for product that will make money. They select the films that they will make or finance based on their guess at what people will pay to see plus a number of films that are payoffs to stars, directors, and others who have accumulated those credit slips by making big money for the group and now are allowed to make their ego projects even though no one seriously believes those will do more than break even in the long run. As business decisions those investments and permissions are often prudent choices because they bind the money-making talent to the company for the other films they are likely to be part of and that are expected to be financial as well as artistic successes. No film is "Hollywood's". It is the product of a specific group of people and often would never have been made by any other group. It is not true to say that all those other people and companies somehow are responsible for this movie and therefore it is unfair to say it. Such a generalization shows a weak mind or someone intent on deceiving by generalizing a straw man. Neither is high caliber behavior.

The unity and the subdivision agreements exist mainly in the head of the speaker who wants to get some additional mileage out of a pattern she has spotted so that she has something to say. The magazine writer notes that three films scheduled for release this fall (out of perhaps sixty total) include a character who loses financial support for a cherished project and is left to scramble for funds. She then informs us that this is the latest hot idea that Hollywood is pushing. That the films were given the green light months apart and in closed meetings of the various production companies is simply ignored since it would undermine the point she has decided to claim. The fact that in one case it is scholarship money, in the second an inheritance that turns out to be less than anticipated, and the third is the result of a corporate bankruptcy so the cases have only the most tenuous resemblance to one another is also sidestepped. "They have a common theme" is her trumpet call. That assertion justifies her filling half a page with blabber about this trend that she has fabricated and is what drives the rest of the article without appearing in so many words on the page.

In a comparable case, there are those who believe, or at least say, that all churches that call themselves Christian are parts of a single entity. They claim that therefore all Christians support and are responsible for every outrageous proposal or position taken by any far out of the main-stream preacher anywhere, whatever her denomination. Do you agree? Those who oppose the group (or religion in general) may claim so, but most people, when they make the effort to consider the realities of life, will separate the individual from the group she represents. In the same way they won't buy into any claims that everyone in law enforcement or the military or various other groupings all think and operate in lockstep.

Washington D.C. (and any nation's capital) has the distinction of being the regional city or location that routinely attracts absurd, untrue, and unfair generalizations about the people in government jobs the way that porch lights draw bugs on a summer night. "The Press" and "the news media" are big attractors as well as dummy group utilizers.

Perhaps these cases are less than critical to social life because usually the observations and objections are being made by persons with a fairly obvious agenda which should put most alert people on guard, but they still cause a lot of confusion and even harm because not everyone is smart enough or paying enough attention not to be taken in.

Why are these unreal unities alleged? Some of the that-group-is-guilty misrepresentations are deliberate distortions or slants; some are inevitable losses of exactness accepted in the name of simplifying; others are innocent details in cases where the speaker is not much concerned with this topic but feels she must scurry across this terrain in order to get to the things she really wants to make points about.

Often these accusations are made precisely with the expectation that their supposed existence will frighten, anger, or fascinate those who cannot or do not think well for themselves. If you want to make a point about something that is included in a film to a group of lawyers, you specify the company and other details because this audience likely won't let you get away with looser references. On the other hand if you want the blue-haired ladies with more money than sense to send you their dollars to support your lavish lifestyle you decry and condemn "soulless Hollywood" and the "mongers of sin". These pious donors won't question except to ask if you will take a personal check after their social security payment has arrived. The evidence all around us suggests that, at least in America, it is very hard for you to stay poor if you appeal for help "to do the work of the Lord", whatever you choose to apply that label to.

Few of us can resist the temptation to recruit masses of people to our side in a debate or controversy even when we know this is stretching the facts as we know them. How often have you asserted that "Most people think..." or some variant on it to bolster your position without anything more that a "feeling" or "a sense of the common mind" that this is so based on the views of two or three individual? When the other side does the same thing there's a temptation to demand more substantial proof of their assertions, some objective polling or the like, but you recognize that with the same kind of evidence required of you your claims will be as shakily supported as your opponent's the common result is that both sides accept the unspoken compromise of making claims and letting it go at that. Let the audience (who are almost always the ones we hope to influence or convince, not the opponents themselves) draw their conclusions based on their prejudices or the impact of your clever turn of phrase or your claim that someone they admire is a co-defender of your position since by that point a descent into facts which might lead to an obvious need to correct yourself will be too dangerous to your position.

Another advantage of supposedly quoting "the people" or some such dummy group is that they never make unified statements (since they can't). Consequently, with little danger of being caught out, you can put any words you want into their mouths. You take any poll result and make it a statement of where "the people" stand, no matter how many other polls show something quite different. You tell people that based on your experience in dealing with a variety of people you have the *sense* that the masses think this, that, or something else. "From your reading" you get the *impression* that such and such is a widely held attitude (although if you read more widely you might not think so). Seldom will you be challenged to say how many you talked to or to demonstrate that those are in any way a representative sample of the population to which this position is being attributed. If that were commonly done the strategy wouldn't be used as often.

The easiest case is when you simply blandly assert every time you make a public statement that "the American people" think or want what you are saying. If it is your news conference or one you can easily walk away from then no one is allowed to disagree or to ask unapproved in advance questions. You always have places that you have to be and people you have to see which allows you the speaker to control the event since the reporters need something to report and quotes are the easiest way for them to fill airtime. You may not be able to control the reactions as much as you would like, but you are able to shape the news to a greater degree than you could in a more open situation.

Do yourself a favor and condition yourself that any and every time you or someone else slips into a dummy group generalization you think, or better say aloud, "sloppy thinking leads to in sloppy talk". You will still do it from time to time yourself but you'll catch yourself more often. You'll also semi-automatically reject what the other says using those false claims too. This is one of those slippery slope things - in this case the chute is the one to unfair and less effective persuasion.

Frequently there are complaints that the bad actions of just a few individuals (whether cops on the take, military officers sexually harassing soldiers, lawyers arranging to buy a jury for a mobster – the shelves in the history sections of our libraries sag under the documentation of the many instances) make the whole group look bad and, to a degree, they should. The bad egg among them is not something the collective is responsible for unless the group (through its leadership) oppose outside supervision or regulation insisting they don't need that, they will police themselves. However, when they take that stance - and the membership agrees - and then they collectively fail to do the job effectively they are collectively responsible even if most of them members have no direct involvement in that. When groups organize to the point of becoming legal entities they take on a life of their own. People develop cancer because some of their cells malfunction while the majority continue to operate as they should; groups can become corrupted while most of the members continue to do what they should and without approving of the actions of the few. How many of them knew, or should have known, that the bad stuff was happening but kept quiet and did nothing to stop it is always a major concern. That, probably more than the focal bad stuff, is what erodes the public's confidence in and admiration for the group. Citizens validly wonder and worry about how far the us-versus-them mentality extends within groups like their local police force.

Note the interesting fact that a few individuals who are doing an exceptionally good job have much less effect on the image of the group overall. They are praised more as individuals than as representatives of the group. Is this accurate? Is it appropriate? I specifically avoid asking if it is right because that introduces a group of largely irresolvable questions related to what *right* means in a case like this.

Is it an accurate to say that the bad ones attract more attention than the good? I think so but I have no scientific data to prove it. Is it appropriate if true? I think so because most of us tend to focus on groups in terms of their effects on us. We ask whether they are doing their job or are creating problems. Especially we wonder and worry whether they are ripping the rest of us off. These are the questions that history has taught us to ask. If there are problem members of the group, they are probably harming us as well as damaging the group, at least to the degree of lowering our level of approval of the collective behavior.

As long as there are no recognized "defective" members in a group it stands up to scrutiny; it is what it advertised itself as being. We don't give special praise to those who do what they are supposed to do; we reserve the special accolades for those who do more than the basics. Living up to your professed or advertised performance level is a basic obligation, not a cause for special rejoicing. It makes sense that in evaluating any group we would compare their actual performance with the level that they promised or accepted a contract to deliver. Anything less is failure to deliver and is not worthy of praise; anything more is nice but not essential. If a higher level of performance were essential we would set that as the minimum level, not something less.

Like cells in our own bodies, members of a group work must as individuals but by cooperation and various degrees of coordination they achieve a higher level of activity than a smaller or less organized number could. We can either focus our attention on the overall level of activity or the individual level. They are going on simultaneously and the one is essential to be other, but they have differences. If a few cells are inactive, the organ will often still function but it is less efficient. If a few cells turn malignant, they can soon destroy the whole body. A few cells that are performing especially well have little effect on the overall impact.

When we organize a group like an army we have to be realistic in establishing our expectations. We must be able to predict the minimum sustainable performance level in order to predict with any reasonable confidence whether this group can do what needs to be done. A group of illiterates won't be able to check credentials and shipping invoices at a border and a group of tone deaf persons should not be assigned as music critics.

Therefore we establish minimum standards of performance for applicants for our groups, minimums that aim to assure that the job will be done. Any performance less than that and the job is not being done and we owe it to ourselves to keep an eye open for that so we can correct the situation as quickly as possible. Therefore we focus on detecting defectives and we recognize that the more of them there are in the group, the less effective it is in doing the job it was assigned or took on itself to.

We ourselves recognize that we seldom view groups as masses of indistinguishable units. We are always looking for the individuals, the faces in the uniforms, the approachable and identifiable. You may stand in awe of an army on the march but you cannot identify with it. You identify and therefore empathize or otherwise emotionally interact with specific soldiers. In that way you may decide you want to be part of a party in the local park but you look to the individual participants for the clues you need about what to wear, how to act, and what to expect.

Some failures of groups are group failures rather than just failures of members within a group. These are the cases where those with official or accepted supervisory and leadership collectively fail by advocating or allowing inappropriate behaviors within the ranks. These officers don't have to participate, they only have to tolerate. Part of group reality is that inevitably there is a power structure evolved and a few individuals are ceded power to decide what is acceptable behavior for the whole group. This power brings with it two obligations. One is to assure that the agreed upon performance goals are achieved; the other is to discipline those who deviate from the agreed upon limits of behavior so that those few don't undermine either the overall goals or the groups' self or public image. By accepting those positions the officers take on the responsibility to see that members do the right thing and don't do the wrong thing.

Failure on either part constitutes group failure if it is tolerated by an effective majority of the leaders. Some or even many of the members may be toeing the line, but the group as a functional unit is failing to meet its obligations. Therefore the group is more than the individuals, but the individuals contribute to and collectively shape the group. This argues that within a group each member must accept some responsibility for the others' performance in addition to his or her own.

No one likes to be the one who reports another member's breach of conduct, but failing to do that makes you individually even more responsible for the tarnishing of the group image that may result. It also means you accept that this person's actions are realistically diminishing the effect of your own actions within the collective setting. So you insult yourself at two levels by tolerating less than minimum performance by any other member of the group.

No group is going to succeed for long without mechanisms for dealing with accusations of failure by its members. It will be too obvious to too many too quickly that the group is a collectivity out of control. Failure of those in the officer positions to deal effectively with problem members is a prime cause of group failure. A major reason for the organizational structures accepted by the membership was to keep intramural discipline restrained, since any group without such a framework will soon tear itself apart as this member (and her allies) fights with that one (and her allies) to restrain certain behaviors. Applicants to the group agree, at least tacitly, that disciplining of themselves and other members is delegated to the officers and their own hands are tied to a greater or lesser degree although they may call for changes.

We should consider the difference between *Group Think* and thinking about groups. This is a convenient example of how similarity in the descriptive terms might lead to the thought that they are more similar than they are. Since you can be a member of a group without losing your personal identity, there are some inherent stumbling blocks in talking and thinking about groups. You may be a member of a group but unless you are the group's "poster person" in the public mind, you alone don't determine its image. You also do not automatically approve of and support the details of every action or position that any or many of the members embrace simply by becoming a member.

Group think is usually taken to mean that the individuals do agree to certain actions or attitudes because the other group members signal that they do. This is an abdication of the proper responsibility to think, evaluate, and make decisions yourself that you make because you agree at some level to "follow the crowd" and let the group organizers (leaders is only sometimes the appropriate term in such cases) decide for you. This is most often at most a semi-conscious decision, more often a matter of not bothering to focus on the subject and opting to follow the path of least resistance rather than a deliberate choice, but that doesn't make it less effective for the organizer or the organized. Those who strongly embrace this mode tend to be or to become zealots for whatever cause is involved and can be dangerous to everyone else. It is an appropriate caution to think of Nazi or North Korean troops in lockstep parade as images of the far end of the path when group think becomes dominant in a society.

Facts. Facts. Who has the facts? In our common speech facts are taken to be true and valid statements of what and how things are in reality. And therein lies the problem because a great many of the "facts" that get tossed around in conversation and arguments are not true or are not valid and sometimes are not even about real stuff. Sorting out the real facts is a nuisance and often rather frustrating but it is also an every day, on-going necessity.

If you are honest with yourself you will probably easily remember some recent conversations, especially those of a confrontational nature, in which you tossed out some suspect-to-outright-imaginary "facts" to support your position. Those were claims you were not at all sure were accurately stated, but were comfortably sure that the others wouldn't know enough about to contradict or even question. Some may have been true but they didn't actually apply to the point you were making yet you tried to force them in there anyway by glossing over the details and trying to leave the impression that you had actually made a sound argument but didn't want to dwell on it and rub it in. Or you may have manufactured some claims out of thin air, probably with a vague recollection of having read "something like that", but where you literally picked out some numbers or details that you thought sounded reasonable and which reinforced your position but which you knew would be unverifiable and probably unquestioned. If even you have done, and probably still do, such things it can't be too shocking to realize that others also do them.

Here's an example of a fact that on examination isn't at all when it seems to be when briefly mentioned. We all know only too well how readily a few words taken out of context can be trumpeted as a speaker's position when an honest reading of what was said won't support that interpretation but might seem irresistible to some partisan operative. I came across a quote attributed to President Ronald Reagan where he said, "Facts are stupid things." Out of curiosity to understand the context of the comment I went to his recorded speech to the 1988 Republican National Convention (the reference conveniently and appropriately supplied by the author who included the quote in his book).

In the text of the speech I learned that Reagan did indeed speak those words - apparently by mistake. In his prepared speech he quoted

John Adams saying, "Facts are stubborn things." He repeated that quote as a theme in the next four paragraphs of his speech. Between the second and third paragraphs the record of what he said indicates that he said, "Facts are stupid things - stubborn things, I should say." He makes no further comments about facts being stupid but repeats the quote from John Adams in the next two paragraphs of his address before he goes off in a different direction. So did he say the words? Yes. There is no attempt to hide or dispute that. Did he mean to say those words? In my opinion (and I'm not his fan or defender) he didn't, he simply misspoke. I suspect that an audio recording of the speech would make that even clearer. If he meant to say it I believe he would have said more to flesh out and defend his position but he wasted not another word on it. The moral of the story is to wait a few days until the after-flak settles before you accept what was uttered as what was actually said and then as what was meant by the speaker.

It is distressing how easily statistics and data can mislead us. In a TV news report it was stated that only 9% of those over 65 are poor, but 21% of children are. Among other questions these numbers raise is, Are these in the same families? If so, the data tells us something about age distributions but little about poverty; if not, it still may not tell us much of anything useful.

Adding numbers to a statement turns out to be a big deal because that mention of a measurement almost automatically gives the whole point greater impact and credibility to many people. In his book *Anti-Intellectualism in American Life*, Richard Hofstadter writes, "The American mind seems extremely vulnerable to the belief that any alleged knowledge which can be expressed in figures is in fact as final and exact as the figures in which it is expressed."

In his 2010 book *Proofiness: The Dark Arts of Mathematical Deception*, Charles Seife defines *proofiness* as, "the art of using bogus mathematical arguments to prove something that you know in your heart is true - even when it's not." In the book he emphasizes that "...numbers can be a powerful weapon. In skillful hands, phony data, bogus statistics, and bad mathematics can make the most fanciful idea, the most outrageous falsehood seem true. They can be used to bludgeon enemies, to destroy critics, and to squelch debate."

Proofiness can be pulled off using a variety of techniques like creating meaningless statistics or misleading charts or graphs to sell a claim. One subtle form of proofiness is *disestimation* is in which we are led to trust a measurement beyond the point where it should be trusted. It happens when we take a number too literally, understating or ignoring the uncertainties that surround it. This gives the number the appearance or aura of greater truthfulness and precision than it deserves. It dresses it up as absolute fact instead of the error-prone estimate it is. Distorting the numbers this way by ignoring their inherent limitations turns them into falsehoods.

In some cases the trick used is to make up scientific-sounding measurements that are distorted or even outright fabricated out of hot air. In other cases what are expected to be valid estimates are distorted to fit someone's agenda. There are for instance always those with a vested interest in making the size of the crowd attending a public event seem large to the many who weren't there as well as to those trapped in a corner by the crush of the gathering where they have no objective feel for and no wider range view of how big the group really is because they can't see for any distance.

Presenting only a select sample of the available data to emphasize what favors your view while underplaying the problems or dissenting facts, putting the data items in the wrong contexts, comparing apples and marmalade, and confidently presenting measurement figures for things like intelligence that are only poorly defined so any measurements of them should be seriously questioned and doubted are all common manipulations.

Are reporters or commentators a valid unofficial class of experts sorting things out for the masses? If so shouldn't they be up front about that fact so that they will do the job well and expect to be held fully responsible for that job? An expert (i.e., anyone who has tried to search out and organize as much information and as many informed opinions and projections as feasible) cannot objectively present the facts in the majority of cases that have any real and substantial consequences. There are always pros and cons - and which of those are which depends on your assumptions, prejudices, vested interests, and other factors.

An important reason that humans have developed societies is so that the collective can attend to many of the essential details and allow each individual to focus on a subset of those. Put yourself in the place of an animal of a species with little or no obvious social structure (a hard species to name now that we know more about the lives of so many species). The true lone tiger or polar bear? I can't think of a vegetarian mammal that has so little social structure and interaction. Maybe the giant panda? Although when confined by man they seem to be okay in groups at least when young. Spiders? Snakes? Octopuses?

As such a solitary animal you must stay alert about and make all the decisions about everything important to your survival. Where can you be safe with minimal risk from the weather, predators, and other natural dangers both while you are awake and asleep? Where can you find enough food? What places or other animals must you avoid because they are too dangerous for you – except when you must deal with those risks to avoid bigger or more imminent ones? Living like that you can't think beyond tomorrow, concern yourself with art or anything that is not essential, or become a specialist (unless that specialty means adapting to a place and conditions where others species cannot survive). It is actually hard for most of us to imagine this situation because as soon as we make ourselves the subject, we automatically think of a member of a group doing at least some sharing of the tasks and responsibilities. Cavemen lived in groups. Truly solitary hermits have always been rare and could only adapt that life style once there were adults. For anyone younger to survive entirely alone would strain the odds of extreme good luck that would be required.

Perfect and ideal are seldom available. The skill for contributing to the maximum to a group and its collective functions is the weighing of pros and cons, the recognition of what could be done differently and the near and longer term consequences of doing that, and what is the least damaging or problematic of the possible choices. Including the choice of doing nothing.

Third best by some criteria may be the first and best choice by others so we should resist getting into the blinders of conditional ratings.

It says a lot about all those concerned that the masters of political manipulation are routinely at least credited for their apparent successes by some in the mainstream media and publicly praised by the operatives who implement their schemes to get enough people to support them (usually with their votes) or to agree to not oppose them (by not voting or by not speaking out publicly against them). Nonetheless year after year, election after election, they continue to use variations on the same strategies to succeed even as many of those who let themselves be used by them regularly complain about those strategies which they have observed and even had explained in detail but those who listened still let those manipulators work against themselves.

When confronted with unanswerable questions, be cautious. The unanswerableness of the questions, like those on the envelope of a subscription solicitation for a publication that purports to get below the camouflage and to the facts, lies in the statements themselves. They say too little to be meaningful because the printed questions mean any of several different things depending on what and how much you read into them. Taken at face value any answer to the questions is simultaneously both correct and incorrect depending simply on who is playing authority and deciding what the phrases do and don't mean to allow that answer.

Consider two of the questions posed on the outside of that envelope. True or false? Plutonium is the most toxic substance known. True: it is the most deadly chemical in that a very small amount, a few pounds evenly distributed among the human lungs of the world would kill the entire human population via lung cancer or fibrosis. False: if you take toxic to mean it is a fast-acting poison that will cause death within minutes, hours, or a few days. A lot of other materials will kill you faster and are more certain to do so if you are exposed to them. The statement is also false if you interpret the question to mean "Plutonium is the lethal material currently adversely affecting the largest number of people worldwide."

True or False? Minimum wage laws help minorities and the poor. True, if we are comparing the conditions of those in the bottom levels of the job market with and without such laws on the books. False, according to this publication, because "Every time the Federal minimum wage has been raised, Black teenage unemployment has jumped, tripling since WWII. Note first that this statement has shifted the consideration from the advantage of minimum wages to job opportunities, something these laws do not control. Only those determined to exploit the poor for their own financial benefit control those. Also note that the tripling of Black teenage unemployment cited doesn't consider the population increases and shifts, which are substantial, or the deficiencies of our tabulation of such unemployment figures in earlier decades. So is that a fact?

We are told by way of recommendation that articles from this publication have been reprinted in the *Congressional Record*. That may sound impressive if you don't know that any member of Congress can have essentially anything inserted into the *Congressional Record*. Once you know that, the boast sounds rather empty because it may well mean simply that some congressman liked the article because it supported some point he was making or had it inserted as a favor to someone he wanted to please. If you check what all gets printed in the *Congressional Record*, the honor and significance of being included there seems very much reduced.

I also noted that the publisher of this magazine in his invitation to subscribe tells us that, "Our editors respect your intelligence, they don't expect you to take things on faith." This after he's told you that all five statements on the envelope are false without giving any explanation of that assertion for two of the five and playing the kinds of word games noted above with the other three. So the only thing the reader can do is to accept on faith his assurance that the statements are false - or laugh and drop the thing into the trash as I did.

One constant communications problem area is the differences between my technical and qualified definition versus your loose and possibly colloquial definition. This seems to be a special problem for news reporters. Probably the focus on controversy and scaring the audience to get them to tune in that many of us judge to be major guiding factors in much media coverage and presentation is behind this but that is not my focus here. I encourage you to think about it though.

Is the economic climate improving? Government statistics, which have known and established criteria even if not everyone likes those, may say the numbers indicate yes but the news anchor delivering the report is pretty close to certain to simply imply that those are at least meaningless, if not a deliberate misrepresentation, because he can show you people who are still in dire straits.

A typical example would be the question, Are we in a recession? If the news anchor asks the question but doesn't specify the definition that his report will use for a recession to let us know from the start whether he is talking technical economics or loosely applied street term you know going in that the report is worthless because it is freely and deliberately mixing orangutans and oranges to amuse you and maybe let you think you know the state of the economy. In the context of that news report, does effectively say that "any condition less than full prosperity for every adult in the country means we are indeed in a recession" make the grade as factual? The professionals may say that the current state of the economy don't fit within the technical definition so we are not in a recession. The guy on the street looking for work may say he doesn't see already in place what he thought should have happened if we were in good economic shape so we must be in whatever name was mentioned that sounded like it meant that things aren't in tiptop shape.

Does presenting those two views answer the question or only add to the confusion? Would it make more sense to you as a general citizen, not an economist, to have it all asked as separate questions with different answers without seeming to suggest they have equal weight and reality? In this case the news is that there is confusion and disagreement and this report has done nothing to help clarify the situation.

It is pretty evident that the news people are always looking to "balance" the news and therefore always strive to include some comment from someone (the *who* often doesn't seem to be of that much concern to them) who opposes or denies the claims or the seeming implication of the basic news item. Are you one of those like me that reacts to some reporter saying, "but not everyone agrees with that" by shouting out a loud and jeering "Who but news reporters thinks everybody agrees about anything?" Good for you if you do that. You get to vent a bit and set a good example for everyone within earshot at the same time.

In an article in *Harper's Magazine* in 2012 John Lukacs writes, "The histories of words amount to more than the evolution of language; words are both causes and effects, origins and results of thinking, including political thinking." Our words are the basis of our official communication. We may get across some ideas with gestures, facial expressions, or grunts, but those can't be written down (usually only someone's interpretation of what was meant or intended is recorded or reported) so I am prepared to argue that too often the words we use complicate things. Words have definitions, although those are seldom carved in stone for long in a living language. That is unfortunate for exactitude, but convenient for getting by with more efficient sized vocabularies, except perhaps for very technical areas, if even there. Those definitions have some looseness about them and that wiggle-room is often what sets up the misunderstandings and inadvertent or intentional distortions of what is meant by a particular word or phrase in this particular situation. The screaming frustration is that you don't find out who will misunderstand or twist your words until they've done so. Yet if you had to make your oral statements about less than critical matters with all the qualifications and specifics right at the start, nothing would get done because the hearers would get tired of listening. It is a bit easier for material in print, electronic or ink, but only a bit.

Considering the time and effort that often goes into preparing the statements to be made public by politicians and industry spokespersons, is it unreasonable to expect the speakers or their consultants or handlers to find someone to preview the statement and point out the few words or phrases most likely to be misunderstood or not properly understood and then carefully rephrase the text to eliminate or clarify those points before the statements are made public? Not doing that with prepared and vetted statements makes it seem suspiciously like the confusion is intended. Why the person or group might do that is wide open for speculation and reaction by you - which is as it should be but probably not what they wanted.

The current mode of viewing all political meetings and statements as battles with declared winners and losers is big on trying to slant the opinions of others but a big loser in any sincere attempt to help people get a fair and honest idea of what is happening. Who won the debate? If you don't know that that is a meaningless question because, unless there was some actual mechanism in place for keeping score, there are only opinions and to present those as more than that is deliberate deception even if it is done with the intent of "simplifying the news", you get misled. If you think about its effect, the strategy of reducing the news to declarations of winners or losers (which of course will depend on what news source you are looking at) means making it more likely that the audience can be persuaded that they know how to judge the event since they didn't have to do any mental work to arrive at the answer that someone intended them to swallow whole (although of course this second part isn't said out loud). Gasp! Silent expression of shock at that idea. Who can imagine anything like that in a political discussion! Did the president win or lose with his speech to some group? Huh? Such declarations by anyone, whether news employee, political party or industry flak, or private enthusiast at the barbecue pit, deserve to be laughed at with disdain for his air-headedness. Even more so when he delivers that judgment with a smirk and/or when it seems clear he expects to shape your thinking using that kind of statement as his tools.

What is the useful information in a news report that a candidate "won" a state's primary election when by the mechanism used by that state to allot convention delegates based on the election results he gets no more delegates that his opponent? It is highly likely though that *he won* was the headline bit, the rest of the stuff mumbled after many had already stopped listening. Was that in fact what was intended to happen? Who authorized or approved that headline? Discuss.

How often have you heard a pundit or news reporter specify the criteria he is using when talking on air or in print about such victories and defeats? Note that there are no official, or even generally agreed upon, check lists of factors to validate claims for what *win* or *lose* means in that case and context unless there were ballots of some sort counted. It would be revealing to secretly listen in on the news staff conferences about why they decided to go with a particular topic in a particular way on that day. What were their guiding principles? Unfortunately if we ask them to tell us that we can't be certain of the completeness or the honesty of the answers.

Can we make the news people and pundits do a more accurate job? Not likely since in many cases their employers want the distorted messages dispersed as part of their political agenda. (Can you spell Rupert Murdock and *Fox News*?) That means, to a degree (and people can and will argue how big a degree until the proverbial cows come home), you can't pressure them by turning off their shows or by not buying the products of their sponsors as you sometimes can with backers who are only concerned about the ratings (and their translation into dollars), not a political agenda that is more important that money to the owners.

There are occasional conspicuous exceptions to my generalization here and I am happy to see them. Each successful pressuring of sponsors and show airers that evokes an apology (no matter how obviously reluctant and of questionable sincerity) is a lesson to the public that the yowlers can sometimes be countered and this is one effective way to do that. Should we pity the pundit whose financial success depends on provoking talk about him when that talk turns against him? Nah, we should use what tools we have to insist that people like that be kept on short leashes. Not censored by keeping them off the airwaves, but with strings attached that lead clearly and directly to those who are responsible for making their voices widely heard.

You can have some impact by publicly actively dismissing those sources as tainted and unreliable when they come up in conversation, but don't expect to have a big short-term effect. That doesn't mean you shouldn't sow those seeds of dissent even if the other person won't promptly change his position. He may still do so quietly later as a result or he is at least now thinking about the matter with more attention. Recognize that after that though the minions of the distorters will see you with a target on your back, so be aware of that and ready to challenge them and force them to be sneakier and sneakier, which will influence the opinions of others against them, and therefore what influence they have.

Only the pathological few like, or have much stomach for supporting, sneaks and exposed distorters.

Would things improve if we could somehow pressure the talking heads to always define the terms they spout? Probably to a degree, yes. The on-going problem is that it doesn't seem possible to exert that pressure. Plus, of course, as soon as an official listing of definitions for terms that can be used in media presentations is proposed the massive effort to build in the distortions to those definitions would begin. If we should have learned anything by now it is that the moneyed interests always have an outsized impact on any rules or regulations that finally become official. They can to an often distressing degree control the legislated rules but they can only try to control the citizens by tweaking those rules when enough people are lulled into believing that having an official rule book that the potential abusers solemnly promise to abide by (as long as it doesn't have legal teeth) means they don't have to pay as much close attention to the statements anymore.

It makes good sense to focus on and evaluate the sources from which you are abstracting the information you are using to decide what is happening to and around you, why, and what the possible consequences are in this consideration. To a substantial degree (which means more than some degree without putting a numerical value on it) your decisions can only be as good as your sources of information (in the broad sense) allow. Much of this we can and often do more or less automatically so my point is simply to encourage us all to do it more consciously so that degree of being properly critical becomes even more routine. There is always a danger that if we start to do anything automatically it will become less deliberate and focused and thus less effective.

In a general way we can group our sources of information into three categories: our gut reactions; our personal experiences; and the various outside-me sources. Then those can be subdivided into a variety of schematics.

You have some basic and innate feedback info from your body that we often call your gut reactions even though often their most notable element is the little man in your head who whispers to you that he's wary of this person or idea but not ready to spell out why, and he also likes this other idea without giving you a detailed analysis of why. These are aspects of our awareness that most of us gradually develop some awareness of and then, based on our experience when they were helpful, decide how much weight to give in analyzing situations. As behavioral scientists devise more refined experiments, they are showing more and more that there is an aspect of our neural functioning (still poorly understood in detail but becoming more so all the time) that makes those subconscious reactions a substantial contribution to our conscious decisions.

What the experiments seem to show is that your built-in and somewhat automatic reaction is a valid and important factor to include in deciding what to do or not do. It seems prudent to always consider your gut reaction to a situation (if you detect such a reaction) and factor it in, but not to operate entirely on that basis. The latter restraint is because in many social and technical situations we may recognize (in part due to our gut reaction) that there are dangers or doubts but if we already know that from other sources anyway and feel it necessary or okay to accept some risk for what we guesstimate will be the more likely and big benefits, we regularly decide to act in spite of the cautions. We opt to proceed with caution in spite of them, not to totally ignore them. A strongly negative gut reaction deserves special attention. You may decide to act against its warning but you are at least more wary and possibly can minimize any negatives if you react in time.

Beyond those seemingly built-in screening and advisory reactions, we depend on experience to guide our decisions. This large body of information includes all that you learned, consciously or unconsciously, from everything you have been through. All the lessons from your parents' examples and words, from reading or various entertainment and education media, and in formal class situations. Plus what you picked up from observing other people and situations, near and far; what you heard in conversations; what you felt when you ate the food that didn't smell quite right but you ate it anyway; what you thought and felt when without warning you got hit by the stream of water from a hose; or your varied reactions when you went down a sliding board for the first time. You cataloged and stored those impressions as memories, now you scan those catalog headings for any relevant bits with each new experience.

We go to theme parks or to learning centers to experience new sensations for the thrill of the moment and the benefits of having a more diverse experience background but survival, as genetically programmed into us plus whatever other evolutionary factors are involved, argues for preferring the known and expected most of the time. Being forced to live in a constantly unpredictable world would strain us enormously and would make any level of function beyond basic survival somewhere between unlikely and guaranteed impossible. Culture (a bit of leisure or at least periods of reduced anxiety from fear) only becomes possible when we get familiar enough with our local environment that we feel we can predict the range of things that can and might happen and we feel we are prepared to deal with those problems.

When, as is often the case, we must get essential information from others there are a few routine questions we should ask about those sources. Here again we often do this automatically but the more often we focus on what we are doing, the more likely we are to hesitate and do it more consciously but still automatically enough not to disrupt things too much at least at first whenever we are faced with a matter of substance. Several considerations are routinely examined and it is useful to double-check them in any case where they might be of special weight.

What are your sources for this information? It is often surprising but enlightening to realize that we don't remember where we picked up certain attitudes or bits of information that we consider to be "facts". This is a caution flag. It means that, depending on how major the topic is to you or the common good, you should make an appropriate effort to verify or validate the information from neutral or trusted sources. Maybe the info is as good as is available; maybe it is outdated, prejudiced, or flawed because you misunderstood it when you first encountered it, or maybe you are not remembering it accurately. If the topic is an important one, it is worth making the effort to check your facts before you foul up the decision-making process or make a fool of yourself.

How reliable are your inputs? If your information sources are largely or totally limited to a single individual or collective entity, you would want to try to verify their credentials from neutral or trusted sources. Among other things, consider where you were when you meet the source and got information from him? How reliable is the guy who accosted you and everyone else who would stop and listen on the street to push his claims? Is someone you met at a clearly partisan gathering a safely reliable source? But nothing of real consequence is easy, so you must start by deciding what credential would be meaningful in this case, based on whatever information and criteria you are comfortable with. Then you need to determine how to reliably verify the person's claim of having particular credentials since it is easy (and a standard ruse) to claim to have such official vetting and approval without actually having them.

Especially in short-term fast action cases it's expected and proven again and again that making false claims often lets you have more impact in the short-term but then after the official decisions are made it is almost unheard of for those to be altered or reversed when it becomes clear and proven that lies and distortions were a major factor. Plus there is seldom any penalty other than a few *tsk tsks* for those who made the false claims or those who benefitted from the distortion. Sadly, this is what political consultants depend on and how they make their money and too often have the effects they are hired to produce.

It may be worth your while to spend a bit of time and energy winnowing through the mass of claims and counter-claims to identify a roster of sources you are usually willing to trust to guide you in checking the credentials, claims, and even actual identity of sources. This has become vastly more important in the age of the Internet because of the massive increase in claims, information, and disinformation, whether deliberate or inadvertent. Especially when much of the material is anonymous and traceable only by those with time and hacker skills to devote to that rather than material that is offered by anyone ready to be identified, to reveal his sources, and to accept responsibility for it. At least the Internet facilitates the searching for other views even though the ultimate decisions about which sites to trust is yours and often not an easy call. It is easier than ever before to begin to begin the process of learning about almost anything when you have a search engine collect a long list of places with some reference or relevance to the subject for you. More computer-searchable public records are becoming easily available all the time. Use the resources.

One definite advantage is when your source can name or identify his own sources and refer you to material from those in print or other-wise stored and available that you can check out to learn more about a topic of interest or to get new ideas about the possibilities of what you already know or have heard of but haven't found useful information about. Even better if there are others that you know and trust enough to give you their opinion about the reliability of this source. Be cautious about asking only those individuals that the source suggests you ask about him though if you aren't able to do that checking through other trusted or neutral sources. That's not being untrusting, it's common sense. Con men and liars often work with accomplices because that multiplies their success rate.

When you examine your information base it is important for you to consider as honestly as you can whether and to what degree your ego is involved in a matter. That is a warning flag signaling that you may be consciously or unconsciously overlooking or overemphasizing some sources or facts and that you need to be more objective if you want to be realistic and safe.

Be skeptical, but there is seldom a need to automatically and overtly reject a source or the information offered there unless you feel that the source is pushing their claims too hard and therefore making their honesty and impartiality suspect.

The same communication methods and avenues are the basis of the parallel channels of advertising - those messages that are intended to sell us products, and those that are intended to dispense ideas, attitudes, and information. Both types involve persuasion but in sales the focus is largely limited to the product while the other type want to influence our attitudes and behavior beyond strictly economic considerations. Sales advertising is aimed at making you aware of a product and convincing you that you want or need to purchase that even though you may not have realized that until now. This calls for a minimum of information and that with a focus on subtle or blatant emotional (in the broad sense) persuasion, much of it actually intended to downplay and distract you from thinking about the facts and rational factors and in favor of the fantastical and imaginative.

Informational advertising wants you to know about some topic in order to help shape your decision about whether to engage in or avoid certain behaviors (like drinking, smoking, and taking recreational drugs) or about which of several competing candidates or policies to support or oppose when you go to the polls or however you will express your opinion about those things. It is important to recognize that there are those parallel paths of selling and shaping and to adjust your expectations accordingly.

When the political ads are presented tarted up with the same bells and whistles as those trying to sell you snack foods you are on notice that those behind them have little respect for your intelligence but figure they know how to push your buttons and get you to react the way they want and that you won't do more than whine about it later when you are paying the price for your poor decisions.

A sobering reminder that the conclusions accepted as facts today based on published research may not hold up over time is the review study "Deterrence and the Death Penalty" published in 2012 by the U.S. National Research Council. They examined dozens of studies published after 1976 (when the U.S. lifted a four year-ban on capital punishment) that examined whether the threat of the death penalty discourages potential murderers. The report concluded that we can't learn anything reliable about the focus question from that thirty years of studies because each of the studies either didn't take important factors into account, made unwarranted assumptions that skewed the conclusions, or had other significant defects. The government officials who made hard decisions during those years appropriately relied on the studies to guide them. Unfortunately, apparently no one with sufficient clout to be noticed examined the proposed setups of the studies, spotted the flaws, and said that as designed the studies wouldn't tell us what they claimed to be intended to. "Facts" that are based on judgments and sincere educated guesses have their place when decisions need to be made and can't be put off for long but they are always only "facts in progress" and need to be reviewed and adjusted as better information becomes available.

The fact that something is widely known doesn't mean it is widely understood. An important component of modern knowledge is scientific information but relatively few people in public life and out of it show much understanding of the limitations and qualifications that go with science.

The most general misconception is that scientific information is absolute, certain beyond doubt, and carved in stone. Nothing could be farther from the truth though. Scientific explanations are, simply but helpfully, educated guesses about how the natural world operates and therefore about the cause and effect relationships that exist. The practical result is that, for instance, we can understand the connections between various internal and environmental factors and some diseases and learn not to do the harmful things and thus avoid or even cure those diseases.

The uncertainty aspect of scientific information is confusing to those who want and (erroneously) expect definite and final answers to important questions. Any scientific study is a sample of the results of what happens in the natural world, but generalizing from there is full of pitfalls. The crux of the problem for most people is that one week they hear a report on the news that "Science" has determined that eating Substance A causes cancer. The next week it is Substance B so identified. A month later there is a report that eating Substance C protects you from cancer and A and B may not be so bad after all. The listeners throw up their hands, pull at their hair and foam at the mouth. Why can't these darned scientists make up their minds?

First there is the same problem with *Science* and *Scientists* that we considered in the last chapter. Science is an ever-growing body of knowledge about the natural world and processes, not an ownership or regulatory group. There is no single and official body of thinkers and researchers who all reach agreement on what and how matters should be investigated and how the results of experiments and clinical studies should be interpreted so there is no *Science* in the sense of group who own, control, or regulate what is studied but there is a science in the sense of the collective of those who investigate and amass information and knowledge using the scientific method. Science is only lots of scientists with their own judgments about the meaning and relevance of the data and no one with the ultimate say. Each individual, investigation team, or sponsoring institution does its own studies and publicizes its own results and interpretations - which is part of the established process for getting research grant money to do further studies. Therefore many diverse groups are tossing information and interpretations onto the table for public perusal. Since there is not and (from a practical point of view) could not be a single body that approves what may be made public, it is inevitable that there will be contradictions, duplications, and confusions.

A huge mass of scientific data is newly generated every day. The normal communications channels, especially to the general population, have limited editorial time and space and the majority of that audience have limited background or preparation for sifting through scientific or in fact any kind of complex technical language and information. As an inevitable result the information gets sorted and shrunk to fit, which means that all the important qualifications and special notes get thrown out and the whole is reduced to a headline that *says it all* even though that process in fact enormously distorts the information and interpretations. The practical reality is that (outside of a narrow field of those working on this particular problem) any study report is today's news only - and that for ten seconds. Next week something new is required by the news media editors to reassure or alarm, and once in a while to amuse, their audience. That guiding motivation further sorts out what the editors or producers decide are the juiciest of the studies first released each week to report on. You might notice that many news outlets will do their own reports on a report that sounds shocking, controversial, or scary. You get to decide if that's really the most important report of the week.

"Scientific" information means what is derived from and depends on experimental and observational evidence rather than statements of any unquestionable authority. The important and appropriate controlling authorities are things like: prescribed guidelines for doing that particular kind of experimental work which were developed after earlier work made it obvious how such studies done otherwise could easily lead to wrong conclusions that would result in harm; the correct ways to interpret the results of statistical analyses; and other similar good sense restrictions. Part of good scientific work is staying alert for how the procedures and materials can affect the results. The goal is to get the most neutral picture possible of how things happen to best understand how to predict and possibly regulate or alter the processes for useful purposes.

Scientists understand that scientific conclusions can always be questioned. That is a standard part of the methodology and is especially true for the assumptions built into the working definitions. All the conclusions are always subject to revision as new or better evidence or better explanations for the processes that we have observed are what happens in Nature are found. Many areas of science undergo such revisions regularly because we are still in the early stages of understanding the details of how to best explain the observed phenomena and new tools and technologies keep expanding the views that are available to us. What some new forms of microscopes and telescopes allow us to literally see today are staggering compared with the views of things at both ends of the size scale that we had a only few decades ago. And they do that usually without making the earlier views irrelevant or wrong - although the earlier interpretations and explanations for them might be. We can now simply see the bits and pieces better and therefore can explain how those interact and thus we can produce more precise explanations. Working parts that earlier we could at best guess must be in the closed boxes that were the smallest details we could see are now revealed so we can figure out how many types there are and how they interact with one another. It all makes a more exciting story and allows us to better understand why changing some factor can result in good or bad effects.

As Tom Siegfried, editor in chief of *Science News* wrote, "In the operas of science, the fat lady never sings". That is, scientific knowledge is never final and unquestionable, it is always open to challenge by better data or other interpretations of the conclusions. In one issue of his popular level science magazine in 2012 they reported on two cases where the original findings were overturned so that the records needed to be corrected. In one case a claim that a particular bacteria type are able to metabolize arsenic instead of phosphorus was contradicted by follow up studies that could not reproduce the reported results. Those studies confirmed that these bacteria can survive in the presence of usually toxic arsenic, but found no evidence that the species requires arsenic or that it builds it into its DNA as the original report suggested. As is often the case in science reports, the new critical results depend on interpretations as much as the original study did. Also there is a problem about the rejection of the report because some of the critics feel that the original paper made certain claims although not flat out but the original author denies making that claim which others chose to read into the text.

In the other case when one team using a different telescope looked at the spot where another team had reported finding the first exoplanet (one outside our solar system - in this case 25 light years away) in a photo taken several years earlier with the Hubble telescope, but the second team reported that since the tiny spot didn't act in one way that exoplanets are expected to, they doubt it actually is a planet. No one can say for certain but the original claim is now considered to be in doubt. Less certain and definite than it was considered to be for the time between the reports, but still a valid topic for further research.

Scientific "beliefs" are properly "so far uncontradicted or refuted claims based on some data and analysis". To scientists they are not "beliefs" in the same sense as those involved in religion or other areas (which those scientists may hold too for those areas) although they may sometimes use the term or feel they must tolerate its use even though they know it can lead to arguments and misunderstanding.

Even long-held assumptions based on initial observations and the failure to find contradicting evidence until now are overturned when there is better evidence. For instance, it was long accepted that humans are born with all the brain neurons or nerve cells that we will ever have and that from the start we make new dendrite connections between those but some are also dying so that our total number of brain neurons goes down as we age. More recently studies in different animal types, and using techniques not available to the earlier researchers, have found evidence that new neurons can be produced, likely as a routine and regular event in those species. So the detailed work moves on to closely examining human tissue for evidence of similar capacity in humans and a growing body of evidence that it does happen in us.

Another such long-held assumption is that those who develop type 1 diabetes (often called early onset type) stop making their own insulin within about a year of the start of detected symptoms. A recent study though found evidence that some of the cells that produce insulin survive in 80 percent of those diagnosed with the disease less than five years ago and even in 10 percent of those diagnosed more than thirty years ago. This is important news because it suggests there may be ways to cure the disease by learning how to induce the surviving cells to reproduce or at least how to protect them from further destruction by the mechanism that produce the disease.

Each new report put out today should be understood as a new piece presented as a part of a jigsaw puzzle. Maybe it will fit securely;

maybe it will be only an approximation of the shape required; maybe it will be recognized on closer examination to not fit the pattern at the spot it was proposed to fill after all.

It may take many years before the right bits of data to become available to clarify a matter that is beyond direct investigation because of the time factor. An example are white horses with leopard-like dark spots that are depicted in 25,000 years old cave wall paintings in France that were initially dismissed by some as symbolic or fanciful. Recent genetic analysis of horse types with long histories finds that the genes that produce such patterns in some modern horse breeds were present in the DNA recovered from horses of those ages. Genetic analysis of genes known to affect coat color in horses in thirty-one ancient horse fossils from various areas of the world found that six of the fossil animals from European sites had that gene

Scientific methods can't be applied to all areas of human interest to the same degree. In the strict sense, science is restricted to what can be measured and observed - even if at this time as much as can be seen are the end results, not the actual detailed mechanisms in operation. It is in getting better views into the detailed parts in action that new technologies are regularly changing.

Note that even much supposedly sacrosanct and above doubt or question (to the devotees) non-science stuff is in fact questioned and reinterpreted over time. Thus the libraries full of translations (often with what those close-in identify as significant changes in tone and color or meaning) and interpretations (whatever term is used to disguise that that is what they are) especially for those who claim that all the truth is there and needs no interpretation except their own.

The assertion is sometimes made that the more scientific we are, collectively and individually, the better off we will be. Expanded a bit for clarity, that belief is that the better we understand how the natural world works, the more likely it will be that we can deduce what is going wrong or is likely to do so in the future as we see changes within and around us. This won't help with everything that affects us, but it at least opens the way to helping ourselves in most of our basic survival needs. Scientific knowledge doesn't yet and likely never will give us complete insight and control but comparing our lives now with what we know from recorded history about the conditions our ancestors, distant and even fairly recent, had to survive and what they knew or thought they knew about how

Nature works the scientific method seems to have definitely improved our lot so far.

Theories and hypotheses. These terms are related but not really equal and unfortunately each has both a technical scientific and a general use meaning which regularly leads to confusion and misunderstanding. In science, a hypothesis is a testable educated guess about the way that something in the natural world works. It is developed after a close examination of the natural system. A simplified example would be that I push a videotape cassette into the slot on the front of the VCR machine and after a *whirring* sound a moving image appears on the TV screen. After a time the picture turns to a random dot pattern, then it freezes and after another *whir* the tape slides partially back out of the slot. If I push the tape back in there is a *whir* but no picture appears and the tape is ejected again.

From what I know about how other systems work from previous scientific analyses by myself and others, and possibly some new idea that pops into my head about how changes could occur in an orderly and predictable manner, I conclude there is an automatic end-of-tape ejection system involved. Then, without opening the cassette unit, I propose a mechanism, an explanation of the details of what is present inside and how it works. Or I go at the matter from another direction and open the cassette and propose an explanation for why the parts I find in there are designed and interconnected as they are. Then it's time to experiment.

I must devise a test that will show that my mechanism is not the correct one if it is not. Any experiment that is not able to demonstrate that my hypothesis is incorrect, that things don't work as I said I thought they might, is of no scientific value. Please notice that I avoid saying the experiment will *prove* anything since that is a taboo word in scientific analysis. The scientific method is based on the reality that there always might be other explanations, either already proposed or still waiting to be thought up, that better explain what happens and what doesn't happen, so scientific explanations are always open to revision and correction when better evidence is recognized. Those who don't grasp the basis of scientific statements regularly allege that this strong point of science is instead evidence that science is flawed. These people insist they won't accept (and of course therefore no one else should either) statements that are not absolute and never changing. Therefore they look for (and of course therefore they say so should you) answers where those claims of absolute certainty and finality are freely made and where no serious questioning is allowed.

Another example. People and dogs with the symptoms that we call diabetes were found at postmortem to have abnormalities of the pancreas. This led to the hypothesis that a healthy pancreas is essential to avoid diabetes. This idea was tested by removing the pancreas from a healthy dog to see if it would soon develop typical diabetes symptoms. It did, therefore the hypothesis was supported. Now more detailed studies were begun to identify exactly what part or product of the pancreas was responsible. At each step a hypothesis was proposed and then tested to guide the growing understanding of the details of the process. Such a grasp of the details has given us insights into ways to prevent, to control, and maybe one day to cure the disease.

Suppose that someone else had hypothesized that it is a high level of the male sex hormone testosterone in the blood that causes the symptoms. This idea could be tested by giving injections of testosterone to a dog with a healthy pancreas and watching to see if it developed diabetes symptoms. It would not, so the hypothesis would not be supported. Consequently that line of research would be abandoned as incorrect without wasting more time on it. This does not tell us about what effects the hormone in question does have, only that it does not seem to affect diabetes in what for now we conclude is a reasonable test. If at some future time we learn from other work that there might be some physiological mechanism that would cause the testosterone to interact with something else and affect the blood sugar regulation and in those cases cause diabetes we always can and likely will come back and reconsider the hypothesis, but a level of common sense practicality rooted in what we know until then is a guiding principle for what lines of investigation to spend time on now.

A hypothesis is a testable educated guess about cause and effect. If this hypothesis is based on confirmed results of a series of earlier, more generalized ones, we have more confidence in it than in one that is concerned with a previously unstudied phenomenon. Every hypothesis is always and specifically intended to be tested though. That is an essential step even when it may be years before the ideas or the technology and equipment to actually conduct such tests are devised. Until then it is accepted that such testing must be done when that becomes possible and until then this hypothesis is considered weak and there will not likely be much interest in building on it until it is verified. Each hypothesis had a basis in direct or indirect observation but it is not *proven* even when the experiments *support* it since a different explanation, even a radically different one that no one has yet thought of, might explain things as well or better. The test results do though support the hypothesis and others interested in or concerned about the topic recognize that as a go-ahead to dig deeper into the details behind the hypothesis with a better hope of understanding how the system operates.

A piece of bread placed in a box made from a special metal alloy with several quarter-sized holes cut in the sides and left in the basement of an old house might have disappeared because the metal "concentrates earth energy" and incinerates a substance like bread without smoke and leaving behind no ashes. Or maybe it disappeared because mice got in through those holes and ate it without getting so excited at their feast that they didn't leave their own traces of the visit behind.

Often what the researchers lack is a model to engage and prod their imaginations, some other system that they can understand and then recognize has structures or functions in common with the one they don't understand yet. When mechanical water pumps were developed the function of the heart was soon recognized. It isn't the center of the soul or the center of thinking, it is a muscular pump.

What we have at each moment then is the best explanation that anyone has come up with so far. The greater the body of evidence that supports it, the more confidence we have in it. But we don't mistake it for proven beyond any doubt. Science can never prove things beyond any doubt although it may teach us how to produce repeatable results in the lab, the kitchen, or the factory. The data and observations amassed from a study that was conducted and intended to be taken as scientific is never sacrosanct. We can and do toss data that is subsequently shown to be incorrect or flawed in some way that can't be corrected for, especially data convincingly shown to have been falsified.

In scientific terminology a theory is precisely a hypothesis that has withstood a lot of scrutiny and testing so we have great confidence in it. The likelihood that it is true and accurate is quite high. It is as close to certain as we can get in science.

Unfortunately there is confusion because in common usage we talk about something being "only a theory" to suggest it has minimal rather than maximum likelihood of being correct or to refer to some preliminary idea about how things might work rather than what is the culmination of a significant amount of study. To confuse things to the max, in general usage a hypothesis is considered the same as a theory and neither has the emphasis on the need for testing by experimentation. "Only a theory" is an accident of the evolution of terms. Had some other word than theory been used early on to mean what that word is taken to mean by many non-scientists, there would be no confusion. Alas, such things happen and we end up with misunderstandings based on our terminology for decades or centuries.

Scientists generally agree to disagree until someone produces more or better data on the subject (although there can be rancor when big egos are involved - but that's vanity, not the science). The scientists seldom form splinter sects and go to war about the meaning of some quote or which of several interpretations of a text must be accepted under pain of terrible punishment though.

The difference between scientific truth and scientific accuracy is another potential semantic stumbling block. Some statement or under-standing about a natural phenomenon or process can be true in the sense that it has a foundation in observation, careful measurement, and well designed experimentation but yet be inaccurate in the sense that it predicts that the factor being studied will produce some effects that don't show up, it doesn't predict all the effects that are seen, and/or those are not within the expected measurement range of how big the effects will be. To those conducting the study at the early stages the fact that some expected results are detected is encouraging. They now examine more closely the bits that their tests suggest are the most important elements in causing the detectable changes and they try to envision a mechanism that might better explain those results before they try to devise new tests to see if they are still in the ballpark and maybe closer to a useful answer.

A typical hypothetical example would be that someone notes that when Substance Z is applied to a bacterially infected wound there is rapid healing with a minimum of the permanent damage seen in patients who survive an infection by that particular kind of bacteria (that was identified and studied in earlier research by others). The initial hypothesis is that somehow Substance Z kills that kind of bacteria and thereby saves the patient. If that is true and nothing else is ever known about the details of how Substance Y kills those bacteria there is still a useful therapy added to our medical arsenal. What is most likely to happen though is that researchers will focus on Substance Z, try to understand exactly what chemical effects it has in living cells and thence how it interferes with some essential process in this kind of bacteria and kills them. That will likely involve a series of steps, each a confirmation or rejection of an educated guess about the chemical and physiological details, that piece by piece give us a more and more detailed understanding of why Substance Z has that effect, what other bacteria types it has that kind of effect on and why it doesn't kill all types, why it has any unpleasant side effects in the patient if it does, and how to minimize those. Then they investigate what similar molecules might have the same effects as Z - or better ones so that those substances are even better therapeutic options, or are more toxic so they need to be avoided even though they seemed before the tests that they should be much the same.

If scientists considered any matter closed and unquestionable when no immediate contradicting evidence was found much of the progress we have made in science, and medicine in particular, would not have happened. The open-endedness is a critical part of the process, especially since often the follow-up work is not done for a long time because there isn't money to pay qualified people to do it since it is not judged by those with the important task of allocating resources in order to get the most from them to be important at all or at least not as important as other projects. Often the delay is because the technology to do the probing or analysis does not exist or is not available (the latter again often a matter of money).

An important element of scientific results and conclusions is that they are not given serious consideration until and unless published so that the methods used, the assumptions, and the results can be examined and questioned by any and all others. For several centuries publication meant in a specifically scientific journal or as part of the proceedings or records of a scientific society but the essential point was and is that what you keep to yourself has no impact on science. It may not be a matter of publish or perish, but it is a matter of publish or you have no impact.

This part of the process has kept up with the new technologies. Today many of the scientific journals and society reports are done online and may never be printed except by those who want a hard copy for their own files. The underlying rules remain pretty much the same though. What you post on the Internet at your own or some casual site will likely be ignored and even if science workers become aware of it they probably won't give it much consideration. Part of the winnowing process that attempts to keep useless or defective and therefore damaging reports from clogging the system is that one or more independent scientists with some knowledge of the particular area of your research must read your report and agree that it follows the guidelines for how the research should be done (matters like what assumptions you may make and how clearly you must list those in the report) and that your conclusions don't have obvious holes in them, before the journal or group will post or publish the report. There are a large number of journals today because there are a large number of studies being done and those all go effectively nowhere if they are not published. Part of the reason for the number of outlets is so that those seeking information about the latest work in a narrow research area may be able to find that in concentrated form in one or only a few journals rather than having to glean the results from a large number of journals that each only occasionally include reports on this small specialty area.

Another important and useful element of how science is done it that generally the doubts and disagreements about the reported results of studies are done in the open and that is considered a standard part of the process. If nothing else, this alerts those looking for the latest take on a particular area that while some new information has been published about it, that does not mean it is accepted as accurate or useful even by the editors of the journal or other outlet that has presented it for public consideration.

A side effect advantage of the science report publication system is that when questions about the results in a study lead to an investigation which concludes either that the researcher made significant errors in gathering or reporting her results, or she fabricated her data to fit the results she was certain should happen even though she hadn't found that to be the case in her experimental tests, that journal can report on the controversy and alert at least the core audience who learned of the original claims there that the reports are being retracted, rejected, or corrected. The mechanism is a reasonable correction process for what cannot always be avoided by the reviewing process when the reported results are literally new ideas and claims so there were no previous studies for the reviewers to compare the procedures and results of this paper with before they approved it for publication. It is an interesting and reassuring fact that in several cases known to many scientists if not the general public, the giveaway that the data was made up in order to fit the researcher's expectations was that it fit the ideal pattern to support her conclusion too perfectly. Statisticians and mathematicians pay attention to things like that and we are all safer for it.

By its very definition, accuracy means being errorless, conforming exactly to fact. By its nature scientific information can come closer to matching the facts about the structure and function of the natural world that any other known method of analysis, but since there is not a better source of detailed information about that subject to compare them to there is no valid way to say with absolute assurance how close our recent explanations come to corresponding exactly with how things are. That is, claims by a few individuals who should know better aside, we can never say that scientific information about any topic is errorless because we don't have a proven and unquestionable model to compare it to.

We can, however, say with confidence that scientific information gives us the possibility of coming closer to matching the facts of the natural world than any other system we know of or have any record of people ever having known and attempted to use. Science gives us total breadth about natural structures and phenomena from submicroscopic to the super-galactic (both interesting designations that reflect how much we have developed tools to observe the world in both ends of the size range in the last five hundred years or so). It has a built-in self-correcting mechanism, is available to anyone willing to follow the basic procedural guidelines that were developed based on the experience of earlier studies, and has openings for many specialties and skills so it can be developed and adapted to use at all levels of our world and lives. It is limited to understanding of natural phenomena so it can't answer all our questions and those who understand its nature don't make or support claims that it can say anything useful about any subject that cannot be analyzed, tested, and possibly disproven. It is scary to think back to how our lives likely still would be without the several hundred years of its evolution into a major foundation of our understanding and thinking. A simple example to prompt you to cheer the scientific method is to remember that only with the development of the germ theory of disease followed by the discovery or development of antibiotics and related materials that only became generally available in about the last seventy-five years any scratch that got infected had a real chance of killing you. The 1918-1920 Spanish Flu pandemic - before we knew how to make effective vaccines - is estimated to have sickened more than a quarter of the entire world's population and to have killed at least 50 million people.

Communication is essential to our individual and societal survival but it isn't always desirable to communicate too effectively or completely. Sometimes you put yourself at a disadvantage by unnecessarily giving away your secrets. Sometimes you can avoid a socially awkward situation by not saying everything that you might. And sometimes people inquire about matters that are none of their business but it may be easier to sidestep them than to cause a fuss by openly refusing to discuss those topics.

It's hard surviving in this complicated world that doesn't readily acknowledge, much less properly credit, our individual accomplishments and talents. Succeeding in that world calls for every tool and ploy in our social species adaptive repertoire. We all want to be loved and we also want to be respected. A few would even like to be idolized. These latter want to be quoted at cocktail parties and in the press, given preference in public places, and pursued for autographs and the mere touch of their smile or hand. If rock stars, movie directors, and millionaires of every persuasion can get it all why shouldn't you and I - if we want it, since not all of us do? But what tactics can you get away with? And can you live with yourself if you use them?

Throughout history people have developed an array of verbal and non-verbal devices for projecting themselves in the best possible light. They even found ways to grab credit for results they didn't deserve, while carefully distancing themselves from all blame. Our society and our subsequent psychology being as they are, we are strongly tempted to manipulate the truth by exaggerating our good deeds and hiding our bad ones rather than sticking to actual improvement of our performance.

When any one of us makes a statement, the claims made may fall into any of a number of categories. The following list simply points out the range of possibilities, it is not presented as an exhaustive catalog of the categories. For some of these we will note the benefits, the risks, and the costs of using this type of statement while we are focused on them.

1) *Truths.* These are accurate statements of objective reality, at least as understood and interpreted in the cultural-philosophical frame-work of the speaker. This is the desired ideal and what we generally try to project most of our statements as being no matter which category they

actually belong to. We also tend to hope that other people's statements will fall into this category but we are alert enough to realize that they don't always qualify even though they are presented as truths.

It is relatively easy to speak truths about simple matters that don't involve our personal welfare or interests. It gets progressively more difficult as the topic becomes more complex or as our interest becomes more substantially involved. Anyone well versed in any technical field, for instance, knows that it is hard, if not impossible, to speak simple truths about these subjects because there are so many variables that the expert can think of which could change the situation and therefore the answer that should be given. We all know the mental searching we do for a way to answer a question about something in which we have a particular interest in order to cast it in a favorable light but still accurate or honest.

2) *Received "Truths".* This category are the commonly accepted and believed generalizations of and in a particular religion, ethnic culture, or other group. On close examination these are often found to be based on inaccurate observations or worse but they persist. Many "truths" are true only if you accept the assumptions (often prejudicial about race, gender, history, etc.) that are behind them. Thus everybody supposedly "knows" that women are the weaker sex, sailors make better lover, blonds have more fun, and Christopher Columbus discovered America.

3) *Half-truths.* These are insidious since they so often mislead people either intentionally or accidentally. These statements contain an element of truth but then either twist that truth, contradict it, draw too many or the wrong conclusions from it, or only tell half of it.

Many of the half-truths are deliberate. This is the special province of advertisers, public relations flacks, politicians, and anyone else who might like to lead you to draw the wrong conclusions (and therefore believe what he wants you to believe) but without actually lying to you. That way he can claim innocence and virtue if you catch on to him and try to come back at him. Half-truths are often statements that suggest something, often strongly, but never actually say it. If we all became just a little better at noticing these we could revolutionize our world in short order by making the people in positions of responsibility responsible. It isn't that hard when we pay attention but it does require us to focus.

4) *Errors.* These are honest mistakes made because of faulty data, miscalculation, lapses of memory, or a whole list of other factors. If not detected they can be as damaging as lies and other warping of the truth, but in these cases we can't accuse anyone of deliberately distorting the

situation for his own purposes. The harm done by errors can often be rectified fairly easily since in many cases no one has any personal interest in preventing their detection and correction. Errors will tend to be more or less random and, at least initially, no special effort will be made to cover them up. Once they are detected and egos and jobs are on the line, however, the b.s. may start to fly.

5) *Outright Lies.* These are deliberate distortions of the facts that are made because someone hopes to gain from them either by making things work out the way he wants or to cover up his misdeeds, mistakes, etc. An honest mistake is not a lie although it may have the same practical consequences as one. Similarly a bus is not a train but both may move you to the same destination. We often find ourselves more angered by a lie than by a mistake that produces the same effect because the lie involves someone deliberately trying to use or abuse us and only some of us are willing to take that screwing over with equanimity.

There are verbal and non-verbal lies. A shrug, shake of the head, or accusingly pointed finger may speak volumes. As often noted, there are lies of commission and lies of omission. I may accuse you of a crime that I know you didn't commit, or when asked by the police I may fail to reveal that I know you couldn't have been at that place when the crime occurred because my doing that might raise questions about why I was where I happened to be that I know where you were. In either case you may be prosecuted.

A lie is easily defined in theory but deciding which verbal or non-verbal behaviors actually fit the description is almost eternally arguable. At least thoughtful people have been arguing about the matter as far back as we have significant written records and they are still at it in thousands of court rooms and millions of living rooms and backyards every day. That suggests that we can assume that universal agreement has not been reached yet. To lie means to knowingly assert what you know or believe is not true. The critical elements in that are a) *communication*, b) *non-truth*, and c) *knowingly*.

Lies are very useful when you want to manipulate the opinions of others because (until detected as lies) they reshape the world as perceived by the others. What could be more effective in controlling minds than literally reshaping what they think the world is like to fit our purposes? A litany of lies comes to mind. "I wasn't near it when it fell over." "I didn't hear anything about it so I didn't know assistance was called for." "I taught him everything he knows." "He said I should do it."

What is wrong with lies?

A) They're not "nice". There are and through history have been almost universal prohibitions against them (in spite of which, they have shaped a lot of human history). They are bad for your image unless you are either very rich or very powerful - and even then if you ever decide to run for elected office or are indicted for a serious crime.

B) When you get caught in them people tend to distrust you for long periods thereafter.

C) They "prove" you intended to deceive and cheat - which is best left as an unproven and, you hope, unprovable suspicion.

D) They can be shown to be falsehoods in many cases where facts, objects, or witnesses are involved. No one has to prove what you intended, only that your claims or statements didn't match the facts as you did or should have known them to be.

E) Because they are usually definite statements, they may have to be followed up on with more lies and ones that don't contradict the previous ones. Part of the heavy cost of lying is the necessity of keeping straight and in mind the two or more versions of reality that you have proclaimed to someone or everyone. It can all get very complicated in a hurry. Some people seem to be oblivious to the danger of contradicting themselves in embarrassing way; most, though, sweat out their lies.

F) They don't look good on your resume - i.e., they may follow and haunt you.

6) *Little white lies* are the category of deliberate manipulations of the facts or the truth which are intended mainly to prevent unnecessary friction in day-to-day life. White lies are social lubrication. These are the little "I love it" comments about the friend's shirt that you hate and the "Glad to see you" when this is the last person in the world you wanted to meet but the encounter is only in passing and any unpleasantness would ruin the event for others who are its focus. There is a problematic gray zone where white lies transform into outright lies.

7) *Misunderstandings*. These result when one person "hears" something other than what the speaker intended to communicate. I am using the term in a limited and literal sense here to refer to those cases that involve an actual mistake in receiving the message presented either as verbal or body language communication. These are generally honest mistakes and while they often cause hard feelings and complicate our lives they aren't as damaging to our interactions as lies or deceptions

because some objective third party can often make everyone involved see that a literal but unintentional misunderstanding has occurred.

8) *Misinterpretations.* These overlap with misunderstandings and a clear-cut distinction is not always possible. I am using the term here to include all cases where we have to take the information that we have received from another (presumably without errors in that communication - i.e., no misunderstandings) and decide what it means, implies, or suggests. This is always a touchy operation because we each bring to the task a background of experience and education that is different from that of anyone else. Words or phrases have emotional as well as factual connotation for us and these color our use of spoken and written messages, our body language, and our interpretations of that meaning for us. Here the cultural differences in body language (gestures, facial expression, social distances) all become important. If you have never encountered the books of Edward T. Hall on such differences I can't recommend them too highly as fascinating and instructive reading.

What may be a harmless and meaningless gesture to you may have a crude and insulting interpretation where I come from. To me any reference to detectives may suggest that you are aware of some illegal activity that I have been involved in but which I didn't think anyone else knew about, so when you innocently make some joking reference to calling in the detectives I am immediately alarmed and uneasy. I wonder if you are trying to subtly tell me that you know about my activities and if so, why? Are you trying to blackmail me into agreeing to whatever you are proposing? Often one word in a conversation can twist the whole thing out of kilter if that word is charged for one of the participants. We often seek signs from one another about what is known but is not going to be made an issue of. We expect such signs to be subtle so that only you and I will get the message. It is no wonder then that, sensitive and straining for some clue, we can so often find something in a conversation which we can and do interpret as a signal.

Misinterpretations are harder to deal with than misunderstandings because in most cases, at least for the key words involved, the people on the two sides are actually speaking different languages. Each has an aura of meaning for each term he uses, a complex set of colorations and associations that he makes with the word based on his unique experience in life. When two people define a term they do so by agreeing on the core meaning, the *point* of meaning, but usually they don't think it necessary to talk about the *color* of meaning of the word for each of them. They can readily agree on the basic meaning, what the word denotes, and still have different connotations of it. One person may understand it to be a demeaning term while it seems quite neutral to the other. Getting to where the two sides in a discussion will thrash out the psychological overtones of the terminology is hard because there is a tendency to assume that because everyone is speaking in the same linguistic tongue they are all "speaking the same language", which is often not the case.

In a common case, a man is likely to refer to any other man he knows well enough to call by name as a *friend*, the term being a very loose and general one for anyone he knows for at least half an hour and currently has no bad feelings toward. A woman is more likely to reserve the term friend for someone she knows and likes much more than just a casual acquaintance.

Some terms have a technical and a general use sense that while not unrelated are nonetheless different in the degree of detail. To Jack the golfer the *habitat* of some bird he sees while on the course is wherever he happens to spot it standing, but to an ecologist its habitat is the type of area it normally spends most of its time in by preference - whether that is a swamp, a rocky hillside, or open grassland. The golfer assumes that the egret standing on the putting green is normal; the ecologist knows it is a fluke.

9) *Facts*. These are observations of reality that correspond to the reality. These are reports on happenings in the world around us as we perceive them to be. Ideally, they don't involve much interpretation, analysis, or other subjective manipulation but inevitably they are always influenced by our expectations, philosophical background, physical health and functioning, and conscious and unconscious prejudices, so they are less solid and resistant to dispute than we prefer to think of them as being. Today there is talk of fuzzy facts (somewhat related to fuzzy math), items that have a factual reality but which are slightly different in the details depending on the context because they adapt to the particular case. These complicate things in some discussions or negotiations while simplifying them in others.

10) *Opinions*. These are facts as they exist once we have processed them. They are what we consider to be the truth and the facts as we believe they exist or would prefer to have them exist. The distinguishing element of opinions is the subjective one. The facts may be unclear or in dispute or there might be arguments about which is the best path to a particular objective, so we have to make a decision about which position

to take. We then do that with the acknowledgement, specified or not, that this is an uncertain or disputed point which means disagreement with us is not heresy (even if we are not encouraging it). Our opinions are our votes in support of particular matters that are not currently resolvable by indisputable evidence. We present these positions as the ones we accept or support and we thereby add our stature to their weight. The claim is then that we put our reputations on the line for this position.

11) *Guesstimates.* These include both our outright guesses and our educated guesses. Raw guesses are worth as much as the track record of the person guessing or any random event. The educated guesses I refer to here are the same as those involved in a scientific hypothesis but either there is, at least with existing equipment and ideas, no way to test them or there is no inclination to do so because no one is prepared to fund that work when the consequences are not that great and there are many other studies competing for funding and attention. Whichever is the case, we have some confidence in the facts since they are based on observation of the phenomenon in question and they probably incorporate ideas learned from the study of comparable systems, even though they leave us less certain because they are not yet fully tested.

12) *Dreams or wishes.* These have a high "I want it" rating but low certainty status. They may be of value to the person in order to keep his imagination engaged and his hopes alive, but as credible evidence of reality usable by others they are of only limited use.

We might recognize the progression of states of credibility that influence us - from *possible* to *probable* to *provable* to the ultimate level, *true.*

To persons who take pride in conducting their lives in a critically considered, deliberate way any lies, misrepresentations, and false allusions are especially offensive because they are attempts to undo the effort being made to arrive at the most workable positions and decisions. Lies cause more trouble for thoughtful people because they raise doubts about everything the liar says. They threaten to undermine much of our social and business system, which is built on a degree of trust and the value of a person's word - backed by the power of the law. That latter is a necessary element of self-defense since we know from sad experience that there are lots of liars and cheats in the world.

The problems of veracity and verifiability in official and casual human communications are never ending. Both verbal and non-verbal messages leave open the door to deception, whether that is intentional or accidental. Often there is no practical mechanism for getting independent verification of whatever statements are made in private conversations or even in standard business dealings, so we are at the mercy of our own sense of the situation and of the other people involved. Sometime we can recognize a deliberate lie because of the liar's facial expression or his behavior or because we know enough of the facts of the case. We also learn from our own and others' experiences to identify some individuals who simply can't be trusted to tell the truth. But we can only wonder how often we have been deliberately misinformed to our disadvantage and to the speaker's benefit and never realized it. A critical thinking approach will argue that it is not productive to spend energy worrying about injuries that you have no awareness of because they are probably not doing you any significant harm if you don't know about them. You have little chance of changing things at this late point anyway. Save your energy for the problems you can identify and are in the here-and-now or the future.

Here's a particular area that calls for special consideration. Do we sincerely want politicians to tell us the truth? We say so regularly in polls and interviews. but I have my doubts based on observations that voter approval seems to be closely tied to making the masses feel good about themselves and their country even if the sentiments have little basis in reality. A candidate who says, "We're great and we're proud!" and wraps himself in the flag usually gets elected without apparent concern for his integrity or his position on important issues because a sufficient majority of those who exercise their right to vote want to hear this *rah rah* talk above all else. When speaking theoretically many say they want leaders who will do what is necessary to deal with the perceived problems of the modern world yet somehow those same people (at least statistically the same ones) seem unwilling to actually elect leaders who will make those changes, preferring those who will speak empty "proud" words instead.

Part of the down side of democracy is that a simple majority of ignorant, misinformed, or dumb voters can burden everyone else with a government of fools or con men. This is the scary part because the evidence suggests that large numbers of voters decide on the basis of either superficial factors or distortions, half truths, and deliberate lies. Do we get the government that we deserve in a democracy? Should we?

The unfortunate consequences of lies told for political reasons, even those that might seem justified (for example to protect delicate international negotiations, etc.), is that they reinforce the accurate perception that we can never fully trust what we are told by politicians and others in decision-making positions. Unfortunately many of these questions elicit lies or obfuscations because political opponents or people in the news media insist on asking questions that ought not to be asked or answered. Those situations touch on the enormously thorny problem of what we have a right to know in a democracy, what it is properly and often critically important be kept secret, and who is to decide what is out of bounds?

Don't let yourself be as naive as the news reporters who ask the obvious questions that are never going to be answered (at least not accurately and honestly) and then act as if the evasions, denials, or lies are news. In some cases the answers (if honestly given) would incriminate the respondent; in other cases they would compromise activities and therefore national security by alerting enemies (in any sense) to some impending action against them. In many cases we the audience must sit and watch some reporter on the TV news asking a government official what the response to some emergency like an on-going terrorist action will be while we hope the answer will be so ambiguous as to be worthless because we know (the reporters and their editors seldom evidence much awareness of the fact) that the enemy or whoever is on the other side of this matter is waiting to find out the plans and intentions in order to take evasive action, somewhere between possibly to probably to our common detriment depending on the specific case. And of course if what the official says is not the actual intended facts he is, and will likely be reported by the same news outlet as, a liar - further eroding the public's confidence in their government - and in the good sense of the people in the news media.

In a literal sense each thing we do is being done for the first and only time. It may be recorded in memory and on film or tape so that we can replay and relive the moment, but that is not a repeat of the act itself. You may perform that kind of act many times, but each time is a unique event. You can perform each type of act for the first time only once. Doing something for the first time or doing it with particular persons or in particular circumstances for the first time tends to be scary because we aren't certain how things may work out even if we know what results are expected. In some cases there is the added worry that our performance may be a matter of public knowledge or even record and we don't want to embarrass ourselves with a less than adequate performance. As a result of these hesitations and concerns we tend to want to have the guidance of our own experience and that of others before we decide how to proceed. Today many of the bits of information that we want to use to guide us come in the form of numbers, either raw data, poll results, or comparisons reduced to some numerical form.

Being able to reduce something to a neat quantity reassures us that in some sense the matter must be within our control. Statistics fascinate many of us for the same reason. Being able to get what can be represented as yes-no answers by processing events reduced to numbers is an exciting idea. The next step from there is poll results, which are response-based statistics. We like to believe that we can even take the opinions or preferences of the population and reduce them to simple *Do this, don't do that* guides for all the important decisions. A danger with this is that the simplification of the task of making difficult decisions will dumb down our critical defenses and make us vulnerable to being misled by numbers. There is no question that statistics, especially polls, can be manipulated to make them show pretty near anything you want without simply making them up. Even when they are not being deliberately slanted they can easily be misread or unconsciously misinterpreted.

Humans are wired to expect certain patterns that likely have had significant survival value during much of the evolution of our species but that can create pitfalls for us in the world of sophisticated data analysis. In his 2011 book *Thinking, Fast and Slow*, Nobel Prize winning economist Daniel Kahneman explains that humans operate on two parallel thinking systems. System One, the fast thinking or intuitive mode, is mostly involved with things like reacting to loud sounds, understanding simple sentences, and driving on empty roads. System Two, the slow thinking or analytical mode, is used to deal with activities that require more mental effort - like doing your taxes, comparing different brands of a major appliance before you buy, or driving in traffic. He notes that, "System One is inept when you have to deal with statistical facts that change the probability of outcomes but do not cause them to happen."

We are always looking for causes of what we see and therefore we sometimes attribute more meaning than we should to events that are actually due only to chance. Kahneman notes, "We do not expect to see regularity produced by a random process, and when we detect what appears to be a rule, we quickly reject the idea that the process is truly random."

He suggests this example. The genders of the next six babies born in any hospital on any day might be the possible sequences BBBGGG, GGGGGG, or BGBBGB among others. Are these three sequences equally likely? Although it seems counter-intuitive to most of us, the correct answer is yes, they are equally likely. Since the events are independent (different mothers delivering more or less at random in relation to one another; boys and girls are born with approximately equal frequency) any possible sequence of six births is statistically as likely as any other. He writes, "We are pattern seekers, believers in a coherent world, in which regularities (such as a sequence of six girls) appear not by accident but as a result of mechanical causality or someone's intention."

Kahneman points out that, "Statistics produce many observations that appear to beg for causal explanations but do not lend themselves to such explanations. Many facts of the world are due to chance, including accidents of sampling. And causal explanations of chance events are inevitably wrong."

Statistics and polls are widely quoted by the news media because they reduce a possibly complex issue to a tidbit that can be both reported and commented on in a sound bite. Plus they have an aura of authenticity or scientific certitude draped over them because they are supposedly objective and, critically important to this perception, their accuracy can be estimated in numerical form. As a result, right there we have an essential point that is commonly misunderstood. Most people would say that the accuracy is expressed by the plus or minus figure included with any good report of a poll result. But that would mean that the value is actually and accurately known and assured to a greater certainty than the statistics support. Rather the value is *estimated*, signaling that there is a real and recognized possibility that the numbers are not accurate. This isn't a major concern for most people because they don't pay much attention to the error estimate numbers anyway, they simply feel reassured about the reliability of the poll results by the fact that those numbers are there.

Problems arise when the certitude implied by the statistics doesn't exist because the statistics were used improperly. Seldom are statistics wrong in the sense of coming up with an incorrect number, rather they are meaningless because the assumptions that are essential for their validity don't hold. You can take any group of numbers and plug them into a statistical formula and get a number out as the answer but unless specified assumptions held true for the data you plugged in - for instance that the sample was truly randomly selected - the answer means nothing to anyone who understands the basic ideas underlying statistics. Yet it looks just as good as any statistical number from an accurate study. A number is a number is a number, but not all numbers are valid and therefore meaningful answers to questions asked using statistical tools.

Opinion polls are a journalistic tool that politicians and business have glommed onto because it serves their purposes too. It seems that the first poll was conducted by a reporter sent by the *Pennsylvanian*, a Harrisburg, PA newspaper to ask people in Delaware what they were thinking about the candidates in the upcoming presidential election between Andrew Jackson and John Quincy Adams. It is obvious that today polls are a major part of contemporary political life in many parts of the world. Stances are assumed, backs are scratched, and speeches and media events are tailored to put this politician or other person where the most recent polls seem to indicate that the majority of the populace - or at least those relevant to his interests (like those who will actually vote, buy, or whatever) stand on a particular issue. Probably never before in history has a political strategy made such jackasses of so many so often. (Sorry, there goes one of those data deficient generalizations I warned against in Chapter 20 again.)

Note that questioning the validity of the statistical procedures used to generate the reported values is not the same as questioning their accuracy. I see no reason to question the fact that within the realm of the mathematics of chance the established methods are valid, but it is still possible to question whether those assumptions hold true for activities like human decision-making. The validity of the procedures used to collect the data can also be questioned. The validity of any statistical conclusions depends on the design of the study which must incorporate certain factors or assumptions for the statistical analysis to have any meaning. Statistics is a world of smoke and mirrors in that the only hard or fixed elements are the formulas used for combining and processing the numbers. No objects or even facts go into the calculation, only numbers. The math techniques allow us to *estimate* the likelihood of particular outcomes if chance is a major factor, but they don't make things happen and they are never more than probability statements. If the study is properly constructed and processed, conclusions can be drawn about what *probably* would or would not happen in the real world. Again, statistics is all and only about probabilities, never actualities or certainties. In some situations they yield valuable information, in others they may give us false confidence. Any time that statistical inferences are described as more solid than that the process is being misused.

My statistics professor made a regular practice of bringing in the most recent issue of the major scientific journal *Science* to point out the various research reports that had used the wrong statistics and why those used were not valid for drawing the conclusions in those studies.

Consider this situation. As a result of some exotic idea he gets from reading the headlines in a tabloid newspaper at the supermarket check-out line, your brother-in-law announces that his statistical analysis of twenty-seven famous men from recent history shows that if the digits of a man's phone number and his birth date add up to an even number under ninety-nine he will lose all the hair on the top of his head before age thirty. You, a male at age twenty-eight, add up the referred-to digits and get seventy-four. Two years later you still have a lot of hair on your head. What happened? The number was accurately determined to be an even number less than ninety-nine, but the assumptions that no one could comprehend when your brother-in-law explained them did not in fact reflect the reality of human physiology.

Opinion polling is based on statistical theories which say that a random sample of X number of people will give a true approximation of the range and magnitude of opinions among the larger population being assessed. The mathematics says it should be so, but time after time we see the result of several different randomized polls on the same topic taken on the same day among the same large populations but they don't come to the same probabilities. If the polling techniques do what we are generally given to understand they do - and what most people, including the political groups shaping their strategies based on them, believe they do - how come they don't agree? Common sense argues that there can't be four different non-overlapping value ranges for the approval rating or whatever is being asked about. There can of course be any number of wild or educated guesses and if that is all we get from the poll we need to make certain that we don't believe or claim to have more. Or we need to be certain that we are not misled into thinking there is more sound and useful information even when those with a vested interest in persuading us with these poll results try to make them sound like more. Having studied statistics for research design I understand a bit about the *ifs, ands,* and *maybes* that underlie statistical theory but that is not what I see coming across when most statistics are used both in propaganda and in decision-making.

Polls are inherently untrustworthy tools of public opinion since they are too easily made selective, slanted, and short-term. Unfortunately they are often the best available or only practical way of assessing that opinion. That is why those concerned about having a trustworthy method work constantly both to find new or better ways of assessing the numbers of those among us with each opinion, while those who are concerned with statistical polling as a serious tool of analyzing and planning work to improve the techniques of structuring the questions and try to police the misuse by pointing out the problems.

There are three questions we should pay particular attention to when we consider poll results. First, *exactly what were the people asked?* Is the data being gathered actually about this matter? If the poll asks, "Do you think that X is the ideal possible policy?" and then reports that 54% of the population rejects X, you may be misled. Some of those polled may have felt and even said that X was not the *ideal* but it was the best and most workable policy available so they support it but that didn't come across because of the way the question was asked and the limitations on how you could answer. You must look at the exact wording used in the questions when you try to evaluate the meaning of the responses. Be skeptical of any and all poll results if the report doesn't include the exact wording. Also, before you accept the results as important, ask yourself if the wording used gives you any worthwhile information. Just because a poll was taken doesn't mean it has anything important to tell you.

Opinion polling is based on the responses of a random sample of people to carefully worded questions which may have a variety of implications or ambiguities but the polling procedures permit only some equivalent of *yes, no,* or *no opinion* responses. This is essential if the responses are to be reduced to numbers as they must be for statistics, but it also distorts your thinking by not allowing for nuances or reservations. You can't qualify your response and you can't get any clarification. If even a significant amount of our day-to-day business communication had to be done in this way the world would be in even greater chaos than it is now. If any significant part of our social discourse went this way there would be civil wars everywhere all the time. In fact many of our social ruptures and disagreements are precisely the result of this kind of failure to communicate which results from not being able or willing to clarify and qualify our statements and stances.

The questions asked in a poll can be deliberately constructed to produce a pre-determined response. If I want people to support the switch over to use of the latest type of high efficiency light bulbs in all municipal buildings I might ask, "The use of the most efficient light bulbs on the market would save the city 15% on electricity and over the extended life of these bulbs 25% on bulb replacement costs, so all city buildings should have them installed as soon as possible." *Agree! Disagree! No Opinion.* If I don't want the bulbs used, however, I will ask, "The proposed use of a new type of light bulbs will require an immediate cost of X dollars to buy the bulbs that are more expensive than conventional ones and newer and even more efficient types may come on the market before these wear out which will delay our switching over to the most cost effective types so we shouldn't install these bulbs." *Agree! Disagree! No Opinion.*

Polls also involve some confusion about what is said versus what is meant by the respondents. For instance, three shoppers might give the same answer but for different reasons to the question, *Is price an important consideration in your decision to buy this waffle iron?* One might actually have said, "Yes, I wouldn't consider buying one costing more than X dollars." The second might have said, "Yes, I won't pay that much extra for the little extra feature on that one." While the third might have said, "Yes, prices vary from store to store so I've been shopping around." The poll may have been conducted to provide feedback to guide the manufacturer in pricing policies but the company manufacturer has no way to know the actual thoughts of the consumers from this yes-no data. Because of the general nature of the question *Is price as an important consideration?* there is little focused information in the responses and lots of opportunity to misread the results any way you want.

The questions asked may mean quite different things to people of different backgrounds. In some cases the pollster (we hope innocently) may phrase the questions in ways that produce a cultural confusion that is twisted by the polling procedure into a false assessment of what the population thinks on a topic. Technical or outdated terms or emotion-laden phrases may be as misleading as are culturally embedded ones.

By outdated terms I mean ones that are either remembered from the pollster's youth, but no longer in use and therefore meaningless to younger persons or perhaps ones having a different meaning to them. They may also be the reverse, the *In* phrases in some age group or social set, but not understood with those overtones by others. My point is to emphasize that we can never be certain that all of those who responded to a poll were answering the same questions although the same words were used by the pollster. We each tend to assume that everyone else thinks and understands things pretty much as we do and are genuinely shocked when we run into a problem because they don't. At such points we get a glimpse of how the same words can mean different things to different people of good will. It is a maturing experience because it makes anyone who is ready to recognize the lesson aware that we exist in a very diverse world.

The second question to pay attention to about any poll result is *How many people were polled?* This point is one easily overlooked. The mathematics may claim it makes no essential difference as long as a certain minimum number that is determined by the math were polled but it does affect the credibility many of us are willing to extend to the results. A poll of twenty people that is interpreted as a valid cross-section of the views of a large population will, if that fact is in focus, carry less weight in a voter's decision-making than a poll based on a random sample of 2000 people. Statistics stretches things and only you, the person deciding on important matters, can decide how much is too much stretch for you to accept.

The third question is, *What is a significant difference between response groups?* Is there a real difference between the different groups? Significant is a statistical term that permeates much of our scientific thinking and I, as a trained biologist, am steeped in the concepts and terminology even though I distrust them. This is one of the thorniest problems in many topic areas but here statistics makes things somewhat simpler by asking the "understood" question, *Is there a difference between the data categories being compared that are likely to be the result of factors other than chance variations?* The math then establishes tables of numbers against which we can compare the number we got when we processed our data and the table will give us the estimate of how statistically confident we can be that the value is not the result of chance events and therefore represents something real. It is standard to proceed on the basis of the data only if we have at least 90% confidence based on the tables. It is even better if we can claim 95 or even 99 percent statistical confidence. However, whether or not the fact that this matter is highly likely not to be the result of chance events, we are still left with the larger and not reducible to a number problem of deciding whether it is of importance in the real world that we must be concerned about.

Sometimes we are told on the basis of some poll that "America favors..." A careful report will include a statement about the estimated accuracy range of the results. For instance, "These poll results are accurate within plus or minus X percentage points." If a poll is accurate within plus or minus three percentage points, and for one question 42% were in favor (thus an accuracy range of 39-45%), 40% were opposed (37-43%), and 18% (15-21%) were undecided, there is no real statistical difference between the numbers in favor and opposed since their ranges overlap. It is therefore not accurate to report that there is a statistical difference. Not that that keeps even supposedly responsible news outlets from doing so regularly. In particular every time you see results reported as meaningfully different that are only one or two percentage points apart you should be very skeptical about the worth of the poll - and the report.

A potential problem is that the results are going to be interpreted, paraphrased, and then generalized by persons and groups other than statisticians. This means that the subtle restraints on the interpretations may be lost and the meaning of the results may be misinterpreted, misstated, and manipulated by impartial newspersons and others who are trying to simplify it for the readers/viewers as well as by those on either or both sides of the issue who want to deliberately mislead people for their own purposes. The majority of people who hear or read about the poll will be exposed to only a synopsis of the results, often reduced to a statement of who won the round, whatever it was, and therefore of course who lost. More details would take up more page space or air time and the presenters seem to believe - and they may be right about this - that the majority of their audience only care about being told who won and who lost. A scary reality.

A further complication is that those who are assigned to report on poll results are under some pressure to say that some difference was found. Otherwise why bother to report on it? There is good reason to say there was no difference when that was the case, but many of those not tuned into statistical thinking would miss the point. Also the report wouldn't get good grades as the "exciting news" or "you must know" information which is the bread-and-butter factor for those performing to inform and entertain the public.

There is a proverb that warns that comparisons are odious. This is derived from the comment of one of Shakespeare's characters in *Much Ado about Nothing* that "comparisons are odorous." They say pretty much the same thing, using only slightly different words. However comparisons are also often widely used because they can be instructive and helpful even though the wrong ones can be ridiculous.

Why do we compare things? (1) To see which one is superior in a particular characteristic or accomplishment or, more dubiously, which is better overall (which is harder to define).

(2) To look for similarities both to decide if the entities are in fact different, and to identify areas where the analysis of a feature in one system may be helpful in understanding the comparable one in the other system even though that was not superficially obvious.

(3) To evaluate one or more of the entities while we decide whether to purchase it with our money, our vote, or our approval and support. This is a way to estimate if it will do the job at least as well as other available systems. We can also get a sense of what limitations or problems are likely that might not be there with another system (that would have its own weaknesses)?

To be acceptable and worthwhile a comparison must be valid and either substantial or relevant.

What does it take to have a *valid* comparison? Similarity in at least some of the points relevant to the consideration. Total similarity would be identity and comparing a thing with itself is of very limited use. Patients diagnosed with a disease and receiving a new medication can be compared with patients with the same disease not getting this medicine to assess the value of the compound. Those patients compared with people who don't have the disease would be of no value in assessing the effectiveness of the medicine but could give an idea of the effect of the disease on survival or on the safety of the medicine. When someone proposes a comparison between apples and watermelons we should go on mental alert and automatically focus on the limits of the similarities between these items. There are some similarities, but they won't make many useful points so what is the person trying to accomplish with this? When you focus beyond the amusement level - or is it intended to be the *This isn't anything to pay attention to* level - you are less likely to be taken in.

The similarity must also be *substantial* or *relevant* before we should consider differences in degree or kind in other aspects to be instructive and perhaps persuasive. The fact that different plant species all have yellow flowers may be relevant to studies on flower development or pollinator attraction, but is probably meaningless to studies on their rate of root growth. The fact that all the men fifty years or older recruited for a study were raised in what are today inner city poverty neighborhoods is irrelevant to various questions about the effects of growing up in those neighborhoods these days on success or social development since those areas were vastly different when these men were children. But it might be relevant to a study of the amount of DDT or lead they were exposed to in those areas and how much of that is still stored in their body fat.

Comparisons can be rigged and therefore may not be fair. Careful selection will allow a well versed individual to select entities to compare that have a superficial similarity but that are actually so different that someone in the know would veto this comparison as worthless. Dogfish (a type of small shark) and dogs both have tails but there are few useful comparisons in their uses of those appendages. Pigs and pygmies have little to usefully compare.

However, if the points being compared are carefully defined, it may be as valid to compare apples and oranges as two types of apples. What can be compared differs, but as long as we agree at the start what the points of focus are intelligent people should be able to work through this. Thus pygmy pigs and pygmy people actually have a bit more in common (e.g., the genetic basis of small size) that might be instructive. The preliminary process of defining terms and limits serves as a warning to all not to extend the comparison beyond those defined boundaries. Some will argue that including at least a summary of the agreed upon definitions and limits in reports on the results is a waste of time; others will argue that without that information any comparisons are the waste of time and potentially harmfully misleading.

Comparisons of some aspects of a system can be used to divert attention. It is true that the statistical danger of you being killed by a nuclear power plant accident is probably (these are statistics so they only give us probabilities) less than the danger of you being killed by a falling airplane. But if there is such a power plant accident, the consequences of the quantitative and qualitative differences, especially the long-term damage to the whole region, will make this technology seem the poor risk that it is. Also from that time forward the statistical risk of anyone in the population being harmed by a nuclear power plant accident will be calculated as much higher than today because there will be more cases to be counted. The 2011 disaster in Japan makes this case about the damage and risks, although happily not the direct and quick lethality.

A useful and valid comparison need not be simple or obvious. Often the most startling and instructive examples are the ones that didn't strike us until someone pointed them out. Generally they must be realistic, but comparing two fantasy actions might be okay.

The Ripley's *Believe It Or Not* feature carried as a regular item in many newspapers for decades (and expanded into books, films, and radio and TV programs - and today about thirty museums or *Odditoriums* around the world) often included good examples of making very large measurements or quantities understandable by comparisons to common items. So they note that "It would take a line of 33,000,000 people standing hand-in-hand to reach around the earth's 24,902 mile long equator!" The use of all those zeros rather than the word million would give many of us a better idea of large number than the word does although we understand that they represent the same quantity. Also "A twelve inch cube of ismium, the world's heaviest metal, weighs 1,345 lbs. - equal to the weight of ten 135 lbs. adults!" The big advantage here is that the comparison allows an accompanying drawing with ten people sitting on the one pan of a large scale and this small block of metal on the other side balancing them. On the other hand comparing the water pressure in the deep ocean Mariana trench to the equivalent of 800 elephants standing on a small car has striking numbers but doesn't yield a good image because the elephants would have to be in a stack about 17.5 miles (or 28 kilometers) high so in a thumbnail drawing on a page they would simply be a vertical line. That pressure compared to having three SUVs standing on your toe doesn't make a good visual either.

We can do the math and recognize that the comparison is true. In fact it may seem so obvious that you might wonder if it deserves that page space. But a good illustration gives us a more concrete feel for how large that length, weight, or pressure is. Recognizing the validity of a quantity is not the same as really grasping its size.

Superlatives are comparisons which should get special attention. Superlatives are the most enormous caution flags in the entire history of life in the universe. See!

We use them often enough that most of us learn fairly early on to accept them with a fistful of doubt and reserve. We also learn how uselessly distracting they can be if we bother to argue about them. A few superlatives can be somewhat supported by attaching a basic qualifier like "officially recorded", "since we began keeping records of such stuff", or the most useful ones "in my opinion" or "in the opinion of (insert the name of the person or group)". But of course because these qualifiers shrink the aura of authority and absoluteness of the statement they are often deliberately omitted.

In some cases there are complicating technical factors that may only be noted when someone wants to claim a superlative for something she has observed. Consider this example. DNA sequencing suggests that Giant seagrass, *Posidonia oceanic*, that grows in the Mediterranean Sea could be as much as 200,000 years old. That would definitely make it the oldest known living thing. A complication is that the species reproduces asexually so all the plant units are clones. That would mean that the clone or genetic type might be that old but no single unit of it is likely to be anywhere near that old. So does it deserve the title of oldest living thing?

We know from trunk cores that let their growth rings be counted that some redwood and bristlecone pine trees are hundreds of years old - maybe two centuries old but nowhere near 200 centuries old. These are clearly each the same plant, growing and changing but not asexually reproducing themselves on the same spot so are they better candidates for world's oldest living thing? Obviously the definition of the trait being lauded as superlative needs to be carefully defined.

Some people are quick and eager to defend the superlatives they toss out. However, since these are seldom about matters of any real substance except to those hung up on trivia or bar bets, arguing with the claimants is unlikely to resolve the questions and will seldom provide any benefit except to strained egos.

Superlatives are, by their very nature, comparisons. Comparisons can be matters of fact or matters of opinion. As has been said in a variety of areas of dispute in recent times, you are entitled to your own opinion but not to your own facts.

"(Insert name of person or group here) was the (insert superlative here) of all times" is a claim. As an unqualified opinion of the speaker or someone he can cite as making the claim before he picked it up, the claim can be argued against if you have the stomach for that but it cannot be disproved because it is not based on verifiable data. Note how important a qualifier would be because that would reduce the claim to one that can be checked against official or at least extant records. Its truth is that it is the expressed opinion of the one who made or repeated it, not the validity of what she claimed.

To be a valid claim there must be a way to verify it, even if that resource isn't immediately at hand. Any "ever" or "of all times" makes that impossible as a fact but leaves it open as an opinion.

The Sexiest Man Alive is an example of an opinion tarted up as if it is a fact although none of those exploiting the title will bother to argue with you if you disagree. This is all a strategy to attract attention to a publication and sell magazines, not a claim of any political superiority or consumer benefit. As a valid factual claim there would have to be a widely-to-universally agreed on impartial definition of male sexiness and no such definition exists or is ever likely to exist.

Formulating such a definition with a list of essentially mechanical criteria that can be objectively measured as its components is harder than you realize until you try to do it. Definitely this group or individual or that one may come up with such word pictures of their ideal, but making it more than a generalization seems to be impossible. Getting other groups to agree is where it really falls apart. Others may agree that the man defined by group Alpha would be an attractive and sexy guy, but the sexiest? Sorry but he doesn't fit their many other descriptive elements, most of them not reduced to words, so he doesn't win their votes in the contest even though he might be nice to look at, fun to be around, and all like that. You cannot say that one characteristic type is the ideal without saying, overtly or not, that all others are less so. Will a sizable percentage of all the people in the world agree on what body type, skin color, facial features, etc. are ugly or second rate so they must be eliminated as criteria for the ideal?

Then there is the matter that for the claim to be valid all those in the category would have to be observed and mechanically rated to identify the winner. For this title that is annually bestowed by a particular magazine that would be all the men in the world. That factor is the Achilles heel of any and all claims of "ever" or "of all times".

Then there is the question of what happens to this year's selected individual that the title no longer applies to him next year even though he didn't die, become deformed, or disappear into a monastery out of sight of the mechanical measuring machine.

Of course few actually take these claims seriously outside the world of celebrity glitter and the groups who award such titles do usually qualify them somewhere inside as the opinion of their editors or as based on a poll of readers or some such. They can be amusing and fuel for the latest round of hype and silliness to distract certain segments of the population and keep the money and glory trains racing down the tracks. And there's nothing wrong with that.

Such claims are easy to pick on, cases of superlatives with clay feet if we want to bother noticing them. Claims and titles and awards like these are worth noting in passing simply because every time we accept such a superlative without reflecting for a moment on how false we know it to be makes us a little more vulnerable to accepting other claims, superlatives or any others, without considering what they mean or the implication of us accepting them without question or dispute.

Whether a comparison is fair is a always an opinion call and therefore inherently impossible to determine to everyone's satisfaction so there is no value to spending much time on it. You decide whether you judge the specific case to be fair and stand by your judgment. How much you have invested in the results of the evaluation will make the big difference.

It is a fact of life that any rating or grading system can be played (and likely already is whether many are noticing that or not). As a now well known example, it didn't take long for some to recognize that where their company product comes up in the listings from an online search engine - i.e., is it among the top group so it will appear on the first page or two of listings or back on page eight or twenty-two where few ever bother to go - will have a large effect on their business success from online sales.

Once these people noted that the rankings are determined by the number of mentions of their company or product names on blogs, chat rooms, and other online places - with no mechanism for assessing their tone or contents - they recognized that creating a lot of mentions by deliberately generating complaints or warnings about their product or service would result in more searchers checking out their website because it would be a top listed site and many wouldn't notice or would disregard the nature of the listing by others about them. So, within limits, they can have more success by making their customers unhappy enough to grumble about them (which many love to do and are quick to do) than by making all their customers happy (when those folks are less likely to mention the companies they dealt with to others).

Another path to the online top of the heap is to pay people to mention you sort of mindlessly but regularly on their blogs and in chat rooms so those mentions add up without the hired help doing more than sitting at their computer for a while each day.

Those behind the search engines have begun to try to deal with these distortion methods but expect that to be a long-term battle of wits since the distorters have a lot to gain and not much to lose directly, in the sense that they can't be fined or jailed for trying to slant the system in their favor.

Philosophers and others have been aware for a long time of the tyranny of names. It is time we all paid attention to it. I am referring to our very human tendency to put a label or tag on everything so we can handle it mentally. The problem is that the name then becomes our symbol for a reality, but the name is only a rough approximation of the reality. The name *ball*, for instance, suggests something to most of us but it brings vastly different specifics to the minds of different people - a golf ball, a basketball, a large wooden sphere with a trained sea lion balancing on top, a fancy dress dance, or a "really good time". It's surprising that we communicate with one another as well as we do considering the vast leeway for misunderstanding and misrepresentation in the use of names that can be loaded with assumptions, consequences, and overtones.

Words can be powerful and have great impact on us. Sometimes it is the word itself that has the effect. A hate name may be used to deride or demean. A rallying cry or a hero's name alone may inspire us to extra effort. A battle cry may fuse the masses into a nation. Sometimes it is a type of message that matters - like a marriage proposal, a resignation, or an apology.

An awareness of the history of what has worked and what has not often leads those who want to manipulate others for whatever reason to make use of the power of names and labels whenever possible. Most of us do so every so often in conversation or when trying to persuade another to do things our way or because we say so. We would be dumb not to do what is widely, although not too explicitly, recognized as making us more effective.

As with many things considered in this book, it is not feasible to prevent those inclined to use this power against us from trying to do so since that would require a degree of censorship that we cannot achieve, especially under a system of democratic governance, and would hate to have imposed on ourselves too. The defense response therefore is to make ourselves sensitive to the technique and depend on ourselves to scrutinize what we are supposed to swallow unconsidered. To the extent that focusing on this process prompts some persons to switch over to more rather than less attention whenever a title is thrown out as a point of argument for or against something, the use of the technique will end up having the reverse effect. Because it will draw attention to itself, each inappropriate instance of hiding behind names and titles will reduce its effectiveness among those individuals. If those detecting the maneuver bring it to public attention with appropriate disdain for the users and warnings for those targeted, the attempts won't disappear entirely but they will become less effective and therefore less often tried.

Titles work, if they do, because they short-circuit critical thinking. For instance, questions are raised about the knowledge, legitimacy, actions, or political position (in the narrow or the broad sense) of some person not identified by name. When that subject is identified by some title you jump to a conclusion that such a person would or would not do or think such and such. In the standard way of acting, once you have reached a conclusion, you turn off the critical spotlight and move on to the next topic. Therefore in this case the title keeps you from considering the individual. Police officials aren't expected to be crooks and bishops aren't expected to lie publicly. Peons are not usually asked for suggestions in solving complicated business problems and fire fighters are not expected to be arsonists.

Problems often result from our failure to adequately define the terms we are using and names or titles may complicate the situation by short-circuiting our critical thinking about those matters or about those individuals. You may be well aware that a particular word or phrase has different connotations depending on the context. There are different overtones, limitations on its applications, or implied connections of both the precise words being used and the coloring of associations and unspoken assumptions they often have in separate cases. Nonetheless you will probably tend to assume that in the context of this discussion everyone obviously recognizes that it means exactly and only what you are taking it to mean.

You might even fear it would generate demeaning comments if you suggested checking your definitions after someone with a title has in some fashion approved the use of the words. Unfortunately after enough misunderstandings or worse, some people will conclude that you can never trust what anyone says about anything and that is the end of that. Yet a cool-headed review of the unpleasant situations will often reveal that a difference in the use of the terms was the problem from the start.

For any matter of importance, act like a lawyer and insist at the start on a explicit specification of the meaning to be attached to each of the relevant terms to be used in the contract or discussion. Make it part of your trademark to insist on reaching that agreement. Firmly decline to proceed without that step. Others may object that it is just a delaying tactic and a waste of time, but often enough if you then state your understanding of the definitions - along with the firm insistence that those are therefore the ones agreed to by all as the operative meanings - that will bring to light significant differences of interpretation early enough to save a lot of time, anger, and ulcers.

This assumes, of course, that you are prepared to be honest and frank in your interaction. If you are carefully plotting your own words to allow subsequent denial that you made any agreement or commitment based on your own particular interpretation of what was said or not said, then you can ill afford to define your terms.

Thus be wary of others who won't agree to an initial definition of terms because probably a major reason for not doing so is the desire to argue at some later time for an interpretation other than the most standard or apparent one. That might mean you are being set up to be cheated, manipulated, or made a fool of. Why go along with that? Consider also that when you are dealing with another who has polished critical skills, this is what you are projecting to him that you intend to do to him if you are the one refusing to define your terms.

Technical terms and jargon have their place within the circle of people dealing with complex topics. Some of the core ideas can usually be explained without that terminology but many of the nuances that are important to a deep grasp of the subject will not translate in the process and usually it will require more words, maybe many more words, to convey that information. When people want to impress others, or when they want to stifle questions or objections, the technical terms are often trooped out without need and without improving the communication.

For example, if I want to explain the workings of living things to those without a background in biology I must use care in my choice of terms. A "membrane depolarization-repolarization phenomenon" and "a nerve impulse" describe the same occurrence but the first would have no meaning for most non-biologists and therefore might be used to sound more learned than the topic requires. On the other hand to a biologist a *nerve* is a bundle of many axon strands, each an extension of a single individual and largely independent neuron cell, but to most other people it means a single complete nerve cell - what the biologist calls a neuron. And calling the outer layer of the skin the squamous epithelial layer reminds the biologist of several traits of those cells but leaves others scratching that layer on their heads.

You can spend all afternoon in chitchat but if you want to make an important point that will not be written into some contract or record in a forum larger than your kitchen table, you need to trim, shape, and compact your words to say as much as you can in the relatively short attention and courtesy span of your audience. A standard device to help in that process is the use of code words, those key words or phrases that stand as symbols of extensive and often complicated realities. These are useful for both the speaker/writer and the listener/reader. Their major plus is the time saved during a communication session and how readily they can become slogans.

These catch words are selected by groups to simplify discussions, but they are only effective in that role among members of that group. They are often significant stumbling blocks for those who are intent on maintaining an independent position because, despite the fact that this limitation is neither etymological nor historical, these words or phrases are easily interpreted as code words indicating what (and only what) those controlling the group wish to approve or disapprove. To use the phrase is to mark yourself as a follower of the philosophical or political cause since no qualifications, extensions, or limitations are permitted by such groups. The down side is that few people using the same code word actually do mean exactly the same thing by it.

Traditional family values is a prime case. This is a code word for a group of specific and narrow attitudes and programs in the parlance of the political conservatives. It is strongly skewed to mean nuclear family with father who works outside the home and mother who stays home in the kitchen where she belongs and raises the children who are rigidly indoctrinated from an early age not to ask questions or to disagree with authority figures so that they will grow up to be, like their parents, people prepared to support the special, usually self-selected, few who wield influence and power over everyone else in order to preserve those privileges that permit them to exploit the rest of the population to their advantage. As you see, the words can have a different meaning for me than for those loudly promoting this code phrase.

Democracy is a catchword that has or had different connotations or specifics in for instance Mr. Putin's Russia, a range of dictatorships around the globe where they go through the motions for P.R. alone, and in the U.S. or Canada.

Doublespeak is a term derived from the *doublethink* described in George Orwell's novel *Nineteen Eighty-Four*. It is speech designed to allow both speaker and hearer to hold two opposing ideas in their minds at the same time and believe in both of them. Such language is intended to limit thought, if not to eliminate it all together. By all means read *Doublespeak* and *The New Doublespeak*, both by William Lutz, to get a fuller exposition of this topic.

Doublespeak is now widely used to refer to cases where names and descriptive terms are deliberately chosen to confuse and hide some of the reality of what is being referred to. When the government spokespersons begin to insist that proposed legislation is about "revenue enhancements", not new taxes, we are deep in the mud. This is a good example of the process since it neatly shifts our attention from the effect on our wallets to the effect on the Treasury holdings. Surely it would be a good thing to have the government coffers filled so the funds can be used to do what surely the politicians will only allow to be good things. If you stay focused on that aspect you may not get around to wondering where the money is coming from - and then you are more likely to support the legislation rather than question the costs to you (until after the legislation is passed when you may whine about that a lot but for the legislators and promoters who devised and approved it you can be ignored until the next election cycle).

Euphemisms, nice sounding words for not so nice realities, are particularly a standard part of political and military talk. This is what gives us "Peacekeeper" missiles and "vertically deployed anti-personnel devices", otherwise known as bombs dropped on people to kill them.

Is real and literal equality of persons in the sense of political clout, economic opportunity, and social acceptance possible? Probably not. Power, whether political or economic, requires skills of intelligence and manipulation that large numbers of persons simply don't have. The unfortunate Catch is that some degree of these skills is probably also needed to avoid these manipulations.

Especially in politics it is a common approach to try to define and control the topics of consideration and importance. When a politician doesn't want to have to explain or talk about something embarrassing, he tries to redefine the topics to be considered. These days we know that the behind the scenes master political manipulators issue lists of topics and the terms to use to push them or to counter whatever the opposition is saying or planning to the party politicians who then, as if by magic and rather literally overnight, all spout the same phrases and insist on talking about the same topics the same day. They believe, and it often seems they are correct, that the majority of the electorate won't notice that and won't wonder why the elected officials and candidates are all automatons.

If you have the stomach for it you might make a game out of identifying the latest push words and topics and how many and which members of which political party find some way to put those into the public discourse in their speeches, in their answers to questions from the media or others, and on their blogs and websites in a several day period. The challenge is to document this strategy while identifying what day those "servants of the people" got those latest orders from the unelected directors of events behind the scenes. With search engine technology available it shouldn't be a labor intensive game.

An example from the not that distant history. The attempt to bathe Gov. Dukakis in an unpatriotic hue because he vetoed legislation similar to that which had already been declared unconstitutional by the U.S. Supreme Court requiring the recitation of the Pledge of Allegiance in schools is too typical of the technique of *Paint it in false colors*, which is a common political tactic. Or more recently, the condemnation of a national health care program by the politician who helped develop and pass a similar plan for his state when he was the Governor. This involves twisting some action or position of your opponent into something else by exaggeration, false generalization, or misinterpretation. The basis of the tactic is the hard to disprove belief that a large number of those who hear the claims will accept them and will never hear or believe the truthful statements and explanations. Or that those people are so bound and determined to deny the current president credit for anything that makes him look effective and intent on improving life for many of the citizens that they will deliberately harm themselves and their families.

The long list of comparable cases trundled out in the process of choosing a Republican presidential candidate for the 2012 election makes the point but are still at the time I am editing this too likely to sidetrack many readers without benefit to the point of this book and chapter for me to cite many of the recent examples. It is disturbing to learn from a report that, all the facts to the contrary notwithstanding, almost half of those expected to vote in the 2012 Alabama primate election told a pollster that they believe President Obama is a secret Muslim. At least someone gets some usable material out of the nonsense. On his televised *Report* Stephen Colbert could say with his character's straight face,

"Republicans release a new anti-Obama attack ad. I can't wait to hear what country he was born in now."

In an interesting twist, in fact, many of the same closed-minded people who go looking for such claims as an excuse for opposing the candidate whom they reject automatically because of party affiliation, racial or ethnic background, etc. will argue that any attempt on his part to point out the inaccuracies or misinterpretations of their claims is simply whining. In fact they whine that he is a whiner.

It will come as a surprise to very few when I assert that people often try to mislead, confuse, and manipulate us. It will surprise only a few more when I point out that the deliberate misuse of terms, especially emotionally charged terms, is a favorite tool for this purpose. Here the tactic commonly is to play up a word with a large and multifaceted meaning - like *patriotism* or *religious* - and then accuse someone of not being that type. Sadly, the less specific the charges are, the more effective they are likely to be. The intention is to keep the opponent dancing around trying to convince people that yes he is so patriotic or whatever - but often the only way to do that is for him to simply proclaim that the smear is false.

The most obvious alternative for the accused would be to point to specific examples of how he is patriotic. But since the accuser likely didn't specify how or why the opponent failed to be patriotic he can simply keep repeating the general charge and an insecure or unwary opponent will fall into the trap of trying to heap example on top of example until he falls into some error of fact or exaggeration at which point *that* will become the issue. Examples from recent political infighting come to mind with the lingering bad taste still connected to those memories. Of course each repetition of the accusation is considered news so it takes up airtime and print space again and again and again. The news media always need to fill time and space for which reason they don't get bored, they only get another hot story to exploit. The main thing we, as voters, consumers, and honest people, have to ask ourselves is what the ploy tells us about the accuser that he would try to mislead us in this manner or stand silently by while his supporters do the dirty work. Then we should ask ourselves if there are better sources for news that we should be paying attention to and supporting.

The switch between "big title" and "little title" is often a move to confuse a more inclusive term and its consequences for a less inclusive, more specific and directed, term. An all too typical example of how

confusion arises (and is often deliberately cultivated) was during the
debate over one of the various "bottle bills" proposed to pressure people
into recycling beverage containers, both to reduce the volume of material
rapidly filling the landfills and to reduce the energy expenditures needed
to manufacture new containers. Some of those with a financial interest in
scuttling the bills that would cut down on their short-term profits
succeeded in too many areas in confusing the data on the amounts, costs,
and consequences of solid wastes in general - which includes household
and industrial trash with highway and street litter. If you were fooled by
them, shame on you. But notice that that tactic usually leaves you with no
one specific you can focus your resentment on.

Two other made-up examples. "He hates dogs" - because as
mayor he vetoed plans for a proposed new animal shelter. That facility
would have violated the zoning regulations and the site was part of a
toxic waste dump site so it would have made the cleanup slower and ten
times as expensive, but none of that matters if we can make you think
badly of him. "He hates employees" because in response to a question
about his thoughts on those who take a paycheck but don't do any work,
he said that getting rid of the deadwood makes you a good manager.

Especially problematic is that often our name consciousness
doesn't grow with our changing knowledge and experience and the very
names of the things can become barriers to our thinking about them in
new ways. Our childhood associations with terms can become problems.
It is, for instance, only with an expanded idea of *house* that most of us can
visualize an underground dwelling, although there are such residences
around today - and it isn't only Hobbits who live in them.

Deliberately changing the names we apply to things often helps
us to think about them in new or different ways. It is also a common
strategy for trying to keep us from thinking about the subject. Thus at
one point the E.P.A. insisted on calling the low pH stuff coming from
the atmosphere "wet deposition" and all the talk about acid rain got even
more confused because of that new and weird name that seemed to
change the subject. Do you believe that wasn't the intended and desired
effect of the new term? Do you believe that wasn't simply politics? That
slowing and distracting everyone from air quality control issues that the
Administration at the time opposed because some of their deep-pocketed
corporate supporters insisted on that scuttling was not the intent?

A Postal Service letter carrier is a mailman but without the gender
implication. Try thinking and talking about "contributions to the funding

of essential government services" instead of taxes. It takes more page space but it reminds us that not all that money goes to legislator's pet projects or down the drain - without denying that some percentage of it does exactly that. Also, calling your doctor or therapist a "health care provider" emphasizes the end result without bogging down in the details of the individual's training or certification when that's not important to the discussion because those with a range of training and certificates or degrees can give us the level of help that is being discussed.

A special problem is the taboo or sacredness that we may develop about certain beings, institutions, or concepts. Once we have elevated these names to prominence we are virtually unable to question or criticize them because that becomes tantamount to sacrilege or treason. See how some persons will wrap themselves in the altar cloth of religion and cry "Blasphemy!" at any criticism of themselves or their ideas and policies. How many persons have you seen figuratively (or sometimes even literally) wrap themselves in the Nation's flag and claim that any criticism of them or failure to agree with them is unpatriotic, un-American - and liberal!

Since there are no laws regulating such things, those who want to obscure their group's nature while keeping it in plain view so they can't be accused of actually hiding it need only adopt a title that suggests they are dedicated to one thing while they are in fact oriented at a substantial tangent from that. Typical are groups who wrap themselves in patriotic sounding names but who are only advocating their own narrow interpretation of the principles they are hiding behind and trying to take over control of the meaning of the terms in the process. *Freedom* is only "freedom to do things and to think their way." *American* is only "our narrow-minded view of what that is allowed to be". Consider the names of the Super-PACs in 2012 politics for examples.

It is true, and I make no claim to the contrary, that often those claiming such patriotic covers seem to truly believe they have both a right to them and the only true claims to them. They do though deliberately construct their labels for effects which include the deception of the unaware because they know their overt claims won't stand up to scrutiny and will be widely rejected as extreme.

There are not, and in a democracy can't be, any overriding rules or authority that can prevent a person or group from using the name they want except where either trademark or copyright infringement or the accepted norms of decent public speech are involved. Without the latter, some groups who are intent on getting attention by shock would call themselves by the labels their detractors or competitors routinely apply to them in private discourse which raises the tension level and complicates the process of making using those names widely socially unacceptable.

Some names obfuscate to suppress inquiry. They aim to produce a reaction comparable to "What does that mean? I don't know so I can't even imagine what to ask those people." For example, a group intent on sabotaging attempts at passing or implementing specific or almost any environmental protection legislation might take a name that makes them sound like they must be supporters of such legislation. Those not paying much attention send them money for the cause, but are funding the opposite side than they wanted to. When they read about this group of apparent defenders saying that the legislation will do more harm than good, these naive souls may even put their votes behind killing the laws. It is not illegal and it works, so if you are willing to use and make fools of other people for your short-term profit it is tempting.

Scare and hate names are the derogatory ones that I apply to you and yours to make you defensive and in order to distract others from the essentials of who you are and what your positions have going for them. To the shame of those who fall for this tactic, they often work because the reaction of the hearer is not to question whether the claim is true, only to decide to distance himself from such a person. *Liberal. Child molester. Cheater. Supporter of regulation on business and industry! Non-Christian. Cultist. Capitalist. One percenter!*

Names of reassurance are the opposite of hate names but they too are often divorced from reality and are as likely to be used as a deliberate distraction or a short-circuit to the matter of examining this person in detail. *Church-goer. Civic minded. Generous. Animal lover.* Who even wants to question such things? So it is hard not to have them influence your judgment of the person referred to without giving that person further examination.

Some names are value-loaded and are routinely used to attach baggage to a person or group without specifics or qualifications or solid evidence. These are used on both sides of many issues, sometimes as badges to identify oneself to those with similar stances or interests, and at other times as warning labels slapped on by someone else to caution those who might be open to this person's "warped ideas". Typical of the names that have different overtones to different people is *environmentalist.* This is a praise word to some and a condemnation as an anti-business, anti-profit-at-any-cost weirdo to others. I once heard someone describe Ronald Reagan as an environmentalist because "he likes to ride on a horse and get out in the country and that kind of stuff." I believe you will find a lot of other people who would consider him a person to whom that term definitely did not apply according to their use of the word.

Nicknames or titles are often given to public persons, especially political ones. These are alleged to encapsulate the person - perhaps unfairly and deliberately, but that supposedly is how life is so they are okay about whatever distortion they add to the conversation - and once they are in print (in the wide sense) they take on a life of their own. They tend to change only if the person gets noticed for something else. Then the label is changed because he has now "matured and changed" or, more commonly, he has been connected to a new scandal or titillating incident that catches the media's attention. For examples think of the names you have heard applied to any president or member of Congress.

In some cases a general title creates gross inequalities because it fits a wide range of individuals that have more that separates them than the element that puts them under that heading. For instance, those from subsistence dirt scratcher to multimillionaire agribusiness operators are all "farmers". When that makes them all entitled to government crop subsidies that are calculated and paid out on a pro rated basis according to the acreage they (or their employees) work, this broad designation becomes a problem.

If after listening to an emotional political (in the broad sense) presentation or debate you wait for the media pundits and commentators (and even worse, the partisan spin doctors) to tell you what was actually said and meant, and who won, you are a dupe and you deserve no better treatment by those people than you will get.

It is all too easy to assume that the way things are done is the way they must be done, in fact the only way they can be done. Only when we examine our world and our lives with a truly open mind can we see what the real possibilities are. E.F. Schumaker demonstrates that so beautifully in his book *Small Is Beautiful: Economics as If People Mattered*.

We regularly screw ourselves over because of our narrow self-interests. We won't support strong measures to control someone else's damaging activities for a special interest because it is apparent that the same general control principles should, and therefore shortly would, also be applied to our own narrow special interests. In many cases our loss is great, our gain insignificant, but too often that doesn't seem to even be calculated, much less given much weight, by those involved. Such situations are not likely to change much either because the pervading mentality is that "I can't reform because everyone else won't do so simultaneously and therefore I would be putting myself at a greater disadvantage." With everyone maintaining that same position, their perception is true and therefore things change much more slowly that they could. The thinking of many eventually does change, often on a generational basis, and those with the new view - and by then likely the political power, change the ground rules and the goals, often leaving an ocean of resentment against those who resisted the process and those who did the resisting and are now furious that the things have been changed. All that bile seeps out and touches all that those people on both sides of the issue do or try to do later.

Think hard about what any attempt to change the terms used by government, military, and corporations mean. For instance when you hear a politician or industry spokesperson railing about the need to relax or eliminate the state or federal regulations on some particular industry or every business, do you automatically ask yourself just why those legal restraints were imposed? A bit of research online or at the library will likely reveal that, after much damage was done and documented, enough legislators were persuaded that restrictions and rules were needed to protect the populace and future generations. Find out what dangers and damage those regulations were intended to prevent or at least minimize. Also an important aspect to research - pay special attention to when federal regulations were needed to protect everyone because some states wouldn't require restraints to protect their own citizens or those in surrounding states or downwind or downstream. Then ask yourself whether fine tuning of the rules and restraints could not solve any problems without throwing away the whole safety system.

Keep in mind that government regulations have to be written to not be too easy for the abusers to sidestep which means there will always be rules that don't apply perfectly to every specific company or situation. But the only way to avoid those cases is to write the rules so loosely that the lawyers for one side can argue they do apply to this case while the ones being well paid by the other side can argue that they don't apply to most companies, including the ones doing the most conspicuous and blatant harm. Be realistic and ask yourself if you really believe that rules that don't do most of the job they were intended to do because they can't be specific enough to deal with every case are worth even putting on the books so that future politicians (which means those in the next election cycle) or company shills can't try to convince everyone that all those pages-long rules mean government has too much say and needs to be gotten rid of - until we need everything ready to go in an emergency when many of those same people will loudly condemn whoever is in charge that day for not making us better prepared.

Consider that when a politician or industry spokesperson says he wants to get rid of regulations he is telling you right up front and out in the open that he is happy to sicken and kill you in return for the favors the industrial exploiters will toss his way, like the treats for a pet that did an amusing trick on command. Have you seen any politician say he favors relaxing or getting rid of regulations for any other than economic reasons? How often have you been told that all the regulations must be removed so that the people who control the industries will hire you poor suckers who need work in return for your help in killing you, your family, and the strangers down the road? Something to think about before, but especially each and every time that you hear someone advocating tossing the protections that were put in place because the people whose actions were the basis of the problem chose not to make the responsible choices to control the damage themselves. Check the record carefully and you will probably find they promised to do that repeatedly year after year to stave off the government regulations for a while longer of more profits for themselves - and too bad about those they killed or sickened and the cost to the public for cleaning up the messes they made in the cases where that is even possible.

One of the great *slant* words in our language has only three letters but a seemingly infinite amount of suggestion to it. If you want to have deniability, you say *may*. If you want to smear someone or something that you have no evidence or arguments to convict or openly attack, you say *may*. If you just want to air your personal opinions but with an aura of universality and objectivity, you say *may*! And if you want to immunize yourself against inappropriate influence by those with any of these or a variety of other motives always add *not* after each statement of what *may*.

Communicators with political agendas - and that means virtually everyone at some times and in at least some cases - have recognized since earliest times that if you use indefinite terms to state your positions and opinions and you only focus on one set of the many possibilities (in fact without overtly acknowledging that there are any others) you can say almost anything without saying it in a way that you can be held legally responsible for it. This lets you smirk and smear but when the cases where it is shown that you are definitely wrong become a problem you can hide under the umbrella of uncertainty you raised.

Is it possible to eliminate such expressions of uncertainty from most everyday conversations? Not as long as you are discussing future events or present or past ones that are poorly quantified and poorly documented. Possibilities are the things that keep us going. If they are too limited, then everything is predestined. If that were the case the losers would soon know it and have no reason to even try to improve themselves and the world around them.

Would it be desirable to eliminate *may* and other indefinites from our communications? Not unless we want all discussion to grind to a halt since we can't be certain of myriad details. We need to be able to state our reservations, restrictions, limits, doubts, and hopes. When we want or need to communicate our lack of certitude, often a critical item of information, we need these words to do it. They are linguistic tools. My warning about or objection to them is that they are often used to slip things by the conscious guardians of our intelligence. The solution is to stay alert. In fact we should try to condition ourselves to have these indefinite terms trigger in our higher critical faculties. If you are paying attention and you are still misled by the words, you are largely responsible for that. It is your critical failing. The volume and the great variety of communications essential to life and commerce rule against us having perfect control or total elimination of lies, misstatements, or opposing opinions. The responsibility for working through the verbal jungle is a basic part of adulthood and especially of mature citizenship and that duty goes on as long as we do. The fooler can't fool you (except once in awhile, and then generally on a very personal scale) unless your defenses aren't up to preventing that.

At times we use indefinites loosely but then recognize that as a mistake. *May* is potentially misleading mostly when it prefaces a one-sided presentation. "I may do it. He may allow it." Is it possible to innocently use *may* and present a one-sided argument or one that doesn't push a political position of some sort? Undoubtedly. But too often someone that innocent is not someone you can depend on for clear thinking about complex matters and you probably know that from other conversations and dealings with her.

May is useful since it signals uncertainty and thus possibilities. For instance, from an editorial writer it signals that this is a person you need to be careful about and take careful note of whether she gives one-sided statements regularly in her articles or essays. If you agree with this tilt it also can be a sign of a kindred spirit and be useful as such.

Many times, especially in advertising, *maybe* will be *may be*, and is intended not to be accurate. "This may be your last or only chance to buy at this price" (since if this sale doesn't clear our inventory we will sell these items even cheaper next week - but if it does clear the shelves we will repeat this same sale next week as "back by popular demand"). Or, "she may be the best candidate to ever run for this office" (at least in her mother's opinion).

Why is *maybe* so alluring to those dealing in people or ideologies as their wares? Because it lets them introduce all sorts of terms into a presentation that would get them laughed out the door if presented in a more definitive form. The political candidate with serious accusations of illegal actions against her (or these days, any hint of questionable conduct that the opposition can find a Bimbob or Bimbo to support) will tiptoe around claims that she may be a true saint - but maybe you would be correct in thinking she is one of those.

Any comment that includes an indefinite qualifier word invites a speculation (even when that's the last thing the speaker or writer intends) and the best defense against being misled is to make the effort to have such words trigger exactly that response in you. Train yourself to have it raise a warning flag even when the presentation or discussion is intended to run right on by that point. The intent is that you won't be able to validly claim later that it wasn't mentioned, but you won't pay it close attention now or later. If the qualification is valid, and many are, the warning flag doesn't damage the message, it improves it because it makes it clearer where the boundaries of accuracy are. If the qualifier is mainly obfuscation, you have a better chance to reject it on the spot so that it doesn't affect your decisions to your detriment then or later.

It is important to intelligent and informed decision-making to know what is, what could be, and what is only wishful thinking. Anyone who knowingly presents "facts" as other than what she knows or believes them to be is a liar. That's pretty straightforward. The person who raises a dust cloud with *may, might, could* to keep you from grasping the real situation is a less straightforward liar but generally no more trustworthy. But note, if *you* make the decision to accept her claim or statement, *you* are responsible for it. Your burden is to make the effort to penetrate the smoke screen and make as sure as you can that you understand the fact, not just the claims. Any pressure to get you to commit to an action or position without taking the time to fully understand the relevant details - which might include verifying this person's claims with other sources - is a second warning flag that you overlook at your own hazard.

Such subtle qualifier words are often intended to be ignored and to suggest that what was said was more definite - but those traps are easily avoided. Adding the negative to indefinite statements leaves them as valid as before but usually presents the situation in a way that is less likely to lead you into unrealistic expectations. "The nation may suffer a major recession" is no truer than "The nation may not suffer a major recession." Only time will tell but by altering the initial statement in this fashion you may have forced yourself to consider the data rather than the intuitions of this spokesperson or the political agenda of this publication. *Maybe, could, should, some, any, many* can all be misleading in the same general way, although they are not by any means always intended to have that effect. All of them can be defanged if you automatically substitute the negative or otherwise reversed version whenever you encounter them. *Maybe not, could not, should not, many, none, few.*

It saves some agitation to accept the intent and assumptions of much public communication. You may well feel (I certainly do) annoyed looking through a book catalog at all the titles that contain *best, greatest, most thrilling* or *most dangerous* or *most important* twaddlepot knitting circles in the named war, century, or on the named continent, or planet. But consider it from the publisher's point of view. Who would give a second glance to a book with a title like, *One of the Minor Adventures...* or *The Unauthorized Biography of the Cipher Who Was My Uncle Mortimer So My Grandma Will Get Off My Back.*

The extent of the lists of the book titles published and music titles released each year reveals the diversity of tastes and interests and opinions across the land and should open our eyes to how little we all agree on the details about when, even to a degree, we all say that we accept and support some general principles.

We need these indefinite words and phrases to clearly express how definite we judge things to be and to show that we are convinced that these claims are acceptably accurate enough that we have the right to present them as factual. It is always the burden of the hearer to evaluate and decide for herself whether and to what degree to accept any claims. Depending on the topic and the circumstances (which often means whether and specifically who are the audience for your exchange with the speaker), you decide whether to leave her words unchallenged because you intend to ignore them, or to point out the flaws and hidden traps in the communication so that the audience will recognize those too. If you choose to question and challenge her statements here and now that gives the speaker an opportunity to clarify her point. Whatever she says in response is likely to be instructive about her thoughts and intentions, one way or the other.

The verbal extension of the consideration of current conditions or changes and rates of change into the future is a common and an acceptable tactic if the matter of concern is likely to extend into or to have a significant effect in that time frame. It is a risky tactic though in many cases where there is a large human behavior or choice factor. It seems reasonable to say that if climate warming continues at the present rate the ice caps and glaciers will melt and as a result sea levels worldwide will rise. It doesn't make good sense to say that *if the current trend continues,* fifty years from now a loaf of bread will cost sixty dollars - which has the unspoken add-in "at today's relative dollar value".

Strictly by the numbers progression, that might be accurate. But since the many supply and demand factors that would be required for it to come to pass involve human decisions it is very unlikely and therefore it seems weak and silly as part of a serious commentary. We know from history that economic pressures can and do change things quickly as people reassess what is available and the value of particular materials to them. Climatic conditions are not as directly vulnerable to short-term human choices or corrections. If the price of wheat makes bread too expensive for people to afford, many will switch over to other basic foods and not pay those prices for wheat flour based items. There is no argument about it, inflation makes a big difference and ten dollars today buys less than it did fifty years ago but everything has increased in price more or less as a total picture in that time period. The distorting element of the bread cost statement is that it assumes a world in which everything except one small group of elements stays the same while those change - and that doesn't describe the real world. As a rough analogy, *if the current trends continue* change in our mental image is like pulling out a bit of a map and creating an inset to print beside the large map that shows that one area in more detail. The real world situation though is like increasing or decreasing the size of an entire digitized photo image using any of the many available computer programs. The overall size is changed but since all the parts are being adapted at the same time the parts of the image stay in the same relative proportions and positions and there is little if any noticeable distortion.

If nothing changes... statements are weak cautions precisely because history shows that things always change and often in unexpected ways that couldn't even have been imagined only a few years earlier when some new technology didn't exist yet. *All else being equal* seems like a safe cautioning comment but definitely it is a weak one.

The honest and careful people among us try to avoid promising what we can't or don't really intend to deliver. At the same time we are often reluctant to admit too openly the restraints on us which make us look to be too little in charge when we nominally are, our lack of interest in the matter which makes us seem cold and unfriendly or unhelpful, or our unavailability which may make it seem that we are deliberately avoiding this person or that we have secrets (and "everyone knows" that those are likely to be naughty). Things don't always work out as we hope and effect so we routinely make allowances - but when dealing with those who are sticklers, put it in words.

Indefinites vary in how large, certain, or whatever a quantity they designate but except in a contract those are seldom critical figures. The words themselves say *indefinite* or *unspecified* or *unknown* so it is your responsibility as the hearer to not take them as larger or more definite than the context suggests they are with reasonable certainty. They also signal that there are unknown qualities or quantities so if you need more definite designations you need to continue the contract negotiations, not stop here. They may be intended as encouraging non-promises but they are too obviously that for you to claim later that the indefinite nature of the situation was kept a secret or that you were seriously misled about the qualities or quantities you were agreeing to.

Indefinite terms can be rather mindless automatic filler words, intended qualifications, and/or intended cautions. Subtle and somewhat standard words of caution are still warnings and heeding them is the responsibility of the person they are addressed to. Most people are likely to accept the use of indefinite qualifiers as a sign of the speaker's true doubt about a claim or its details and therefore a simple caution. But few will approve of someone using those qualifiers as an attempt at false reassurance in order to get you to agree to something that is not in your best interest.

There are conventions in speech, coloring or overtones of the meaning that are not universally agreed to or followed and that only those fluent in the language are likely to pick up on. These don't change the core meaning of the word or phrase so some short dictionaries won't give them away to those studying English 101 and the more complete ones will likely list them as fifth or ninth usage meanings. *Can* and *may* are an example. To many people *can* has an overtone of capacity - that it is physically, economically, or in some other area possible for this to be accomplished or for me to accomplish it. *May* on the other hand has an overtone of being permitted or approved by me or for me to do. *I can do it but I may not be allowed to do so.*

Could and *might* are another example. *Could* is often used with the implication of what is physically or otherwise possible, not just allowed or approved of. *Might* is a hodgepodge of physically and otherwise possible and what is likely to be allow or attempted.

The fact to keep in mind is that when you are asked to do or to agree to anything of consequence those words may be used by the other as if following the conventions without her intending to stick to that so it is safest to spell out explicitly what you mean by the indefinite words in that particular area. There may be protests later that you must have meant the other sense of those words (because that is what the other person's agenda requires) but if you have been explicit up front you are out ahead on the matter.

Any suggests that there is a degree of universality that the rest of the statement may or may not permit. Often it mainly indicates that the speaker has not thought through the quantitative element or other particulars of the topic. *Some* is indefinite but may seem conspicuously and deliberately vague.

Some words hint at the speakers assessment of the possibility of something happening or being doable. *Can* suggests that the item is doable but makes no promise to do it. *Should* suggests there are some criteria that must be met for the thing to be doable but gives no promise or assurance that it can or will happen even when those are met. *Would* always includes an element of the future to the consideration of what might be done or doable.

Some words suggest the speaker's judgment about the degree of commitment, assurance, or likelihood about what will or will not be done regarding a matter. Some of these words signal an indefinite estimation of a positive prospect: surely, possibly, likely, always, usually, as a rule, most of the time, frequently, periodically, on occasion, sometimes, once in a while. Other words signal a negative aspect: unlikely, doubtful, won't, can't, shouldn't, wouldn't, never, almost never, seldom, rarely, once in a blue moon.

Many simple but indefinite qualifiers are about quantity. These include: any, many, few, several, some, lots, most, nearly all, majority, plurality.

Remember that these are the easiest potential misleaders for you to neutralize. Always promptly repeat the statement to yourself or even aloud with the indefinite reversed. Having the positive and the negative statements both laid out on the table in your mind makes it obvious that one is as likely or weighty as the other.

In our complex world we all have to make decisions constantly and to do that we need information. Often part or all of this information is coming from people who might want to influence our decisions in their favor or against positions they oppose and they can do this by the facts that they present to us and the way they present them. Sometimes we are given blatantly false information but more often the attempts at manipulation are subtle. To protect ourselves from those distortions we need to be aware of some of the ways that information can be slanted and opinions shaped. We like to think that we are mature and intelligent enough to make reasonable decisions for ourselves and these approaches are the ways that other people may tell us that they think we either cannot or should not be allowed to arrive at our own conclusions.

People may want to confuse or misdirect you for any number of reasons. Often their intent is to gain your approval or to make you disapprove of some proposal. Let's consider some realistic but fictitious examples.

First, several cases in which the writer/speaker wants to gain your approval whether in the form of your vote, your praise, or your money.

"Approve the new water treatment proposal. The simplest and most cost effective way to remove a large number of kinds of the most harmful pollutants from our town's drinking water supply is to install charcoal filtration at the central distribution point. Many other processes require separate treatments for each type of pollutant but charcoal or activated carbon removes most of the carbon-containing molecule types in one step and those are the majority of the things we don't want our children to have to drink."

"Approve the genetic engineering proposal. It will mean new vaccines and more abundant, healthful, and cheaper food."

"Go see this movie. If you like to laugh, you'll love *Funny Movie: The Film*. Take two of the comedy world's biggest talents, put them together in a zany situation with a deadpan sidekick to keep things stirred up, and you can't miss."

But the emphasis changes if the person wants to discourage your approval.

"Reject the new water treatment proposal. A group of zealots want to spend millions of your hard-earned tax dollars for a new system that can't guarantee to solve all the problems of our water supply. They want to trust your children's health to an old timey solution for a very modern problem by spending big bucks for something that can best be described as primitive technique, not even properly called a technology."

"Reject the genetic engineering proposal. We don't want to risk epidemics of untreatable disease or monsters in the farmyard that may spread their distortions to people just so a few people can get richer."

"There is nothing worse than a film that keeps trying to be funny but fails at each attempt. *Funny Movie: The Film* can't even get a chuckle when it pratfalls because the sight is too terrible. Most of the audience will be asleep or on their way home long before it is over so they won't be disgusted by how it fizzles out rather than reaching any climax or making any sense. Be warned, I can't think of anything worse to compare this film to in order to say anything favorable about it."

The intent might also be to make you think you were informed in full when you were not, or to deliberately misinform you.

"Scientific studies using tabletop pitchers of water have found that charcoal filtration is adequate for general household purposes but there are no assurances that large-scale municipal systems are even that effective. Tons of activated charcoal would be needed since the system needs to be recharged periodically. That means additional expense on a regular basis. Inorganic compounds would still be a problem and might cause a greater percentage of the harmful health effects after the water was charcoal filtered."

Sorry, but I can't pass up one of my few opportunities in this book to react to three points in this even when I am writing it as an example myself. First, there are studies of filtration systems of various sizes and note that the above statement doesn't say those have been done and found problems, it only invites you to draw that conclusion. If the reason that there is no evidence of harm is because no studies have been done on the topic we have a right to be told that. Failure to note that there is no evidence precisely because there has been no research is sloppy at best, deliberately deceptive in all likelihood.

Second, any other water purification system also requires regular inputs of reagents. What process do you know of that doesn't require some inputs but produces benefits? Since charcoal or activated carbon is cheap and can be produced from a variety of materials that are otherwise waste items, like peach pits from the canning industry and a list of other waste materials from other operations which means that in many areas it can be produced locally and thus eliminate the shipping costs. All that together means this is actually a good way to go.

Finally, simple logic dictates that if we remove most of the many organic pollutants, what is left in the water is what will cause the harm - but that doesn't mean that there will be more harm done overall. Note that the statement above doesn't say it means that, it only invites you to interpret it that way. If we remove one mess of problems what we leave behind is the stuff that was causing part of the harm all along but that is now the only source of the problems so obviously it is responsible for what continues - which is much less because the harm from the inorganic materials didn't increase, only its obviousness. And without the damage from the organics, overall the damage is much less.

Part of a critical assessment of what we are told is to differentiate between the content and the presentation, between the speaker/writer and what he says. Too often we are charmed into letting down our defenses and then taken advantage of. "He's such a nice person. If he says it, I wouldn't argue. Someone with such a nice smile wouldn't do anything bad to us. Besides, he's wearing a business suit not some company uniform so he must be on our side."

There are dynamic speakers with nothing to say and others with something subversive to sneak by you. There are also dull or pedantic speakers who have ideas and messages we would profit from paying heed to even when that takes a special effort. Everyone who has ever so much as thought that some person in the spotlight couldn't be a criminal or other bad person because he "doesn't look like one" is open to being deceived by an attractive speaker without that person making any special effort to do that. Are you ready to trust your own and your family's safety to your ability to spot crooks on sight?

Let me list some characteristics of a speaker that might misdirect us or distract us from the message which is the most important part of the presentation to consider while listening. In themselves none of these is a problem or even a warning, but they are the tools a knowledgeable speaker can use to influence his audience without them being conscious of the manipulation. Many speakers use these factors without being aware that they are doing so and without intending anything sneaky in doing so. But as I have been emphasizing, it pays to stay alert and these are some of the things that you can keep an ear on while you scan the message for content.

A) *Sound Level.* Is the speaker talking so quietly that you are only able to catch part of what he says because he wants you to miss points but he will still be able to claim later that they were made?

B) *Dynamism.* Any good speaker is dynamic. He also knows how to use a change in cadence, volume, or tone to give emphasis without adding any words about that. Is this speaker slipping ideas under the wire by emphasizing the safe points and downplaying the controversial ones?

C) *The structure of the presentation.* Any good presentation will have an internal logic with one point leading to another and those points intended to be best remembered presented last so they are the residues that sticks. Points that don't mesh, or conclusions that don't follow from the arguments made, can still be inserted and those who are not paying close attention may not recognize that disconnect and can therefore swallow wrong ideas wrapped in a covering of sound ones.

D) *Straw Men.* Weak ideas that are presented as the positions or arguments of an opponent and then gleefully dismembered to give the impression that the valid ideas of the other have been shown to be deficient is a standard tactic of those attempting to shape our thinking. If you recognize the straw man as such, the impact is minimal or even the reverse of what was intended since you are likely to resent the attempt at misleading you and wonder even more why the presenter had nothing better to say to try to persuade you.

E) *Use of Generalizations.* As we noted in Chapter 20, these are easily abused since in many cases there are more dissimilarities between the items in a general grouping than there are similarities. An attempt to make us think we know something about a person, idea, or program based on such loose information is sloppy information at best and highly suspect as a try at deliberately misleading us.

F) *Complexities.* When the details of what is being argued about are presented as "too complex to go into except with those who have studied up on it" you are forewarned that you need to do your homework and study up on it or at least reserve judgment until someone knowledgeable on the subject whom you trust has reviewed the details and offered an opinion on the validity of the claims being made. That is because too often this is just a ploy to discourage you from actually looking at the details to see if you can understand them and maybe find out that they don't correspond to the summary you have been given.

G) *Use of Humor.* A joke can relieve tension or make a point that will stick, but it is hard to take seriously an important point that you have publicly laughed about. You need to get your back up to resist the attempt to degrade important and serious points by making them the butts of jokes. Someone arguing a side you are uncomfortable about, if not full out opposed to, that tries to draw you into a joking mode needs to meet stone-faced resistance. Your affability can easily be used against you so save it for other occasions.

H) *Choice of Vocabulary.* A speaker who uses complex technical terms and jargon for an audience unprepared to deal with that is either not prepared for this audience or is trying to produce a snow job. You get to decide which you think is the case. As long as you're not willing to agree to stuff that you don't understand, you are protected whichever is the case.

I) *Authority.* What authority does this person have to make certain types of claims or allegations? What are his credentials? Do the various honors listed in his resume have any meaning and therefore weight in this presentation? Having been the president of his high school class doesn't give us any reason to think he is any better versed in the details of economics or psychology than the guy who was forty-seventh in the class ranking or only made it to the semi-final round in his third grade spelling bee. We should ask ourselves what it says about him or about those promoting him as someone we should consider an authority on some topic on the basis of such lame credentials.

J) *Combativeness.* If the speaker comes on strong, at least you know he's not pretending that the topics to be considered are not controversial. In many cases your own position on the topic will influence how much allowance you will make for attack and negative criticism approaches.

K) *Willingness to address known public concerns and criticisms.* If this is a contested topic but the speaker won't deal with that, you are forewarned that this is not going to be a satisfactory presentation. You are also put on notice that the spin doctors are likely going to claim to the news media that the audience accepted without comment or perhaps even with enthusiasm more than was actually presented by the speaker. Maybe this is an occasion to literally boo the speaker.

L) *Willingness to answer reasonable questions and to respond to reasonable objections.* A moderator or speaker has the right and often the obligation to take reasonable steps to keep things from getting bogged down by statements that were supposed to be questions, or questions that will provide an opportunity for name calling and mudslinging but won't clarify the facts or positions. Clarification is often critical to preventing misunderstanding and we can feel better about the person willing to make an effort to keep things straight in everyone's mind. If the speaker or the moderator tries to block the clarification, you are on notice that someone apparently thinks you shouldn't know the facts in their fullness. You get to decide who that is and whether it is ineptness or an attempt at deception.

A variety of sources all indicate that in matters of consequence - like the selection of leaders and political representatives (categories that are often referred to as synonymous but any open-eyed consideration will see are not) - the fluff and sound-bite propaganda have far more impact than any information of substance. Some claim that Ronald Reagan reformulated the way successful politicians communicate with the public. Some concluded that those politicians justifying and defending the efficacy of government instead of speaking person to person to their fellow citizens make the mistake of not seeing that politics is not about programs, it's about passion and poetry and a search for some common national identity. I argue that the notion of community, of national self-sacrifice or responsibility, is a harder sell than the case for individualism and self-gratification, but there is a case to be made.

If this "fluff talk rules" is true, then when and how do the issues and the details get presented? Or will the majority simply leave that to the discretion of those they like? Is it possible to have a meaningful presentation of candidates, policies, or positions with primarily sound bites and headlines? Is it possible to run the country and the world on that much doctored propaganda or will there be a revolt and demands for better information? Does it matter if Joe and Jane Citizen know anything of substance about candidates, programs, and policies as long as a central core of persons who are primarily concerned about those matters are presented with a fuller picture? We regularly get the impression that the majority of voters know nothing more about what is happening than what they get in ads purchased by the candidates, TV sound bites, and a few headlines and that they are content with that. Is that the case or is that a misconception (genuine or contrived) of the news media that give us that impression?

How can this be changed? It is nothing new that the news media are owned and operated, and therefore influenced, by private interests with political views. That means that almost all of the information we have available to base our decisions on is selected, filtered, and shaped before we have any access to it and therefore it is always suspect. What we find on the news outlets is only that part of the data that some writer or editor or producer decided was what we wanted and/or needed to know based on what he thinks we want, need, or should know. Sad and particularly worrisome these days is the fairly open slant to shape the news presentations to what the audience "want to hear" rather than what they should and need to hear if they are to understand situations they can't directly assess themselves. Why? Ratings and readership numbers. When all the readily available outlets are vying for attention with the latest fluff at the expense of serious stories, we are in deep trouble and need new options.

Here's a scary question. What other sources do we have available to supply us with reliable in-depth information about the people, policies, and plans? This isn't a new situation but have we improved the situation for the majority of us over the years and with our new technologies? Another basic question to ponder.

Sadly, the evidence is that today elections can be bought not in the old fashioned way by slipping cash to voters on their way into the polls but by spending more on advertising than your opponent. This is where we have to wonder how so many can be so blatantly manipulated by what are too often lies or distortions as well as the obvious smears. The answer is that a lot of people are not very critical (in the good sense) and we all pay a heavy price for their deficiency. Then we have to listen to their loud whining and complaining afterwards on top of the working-over their chosen deciders give us all.

It is scary that the belief seems to be that the candidate whose ads are aired the most times gets the most votes. I assume there is evidence to support the idea and only time and a few more election cycles will tell for sure. It is depressing and scary to learn that for the Republican primary in Florida in January 2012 there was so much demand for paid political ad spots that some stations had to turn down some requests because literally every space they could squeeze in was sold.

This idea accepts that the TV ads are often heavily dependent on Internet blogs to supply new controversies and amusements to get wider attention and reactions, but at least for now their direct effect of the Internet items by themselves is harder to measure and track which keeps the focus on the TV material. Print presentations seem to have much less impact beyond sometimes being the sources of the items that can be churned into claims for or against a candidate and provide further justification to the TV news bureaus for wallowing in the muck while pretending to really want to be above that but hey, they're in business to report (selectively but we're not supposed to focus on that) what is being talked about.

In theory this means that if enough people become critical in their evaluation of ads and partisan claims, the power of money (at least in this area) will be reduced but you have to be very optimistic to think that will happen anytime soon. Are there ways to increase the likelihood of that happening? Direct educational exhortations or programs don't seem likely to make a big difference. In fact no single program or drive or whatever seems like an obvious way to do that job without triggering unhelpful resistance. Maybe a variety of subversive stuff might but it is probably better that those who devise such strategies stay under the radar as much as possible because they can probably have more effect when the targets aren't aware that they are being manipulated to face in certain directions where they can ever after be convinced they arrived entirely on their own. Since in terms of their interests there are lots of kinds of people, no one approach will be effective for more than a sector of them but if from early on the expectation and thinking is that there should be many contributing factors, we might come out ahead of the determined users and the empty-heads.

Symbols are natural targets for attack precisely because of their potency. Those who oppose something have the same general intention as those who support it. They want to get their message across to the largest number of people in an efficient and effective manner. Symbols are efficient and often effective communication. Sad to say, in the world of public opinion, slogans are better than essays, and symbols like flags are even more efficient because even illiterates or those only scanning a page or view screen can get their message.

This is the power and the emptiness of symbols. They are idiot talk because they allow no qualifications, exceptions, or explanations. They are used in an attempt to force yes-or-no responses to complex issues with the clear understanding that a *yes* from you in response to a question I pose will be taken by me - and I at least pretend to believe (and possibly do) - by all the others who hear it or hear of it, as your agreement with me on all the particulars and ramifications of the issue involved. Unfortunately you also operate on a similar principle and you take my acceptance of your agreement to mean that I agree with your interpretations of the details. But personal experience and the long blood bath of history show that this is often not the case. We have superficial unanimity or capitulation but no common agreement so that the unity will be shattered, possibly with feelings and accusations of betrayal and dishonesty, as soon as any dispute about the details comes up. For instance, we saw this kind of thing deliberately built into the wording and negotiation of international treaties when some in certain former U.S. administrations let it be known that they were interpreting certain passages in a different way than the preceding administrations that had done the negotiating and signed the treaties in the name of the Nation had agreed to.

Is it acceptable under the American Constitution and system of laws to criticize and even to try to change government practices and policies by peaceful means? Of course it is. That is what made us the model for the rest of the world in political theories. Ask anyone who is out protesting the government policies on abortion, immigration, prayer in schools, Christmas manger displays inside City Hall, or other civil rights. Or better, prepare your arguments to maintain that citizens shouldn't be allowed to protest, petition, and organize voter groups to peacefully coerce changes in laws and policies. Of course if you yourself believe there is any government policy or law, any at all, that is wrong and should be changed, you must recognize that you therefore don't believe existing policies are perfect or at least unalterable but you don't believe you should be allowed to do more than pray in private for them to be changed.

If you recognize that citizens have a right to say that policies or government representatives are imperfect and need to be improved by being changed, it becomes clear that the essential issue in a matter like flag burning is the acceptability of specific modes of expression rather than the essential motivation behind them. The argument is not about whether you can protest, but about what forms of expression you may use while you do that protesting.

When we squarely face the fact that it is the "words" that are the issue, we are often more likely to curb our tendency to exaggerate and pontificate. Since symbols are "words" we must reach agreement on which ones, if any, are so inherently important that we won't allow them to be used to attract attention to someone else's political position. And then we have to refine that to define who the *we* are that won't allow certain activities and how that group will be allowed to enforce their preferences. In a nation founded on the principles of our Constitution and Bill of Rights the reasonable argument must be that no "words" except those that directly threaten the life or safety of the hearers (like shouting Fire! in a crowded theatre) can be banned without the inevitable consequence of *every* word being banned as one group and then another momentarily seizes control of officialdom or the ballot box.

Let up hope that the recognition that the symbols are the issue will prompt the intelligent people among us to focus on the substance-symbolism dichotomy and insist that official policy should not be predicated on superficiality or silliness. Most flag-burners and other protesters aren't proposing to trash the Nation and all it stands for, rather they are expressing their distress at the shameful disparities between the promise and the reality, the theory and the practice, within our borders and spheres of influence. They are also openly rejecting the sanctification of certain items like a flag design and the small-mindedness of investing minor bits of paraphernalia with greater importance than as momentary reminders of the ideals those items have been adopted as symbols for. The snake eats its own tail when the protest is against the right to say what you want about symbols of the principles defending your right to free speech. The few who do want to destroy everything are largely ineffective except in the very short-term.

As the Doonesbury cartoon characters noted about the issue of flag burning back in 1989, once we decide to outlaw "flag desecration" we face the details. Can you tear up a photo of a flag? Can you cut a cake decorated with a flag? Can you wear a T-shirt emblazoned with a flag or are only government officials or employees allowed to wear it on their persons? The practical consequences reflect the complexity of what some would represent as a simple matter. The degree to which some groups work themselves up about even accidental damage or destruction to items like copies of a revered text keeps reminding us that whole groups, prodded by their leaders, can overreact. It is appropriate to question their overall good sense as a result. But check the history books for which and how many other groups reacted in comparable ways over the years before you make rash accusations.

On the battle fields of public opinion, angry people use angry words and get attention; polite people who use meek words get ignored. That is simple reality even if we might wish it were otherwise. That means that people who want to have impact use powerful words and try to make the familiar and the comfortable seem alien and therefore attention-getting. That is effective communication. That is good public relations. It may also be upsetting to some of the audience and be less effective with them.

Any decision to try to influence a group involves making a sort of profit and loss calculation. How much will the specific action help the effort, balanced against how much will it hurt the overall project (where the cost is measured in people convinced, votes, or advancement of the peaceful consideration and discussion of the topic)?

I would like to believe that even most of the reflex hotheads will cool their craniums when expressly facing the issue of peaceful dissent divorced from the matter of symbols but news media "people on the streets" interviews and polls are not reassuring on this point. It scares me to read that at one point a majority of the "ordinary" or "middle" Americans who were asked to read the Bill of Rights (without identifying it as such) said they didn't think those rights should be guaranteed to dissenters. In light of our history and our daily political wranglings, it is difficult to believe that there are any universally agreed upon ideals, a fact that is at the heart of some of our conflicts.

It is certainly a psychological defect when a person always finds fault with everything. Having unrealistic expectations and standards assumes both that the person will not be satisfied and that he will not be taken seriously by others for long. The result then is that the individual has no significant long-term impact on how things are done. But for many areas of our lives and societies it is possible to argue that there are real short-comings and we ought not to accept the status quo too easily. Complaining has minimal effect; suggesting a better way may make a big difference. Hitting the balance requires care and effort. But then everything that is of real value as a human endeavor requires care and effort.

Some things I can change myself; some I can influence change in; and some are beyond any direct influence by me. I need to recognize and accept that fact. To paraphrase St. Francis of Assisi, Let me cultivate the wisdom to know the difference. I can't do everything, but I can do some things if I am willing to make the effort.

There is probably no such thing as the "simple unvarnished truth." Almost everything of human knowledge has an element of theory, belief, or opinion about it. Therefore since we always add our own coloring to our statements, we must all take everything that is said with the proverbial grain of salt and expect others to take us the same way.

At times we may give the wrong information without consciously or deliberately aiming to do so. We may simply make an inadvertent misstatement and not realize it until later when we get feedback on what we are being accused of having claimed. Or perhaps we will never realize the mistake we made but others were misled by it and any subsequent harm still happened even though we don't realize our connection to it. Asking for a playback or even an interpretation of our question when we ask it makes it harder for the other to deny his intent to misinterpret or evade our question without being too obvious and may avoid many of the innocent misunderstandings.

We may give the wrong impression without deliberately aiming to do so if there is a disagreement between our words and body language. We may also give the wrong information or impression by answering the wrong question. That is, we answer the one we thought was asked, rather than the one that was actually asked. Or we answer the question we think was intended but that was deliberately not being asked, but we may be wrong about that. We may answer the question that we can defend ourselves for claiming that we interpreted the other person as asking - so that we can sidestep the one actually asked that for some reason we would prefer to avoid. Or we may not think it appropriate to say outright what we know or think because of others who would overhear us, especially children, rivals, or perhaps in some cases the police.

We may intend to not answer but we give polite phrases rather than get into a fight about our decision. We may avoid giving an answer that we don't feel is required of us by misdirecting the questioner but without lying. We may conveniently misunderstand the question, state what we are answering, then give a useless answer. We may simply delay giving our response so that we can avoid doing so by escaping from this person's presence. We can fall back on that all time favorite solution of politicians and insist that the topic requires further study or inquiry before we can respond. Or we may simply repeat what others have said on the topic without committing ourselves to any position. Lots of options, depending on the exact circumstances and our intentions, self-assurance, and craftiness.

It is a shame that there is such a void between what some people say and think they should be or do, and what they actually are as defined by their actions and deliberate inactions.

An area of concern that we should consider here is the difference between what you say and what you don't say. I couch the subject in exactly those terms to emphasize that you and I spend a lot of time trying to obscure the fact that we don't always tell the truth, the whole truth, and nothing but the truth. And probably we shouldn't or can't do so. We tend to think that the other people doing this are trying to deceive or use us, and sometimes they are. But when we become aware of how, how often, and why we also do it, we will get closer to the point where we will be able to sympathize with them when, for any number of valid and proper reasons, they decide they can't or shouldn't be completely candid or honest. We will then be better able to prevent them from doing so to our detriment while accepting the other instances without undue rancor.

Often, either by design or by accident, we suggest as much by the statements that we don't make as by what we actually say or do. This might, for instance, involve not mentioning certain defects, deficiencies, or costs when we are negotiating about a product or service. Particularly in advertising this seems to be a standard procedure. That makes a kind of sense since the sale is the point, not total clarity and transparency.

Some will argue that you are not obliged to tell absolutely everything that you know about a product you are attempting to sell. In fact few of us really expect a salesperson or advertiser to tell us anything uncomplimentary about the product unless it is important to our health and safety and to the seller's legal liability protection for us to be made aware of a potential hazard up front. Perhaps it is unrealistic to expect the seller to volunteer unfavorable information but you should expect, in fact demand, that you be given accurate information when you make specific inquiries. It is your burden as a consumer to ask the questions that will give you the information you need in order to make reasonable decisions. Only when you sensitize yourself a bit to how much false information you are receiving, either as a result of deliberate suggestion or simply because of what you are reading into what is said, will you begin to actively and regularly seek the clarifications that you need. This will mean you will avoid many misunderstandings while removing one more means for others to manipulate you.

I am arguing that there are universal rules for communication that regulate what correspondence there must be between what you say or otherwise communicate and the external objective reality as you know or believe it to be. My main point is that you will be less vulnerable to being misled after you have thought about what can be done to control the perceived message by careful selection of the signals.

Here are a number of generalizations that might be made about when I might not say all that I actually know.

1) *I don't know enough.* Sometimes I don't feel that I can give an unequivocal answer because I don't have enough of the information needed to let me be confident that I am giving you at least an adequate answer. Particularly when I am an expert on some subject and I know you are only vaguely acquainted with it I may realize that you need additional information if you are to appreciate the true meaning of my statements. But you may feel that I should be able to answer your question with a simple yes or no. I know that if I do so I will give you the wrong impression and you'll probably go off and make wrong decisions based on my response. Later you'll be angry or worse with me, accusing me of giving you bad information. Therefore I hedge. I equivocate. You throw up your hands in frustration and accuse me of playing word games with you. Some matters simply can't be reduced to an either-or, yes-or-no answer and to insist that they can is a prime sign of ignorance in the lack of essential depth of information and understanding sense, foolishness, or knavery.

For example, you might ask me if diabetes is hereditary. I tell you that there are studies that indicate that in some cases it is. You assume that because there is no history of the trait in your family history you can't get it and you end up dead of complications of untreated diabetes.

2) *It's none of your business I.* Sometimes the information you asked for is none of your business but in order to avoid a fight I may put you off with some circumlocution rather than tell you that bluntly. This is especially true if being on reasonable terms with you might be valuable or important to me in the future.

3) *It's none of your business II.* Sometimes I prefer not to give you a direct answer because to do so will reveal something that I prefer not to have you aware of. This might involve specific personal information that you might be able to use against me, something that I have promised

others I will not divulge, or something that I just don't feel you have any right or need to know about me or someone else unless you have the legitimate authority to demand to know it (in which case I did tell you).

4) *I forgot.* Sometimes I don't tell certain events when questioned about an occurrence by someone with a right to know because I have genuinely forgotten them. The problem with this reality is that no one else can confirm that I didn't remember them so I may be suspected of lying about that. I have no way of proving what I didn't remember about the matter at the time, there is only my word for it and that is already in question so this is not a strong position for me even though I know it is true. Realizing in advance that I am in this unenviable position may at least keep me from freaking out when I recognize the signs that my claim is being doubted.

5) *It didn't seem important.* Under the stress of the moment, I may not recognize that some facts I know are relevant to the question I was asked. Later it may strike me that I should have made the connection but it simply didn't spring to my mind back then. It surprises us when it happens but it is something that most of us experience occasionally. You simply don't recognize a less than blatant connection between factors for a period of time, then in an instant it clicks and the fit seems so obvious. That of course is the whole light bulb going on over your head thing. Suddenly you get the idea, and of course it happens in an instant since that is the way our thinking operations work. At any moment you either see the connection or you don't. Like one of those optical illusion drawings where you either see the pretty young girl or the old hag but although the same lines are on the paper you can't see them both at the same instant. Your brain assembles the pieces into one pattern and you see that image; it reconsiders and assembles them into the second pattern and the image that you are aware of changes.

Here also you have only your word for what you were aware of at the time you made your statements, although your excitement about what you have now come to see both ways may help make your case that it is new to you. Again knowing there may be doubts about your claims lets you brace yourself for that since there is no physical evidence you can present to prove your innocence.

A few do and don't suggestions might be useful.

Do stay alert for ambiguous terms. Sometimes it is good not to nail things down too tightly but that is only true if both sides agree to proceed that way. The ambiguities that only one side really agrees to are always going to be points of troublesome misunderstanding, whether that is intended or not.

Do ask all the relevant questions, even when it seems like you're asking about the obvious. The easiest and best excuse for not telling you some relevant bit is that you didn't ask about it. This might offend the spirit of truthful communication but not its letter - and violations of the letter of the law are what get you fined or thrown in jail.

Don't assume that what was said is all that could be said. The moment that you start thinking that what wasn't mentioned can't be a problem, you are in sucker territory.

Don't accept euphemisms if you are concerned about accuracy and accountability. Spell out exactly what you are talking about and insist on explicit responses in kind.

Don't insist on full disclosure about the personal affairs of others (except where it is extremely important to your own concerns) if you don't want them to expect and demand the same from you in return.

Don't let someone else's claim of having been completely open about their personal affairs with you place any weight of obligation on you to reciprocate. Some people have no sense of privacy (or, more often, they reveal only what they want to and claim it is everything) and will try to pressure you to abandon your right to privacy as a result. For this reason it is often better when such a person starts telling you lurid details of her past to tell her that you aren't interested in her private matters. This won't make you her candidate for Most Cooperative Person - but who wants a person like her to nominate them for that title?

Do recognize that you too can use misdirection to protect your privacy. Carefully chosen descriptions are artifice but not lies if others draw erroneous conclusions from them. This is the sticky area. I see no major ethical problem in letting her draw her own conclusions if this information isn't something this person has a right to know. However, I see serious problems in deliberately misleading her if the information is something that she has a legal and/or moral right to know because that data is important for her to make a true and accurate evaluation of a situation that will affect her or others.

How much detailed information is another person entitled to? That depends on who that person is, the matter under consideration, and who or what might need to be protected.

Some persons have a legal right to certain information. An officer of the law while exercising her official duties has the right to ask certain questions and to coerce truthful answers.

The supervisory duty of parents, teachers, and various job over-seers gives them a proper need, and from that a moral right, to certain types of information of even a highly personal nature in germane topic areas. This right is not universal though. The social obligations of the relationship determine the limits, with parents having the widest latitude. Even then though there are restrictions that tighten as the child matures.

Based on the agreement to share their lives that is the basis of the marriage relationship, a spouse has a conjugal right to certain information to which no one else can make a comparable claim. It is, however, dangerously naive to think that mates should have no secrets from each other even though many areas of their lives are open journals to one another. We all need to leave some things buried in the darkness of the past.

Some persons have a *friendship right* to certain information. Your sibling or a friend may have the right to accurate information about things that directly affect that relationship, but not to know anything more about other stuff than anyone else without special credentials.

You should be haunted by your words and actions for all your days. They are part of your history and you should not be allowed to alter or rewrite them to match your present goals. We will give you credit for being prepared to stand behind your words when you spoke them, so we take them to be a valid sign of your true beliefs and intentions at that time. If in fact you were lying for some purpose it seems appropriate that your lies should now haunt you since they in themselves argue against our giving your current arguments total serious consideration.

Intention is an important area where the difference between the Law and the marketplace (used in a generic sense to represent our daily social and economic dealings in the family, on the job, and in the Nation) is critical. A person's integrity is most important because the only way to prove intention, previous knowledge, prejudices, and other factors that might color our understanding of why she said and did exactly what she said and did is if she tells us (which includes having her tell someone else who can be persuaded or pressured to reveal to us what was said).

Courts of law, and often even the court of public opinion, will require such objective proof before imposing any penalties. That makes good sense since otherwise effectively any accusation of prejudice or the like would automatically become fact in the eyes of the court and the people. By insisting on objective evidence we pay a price because some liars will slip by, but we benefit from more assurance and fewer deliberate smear campaigns. We also avoid an even less workable situation.

We know from common experience that even when various types of discrimination are legally forbidden, they are often still the motivation of those who can make a difference by their official or personal actions in hiring, buying, accusing, prosecuting, etc. This presents us with the problem of how to react to what we perceive to be discrimination of any sort, blatant or subtle, social or economic. If we depend on objective proof of the intention to deliberately and knowingly discriminate we are forever stymied and may as well resolve not to even bother considering such matters because our criteria have defeated us in advance. All the guilty party needs to do is to say she didn't discriminate or have the intention of doing so and the only evidence we have are our perceptions and our memories of past deeds, and words of this person or group. With rigid criteria, these always force a hung jury.

What can be done? Objectively (by which I mean in a proven or legal sense) nothing except to try to locate any other person who might have witnessed the actions or heard what was said at that time and place or someone to whom the truth might have been spoken - with no guarantee that there is such a person - and then fight the public relations battle of defamation of that witness, her credibility and her motives. Generally this is not a fight worth the price because it has so small a probability of success. The alternative is a personal one. You decide what you think the intention was and conduct your actions accordingly. If you believe the intention was improper, you must decide whether to buy from or otherwise support this person, maintain membership in this group, or whatever action or inaction you feel is called for.

If you take your position public by accusing the other person of bad intentions, or you organize opposition on the basis of this matter, you risk being dragged into the arenas of law and proof and we have already seen that you are not likely to win there if you have no witnesses or evidence.

So what to do? One possibility is to announce your opposition in whatever way is appropriate to the situation, but to avoid specifying your reason. You simply say no to this matter whether that means voting no, refusing to buy the product or pay the price or sign the contract. You decline to give support, or to allow your name to be added to their list of those approving them. Let the other side try to prove your unspoken intention if they wish. Some will find this unsatisfactory and will pressure you to state your reasons, but once you do so you can be called on the points and your inability to prove your assertions will work against you before any court, including that of public opinion. Stand firm and the other side is in the comparable stymied position with you as you are with them. Who you are in the context and how much impact you have on others and the situation will influence how readily and how acceptably you can maintain this position.

Are you required to state your reasons if you take some stance for or against something? Legally probably not, but in the marketplace it will depend on who you are, what the topic of dispute is, and how influential or important you are trying to have your stance be in the decision-making of others. Generally the more you wish to influence others, the more explanation you owe them.

If you are a voting member of a group and you are interested in making your vote for or against some point count but you aren't trying to influence the decisions of other members, you have no obligation (barring some previously agreed to by-laws of the situation) to defend or explain your position. Someone who does want to influence the decisions of others may try to intimidate, importune, or otherwise pressure you to reveal your reasons so she can jeer, cheer, attack, or adopt them but that doesn't impose an obligation on you to answer her questions.

Can I greatly alter my position on a topic with time? Certainly. Is such a change of position inherently false and deceptive? Not necessarily. It may be very sincere and deeply held. Therefore shouldn't you simply forget my former position and consider only my present one? Not at all. That would be an invitation to deception and a missed opportunity to understand you and your position on the topic. If you have had a change of position on the topic it may be useful to me and others to know why. Not because we don't believe what you say about your present thoughts on the matter (although we may have our doubts), but because your reasons for shifting sides may help us better understand the topic and our own feelings on the matter which may not have been well tested and may need intellectual or morale support.

You may have had a sincere change of heart on the topic but if it is a matter of importance and an emotional issue where battles are being fought for the hearts and political, morale, or monetary support of others, I would be a fool not to consider the possibility that your claim is only a ruse to get some advantage over me and my side. To forgive is one thing; to forget - in the sense of not taking prudent precautions to keep yourself from being duped or hurt again is dumb. We all have the burden of proof of the sincerity of our claims and just saying something doesn't make it so.

Changing some of your positions on major topics as you get more experience of the world is normal and to be expected. In fact those who are most suspect are those who don't change their opinions on at least some subjects with time. They are either blessed with clear-sighted understanding of the complexities and the realities of life from an early age (which is not a widely observed phenomenon) or they are so rigidly tied to a set of positions that they can't be considered functional and mature individuals as adults.

Precision, clarity, and succinctness are characteristics of effective verbal or written communication. They are also all too rare commodities in such communication. These qualities can be achieved in verbal and written communication by giving critical thought to what you are trying to say. Sloppy thoughts produce sloppy talk.

When the talk is limited to polite noise to fill in the gaps in social rituals, the defects don't make much difference. However when this is intended to be a serious meeting of minds to come to a formal or informal agreement, it is important to reach a mutual understanding of all the terms, the color of their possible meanings or implications that is intended in this case, and the limits being placed on the responsibilities of each party.

That this is not an easy task is documented by all the fussy legal terminology that lawyers use to fill the pages of a contract document supposedly guaranteeing that the precise meaning of everything is understood and agreed to by all parties involved. Yet all too often the sides still end up fighting in court for years over what the supposedly precise and technical language did or did not mean in this particular case.

We see what happens also when government officials decide they are going to go back and "reinterpret" the language of laws on the books or treaties with other nations in order to justify or allow their own pet projects which were considered clearly forbidden (or required) under the initial interpretation of the terminology and the interpretation that anyone not intent on justifying the new position at all costs of honesty, good sense, or the historical meaning of words in the language would understand from the text.

Sloppy thought is not the only source of faulty communications, of course. Very often the terminology of a conversation, treaty, or contract is deliberately left ambiguous or vague because the parties involved don't really want to commit themselves to much but for purposes of show they want to claim to have reached agreement. Each side leaves open the possibility of claiming an interpretation of the terms favorable to their interests at some later time, but they shake hands and smile for the news cameras today.

Some lack of precision in legislative terminology is inevitable since the lawmakers recognize that they can't predict every possible specific set of particulars of the general class of behaviors they intend the law to encourage or prohibit. Laws written with extreme precision and specificity are neatly sidestepped by anyone avoiding any single point of the prescribed conditions so there is a proper, even an essential, place for an appropriate amount of generality. This looseness of wording will always be the point of attack by those opposing the regulation but that is an inevitable part of life in a diverse but democratic society. The bad-mouthing of the rule-makers for not making every law applicable to every case is as old as rules and tells us lots about the grumblers but not much about the reality of law making, especially not in a high litigious society.

If the whiners proposed rewording or other changes to the laws they want enforced that have failed judicial review instead of just foaming at the mouth and showing their lack of understanding of how the law works and why and how legislation-based restraints need to be structured to make it feasible to enforce them, they might get more of what they want and in the process set a good example for those upset about other failed laws. Focus your energy on supporting fixing the laws rather than just complaining ineffectively.

Unfortunately some of the sloppy talk is intended to be just that. It is sloppy talk so it can be used to abuse or mislead, but it can't be nailed down or used against the speaker as evidence of a premeditated intent to deceive.

Setting aside the deliberately chosen imprecision and ambiguity, and the appropriate generality of the wording of laws and regulations, a substantial part of our day-to-day converse creates unnecessary anxiety, confusion, and trouble because of the lack of critical care in the speaking - and the thinking. Therefore better critical analysis can make things better in your personal space and that may radiate out like ripples on a pond and improve things for others too.

There seems to be more lying, misrepresentation, and distortion than ever before in history because of modern speedy communications, including but not limited to the Internet. Definitely this speed and anonymity gives the professional distorters more tools to work with. The modern state of interconnectedness means we all hear more of and about the lying and abusing in all its vehemence so we are more aware of it. Careful historians regularly dispute that things have gotten coarser or nastier in more than the short-term though. They remind us that as individual we aren't old enough to have heard, read, and lived through the earlier slur fests. They seldom disagree though that much of our awareness of the wrath is due to new communication technologies (not evil things in themselves) that put the audience more at a distance but vastly expand those who can almost instantly and for a small price be reached with a message that is close to impossible to then erase.

You can't stop it by protests or by legislation, only by making it ineffective. That means becoming a better critical yourself - while knowing that many are being twisted and there is little you can do about that since they aren't becoming more properly critical.

Ever vigilant doesn't have to mean hyper or aggressive though. Those shouting simplistic messages are advertising that you should ignore them because they are adding to the problems, not helping to solve them. If you do much shouting or strenuous button-holing, then that category includes you. What you need to do to be helpful is to seek and disperse useful ideas. That means you have to be open-minded and listen as well as shout.

Within reasonable bounds, everyone has a right to speak but not the right to have others listen to him or agree with him. You always make a quick decision about whether to pay more and closer attention when someone starts making his point. You have no obligation of any sort to waste your time listening to the full presentation of someone's position (and don't kid yourself that the guy who argues that you're obligated to hear him out will do the same for anyone else that he doesn't instantly agree with).

Don't hobble yourself by thinking that free speech means no consequences speech. We may not prevent you from having your say but it is naïve and absurd to believe that we won't and aren't allowed or supposed to change our opinion about you or our actions in your regard because of what your claims and positions teach us about you and your view of how the world should work and who should control everything.

Make it personal. When you see another person acting against your preferences and especially against the common good, identify the person and then ask yourself in what ways you are supporting him. Are you buying from him or dealing with him in business? Approving the use of public funds to support his programs? Recommending or at least tolerating him being invited or paid to address any group for which you have a say about that? Do you intend to continue to do that in light of what you now know about him? Actively working against someone is one thing and not necessarily in itself a bad thing; not supporting them is a critical difference. It is interesting to note how often someone intent on pressuring you to do what he wants will claim that you have a moral duty in that manner yet how seldom he seems to find himself morally bound to act that way when it is someone else's presentation or position being considered. The pseudo-pious are great utilizers of piety excuses to manipulate others.

Can you preach and make it helpful and effective? How active do you want to be, or are you willing to become, about arguing claims and pointing out distortions? The task has its benefits and its downside.

The better practiced you become at staying alert and defensive, the less disruptive maintaining your vigilance will be. Face the fact that vigilance is work but not inappropriate, unnecessary, or bad work. As animals we need to be always wary of predators, whether those are others species or other members of our own.

If you wouldn't take advice from a person about what company to invest your money in or which make and model of car or major appliance to buy, why take his advice about political persons or positions? Is that your idea of being smart?

Whenever possible, let it rest. Wait at least two days to hear the fallout, back-tracking, clarifications, and revelations before you accept the claims you heard made in a public forum. Ask yourself if you are realistic if you say you don't tend to simply repeat, not question, claims and statements after you have once accepted them.

Learn from experience. Don't ignore or forget the incidents in the recent past when claims were made and officials reacted but then the original claims were shown to have been wrong, even maliciously so.

Consider however how often the official confusion that resulted from cases like that damaged personal and/or institutional reputations but the liars and distorters were then rated and to some degree applauded as the winners not only by themselves but also by some of the pundits and some in the news media. The very talking heads who should have been shouting *Go slow!* but weren't now act as if they shouldn't have been expected to get involved except as witnesses with score cards. Shame on them! Why are you still listening to them and letting them shape your ideas about topics?

Recognize which are the slanted sources and let that guide you in evaluating claims. Don't expect honest and realistic claims about business practices and government regulation from the *Wall Street Journal* or *Fox News* and don't expect *The Sierra Club* to tell you that clear cutting is good land-use policy.

The fact that the problems continue to exist indicates that these are personal matters in the sense that you individually must learn to deal with the confusion of complicating information and interests, but that dies with you. In too many cases there is no institutional memory about such things. You may teach others the lessons directly or by example, but they must individually decide whether and how to accept and use them and whether those strategies are still the best or even appropriate ways in their social and technological world as opposed to when you were practicing those.

Each generation we lose part of our collective knowledge and awareness and must relearn and adapt because the accumulated memory is being lost at one end of the spectrum of living experiences and being replaced by new unformed ones that are trying to deal with the old base level matters in terms of the social and ecological world in which they are struggling to survive and succeed under the latest conditions.

We write down rules for what to do, but we know these are of limited use even in the short-term. That is because the general principles must always be fitted to the particulars and those always involve so many specific and often unique combinations of features that the end result is, at best, an approximation of a best answer. We strive for best answers but understand that better ones are often as much as we can really hope for - but those better ones are still worthwhile accomplishments.

The whirlwind media cycle (or circus, your call) isn't likely to be stoppable in the short-term. There are too many hooked on *the very latest* even when that is only hot air and nonsense. Also, the media (in a very broad sense of that term) are in business which means they lead by following the largest, noisiest, and most free-spending crowd. Sadly that crowd doesn't include many of those making the important decisions (in spite of the new batch of political consultants trying, and on occasion succeeding, in influencing some candidate's campaign). That crowd are the reactions because they are the reactors. Even then, generally only the ones who rave, rant, or whine the most have any significant impact because doing anything practical (like voting, not buying certain products, or changing the way they do their routine jobs) seems to be beyond too many of them for one reason or another. That crowd are the mass images on TV screens but collectively they have less real impact than they and those who want to sell them to manufacturers, politicians, etc. want to believe because not enough of them convert their enthusiasm while part of a crowd to personal practical changes.

Being defensive is not limited to and does not require arguing, brandishing your sword of holy wrath, or digging a moat to house a clutch of crocodiles kept poorly fed so they are vigilant. Being defensive means paying attention. How much, depends on the importance of the matter at hand.

In fact it is pretty hard for any adult or responsible teen not to be defensive but you can still be relaxed, playful, and having a good time while still being defensive in the good sense intended here. A parent can be delighted to see the kids falling down laughing at a party, but part of his attention is still scanning the area for persons or situations that could endanger the kids and everyone. They aren't unable or unwilling to share in the good feelings but they've learned as they matured into responsible people that the world is full of dangers, many of which you can sidestep if you stay alert. So they learn to recalibrate their attentiveness to stay always a bit alert for the odd, the out of place, the expressions or body language or small gestures that hint of intended actions that others are not supposed to be aware of.

Being defensive includes a collective aspect. In a group who know one another and share some trust the *on guard* duty is shared so that it isn't necessary for each person to be on full alert every minute. That most often means distributed so that each responsible individual is on duty for a time, then the responsibility is passed along. We see this same defense method in a variety of animals like geese and mongooses (not mongeese, I checked) where the adults take turns watching for danger so the youngsters and the other adults can focus more on feeding and the routine activities of the species.

There are of course limits to this and to every human strategy. There is always the danger that some adult will be sloppy about the job when it is his turn to protect everyone. Another danger is that some individual may organize and deliberately generate the impression of being trustworthy in order to get others to lower their defenses so he can rip them off or otherwise victimize them.

Being wary is closely related to being defensive. For my purposes I think of wary as what you do in advance to avoid or to defend yourself from verbal, ideological, or physical attack by others by not putting yourself in vulnerable position. I think of being defensive as referring more to the actions you take to fend off actual active attacks. You are being wary when you look for where and how those you suspect might want to harass you in some way could do so and then you try to avoid those situations. You are acting defensive when you take action in response to what you are aware is already happening. You may or may not do anything because of what you are wary or aware of, but you are less likely to do anything in a defensive rather than a random way unless you became wary or aware first. The two go together. In fact they can be considered parts of the same process with no argument from me.

Distrustful is part of wary that I am pulling out for a bit of focus so it is explicitly dealt with and is thus less likely to be overlooked. When you meet anyone (and for purposes of this discussion that means a person or a communication), you first search your memory to see if you remember ever meeting him before – and if so, in what context and what was your rating of the encounter at the time and on later reflection on it? Whether you remember him or not, you start to analyze him now. You register your reactions to his physical appearance and the persons, groups, locations, and other environments you connect him with – whether that is his intention or not. You consider your reactions to the details of his expressions, body language, apparel and other ornamental symbols or apparatus. Then you arrive at this virtually instantaneous evaluation. A gut reaction. A first impression. You may reevaluate that assessment later but you make it now even if you might deny doing so if asked about the matter because you did it so quickly and automatically that you may hardly realize what you did.

For animals, including us, survival often depends on at least at first suspecting anything and everything of being dangerous. That shape could be rock or a hungry creature able and more than willing to have you as its version of sushi. This open area may be one that you or your family group have visited regularly many time in the past, but each time you enter it cautiously and examine every corner for anything you can remember that has changed since your last visit. This is also likely an open access area so predators or rivals can have come here and be waiting in hiding for you to return, undetected until it is too late to do you any good but you will be a welcome item on their menu card or your females or territory a nice place for the rival of your species to be at home while you slink off in defeat.

It is normal to be distrustful and concluding otherwise is inviting the users and abusers to advance their agendas at your expense. There are those, usually highly religious and pious souls, who claim that trusting everyone else always and completely is a good, even a godly, way to act. I disagree. There are limits on trust as on everything else (a theme I hope you detect regularly in this book) but beyond some reasonable point too much trust is an invitation to a subset of people (how large a group we can't say with much authority because it varies with specifics) to follow the path of the less than saintly but often profitable for them exploitation of the weak, unwary, or dumb. This is more or less what we see as the common strategy of predatory animals in Nature where it keeps the predators fed and by removing the unfit from the breeding population keeps the prey species from being genetically weakened.

To a degree is the essential and weighty qualifier since there are no absolutes in human behavior. The situation (the exact conditions – location, time, persons or other entities involved, etc.) always determines what is best under these circumstances. This baseline fact understandably makes those who are law-makers and behavior-dictators crazy because their tasks require defined regions with clear cut borders. That means the impossible until/unless you are willing to accept and admit that there will always be some degree of fuzziness.

How can we ever proceed? By doing as we have for a long time, by selecting and then depending on judges of various types to decide he individual cases – with the same "no final absolute answer" results.

For you the individual, *to a degree* is a safety valve and a reasonable reassurance. There are indeed many things that could kill us, often with little or no warning – a nearby volcanic eruption, an earthquake and resulting tsunami, maybe an enemy sneak-attack using weapons of mass destruction. The list can be very long. Most of those aren't things we can prepare for in more than a general way. That means we collectively make the best judgments we can about what could happen that we can be prepared for and put those preparations into place. Human history is filled with cases where we underestimated what could happen (think Japanese nuclear plants and tsunamis) or what would be needed in the aftermath. These were failures but usually cushioned failures. We didn't make exact educated guesses about what could happen even though we often based our ideas about those matters on the size, location, and effects of similar events in local recorded history. That seems like as good a basis as we can depend on without reliable witchcraft.

Note in passing (but think more about it later) the very large and important difference between what *might* happen and what *could* happen - and ask what we expect the decision-makers to plan our defenses against. Then check out the accusations of incompetence or worse when what did happen exceeds what the guessers estimated was likely to be able to happen based on past events. At least we can usually see that the results in lives lost, property destroyed, and long-term changes in the area would have been even worse, maybe disastrously so, if we hadn't made at least the preparations that we did.

The personal justification is that you took the time to consider the consequences of various scenarios and decided on a position. That may not get you totally off the hook but will at least let you feel that you made a reasonable effort even if not the best of all possible choices. You took charge of your life to that degree rather than abandon all the choices to others. That is what becoming mature involves. We make choices, sometimes more deliberately that others. Sometimes with better short-term results; sometimes with better long-term results. Some of our less perfect choices are the result of our expectations and intentions; some-times they are the result of factors beyond our control and maybe beyond our knowledge. Adults understand that life is an on-going series of adaptations. Something works now but the same decision results in failure another time. I am willing to accept a certain amount of risk in my decision now, but at another time - for instance, when I have dependents - that may be more risk that I am comfortable taking. This is the reality of life. You can't coast very far or for long before you have to make additional choices about whether to continue on that path or to make adjustments. Most automatons have limited usefulness because they don't have that adaptive capacity which humans sort of have built-in. Engineers are working to design robots with more of such capacities in at least limited areas so that the machines' uses are increasing rapidly and regularly. The most conspicuous insight of all this is how complicated human adaptability is.

Every so often programs or attitudes are proposed as solutions or defenses against some kinds of problems. From time to time those proposals are unacceptable even when they are superficially good ideas. Zero tolerance policies and other absolutes fall into this category.

Zero tolerance is over-simplified, anti-adult behavior proposed and implemented by those who want an easy way out of complicated situations that don't allow for one. They're anti-reasonable, but positively stupid. If you don't trust those you put in important overseer positions to act responsibly, don't put them in charge. Those who accept the job of being in charge must accept the responsibility for making the hard calls, not say they need rules that disqualify them from using common sense. If you insist that you want zero tolerance, let's have it about everything, not just what applies to select age groups, locations, or actions. If those in charge don't, won't, or aren't allowed to be deciders, stop paying them the top salaries as if they are.

Identify those who instigate, advocate, or foster zero tolerance and never forget or let them forget that they are unacceptable in any position of responsibility ever again. They deserve to be branded with the shame of their failure to act like grown-ups. However, don't be too quick to blame those whose job may depend on them enforcing rules that they didn't make or approve of but aren't allowed to finesse to meet the real world situations with those who established those rules. Too often the enforcers are caught in the middle.

Such policies are often created in the heat of a media firestorm about some event like the shootings at Columbine High School by groups who are eager to show the world and themselves that they are being tough in order to make certain that such a thing can never happen again even though nothing can actually accomplish that and sensible people know it. You can make it harder but not give guarantees. Those who are intent of creating mayhem aren't going to let a rule stop them.

Those calling for and supporting these policies demand simple answers to complicated situations even if that means that no one should have any rights unless they approved on them in advance. These people demand absolute policies as a way to reduce complicated matters like sorting out what actually happened and whether there was any intent to do anything wrong to a simple, unarguable answer. They are especially likely to demand such policies after hearing about such a simplified solution being imposed elsewhere. That brings up the knotty matter of the role of representatives in any democratic system to be smarter and better than any group of scared and angry shouters – and is a case where a carefully crafted rule with the details spelled out would have the same benefits but avoid the unfortunate parts. Those who make the rules usually are not the ones who are supposed to enforce them or they would be more careful and specific. These policies are usually implemented to require enforcers to not be lenient at penalty of being fired. Why? If those on the scene and dealing with the situation are not ruthlessly unthinking enough apparently that makes the upper level administrators feel that they may look weak and they don't want to have to defend themselves and their underlings from hot-head accusations that someone wasn't punished even if that would be a gross violation of justice.

Wouldn't allowing leaders to choose leave some constituents shouting laxity? Certainly. It will also leave others shouting that common sense should prevail in public matters and failure to allow them to choose – or for them to do so when they have the leeway – is stupidity and smacks of fascism. There will always be those who say *too soft* or *too harsh* about any decision, but the general aim is to find a reasonable and defensible middle ground. Neither extreme is going to be workable for a diverse non-cultist group. And absolutes are extremes.

Which group of the shouters (among the various positions that will be discernible) that you allow to rule you and your family and your community will tell us a lot about you. Some will like you for it; some will disdain you. Many will wonder when the process of supervision and governance became so dumb. There is no perfect system if more than one person is involved.

The policies are established and insisted on only by the ones who threaten to fire those who don't blindly do that. In some cases they take that stance because they believe this is the proper way to do things; in some cases they are not imaginative enough to back better solutions. In too many cases they are simply reacting to the loudest shouters after some incident by giving the crowd what they demand as long as it won't directly affect the policy makers themselves. History shows that politics (in the broad sense) has so very often led to bad decisions.

It is tempting to say that there must be and therefore are a few acceptable close-to-absolutes - but trying to name those is hard. Why would there be any question or leeway if an act of violence or large scale harm is involved? Because of the circumstances. Every act is part of a set of circumstances and when those add up to reduced or limited control and therefore responsibility by the actor, it is unreasonable not to take that into account in our reactions. Having reduced capacity to not do the action does not automatically mean the person has no responsibility, but it recognizes that fairness should be impartial but not stupidly blind. Saying that allowing any leeway is wrong is what is wrong. Live your own life that way if you wish and are allowed by others to get away with it, but don't try to tell me and others that we must live our lives that way.

If a private company traumatized you with its stupid but assumed legal rules and procedures, you could sue them for psychological and reputational damage (whether or not you would win depends on many factors) so why not sue any school or other institution that causes indefensible trauma by having a twelve year old taken away in handcuffs for marking on a school desk with an erasable marker or sending an eighth grader to a mandatory drug awareness program for accepting a breath mint? A first grader charged with being a sex offender when he touched another boy's groin as they were playfully grappling? A first grader charged with sexual assault for hugging a teacher's leg? Are there no sensible adults in charge?

Zero tolerance rules are broadly written so why not tighten them up to avoid looking dumb, insensitive, and like automatons rather than adult deciders? A rule against carrying weapons into a building doesn't have to be zero tolerance to keep those with bad intentions from being stopped and dealt with. Yes, defense attorneys will argue at trial that the fact that not every student who was discovered to have a knife in his possession was arrested means his client must be released as innocent. Strangely, that will be done with no distinction made by that attorney between a plastic knife brought to spread cheese on crackers and a ten-inch steel blade hunting knife. But the decision about whether to be sensible is still in the hands of the judge and/or jury so there is not an automatic out for the would-be assassin, only a task we hope the defense attorney finds as distasteful as those who witness it are likely to. But that's his job. That doesn't mean he has to succeed at that though. These are classic cases where regulations are complicated to the point of being useless because those who don't like what happened or don't want to be restricted can and will have their lawyers use even the tiniest discrepancy between the exact wording of the rules or laws and what happened in this case to deny that the rules were violated or to claim that those rules which have so far not been tested in the courts in cases like this or to this degree of minutia are unfairly and illegally restraining their clients.

Here are two interesting and important questions to ponder and perhaps research. Is the imposition or use of zero tolerance a form of bullying by adults with either a political agenda or serious personality problems? Are there any zero tolerance policies that were or are made by groups who don't have to face elections?

Low tolerance can be defended, zero tolerance cannot. Everything happens in a specific set of circumstances that good sense and justice and reason argue must be considered if we intend to impose penalties on those suspected of being involved. A bomb hidden in this man's car blew up and killed people near it. Should he be condemned and treated as a terrorist? What evidence is there that he knew there was a bomb in the car? What evidence is there that he knows how to build such a bomb or has dealings with people who know that? What evidence is there that he had a choice? If he was unconscious or drugged nearby what could he have done?

Weighing the evidence and the possible degree of responsibility takes time but doesn't have to take long. Injustice due to haste cannot be undone and should haunt those involved in it forever. Appropriate delay doesn't have to mean not done, only better done.

Zero tolerance policies set a bad example and send messages in addition to those their makers intend. They say, "There is no place for reason in this society or jurisdiction". They say, "Don't respect authority or justice because those aren't reasonable – so overthrowing them would be a good thing". They advertise that rules you don't know about (and would be little afraid of if you are acting based on common sense) can devastate you and your whole future for an insignificant mistake. They shout out, "Don't expect good sense from governance. They are over-simplifiers and don't deserve your respect, compliance, or maybe even your tolerance." But they allow some to feel they have done something and that makes them look tough and entitled to your praise, too bad about those damaged by the stupid consequences.

What about security TV camera surveillance? You install a system and get poor quality images that may or may not let you identify the perpetrators. Based on what we see on the TV news, that does not happen all that often as yet again the police ask the public's help in identifying the shapes on a tape that could be almost anyone in the world. Fortunately at least once in a while someone does identify the person in the recorded image on the basis of the clothing the suspect it wearing, background items that identify the location as a familiar one, or some characteristic move of the suspect so the images are not totally worthless. You have to assume from those requests that the police can't improve the image or why would they ask us to identify the crappy picture rather than a better one? The bottom line though is that you didn't prevent the crime, you only collected some evidence to help identify and maybe arrests some suspects later. But it seems that mostly what you have are useless images of guys running down the street. Even if you have moderately good images you still have to identify those in them and then catch them. Then you must persuade a judge or jury that that blur on the screen is this person who doesn't look much like that because that blur doesn't have enough detail to look like anyone specific. Locks prevent crimes; taped surveillance pictures seem mostly to only document them - and give those who install them a false sense of security. We have no way to know how often they do give a potential thief second thoughts and prevent them – and there are always people willing to spin numbers out of the air about matters like that - but that is another story.

In cases of violent attacks it seems that the presence of cameras seldom prevents them because those either weren't pre-meditated or the attacker didn't know or didn't care that there was surveillance. Even then they only help catch the perpetrators some of the time. Better than nothing? Maybe - as long as they don't create a new group of problems in themselves. Are security surveillance cameras the best way to go? That's a subject for on-going discussion. Certainly we are eager to hear about as many constructive suggestions as possible to give us alternatives to try.

Except in pretty literally life-and-death situations don't let anyone pressure you to make immediate decisions. Be very suspicious of those who routinely try to set you up to pressure you this way. Try to plan ahead so you don't need to make rush decisions. If you operate that way most of the time, it's up to you to decide whether and how much to beat yourself up too much trying to change. At least make the most of your practice of concentration on the details but accept that you're voluntarily handicapping yourself.

Whenever possible it is prudent to literally sleep on important matters before making a final decision. Controlled academic studies document the long suspected idea that we are better off if we take some time to let our subconscious process the details and let our conscious ponder as many of the consequences, costs, and risks as we can before we commit to a deal. Often without pressure to make a quick decision (again, when a delay will not predictably result in harm or greater harm), we are more likely to realize or recognize the factors that this decision will affect, the various other things that will change one way or the other because of our action in this case, and the alternatives that didn't occur to us initially on the spur of the moment that would have the same benefits with perhaps fewer unwanted side effects.

Who we make a decision for depends on the circumstances. In a sense you are always part of any decision you make but in some cases you are hardly more than the operator pushing the button that makes the machinery turn the merry-go-round ride to the delight of those riding it and those watching. Always take a little time to consider the good and bad effects of this decision on others as well as yourself since those most likely to be affected are your family members. In some cases your business coworkers are positioned to get a good dousing of any splash over too. Your decision may have little effect on anyone else compared to how it shapes your present and future activities and options but it probably has some impact. Most often you decide things that you expect and intend will affect you fairly directly no matter who else might be involved to push the buttons. The more your decision will affect some-one else, the more you owe it to them to consider the range of possible consequences for them even if you don't decide that you must consult with them before making your choice.

To do your best thinking of most sorts it helps to be relaxed so you can let your mind go wherever it wants to in order for you to explore all the areas of your experiences (including all you learned via others) and your imagination. There areas where you want to be more on edge are when you must make emergency or survival-relevant moves and do those quickly and with enough vigor and determination to have a solid and possibly strong physical reaction.

Being rushed creates stress on you. Being under stress causes tension that makes it more likely that you will overlook things and end up making less effective decisions. Feeling tense makes you want to rush to get relief by making a decision. Round and round it goes. Not the best internal environment for new and careful consideration of the details.

By being a properly critical person you protect yourself from some of the exploiters and you set a good example for others. Being critical without rushing (when that is possible and appropriate) makes you an example of a better than average critical thinking person. Not rushing to panic decisions when those are not needed and rushing to snap decisions when those are called for - then recognizing and possibly making it clear to others by whatever method is available that you were able to do that because you were prepared to do so based on your previous unrushed considerations makes you a champ.

Condition yourself to ask, why the rush? Unless the world or some element of it will end, why does it matter if you agree today or tomorrow if you haven't already had good time to consider the details? Sometimes there are reasons and you can agree to the rush; sometimes they are artificial limits or deadlines imposed primarily to pressure you. It makes sense that a contest that anyone can enter has a midnight Friday deadline for the receipt of entries so those running it can then process those and move on. But if you are invited to invest in a supposedly on-going business but must agree in the next two minutes to the terms you have just been shown for the first time because the other party is in a hurry, that deal is suspect at the very least. Ask yourself if this deadline is real. Will this person actually decline to accept your money if you decline to sign any papers until you and your lawyer have reviewed the terms or until you've had a chance to verify the other's claims about his credentials and the alleged connections and details of this company? Do you really want or need this deal enough to risk calling his bluff?

If the other will decline your money because you won't meet his deadline, is that someone you consider to be a sound business partner and someone you want to be affiliated with? Even if you aren't certain if he is legit, do you want to be thought of by potential clients or customers as part of a company that blithely leaves you with a tone of questions about its legitimacy and its trustworthiness?

At the very least give yourself a mental reminder that if you are stressed (whether by lack of sleep, by pressures of various sources, including imposed time limits) you're not able to do your best evaluation and decision-making thinking so you make yourself more vulnerable by doing so at that time. Maybe you have no realistic choice or maybe you are just not willing to withstand the social pressures. Either way you are proceeding knowing your conditions and willingly (even if reluctantly) accepting those. You can't validly claim that someone else should have protected you or that you shouldn't bear the consequences of your deliberate, even if rushed, decisions.

How good a decision-maker are you if you get yourself involved when you have to deal with artificial deadlines that affect mostly or exclusively this specific deal? Have you ever insisted on such limits to pressure someone else to decide? If so, you can at least make an educated guess about the other person's motives and thinking. That lets you better evaluate whether this is a good deal for you, whether you want to do any business with someone who operates like this under the circumstances that you can evaluate, and whether you want this badly enough to accept the risk that it will turn out to be a poor choice when the dust finally settles.

This is not to argue that either side of a negotiation should let things drag out beyond a reasonable time. If you have had good time to consider the details and are "just not sure what to do" the other is justified in essentially saying put up or shut up. A deadline is only suspect when you are not given reasonable time to read the fine print, verify and consult. There are reasonable time limits at both ends of a deal – too little and too long. Their actual lengths are determined by you as you weigh the specifics of the situation and the consequences of your alternative decisions.

It makes sense to learn what we can from the lab research on the factors that affect how we make decisions. This research finds that no factors examined so far seem to be absolute and universal but many are common and at least a few will likely affect some of the decisions you and I will make today. If they were automatic and universal there would be nothing to do but submit but the human behavior research work done so far suggest that if we pay attention, learn the tricks our minds tend to want to play, go slow enough to let our conscious keep up, and scrutinize the automatic tendencies, we can be more in control of our decisions. Several of the suggested readings at the end of this book are focused on the factors that we hardly notice that operate us unless we make special efforts to sidestep them.

Another phenomenon that people have long experienced but had only casual feedback about is the effects on our decision-making of information overload. We handle a staggering amount of sensory input every day. Everything we think about starts as sensory input whether visual, auditory, smell, or whatever type although once it is received and processed it may no longer require new external sense stimuli input to trigger thoughts. The memory storage areas and other parts of the brain or nervous systems or body chemistry may keep the processes going once activated.

There is a limit to how much our brains can process at one time and overload leads to poorer decisions, with the consequences that go with those. Going a bit slower and resisting any unnecessary calls to make hasty decisions helps neutralize this potential problem.

Sorry, but new technologies for actually visualizing and measuring activity in different areas of the brain in real time have shown the claims that we are not using much of our brain at any moment (which never made sense or seemed like it could be true to me from the time I first read it) is not a meaningful or accurate claim. All parts of the brain are on constant alert status to be ready to process the kinds of inputs and actions that are that region's special assignment. You can't make a rocket guidance system that also ties shoe laces or picks raspberries without getting scratched with only portions turned on and at ready status. Our reactions would be a lot slower and our individual and therefore species survival much less likely if we had to turn on each brain area only after we determined that it is needed at that time.

This is a good example of how new and better technologies let us understand what is happening in more detail and consequently allow us to describe the interplay of the parts we understand better and correct our previous interpretations when there was more guess, less detailed data. In the case of the brain we now have several different systems for making the relative activity levels of specific brain areas from second to second literally visible on monitor screens where we can photograph or otherwise record them for examination at any later time.

Another reason to take enough time to think the matter through and then let your mind settle a bit is the recency effect, your inherent tendency as a human to remember and accept or believe the last claim or statement about the topic made before you began the final steps to make a choice. Caution is called for because this mechanism can be used by another to direct you to the choice she wants you to make. It is not an absolute factor but it can be quite effective. Try to think about it and consider whether the choices presented to you are intended to or likely to nudge you to go with the last one even if more objectively that is not obviously the best one for your purposes. When you want to persuade someone else it's not dirty pool it's common sense to structure your presentation so it will have what you consider to be the best effect. If you have to present all the arguments and claims why let chance determine the order in which they come out? If your presentation would remove the other person's ability to think or say no it would be a different thing but recency is one of the factors that the hearer's focused attention makes of only minor influence. If all parties to the decision-making are alert there should be nothing unfair or sneaky about shaping your presentation to have the best effect. Certainly nothing to feel guilty about. Get over any idea that you are not allowed to, or not supposed to, sell your side of a matter. As long as you present all of the relevant information that you are aware of and insist on a level playing field, you are acting normally and appropriately. Each party is responsible for checking things out and deciding whether this is a good or at least an acceptable deal for her. Someone is supposed to win any card game and as long as you aren't cheating there's no reason it shouldn't be you.

At times you have little choice but to make a snap decision. When the consequences of that specific choice are minor there is little loss except perhaps to your sense of self-importance if you make what turns out to have been the poorer choice. Snap decisions that are based on your experience are not usually rash or misguided though. Those experiences include your physical or "body memory" as well as what you thought and felt before, during, and after comparable choices. Sometimes making a fast decision about a matter you have considered in detail at an earlier time works out best precisely because it keeps you from over-thinking it now and tying yourself in knots to no good purpose. Gut reactions are often correct so don't automatically reject them - but don't automatically go with them. Your objective should always be to consider all relevant inputs and be exacting but reasonable in your thinking and deciding.

Studies show that pressure to decide now makes us skip over some of the considerations we would weigh if we took more time about deciding. Even without the academic studies showing this, the sharpsters have always recognized it and exploited it. It's not illegal or obviously immoral to try to set things up so that the person you want to have go along with your terms on an agreement of consequence is at a bit or a disadvantage by rushing her to decide - if she lets you do that. Seriously consider whether the other person's insistence that you must agree immediately or the deal is off isn't sucker bait - and then if you are still okay with it.

As with almost any mental activity making quick decisions means cutting corners and glossing over details. When time is short and a decision is essential now we are equipped to do that by a combination of subconscious genetic based processes, gut reactions, lots of areas of personal and collective experiences (all that we learned from other people whether formally, informally, by observation, or by imitation). Think it all through in some cases at your leisure and you are better prepared to do it at least okay or better in a hurry because you have rehearsed the moves and sort of laid down the tracks.

There are times when you want or need a quick decision. If you are someone (or you must try to prod someone else) who tends to go to a lot of trouble to avoid making decisions and then sticking with them you may want to develop a technique for putting a short time deadline on you or that other to coerce a decision with the determination to stick with it until/ unless you recognize a major problem. The specifics of what is a major problem in this instance will depend on the details of the situation and the consequences of you having made a poor decision.

Having considered what you should avoid or be wary of to not be rushed into things, you can use that information to design your scheme to get a fast response more or less on cue. You must hand-fit the method to the other person's quirks and level of resistance but you can often figure out what to say and not say to have the effect. And come on, you know from experience how to make yourself think you don't realize that you're manipulating yourself to get around your self-imposed prohibitions against things.

As suggested above, when you are not under immediate pressure about the matter it is a useful exercise to think through some decision you made in the past to better appreciate all the many factors that you considered and maybe those you could have but didn't think about at least consciously. Doing it this way lets you gauge its actual consequences and impact rather than just what you hoped and intended to happen. This task is to make yourself more conscious of the many considerations and decisions that were necessary for you to make your final decision. Possibly, even probably, you pushed through the process back then to be done with the stress and pressure to be done with it. For the purposes of the exercise, select a major matter like the purchase of a major appliance, or whether to take expensive vacation, or to remodel part of your house.

What things did you probably consider at least briefly? Almost certainly cost - in the broad sense of money, plus the time to acquire and learn to use and then to actually use the item. That would wash over to a consideration of what continuing inputs would be needed and what continuing benefits you would accrue. All of that likely lead you to classify the item as something you needed or as only something you wanted. Did you foresee it only as a convenience or as a tool that would make an essential difference? A complicating factor was the matter of who else properly had to have input on the decision? If there was someone else then you had to decide how you would present your arguments for or against the whole thing based on your analysis of the costs.

We'll use the example of buying a car. That purchase will mean less money available to buy other things. But having the car may make it easier to get to work and do your routine chores. It means you need insurance if you don't already have that, and possibly changes in your policy if the new-to-you car is more valuable than what you had until now. It may mean a space problem if it is a second car and you intend to keep the first one. It means your family will become more mobile and with a second car you will no longer all have to go to the same place at the same time – which might result in the family collectively getting all the chores done in less time. It might mean that a physically incapacitated family member can now be taken where she needs or wants to go more easily or simply feasibly. All of that and we haven't gotten to whether it will be a new or a used vehicle, a make, model, color - and whether to buy one or two of those little new car smell thingees to hang from the rearview mirror.

Most of what we do with more deliberation (when that will not cause undo problems or damage), that is with more thought about all the parts and processes, is likely to produce better results for us and society as long as we are mentally stable and honest. At least on a first time in our recent history review of a subject area that should mean we will take as much time as we feel we need rather than do it fast and poorly because we mostly want to have the task over and done with.

"Taking time" doesn't mean only or necessarily actual clock time, it can also mean the priority of decisions you focus on and other relevant factors. It is only useful to take your time if you use that focus to make the effort to think more about the decisions that are pending - their consequences, extent, and downside; the complications that are sure, likely, or possible. You don't need to sit at a table frowning and mentally grinding your wheels but going out of your way to distract yourself from any thoughts about the topic is not the objective. Try not to let your focus become so intense that it makes you angry or unhappy when you might slip over the edge and opt to rebel and do something bold - and stupid.

This reflecting time is not meant for doing absolutely nothing (if that could literally be achieved without major brain damage), it is time to do your homework. For instance, checking out the claims made by all sides in the matter, the credentials of those who claimed or were presented as having credible backgrounds or special knowledge on the subject, and any other "evidence" presented in support of one position or the other.

Keep in mind that while doing an online search you are half-blind so look over the descriptions carefully for the details you need to know to be reasonably certain this is as close to exactly what you are looking for as possible. Check whatever feedback or ratings sites you can find that include comments about this source. The Internet is a wonderful resource but also a minefield of dis- and mis-information.

Taking some time to consider a matter isn't restricted to sitting in a chair or lying in your bed. Exercise may help clear your head and sharpen your thinking. Often is it useful to get out of your chair and go do something. Go and look at what you are thinking about since that extra input may help you focus on or to think about factors you wouldn't have otherwise. Literally seeing where an effect would occur, the physical spot, might make your aware - or remind you - of what surroundings will affect the results and in what ways. What will be enhanced by the change you are considering? What is likely to be diminished or damaged by it? This may be an aspect you hadn't thought about. Maybe being there will jog your memory or otherwise stimulate your thinking to visualize alternatives that would make the whole project more effective and/or less problematic.

Whenever you can, in private or very publicly, take the time to consider the possible effects and consequences of not making a major decision until there is more and better information available on what actually happens rather than what the advocates say and even promise that will be (notably with no actual personal or corporate penalties when it turns out other than they said).

As an example much on many people's minds in 2012, what will be the costs if permits to allow fracking to get natural gas from underground deposits are delayed while further studies are done to better understand the longer term and especially the unintended effects? Who will suffer as a result if it turns out to be as safe and non-damaging as its proponents promise but was delayed for a year or two? In what ways and to what degree? Who will suffer as a result if it turns out to be as dangerous and destructive as some indications (like people living over the altered land having their tap water flammable as it comes out of the faucet) suggest because we didn't wait to be more sure? Who will pay for that damage? Who will pay when it becomes clear that whole areas have been made unsafe and unusable for decades or longer? Will anyone benefit overall in that case? Who? Who all will be harmed and to what degree? Lots to think about and exactly the kind of situation where any rush to judgment is questionable. Have we learned nothing from the disasters of the past that were predicted but allowed anyway? What's the big hurry and is that sufficient reason to act sooner rather than a bit later is a bottom line question.

Ironically, having options is good to a point but having too many of them actually works against our thinking and critical evaluating processes. Once we know that having to choose among too many seemingly good and workable possibilities we can help ourselves by trying to sort our options into more workable numbers. We might do that winnowing on the basis of ease of acquisition or use; cost - upfront and on-going; personal preferences; or whatever factors are important to us and our plans.

Everything, including taking reasonable time to make decisions, has its limits. No matter what or how much benefit-versus-cost data and reasoned argumentation is presented a few people seem unwilling to allow things to proceed if that means they must make a decision. I decline to say they are unable - unless they are damaged, in which case the common good argues for taking the right and power to make binding decisions away from them. My feeling is that many decisions are hard but we all have to make those from time to time and society has collective rights that can outweigh those of any individual in specific cases. Early on, societies developed legal systems to deal with these cases.

Don't rush into making decisions unless the situation requires that. Don't ignore your gut feelings about a case but still review the details as rationally as you can. Then decide, act, and prepare yourself for the next unavoidable messy situation.

Saying no doesn't have to mean being rude, unhelpful, or anti-social. It means not letting others dump on you and also not letting yourself become so busy with unimportant matters that you neglect the things of greater consequence to you. So say no! You have the right, sometimes even the obligation. It can even feel good because you recognize that you are putting yourself more appropriately in charge of your actions.

Being negative in the sense of pointing out faults and deficiencies is not unloving, unpatriotic, or "siding with the enemy". It is assuming the role of parent, lover, teacher, or coach in helping the person, group, or institution strive for the best it is capable of being. Who is willing to say he believes anyone who cares for us will leave us in our mediocrity if he could make us better? Maybe you should ask that question publicly of anyone who disapproves of you not accepting others and situations as they are without commenting or pointing that out when you can see that improvement is possible.

Saying no to a request for assistance, participation, or agreement to someone's statements is viewed by some as negative but they are mistaken. Saying a thoughtful no is a positive action because you made a considered decision and your choice was to protect your own time and interests, your personal integrity and your psychological and material resources. The person whom you turned down may have negative thoughts and may well want to try to pressure you to change your mind with murmurs that you are that terrible thing *negative*, but if you stand your ground he will have to try to warp things to a literally incredible degree to make a case that a decision to protect yourself is bad. That situation may be awkward and unpleasant at the time but at least that person isn't likely to bother you with that kind of request again. If he spreads the word and you get dropped from the won't-say-no lists of others, is that bad? Note that no person or group is likely to reject your help when you offer it even if you aren't on their "easy to recruit" list. This puts you in charge of deciding what you will do and how you will make use of the limited time you have available to you. Is that bad? Are you a selfish and bad person for controlling your own time? Do you really care about the opinions of those who say yes to those questions when they are talking about you?

Being negative can mean actions as well as words. It can mean declining to follow social conventions or the usual pattern blindly when those don't make sense or when you view them as harmful or improper. For instance, if there is a speaker, film, or gathering that you feel is improper or objectionable, you are free to show your disapproval by not attending. That is a message, but one so weak as to be valueless in many situations. If the speaker is invited to address some limited membership group to which you belong and whose functions you normally attend, however, it is likely that your staying away will have some influence. If you want to express your disapproval with more impact, you can demonstrate or picket against it. That is a now time-honored mechanism many places in the world. By the same token, if you believe in what is being presented or simply in the right for it to be presented, your very presence in the hall or on the street outside is a message.

In most circumstances don't expect anyone else to defend you from impositions since that would be an implication that they don't think you aren't mature enough to handle your own affairs and need to be spoken for, like a child or an incompetent.

There is a tendency for those who say yes to some things to be asked first and most often for other things. When faced with the task of recruiting help for some worthy project we all know the easiest way to fulfill the task is to ask those who, based on past performance, are most likely to agree. That is a most natural and valid approach. None of us really wants to go through the uncomfortable business of trying to get the reluctant ones to do their share even if we would argue that the burden should be distributed among the group's membership. The result is that one segment of any group does a disproportionately large amount of whatever work there is to be done although, you may have noticed, all the members tend to show up when it is reward and acclaim time.

This is probably the way it has always been in organizations and there is no problem with it as long as those doing the bulk of the work *want* to do so - and for a variety of reasons they often do. The difficulty arises when these people resent being imposed upon.

The problem becomes of consequence to you or me only when we are the ones being imposed upon. As I will maintain over and over again, the problem is one that only the persons involved can remedy and they can do that quite simply - by saying no. Politely but firmly. No excuses. No explanations. Say no and that ends it. You can only be imposed upon as long as you allow yourself to be.

Some will demand an explanation but you have no obligation to say more than "because I said so". You only make the matter more unpleasant by letting this person coerce you into justifying what you say or decide or do - always with the important qualifier *unless he has the proper authority to do that*. Let him do that and let that become the pattern and you are his puppet forever and it's hard to feel sorry for you.

In some cases where you have a specific objection to the task, those who are backing it, or those who will benefit from it (especially when that is deliberately not made clear to the general public) you can welcome an opportunity to publicly raise those issues. The reaction of the person insisting on an explanation will speak volumes about his awareness of the details and his agenda beyond the seemingly innocent one of wanting to get this job done.

Do you really care that much about the opinion somebody will have of you if that person's present opinion of you lets him feel he can try to impose on you this way? Think about it that way when you feel that little twinge in the back of your mind. What does it say about his opinion of you that he will approach you about this matter but not be prepared to gracefully take no for an answer?

Don't make any mistake about it, high-pressure salespersons are deliberately attempting to bully you into making a sale. They don't care about your feelings. In fact they are trained to, and deliberately set out to, use your niceness against you. Therefore it doesn't make much sense to worry about their feelings. Tell them no in no uncertain terms. Don't debate with them. Don't explain or defend your rejection of their sales pitch. Say no and close the door, hang up the phone, or leave their store.

They are depending on you feeling guilty about saying no to them and they intend to play on your guilt feelings to sucker you into buying what you don't want or need. They may approach the matter aggressively or in a wheedling way, but the objective is the same. Don't fall into the trap of answering questions about their product unless you came looking for information on it. Typical is the salesman out to sell you a multi-volume encyclopedia or its current digital equivalent who, when you tell him you don't want his wares asks, "Isn't the education of your children important to you?" Note that there is no real and necessary connection between you buying this expensive reference item and your desire or your success in educating your children, but it is a great opening to make you feel guilty. At least enough to hear him further so he can give you more of the same to persuade you that to avoid feeling guilty later you will have to agree to buy his wares right now.

Note that I am not arguing that an encyclopedic educational item might not be a valuable item to own or that you ought not want to own one, I am simply suggesting that if you didn't feel the need for it before this person began playing on your guilt feelings, you probably don't really need one. If you planned to buy one anyway, the salesman does you a service by processing your order. If he simply makes you aware of a resource you didn't know was available so you can decide whether it will fit within your budget, he has done you a service. It is only when he tries to manipulate you into buying what you don't want or need that he oversteps his bounds in your regard. But of course that is part of what many will argue sales is supposed to do.

It is difficult for many of us to avoid the everyday situations in which others, often strangers, try to impose social pressures on us to support them or their causes with our money, our vote, or our approval. It is even harder when the supplicant you are dealing with is a child or in some visible way handicapped.

You need to remind yourself that you have no obligation to buy this, sign this, or do whatever else is called for and that you will provide the person with a lesson in the realities of life if you politely decline. The lesson that not everyone is going to do everything that he would like them to do isn't pleasant but it is important. It's neither desirable nor necessary to be in any way unpleasant about declining or refusing but you should be prepared for the fact that the other person is likely to be disappointed. That is a natural reaction on his part and one which he set himself up to risk when he decided to approach you.

Part of the problem is that some people feel they have a right to impose upon you and they will complain, usually by pointing out that someone else goes along with them, when you refuse to cooperate. That's a lousy argument but it's still effective with some people. Why should you let yourself be manipulated just because someone else let's himself be used?

It is a favorite ploy of manipulators (although some of them do think this way) to attack you and your position by representing you to the "innocents", their audience of the moment, as completely alien and untrustworthy, and therefore unacceptable for not doing as they insist. For some audiences this is effective precisely because the members are part of this particular assemblage precisely because they don't want to have to think for themselves. They don't want the responsibility for making the important decision in this life and the next. They think they are shedding responsibility for their own eternal happiness by giving up control to someone who claims to represent the higher powers.

There's a problem with those poor and unfortunate souls reduced to (or in a few cases opting to) live on the streets of our cities. Any sign of friendliness or notice almost inevitably is taken as a sign to hit you up for a few coins, which unfortunately reduces your attempt at recognizing them as humans to a strictly mercenary interaction.

Some will feel that I am arguing against charity and human kindness and concern when I recommend that you regularly say no to those soliciting alms from you. I am not suggesting that you never contribute to any individual or cause. I am rather recommending that you do exactly that, contribute but do it consciously and deliberately because you decide this is the best place for you to distribute some of your resources. Done deliberately it is a joyous, fulfilling act. All too often when we contribute because we feel pressured and embarrassed into doing so, we resent the person soliciting and the very idea of the cause they are working to support.

Such begrudging financial assistance may let them continue for now but it doesn't do much for them or us in terms of expanding our horizons and making their concerns our concerns. Many will prefer to simply open their wallets and not have to consider who is at the receiving end of this "charity". That sidesteps asking yourself or the beggars what their true needs are and why they are in this condition of need. It doesn't bother with how my actions - conscious or unconscious, deliberate or very indirect - contribute to these conditions, and what I could do about the situation so they wouldn't need to depend on "charity". I can't bring myself to use this word in this context without quotations marks because I believe our highly organized and formalized solicitation campaigns too often seem too much like businesses in themselves and divorced from the true meaning of charity as a human activity.

I don't believe any of us can, and therefore should, be concerned in a fully involved way with more than a tiny fraction of all the problems of the world. Our solicitation campaigns always work from the premise (or at least try to give that impression with the intent of imposing a sense of guilt on us) that we must all be thinking about all the unfortunates of the world simultaneously. It can't be done. But the more of us the solicitors can inflict guilt on, the more contributions they will receive. It pays to advertise. In the short run this is probably true but once the drive is over and the checkbooks closed, that problem disappears from our consciousness, shoved rudely aside by the next campaign with the next sadly deformed but bravely smiling poster person.

The people who are going to make the real difference in solving any of these situations at the human, personal level are the ones who are going to give the matter more than that passing "I have to give this person something to get rid of him or I'll look cheap" thought. They are the persons who have made a deliberated decision that this is a cause they care about and one that they can do something about, whether with their time, talents, or money. But each person has to embrace only one or a small number of causes or he will spread himself too thin to be of much help to any of them.

You also need to be negative when somebody tries to pressure you to provide a critical assessment at a time or on a matter that you don't want to express a view. The subject of the requested critique may be the person asking or someone or something else. Any number of motivations may be behind the request. Especially when the person wants a negatively critical assessment of someone or something else from you to support his own views or to use against the other, you have every right, maybe even an obligation, to refuse to cooperate. You have probably experienced the transference that occurs in these cases where when you refuse to give the person exactly the support or ammunition he wants, this prompts him to turn on and attack you. If you won't be an ally, then you must be an enemy. This can be a useful moment. Ask yourself how you rate your initial assessment of this person and your decision not to support him now?

It is pointless to present reasonable arguments for refusing to discuss the matter with him. This person doesn't want reason, he wants support and cooperation for his position and nothing else will do. The number of spurious arguments that will be presented to counter your objections would fill volumes so you are better off firmly refusing to get involved in the matter at all. Understand that this will leave some people unhappy and may lose you some "friends" but you and others will be even more unhappy if you get caught in this quagmire.

Even when the person is asking for a critique of himself or his work, you are wise to be cautious about offering such feedback except at your own time and initiation. It is normal and human enough that relatively few people who ask for such feedback really want anything other than praise and approval. Despite your good intentions and the importuning of the person receiving the critique, any negative (in the non-praising sense) elements of such appraisals will seldom do much good. They know you are wrong about those points if your views don't jibe with theirs. So yes, your non-praise observations are likely to put a severe strain on your friendly relationship with the person who now knows you can't be trusted to see everything properly and objectively, i.e. the way he sees things.

Unless you are ready and willing to do so without prodding you will often generate less antagonism by demurring from giving critical evaluations (no matter how many disclaimers you attach to them) than by giving them honestly. (See Chapter 14 for more on artful dodging.)

You may even say no to criticism given to you, whether you say that out loud to the critic then or later, or simply choose to ignore his critique after considering it. It is your basic right to ignore or reject inadequate or inappropriate criticism. It may also be difficult. Difficult, because you must determine that it is inadequate or inappropriate without letting your own ego and prejudices blur your vision. Difficult, because often the criticism is imposed by someone who had societal authority to do so and who has the power to impose penalties on you if you don't comply with the changes in behavior called for. In the more extreme cases, you may be penalized any time you won't publicly state your agreement with and acceptance of the other person's positions and ideas. Difficult, because if you are sincerely looking for help, you may not see any others you can turn to for that so you might feel depressed or inadequate to the tasks expected of you.

Depending on circumstances, it may or may not be helpful to tell the critic when you are rejecting the offered views. With someone in a position of authority or control over you there will often not be much benefit to doing so and possibly some unnecessary aggravation if you do. Why make more unpleasantness when you can just nod your head and go do what you intended? But with someone on a peer level there can be an advantage to clearly and explicitly rejecting his criticism when you judge it to be improperly motivated, inadequately considered, or inappropriately presented. You are then reversing the situation and acting as a critic of that person's skills as a critic. In this case of course, you have the same obligation to be constructive to be effective.

A flawed criticism bestowed on you in a public forum may, and often should, be answered in that same public way. If the critic naively mistook this as a time and place to offer personal criticism, he will learn from the experience. If, as is more likely the case, the critic makes the observations in these circumstances precisely in order to embarrass you and/or to damage your social standing, you have the right and the obligation to defend yourself against the attack and can do so with confidence that what was offered was not intended as an effective constructive criticism.

A good critic always has in the back of his mind the caution that he might be missing some information and that he may be describing something that literally doesn't exist, didn't happen, or (more often) that wasn't intended to convey the message the recipient is picking up. That doesn't make the criticism useless, inappropriate, or even less valuable (since the other is now aware that misinterpretation is possible) but it does mean that the personal intent aspects of the criticism are off base. This can have a chilling effect on a would-be critic because it makes him look like a fool (which, in a sense, he is). This is part of the price to be paid but it shouldn't deter a constructive critic because you can only make your best judgment on the facts and situations as you perceive them and a good critic always recognizes that he can be in error.

Since the possibilities of misreading are multiplied by the number of communication interactions used to convey the information, if a critic's information is based wholly or largely on third person reports (verbal or otherwise) it is even more important for him to think in terms of establishing a dialog with the recipient of the observations rather than making a one-sided presentation of indictment. You probably recognize from your own experiences (if not, it's time you started paying attention) that you interpret what you hear and read based on your expectations and experiences and then you reinterpret it when you tell someone else about it. You add emphasis and draw conclusions about events, motives, and extenuating circumstances. For generations we have laughed at the jokes in which a series of people pass along a verbal message that gets modified at each stage until it is changed into an entirely different message as each person interprets what he thinks he heard into what he thinks it should have been to be a meaningful message. We laugh because we know how true that situation is. The recognition of this reality should make us cautious about third person information, but not so paranoid that we refuse to accept any such input. Generally the import and the impact of the information should guide us in accepting it and operating on it.

The aim of maturity as a person is to be responsible for yourself, for all of your decisions and actions. That means taking steps to protect your time and reputation from exploitation by others beyond the extent that you decide is desirable, and to let you focus on doing your chosen activities. Every time that someone else coerces you into accepting a decision, you have less control than you might prefer, whether you might have arrived at it yourself or not. Being responsible for yourself doesn't mean you think only about yourself and what you want, but it does mean that you ultimately make a conscious decision for or against each option you consider rather than simply acquiescing (which is a decision, but a weak one).

So practice. Say no today. It is quite likely that you will have one or more opportunities without going out of your way looking for them. You will probably find that it gets easier with practice even though you may never especially enjoy it. The goal isn't to say no to everything but to do so often enough in situations where you feel imposed upon to trigger you to think in every such case in the future that you have the right and the ability to opt not to comply. You reflect on that reality for a moment, consider the circumstances this time, and decide what to do knowing that you have options.

Practice saying no in order to get used to calmly making decisions despite pressure. It is good practice for holding your own in other hard-to-do situations. Once you have thought your way through the ideas and accepted that you have the right to take this stance and maybe even the duty to do so to protect yourself, you won't have to go through as much turmoil - or even none at all - to reach the same conclusion in the future.

Practice will improve your performance in saying no graciously. There is seldom a need to raise your voice or get angry while doing so (although there will often be provocations that tempt you to do so). It is also harder for the other person to get angry when your refusal is polite but firm. They would have to play the part of the unreasonable person to do so, and they are trying to avoid that. You also set a good example for this person and all who witness your exchange. *I don't need to let myself be exploited against my wishes. I am demonstrating that I can say no without becoming upset or generating tensions. This is the adult way for me to act.*

Practice to avoid the times when you are asked to do the work that the other person is responsible for but simply doesn't want to be bothered doing. Especially in those cases that are no big deal for the other person and would involve no big time loss for you but where you would be used so that he can get the benefit at your expense, you owe it to yourself to draw a line. You will like yourself better in the morning.

Saying no includes standing firm on the principle that actions do and should have consequences and when the consequences are penalties those ought not to be lightly absolved or they are meaningless or worse. Prescribing penalties for specific actions but not routinely imposing them on the violators sends the signal that the rules and restraints are simply hot air since the threatened penalties will not be imposed and therefore only fools take them as having any real teeth and meaning or relevance.

In various areas but especially in politics the lying, smears, and deliberate distortions can't and therefore won't be less common and damaging as long as there is no swift and significant punishment after the election or voting on the passage or defeat of the specific legislation for those who do those things to get elected or to gain other power by doing such things. If being shown to have mislead people to get elected would result in the deduction of a preset percentage of votes and thereby possibly reverse the election before the person is sworn into office or the passage or failure of the law before it is implemented, those using such tactics might pay more attention (and hire more lawyers to find ways to block or confound the law or its effects for their side) but that would create major chaos. The chaos would result in long and distracting legal argumentation that would be needed to reach a decision against the abusers in each separate case. Inaction would likely drag on to and even beyond the next relevant elections cycle or vote on the issue with the inevitable ever on-going confusion about who is actually in charge and able to take binding action at any moment.

A start in changing the situation would be to make the candidate and no one else responsible for publicly answering all questions about what was done since he is the obvious beneficiary from the mess even if he is viewed by the party as a mere puppet,. That is, literally he alone, no surrogates being well paid to take the blame, no spokespersons, no phalanx of lawyers and advisers, must appear before a panel of citizens where the nation and the world can see them all on TV but no one else can interfere, shout out, or otherwise disrupt things. This would of course profoundly change the game by making the candidate the boss rather than the tool or the *product*. Only those with real organizational skills or the leadership and smarts to select campaign workers who wouldn't jeopardize their careers by doing unacceptable stuff would succeed as candidates. Would this be a bad thing? This doesn't say they must do everything themselves but does say without adornment that the buck stops with them. If they don't trust their operatives to stay within the rules they either hire others they do trust or they accept that the help, who are likely to have their own agendas, can bring them down as easily or maybe even more easily than steer them to success.

The obvious but admittedly not attractive way out of the mess is for the candidate to publicly denounce and distance himself from the illegal or unacceptable deeds as soon as he learns of them - before the voting, not months later. In the time frame when the impact that those actions by others can still be offset and deplored. Is this a workable solution? Not likely, since those responsible for the dirty tricks will simply officially distance themselves from the campaign to protect the candidate as we see already in the first round of national elections when SuperPACs are legal. The effective solution would be for enough of the potential voters to decide a penalty is called for and change their votes. That is complicated by the need for each such voter to recalculate the pros and cons of the candidate since it is unlikely that the matter alone will be a make-or-break one for many. Plus, if enacted into law the lawyers will tie it in knots for decades when it might have helped made politics more responsible and honest. Those deeply involved have many other things to focus on though so this aim gets lip service but politics has a long history of not changing much in the short-term and of always seeming to accept whatever works for the current election cycle as the standard procedures, ethical considerations be damned.

The start place for reforming any process that rewards cheating or other bad behavior is to recognize in general terms the nature of the failure and then to seek reasonable (that is, neutral, open and overt, simple enough that all who need to can understand) changes to the procedures, including restrictions and prohibitions where those will help, in order to make the process work better. An immediate stumbling block is to define exactly what *make the process work better* means.

As with any attempt to restrain partisan behavior, agreement on even general principles and limits will be hard to reach; agreement on any changes with actual teeth so they might make a major difference are even less likely. But that is the only obvious way to proceed. Short of absolute takeover by a ruthless dictator, it seems to be the only possibly helpful task. I for one would be eager to learn of suggestions for alternatives but

I am not confident there are any that aren't simply cosmetic variation on this core idea. In particular I am prepared to reject close to out of hand any changes that depend on the "good heartedness" of the participants or any form of "self-policing". If history should have taught us anything it is that "trust me" and "we'll regulate ourselves so no government rules are needed" are signals that the proposal it not to be taken seriously. Without clear and emphatic definitions and limits and, maybe most important, quick and certain and definite punishment for violators to what were freely chosen agreements, the con men and liars will leave the *nice* people in the lurch and paying for their own screwing over just about every time.

Those intent on using others have always succeeded by operating on the assumption that enough of the population for whatever area they are operating in won't go to the trouble to check on claims, candidates, credentials, or their credibility to keep them from persuading enough people to hand over their money, votes, or other approval for what will profit the users at the expense, to a greater or lesser degree, of those who are inattentive or too easily swayed. The others, who are part of the larger entity but were outvoted despite their efforts to make the others pay attention to the details of what they were agreeing to commit them all to, pay the price too. Their only consolation too many times is that they did what they could under the circumstances.

For users and abusers, making a matter at least seem complicated is a standard and highly effective strategy. When the topic gets technical many, appropriately, look for guidance on what it all means in simplified terms. The attractive - which will usually be the seemingly simplest explanation - will carry the day with many. The conscientious advisers try to give an honest and correct analysis in the simplest terms that support the actual reality; the users don't care if their claims are later shown to be grossly distorted and inaccurate since they will get the result they want *now* knowing that things will almost never be reversed later even though the deliberate manipulation can be proven. "That's politics" is the out since many assume, maybe with some basis, that even if they won't say it out loud and publicly, many groups want to preserve the option to use such tactics, with the thought that they may want to resort to them themselves in the future.

A mantra for an effective critic is: Pay attention; Draw attention; Demand attention.

The *pay attention* is directed to yourself. The process I am calling going critical starts with you observing what is happening to you and around you and deciding that some things are not acceptable or at least not as good as they could and should be. It is possible to live in a fog and not notice a lot of bad stuff chipping away at your resources, your rights and freedom, or even your personal safety. Not allowing yourself to admit to yourself that you notice has the same final effect but is a more complex psychological phenomenon. Too often we only focus on such stuff after a lot of harm has been done. It makes sense to catch this destructive stuff early and limit the damage but that requires that we routinely stay alert and pay attention. Therefore the mantra's exhortation and admonition.

Draw attention means to focus others on the things that can be, and you believe need to be, changed when they are more than items resulting from your personal decisions and actions alone. This is a call to make the world at large, or as much of it as has any connection with this topic, aware of what you see as a problem so others can decide whether they agree and whether to join you in calling for or implementing the appropriate changes. Some things you can do by yourself, but most problems of more than a personal nature are more effectively dealt with by the combined effort of as many of those affected or interested as possible. Noticing a problem and keeping quiet about it lets you protect yourself but probably does little to correct it or to protect others from it. A good critic wants to have all three of the mantra's effects so she will do whatever seems most appropriate to her to draw and focus the attention of everyone interested and affected by it to the matter.

Demand attention should be understood to include "from those who can fix the problem." Many people may be affected but often only one or a few are in positions where they can change things directly. That person may already know there is harm being done but because it would be difficult, inconvenient, or costly to do things differently she may choose to act as if she is unaware of any problem. When pressured, she may cite statistics or testimonials about how much people approve of what is presently available and may claim to know of no dissenters except you. The task then is to be a dissenter in a public enough way that you are noticed by the many and can't be ignored or denied by those in charge. Then stand your ground.

A common strategy in these cases will be to try to buy you off. Give you some small gift or a pat on the head and escort you out the backdoor with a promise to "look into it." Your task it to use whatever reasonable tactics are called for to require those persons to acknowledge that there is a problem and to pay attention to it. You often can't force them to provide instant resolution to the matter and therefore you need not impose the burden of doing so on yourself, but if you make it clear that you are in the game for the long haul and will be beating your drum to focus public attention on them tomorrow and next month and next election day or at the next public meeting about the topic you are likely to have some effect. If the proposed solution isn't acceptable or if the response is to claim that there is no problem, you can clearly see your job - more of the same. Keep up the pressure. Demand attention from those farther up the ladder who have some control or influence in this area and step up the efforts to get more people riled up and demanding attention to the matter.

So the mantra generates three spheres of influence we need to consider when we find something unacceptable - ourselves, the public (whatever parameters that term has in the particular case), and those who can fix the problem directly. It also suggests a working idea of the sequence of actions. To start, we must become aware of the problem ourselves. Then, after some examination of the matter, we must conclude it can be changed without making the situation even worse. Only then should we resolve to take action ourselves to bring that change about. Next we may want to test the waters a bit to find out if any or many others also see this as a problem and if they agree that the proposed change would be better than continuing with the current process. Once you are convinced that you are more than a crank whom no one else is likely to support, you will be more confident in going to those in charge, especially if you can now guarantee a public uproar if there isn't a satisfactory response from them. If it seems that you *are* such a lonesome crank you have to consider other options.

Often those in charge are as interested as you are in resolving problems as soon as they are pointed out or as soon as someone can suggest a workable alternative to what is currently being done. In those cases generating a fuss before contacting them is counter-productive. This is a judgment call by the critic. In most cases it is not essential to success that those in charge be the last ones consulted and there is nothing that says you can't go public if and only if the initial official response isn't satisfactory. Often you will likely be better off starting with the belief that you will get a satisfactory response from those in charge and therefore you can limit your contacts with the public to the research on the opinions of others suggested above. You can always turn up the heat, but if you come on like a blowtorch every time right from the start you can do a lot of harm without compensatory benefits.

Criticism at some levels requires that it boil over into activity if it is to be of value but then it may have impact out of all proportion to your expectations. In many cases your personal critical evaluation is worthless because the only people that know of it are yourself and your weary-of-hearing-about-it friends. When it boils over into a letter of protest to a government official or a corporation's representative or the editorial page of a newspaper it gets to the right place. Perhaps as a follow up, with the text also posted on a blog when you send the letter or if there is no acceptable response in a reasonable time. No matter how often we are told of its effectiveness, too many of us are too "polite", too "busy", or too convinced that it won't do any good to take the time to write a good critical letter to the people who either can do something about it or who can bring the situation to general attention. In this respect, it is more than time that we stopped being so nice.

Such a letter is a true test of your ability to criticize. Draft such a letter - perhaps in the heat of your emotion - then when you have cooled down ask yourself if it has the earmarks of a good criticism. Is it to the point? Not a generalized "the whole business is garbage" screed, but a specific listing of the objectionable procedures, events, or whatever. Is it reasonable and clearly stated and not just a tirade? Is it constructive at least to the point of suggesting that no action be taken until the matter is better understood but that such study of the topic is important and needed now rather than later when more irreversible harm will have been done? Even better if you can and do suggest an alternative that would eliminate or minimize the objectionable elements. Is it criticism of the deed, decision, policy, etc., not the person? That is of course unless you do feel that you can argue to the addressee that this problem follows directly from some flaw in her own personality or action or that of some other identifiable person and doesn't represent the action that is desired by or in the best interest of the people being affected.

No matter how hard you try to prevent it, you can expect to be misread, misunderstood, misquoted, and misinterpreted. Remember though that you are likely to do the same thing to others and their replies unless you are very careful and disciplined.

This letter that you compose may be the first time you have forced yourself to think the matter through. The exercise is valuable if it does nothing more than this. Very often we only really begin to solidify our thoughts on a topic when we have to put them into words, especially into writing. The regular application of the techniques of criticism have this effect of clarifying our thoughts and positions, making us less likely to let someone else do our thinking for us.

Critical letters to public figures (which here refer to politicians, corporate representatives, government and private agencies, and the like) are megaphones augmenting the impact of your stance since these persons are usually collectively somewhat sensitive to and therefore interested in the reactions of those they depend on for approval in the form of votes, purchases, or support and cooperation. A letter to the editor published in a newspaper or magazine, or a verbal letter put out over the airwaves via a call-in radio talk show - or, these days, especially a posting on a well chosen Internet site - has an even greater impact because it lets others in the public in on your thoughts and observations. This may prompt some of them to take a similar stance or at least make them aware that this matter can be considered because it can be changed if there is sufficient pressure to do so. Some of those who hear of your actions may decide to shift their own votes, especially the economic ones, to apply pressure for changes for what they agree with you is the better, even though they may choose not to join you in writing letters, picketing, or other overt pressure activities.

You might choose to give stationery as gifts to encourage others to write letters to government and business in support of their ideas and rights. Some will find it helpful to establish a personal quantitative goal - a weekly or monthly protest budget of time allocated for blog reading and research, for sending messages of complaint, protest, or support to persons in positions to make the decisions that can make a difference. So much money set aside for stationery, postage, phone bills, transportation to demonstrations, and other activities.

Remember that praising and encouraging those doing a good job is as important a part of the critical process as any negative feedback. Those calls and letters will get attention and be appreciated too.

You might find yourself driven to write a complaining letter in order: (a) to criticize and suggest improvement in the performance of a person, group or company, (b) to complain about being wronged or cheated, (c) to demand a refund or other resolution or compensation for an unsatisfactory product or job, or (d) to give your views on a topic to others, especially those who are the larger scale decision-makers.

Here with a few generalizations to keep in mind if you want your letter to be effective.

1) *Avoid shouting and name-calling.* It may make you feel better to get it off your chest that way but it won't prompt the reader to take you seriously or even to bother reading the rest of your message.

2) *State your case clearly.* Ranting and making unprovable or too general claims won't help. Be as explicit as possible, specifying date, time, location or any other relevant details without dragging it out. Perhaps mention that you have extensive details if the recipient wants that information. Anyone who reads your letter even casually should be able to state what the topic of concern is and what your basic position is even if they don't remember or even grasp all of your arguments pro or con. A muddled grumble goes into the trash; a clear statement is more likely to at least go into a file or pile and be counted.

3) *Direct your message to the appropriate person.* Don't make the put upon assistant's day any worse by complaining to her about what her boss did - unless the boss has arranged things so that this assistant is the only route to get the message to her. If the assistant is designated to screen the boss' messages she is in the line of fire, but make it personal against the boss not the assistant.

In theory it should be most effective to take your complaint to the immediate supervisor of the level that you have found deficient. That gets to the heart of the matter without upsetting the higher administrative levels who may appropriately expect certain kinds of complaints to be resolved at lower levels. There are at least two potential drawbacks to this approach. First, you may not get satisfactory action at this lower level because this supervisor doesn't want to have to get into a hassle with the worker involved and may opt to simply hope it doesn't happen again. Second, the people at the upper administrative levels may have little idea of how poorly the company is being perceived and how many disgruntled customers or clients are bad mouthing them to friends and associates. Deciding how high up the ladder to aim your letter is an imprecise art complicated by the reality that in the corporate offices, messages are likely to be screened and not reach the top people even though addressed to them.

4) *Say what you want done.* Your letter is more likely to generate an effective response if you specify what you think or expect should be done to resolve or correct the problem. Even if your suggestions aren't workable, they provide an opening for a calm response from the recipient explaining why they won't work but opening up a possible dialogue on what will. The fact that you did more than simply shout, "Fix the mess, you stupid jerks!" indicates you are at least as interested in resolving the underlying problem as you are in calling people names and demanding that they be fired or placed in the stocks in the public square.

5) *Don't pick a fight.* Assume you will receive a reasonable hearing and a rational response. You may destroy your chances of being effective if you start screaming and accusing them about what you think or expect they are going to do or not do. It will be even harder not to expect a poor reception to a second letter if your first doesn't elicit an acceptable response, but it is better to give people the benefit of the doubt that somehow your letter never did reach the designated person than to poison the atmosphere with recriminations. Of course your message getting lost in inner space might itself be good reason for another complaint about the inefficiency of their operation. There will usually be plenty of time for ranting and raving if you still don't get satisfaction.

6) *Don't make threats.* Don't threaten people unless you are able to follow through and you actually intend to do so, otherwise you make yourself look silly. Even governments would do well to pay this point more attention since what comes across as insincere saber rattling often makes a government sound like an angry nine-year-old geek on the playground.

7) *One complaint per letter.* It is probably best to follow a modified paragraph rule for complaining letters and limit yourself to commenting on one problem in each letter. A shopping list of criticisms or complaints will promptly switch off the attention of most readers. It is more trouble to write three letters about three problems but it will generally be more effective. Among other things each letter can be sent by the supervisor to the most appropriate underling for resolution without the need for her to write separate explanatory memos to each. It also keeps you sounding

reasonable and not like a mad complainer while registering as three separate complaints on the group's running tally count that is the only factor what many at the upper levels are briefed on, not the particulars. The major exception to this rule would be a letter sent to someone that already knows you and is willing to hear all you have to say because she respects your intelligence and honesty.

8) *Keep your letter short.* Make the letter only as long as it needs to be to make your point. If it only takes half a page, only write half a page. If it takes three pages then send three pages. If it takes ten pages maybe you need to reevaluate whether this isn't a global rather than a specific complaint and if you can't and shouldn't break it down into its relevant parts and decide what your real concern is. Don't burden the letter with a lot of irrelevant details. Provide only as much background and setup material as you need to make your point clearly - with the comment that you have a more detailed account when this person is ready to see that. One page with some white space is the goal to aim for. The discipline needed to be succinct is good practice for all public presentations.

9) *Take responsibility.* If you aren't willing to sign the letter and put your return address on the envelope, don't bother to write it. If you expect someone else to accept responsibility for her actions, you must accept the responsibility for your own. Anonymous letters, accusations, and the like are garbage and should be treated as such even though much of the controversy that drives parts of the news media and the online gripe, smear, and titter sites would collapse without it.

This is a touchy matter when we are dealing with whistle blowing in government or industry because the welfare of many people might be jeopardized and the command systems are designed to protect those in power. Whether to risk reprisals in these cases is a tough decision that the individual must face. For very good reason many of us consider whistle blowers trying to protect us all to be true heroes.

10) *Vent, then edit.* Beware! Write it in anger; rewrite it when you have calmed down. When you have cooled down your tendency will be to deposit your critical letters in the trash rather than in the mailbox. This is probably because you were taught not to be "nasty" or a "troublemaker". Don't discard the letter. Discipline yourself to follow through by at least rereading your angry notes. See if you still think that your ideas are reasonable and valid. This may give you some insight into yourself. Do you fly off the handle and make a lot of fuss about matters of little or no consequence? Do you let the circumstances of your day color your

perceptions and proper decisions? These are common reactions but they make you come across as a less rational and perceptive person in your letters and comments.

Perhaps rework the ideas to make sure that they accurately represent your thinking if you think that desirable or necessary. Edit out the ranting but keep the calm anger and the dismay that this problem exists and is still in need of a resolution, then rewrite your ideas as a reasoned, thoughtful letter and send it off. Few of us pay much attention to the immoderate ranting that we encounter. Few of us though are unmoved (at least to reconsider our own positions) when faced with a calm, reasonable suggestion that our positions may not be the best, the most effective, or the only reasonable ones. We're also more open to the suggestion that our positions may have interpretations or effects we didn't foresee and haven't recognized until this person made us aware of them.

Beyond sending out your messages it is good practice to keep yourself aware of the messages that you are being bombarded with. On the assumption that the old educational adage that the more senses you use in acquiring information, the better you learn and remember it is accurate, I advise also using your critical faculties to reject or repel any inappropriate information. Yell and jeer at your TV or other device when stupid, misleading, or repulsive claims are made in the material it delivers. I especially recommend conditioning yourself to laugh out loud at the nonsense and the decisions of those who chose to manufacture and disperse the crap. Make it a game for yourself to laugh at the attitudinal blather of paid/ published commentators to remind yourself of their true value to you and keep that evaluation in mind when you discover anyone who takes those rumor mongers and scandal enhancers seriously - especially anyone who actually quotes such sources.

When you laugh at it, you automatically mentally stamp the in-formation, claims, or interpretation as faulty or worse so those are less likely to affect your thinking and reactions the way they may have been intended to. Laughing at, not with, an idea signals you to erase the item from the *approved* or *uncertain so willing to be persuaded* files in your mind but leaves a smudge that reminds you that you found this source or matter flawed. For someone aiming to subtly manipulate you, having you focus on her tactics is a disaster since you will be more resistant because you are aware of her actions and intentions.

Focus by the targeted person on what is being attempted is the enemy and the remedy for subtle manipulation. Make yourself notes on the subtler manipulations being aired. This improves your ability to see the falsehoods and you can use your notes to help others open their eyes to the same things and as the basis of protests against the attempts at misleading and manipulating you. How fast and how thick that pile of notes will become may be distressing but an eye-opener and possibly a prod to get you to take action.

Always be open to what you judge to be the positive side though. Literally cheer and applaud whatever presentations, explanations, or suggestions that you judge make their points clearly and honestly even if you have no intention of climbing aboard those bandwagons or if you actively reject those. You should respect someone who presents her positions openly and succinctly even if you reject her ideas; it is hard to respect anyone who dispenses statements riddled with code words, hints but nothing she is willing to stand behind, or glib distracters rather than answers to questions.

Openly and physically reacting to presentations (when and to the extent that is appropriate to the situation and not disruptive unless that is called for) connects you more strongly to your decisions and sets an example for others who were not paying close attention so they missed the errors, deliberate distortions, or attempted snow jobs, or who for whatever other reason have no idea what stance to take but now have one to imitate. The Tea Party people with their noise and their quaint costumes showed that they got the *impress it on me, I'll try to impress it on you* (aka monkey see, monkey do) part of their positions right anyway.

What can you do when you find fault with a policy or action of a business or a whole industry? Your letters or calls of complaint are probably going to someone paid to either make them disappear without a trace or to respond in a sweet and reassuring tone that promises nothing but fills up a page so you will be placated that you got your message across even if your punch is minimal. To have impact you must hit them where it hurts. Don't buy their products. This may be difficult because the large conglomerates have their fingers in so many products and companies. The only real contact you have with them is those products which means that you vote against the corporation by buying from someone else or doing without. Every time you buy a book, attend a movie, or watch a TV show about some crook or anyone more interested in herself at the expense of the common good, you are promoting that point of view. You make the decisions. It is one thing when you are educating yourself with a view to understanding how bad stuff happened and what to support to prevent repeats of such stuff; when you are consuming this material because you think the subjects deserve to be held up as role models, you are sending a different message to the world. Your decision to go along with the line that of course your fascination with them is only so you can revel in their downfalls may convince you but it doesn't ring true to everyone. We can all see what books are bestsellers and what movies are the weekend box office hits and draw our own logical conclusions.

If you want your decision to have resonance let those you are not happy with know you are not buying their products and why. No threats, no name-calling. Simple economic fact. I am deliberately taking my business elsewhere for the specific reasons that I have listed here. No response from you is required. This is the only sure way they have of finding out what they are doing to themselves and simultaneously it is the way that lets them know how to improve their customer relations which is usually of concern to them and their long-term business success.

To have more impact, let others also know that you're not buying this company's products and why. This could include stockholders, your political representatives where appropriate, letters to the editor of newspapers and other publications, as well as your circle of friends and acquaintances. The more people thinking and talking about your points, the greater the likelihood that changes will be made and in a timely fashion. Being just one more name on an organized group's complaint form is less effective that sending your own personal letter, not just a copy of someone else's prepared text.

Be considerate though. If you are waiting for a bus and bitching loudly about delays or poor service you don't make the bus arrive even a second faster, but you do make yourself and those around you more unhappy. Who gave you the right to impose a further burden on those people like that? Complaints about the bus service or whatever are of value only when directed specifically to those responsible, those who can do something about them if in fact they are accurate, reasonable, and matters that those operating the system control. Complaints because the bus was late when there was a major traffic problem let those who need to vent do that but don't improve the transportation system or the opinions of most who can't escape hearing the complainer demonstrate her stupidity waiting about the fact that shit happens.

Reporting the direst predictions of the possible outcomes is often considered the best journalism since it gets the reporter airtime or page space. Many will argue that there are times when we are justified in painting the extreme picture to make a point or to get people's attention on topics that we feel are critically important, like pesticides on certain foods or crumbling bridges and other infrastructure.

The other side of that coin is that hype begets indifference because the words, decibel level, and other signals are overused. Cry wolf too often and you may find snarling wild canids at your door with few people noticing that. Think about the needed balance to get attention for your point without adding to the confusion.

You can't force people to arrive at only good ends using their freedoms. You can constrain people by force, but you need something positive to entice them. We need to consider how to establish role models that make it fashionable to arrive at sensitivity, responsibility, and caring by your own route. This is an individualized task, not a *one method fits all* process. Which also means it is a never-ending job since each new person must learn to do it for herself at some point in her life.

Every time that we organize a movement like some kind of a consumer self-protection group we gain clout through numbers, but we lose individuality. In little time we are back to the point of having only representatives and consensus positions. Therefore it's not enough to just support organizations, we must also foster constant individual decision-making and pressuring through our purchases, our financial and ballot box support of candidates, and the many other outlets for our influence.

To recap, first, you have to analyze the situation and decide what seems to be needed in order for you to accomplish some end.

Second, you find out what you can about your options. What already exists to accomplish that end that you can simply make use of? Are there buses or trains to where you want to visit so you don't have to drive your own car? Are there prepared versions of this food items you want to try, or local restaurants that have it on the menu, so you don't have to find sources for the exotic ingredients called for in the recipe? What do those with more knowledge or experience about the focus subject suggest or recommend about your options in your specific circumstances?

Third, you make what you want to at least tell yourself is an informed choice and act or refrain from acting on the matter.

For your own sake don't rise to every bit of bait that is dangled before you. Consider your status and the limitations of your time, energy, and other resources. Respect the right of others to have opinions that contradict yours. Don't kid yourself that many of those who sound off publicly are open to being persuaded.

Read and listen, but selectively and critically. Keeping up with the latest findings on how people think, choose, and react will help you figure out how to have the most impact when you want to make points to others and how to best protect yourself from your own somewhat automatic reactions to ideas, claims, and comments because of the terms used or the context in which you encounter them. We all want to be effective when we do things so it helps to know that, on average, certain categories of people respond positively to what is presented as one set of choices but those in other categories respond negatively to the same options. It is fascinating to learn how these insights were determined but it is worth evaluating even without knowing that part of how those researchers pick apart the details of how we operate if it suggests that how you are presenting ideas is ineffective and how you can reshape your presentation to push the right buttons or to at least avoid pushing the ones that undercut your intended results.

To the degree that you can stomach it, reading the letters to the editor of a print or online outlet can be instructive about the range of interpretations (or you may quickly decide misinterpretations) of any and every statement made by anyone else. This may disillusion you about the intelligence and honesty of "the masses" or "those people" but it is useful for that reason. It's a zoo out there so you need to reevaluate how much weight to give to analyses and reports on what "the public thinks". Reading the missives is one place to start. Always keeping in mind though that an editor selected the ones to print and her job is to keep you coming back day after day so, to a point that doubtless varies from outlet to outlet, controversy sells and outrage outweighs calm and reasoned presentation - although the selectors will of course say they are interested in presenting a balanced selection.

Another lesson to be absorbed from a few consecutive days of such messages is that today's furor is likely to be spent by tomorrow (again with no way to know how much of that is editorial selectivity). The attribution of traits or actions to whole groups and wildly exaggerated claims about what will or won't happen if this group or that one is or isn't stopped are standard elements. A comment made by one person is attributed as the position of whole groups whether the commenter has any connection to the group or not. At least you are likely to come away from the task of slogging through the stuff with a more realistic idea of why reaching a workable consensus on any matters of importance is so hard and how tempting it is to some to roil the waters trying to prevent that state of relative peace and calm if they can't get their way and nothing but their way.

It has likely always been that way but with so many having such easy access to outlets where many others are exposed to their views and comments it seems like the din must be louder and maybe nastier than ever. The accuracy of that observation is irrelevant except to historians; the reality is that we are inundated with inputs claiming to be important information and consequently at the most basic level our choices are to either do nothing and suffer the consequences (with limited permission to complain) or we have to sort through it all and decide what we think should be done, what we can see how to influence to get that done in the short-term, and what we can't see how to fix but at least will focus on enough to give those who can see the possibility of solutions permission to develop their ideas and proposals.

We at least want to believe that bad policy is often the result of errors in establishing, defining, or enforcing the rules, not evil intention.

You can't force politicians and their handlers to tone down the smears, misrepresentations, and deliberate attempts to confuse us about the facts by law, only by publicly chiding them for it en masse to their websites and those news agencies that repeat their noise but that also want to report on how the garbage is going over.

Position yourself and stay alert to use every man-on-the-street feedback opportunity after any public event or political gathering on any subject of consequence. Each of these is your opening to tell the public what questions weren't answered, were answered incorrectly as a check of various records will verify, or were brushed off with a comment about an irrelevant tangent instead of answered. Also feel free to suggest whether you are under the impression that some out of left field response was an evasion or an example of the speaker not knowing her subject.

Get right to your message and stick with it. There is no guarantee that you will get more than a minimum of airtime or page space, if that, but it's worth trying for at least that much. Don't waste time answering the specific lead-in by the reporter if that was more than "What did you think?" or "What points did you notice?" Use common sense though and don't rush to bad mouth the performance of the third graders' skit or the new garden dedicated on Earth Day in the town center park. Stick to matters of real impact and importance.

Remember that today the news coverage is largely based on sound bites, which means keep your comments short and pithy. Often you can predict a short time in advance that you may be asked for a comment, therefore prepare and edit that in your head so it will be too striking for the editor or producer to decide not to include it even if she was looking for something either blander or leaning more to favoring the other side of the issue. Think the long flowery introduction but as soon as the microphone is aimed at you blurt out in clear and adequate fashion the core message of what was or was not presented. Chances are good that you won't even be given the chance to go on for long so lead with your big points because they will likely be as much as you will be given time to present.

It may not seem that you are being heard (which would mean that someone from that camp sends you more that a routine boilerplate message that your message was received) and the shouter advocates will publicly claim you are not being heard (can you spell P.R. cover our asses?) but you are. When enough similar messages are received, changes will be made even if the honest reasons for doing that are unlikely to be given and even if it was because of your (collective) chiding that is likely to be actively denied.

You don't have to preach (although if appropriate opportunities arise that is not forbidden) but you will likely have many small chit-chat openings to comment about your concerns and opinions without being aggressive and contentious. You have come far when you refuse to get into useless arguments by agreeing that the other has a right to her own opinion (but not to her own facts, including established matters of history) - or to her own right to be wrong when she wants to keep fussing.

Without preaching (except to mimic and offset others who are doing that to the detriment of the process) talk about your estimations of persons and policies among those whom you recognize tend to be followers and me-toos so that you subtly give them the good examples to latch onto and become proud and protective of. This uses their weakness but not against them, rather to make them better contributors to the common good.

Keep in mind that you choose how you will decide and act which means that the more aware you make yourself of the meaning and consequences of the matters that need to be dealt with, the more good you will do. Set a good example and sleep a little easier because you've done what you could.

The bottom line is that there are lots of attempts to communicate in order to shape our thoughts and decisions and it not realistic to think that we can control any except the most blatantly dishonest ones by legislation or self-imposed rules adapted by industry or other groups to reassure us. The critical recognition is that we individually still make most of the decisions so if we don't let ourselves be distracted or distorted by those inputs the results intended by the users and abusers that depend on our actions alone won't happen. Being aware and critical can protect us from many of the attempts at using us for the purposes of others that are not in our own best interests. There are still the many problem areas where working majorities of various groups that we are part of make decisions that negatively affect us no matter how astutely we ourselves avoided being individually misused and we need to decide individually what and how much we can do to alter those situations. Life goes on and protecting ourselves is an on-going, never finished process. If you think it's probably not worth the hassle, consider what your life would be like in North Korea.

Going critical is a start, not a complete solution and it is not guaranteed to lead to suitable solutions. At the end of the process that provides the impetus to be consciously critical you make decisions about the specifics of the topics of interest or importance to you and those decisions are what will lead to the effective solutions or fail to do so. What is the best life for me is what is most workable for me, not some ideal existence.

I don't expect you to agree with every position I take but if I have provoked you to consider more closely what you think about some topics and why, then I have accomplished what I set out to do. It is likely that if you deliberately revisit a topic you will end up with a more considered stance relating to it and that will be good for everyone. Too much of what guides and regulates the world is poorly thought out reactions and beliefs so each subject that is more intensively and deliberately analyzed, weighed, and re-decided is a good thing. That is true even for the other people who judged your positions to be weakly whacko before and now find them definitely and defiantly objectionable. The more solid the foundations of your thoughts, the better the chance that you can defend them clearly and with reasoning rather than emotional blather. Your better explanations and defenses give others insights into your thinking and positions whether they decide to embrace or reject your conclusions. Less fog, more solid communication - even if only the equivalent of spider webs - provide better raw materials from which to construct the consensus needed for peaceful civilization.

Don't automatically accept or reject, consider.

Some Suggested Readings

Ariely, Dan, *Predictably Irrational: The Hidden Forces That Shape Our Decisions* (Harper Perennial, 2009)

Bach, G.R. & Goldberg, H., *Creative Aggression: The Art of Assertive Living* (Doubleday & Co., 1974

Baggini, Julian, *The Duck that Won the Lottery and 99 Other Bad Arguments* (Granta Books, 2008)

Chabris, Christopher & Simons, Daniel, *The Invisible Gorilla: How Our Intuitions Deceive Us* (Broadway Books, 2009)

Charles Seife, *Proofiness: The Dark Arts of Mathematical Deception* (Viking/ Penguin Group, 2010)

Damken Brown, Claire & Nelson, Audrey, *code switching: how to talk so men will listen* (Alpha/Penguin Group, 2009)

Dimnet, Ernest, *The Art of Thinking* (Simon & Schuster, 1928)

Elgin, Duane, *Voluntary Simplicity*, (William Morrow & Co., 1981)

Gallagher, BJ, *Why Don't I Do the Things I Know Are Good for Me?* (Berkley Books/Penguin Group, 2009)

Hall, Edward T., *Beyond Culture* (Anchor Books, 1976)

Hall, Edward T., *The Hidden Dimension* (Anchor Books, 1990)

Hall, Edward T., *The Silent Language* (Doubleday, 1959)

Hall, Edward T., *Understanding Cultural Differences: Germans, French, and Americans* (Intercultural Press, 1990)

Halli329nan, Joseph T., *Why We Make Mistakes* (Broadway Books, 2009)

Hofstadter, Richard, *Anti-Intellectualism in American Life* (Vintage Books, 1962)

Isay, Jane, *Mom Still Likes You Best: the Unfinished Business Between Siblings* (Doubleday, 2010)

Iyengar, Sheena, *The Art of Choosing* (Twelve/Hachette Book Group, 2010)

Kahneman, Daniel, *Thinking, Fast and Slow* (Farrar, Straus and Giroux, 2011)

Lukacs, John, "American Nationalism", (*Harper's Magazine*, May 2012)

Orwell, George, *Nineteen Eighty-Four* (Harcourt, Brace & Co., 1949)

Schumaker, E.F., *A Guide for the Perplexed* (Harper & Row, 1977)

Schumaker, E.F., *Good Work* (Harper & Row, 1979)

Schumaker, E.F., *Small Is Beautiful: Economics as if People Mattered* (Harper & Row, 1973)

Schwartz, Barry, *The Paradox of Choice: Why More Is Less* (Harper Perennial, 2004)

Tannen, Deborah, *I Only Say This Because I Love You*, (Ballantine, 2001).

Tannen, Deborah, *Talking from 9 to 5: Women and Men at Work*, (Avon, 1994).

Tannen, Deborah, *That's Not What I Meant! How Conversational Style Makes or Breaks Relationships*, (Ballantine, 1986).

Tannen, Deborah, *The Argument Culture: Stopping America's War of Words*, (Ballantine, 1998).

Tannen, Deborah, *You Just don't Understand: Women and Men in Conversation*, (Ballantine, 1990).

U.S. National Research Council, "Deterrence and the Death Penalty", (National Academies Press, 2012)

Weisinger, H. & Lobsenz, N.M., *Nobody's Perfect: How To Give Criticism and Get Results*, (Stratford Press, 1981)

Made in the USA
Columbia, SC
29 December 2023

29644773R00212